URBAN ECONOMIC PROBLEMS

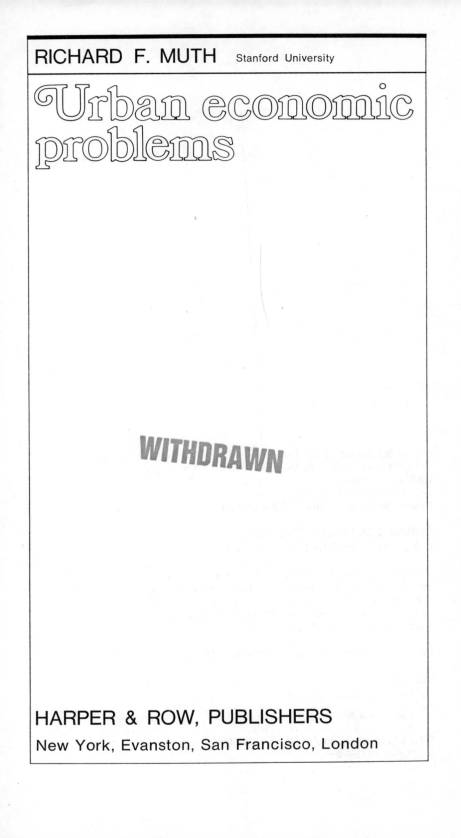

RICHARD F. MUTH   Stanford University

Urban economic problems

WITHDRAWN

HARPER & ROW, PUBLISHERS

New York, Evanston, San Francisco, London

Sponsoring Editor: John Greenman
Project Editor: Elizabeth Dilernia
Designer: Gayle Jaeger
Production Supervisor: Will C. Jomarrón
Printer & Binder: Halliday Lithograph Corp.

URBAN ECONOMIC PROBLEMS
Copyright © 1975 by Richard F. Muth

Library of Congress Cataloging in Publication Data

Muth, Richard F.
    Urban economic problems.

    Includes index.
    1. Urban economics. I. Title.
HT321.M87   330.9′173′2   74-14346
ISBN 0-06-044705-2

CONTENTS

PREFACE

This book is intended as an elementary economics text on urban problems. I am one of an increasing number of scholars who call ourselves urban economists and who feel that our specialty is defined by a set of problems that occur in urban areas. Others, however, prefer to think of urban economics as consisting principally of those special features of economic theory concerned with the internal structure of cities and their relationships to the national economy of which they are a part. I find both aspects of urban economics fascinating, and much of my own work has been concerned with the latter. In my experience, however, students seem to be far more interested in urban problems themselves than in the economic theory of urban areas.

Much of the interest in urban problems exists among students who are not economics majors. At the same time, in my experience, few undergraduate majors or even beginning graduate students in economics are familiar enough with the more advanced techniques of economic analysis to use them in studying new material. For these reasons I have tried to keep this book as free from the technical artillery of economic analysis as possible. Though I have used simple algebra in a few spots and included a set or two of cost curves, the major theoretical apparatus used is the law of demand and supply. Given these self-imposed limitations on analytical techniques, it is not possible to give a rigorous proof of every proposition discussed. I have tried, though, to describe propositions clearly and present intuitive explanations for them.

This book begins its discussion of the economic function of cities and their place in a closed economic system in Chapter 2. Chapter 3 considers the internal structure of cities, especially residential land use, and Chapters 4 and 5 discuss housing problems. Chapters 7 to 10 deal with those aspects of labor economics, and Chapters 11 to 13 public finance, that seem important to me in understanding urban problems. An alternative ordering of topics would be to begin with Chapters 7 to 10. The book covers a slightly greater range of topics than I have been able to cover in a one-quarter or one-semester undergraduate course. Because many of my perceptions and policy conclusions are not universally shared, I would imagine

that most instructors using this text would want to supplement
it with other readings.

I believe that progress in solving urban problems can be made
only by understanding them. Understanding them requires
far more than humanitarian intentions. Indeed, the zeal
to do something about urban problems without understanding them may be counterproductive. Hastily designed and
ill-considered programs at best delay solving problems, and
at worst may actually intensify them, as many efforts in the
United States have done. What seems to be most frequently
lacking in discussions of urban problems is careful and systematic thought coupled with taking empirical evidence seriously.
It is this latter point of view that I have attempted to foster
in this book.

Many members of the economics profession have contributed
to this book through their professional writings and personal
contacts. I am especially indebted to Michael Boskin for
reading Chapters 6 and 11 through 13 and to Edward Kalachek
and John Pencavel for reading Chapters 7 through 10. Their
critical comments have been most useful to me. I also wish
to acknowledge the assistance of Allan Meadows for his aid in
preparing the preliminaries of this book. I owe a special debt
to my secretary, Beverly Hallak, for typing the manuscript and
for helping in its preparation in many other ways.

Richard F. Muth
Stanford, California

URBAN ECONOMIC PROBLEMS

CHAPTER 1

Economics and urban problems

THE NATURE
OF URBAN PROBLEMS

Urban problems are of vital importance in the United States today. They seem complicated because they are not well understood. Like fractions, logarithms, or even calculus, when understood they seem simple enough. In this section I wish first to identify what I believe to be the fundamental urban problem. Next, problems of less importance will be considered. Finally, I wish to comment on two aspects of cities that I would characterize as conditions rather than problems.

Poverty

Simply stated, our fundamental urban problem is the low income, or poverty, of many of the residents of our cities. In the 1930s President Franklin Roosevelt asserted that the South was the nation's number one economic problem. Today many would argue that our cities are. What has happened to change matters? The problem has moved from the rural South to the urban North. Particularly during the 1940s and 1950s, large numbers of families, especially poor and black families, migrated from southern farms to northern cities. The poor have thus come to be increasingly concentrated in urban areas, and their poverty has become more visible to the nonpoor. It is thus understandable that some mistake a problem occurring in urban areas for a uniquely urban problem and infer that the problem is becoming worse over time.

Actually, poverty is more intense outside urban areas and, if anything, has been reduced in the aggregate by the migration from farm to city during and after World War II. (Data supporting this statement are presented and discussed further in the following section.) Failure to appreciate the truth of these statements is partly due to the fact that, as urban dwellers, many have seen city slums but not the squalid living conditions of many of the rural poor in southern states. Yet in 1949 the average income of nonwhite, rural farm persons in the southeastern states was only $486 per year. The average income of nonwhite urban and rural nonfarm persons in the Great Lakes states, however, was almost four times as high—$1753.[1] Migration of the southern rural poor into the urban North is thus no surprise. The only real question is why this migration did not occur sooner.

In *The Unheavenly City,* Edward C. Banfield draws attention to the true nature of urban problems quite nicely when he states:

> If some real disaster impends in the city, it is not because parking spaces are hard to find, because architecture is bad, because department store sales are declining or even because taxes are rising. If there is a genuine crisis, it has to do with the essential welfare of individuals. . . . It is clear . . . that poverty, ignorance, and racial (and other) injustices are among the most important of the general conditions affecting the essential welfare of individuals.[2]

It is hard to add to Banfield's statement. I can only ask the reader to weigh the irritation caused middle- and upper-income persons by occasional freeway tieups on the way to or from work, or even the loss of income suffered in some cases by the decline in demand for goods and services in large cities, against the human misery associated with poverty.

Lack of income is the primary reason for poor nutrition, poor clothing, and poor medical care. It is almost wholly responsible for poor housing quality. Despite frequent assertions to the contrary, though, there is little evidence that poor housing contributes to poverty.[3] Indeed, the special concern for poor housing probably results from the fact that it is the most visible manifestation of poverty. It is all too easy both to become aware of poverty by observing the housing of the poverty-stricken while driving to work and to feel that the problem has been solved by demolishing the housing in which poor people live.

Many other problems are closely related to poverty. Those of racial minorities are certainly not wholly due to income differences. Several studies, for example, suggest that only

---

[1] Harvey S. Perloff et al., *Regions, Resources, and Economic Growth* (Lincoln: University of Nebraska Press, reproduced from the 1960 edition in paper), table 163, p. 498. The regional classification of states is identified by figure 86, p. 492.

[2] Edward C. Banfield, *The Unheavenly City* (Boston: Little, Brown, 1968), pp. 10–11.

[3] Richard F. Muth, *Cities and Housing* (Chicago: University of Chicago Press, 1969), chap. 10, especially pp. 278–283.

a part of the residential segregation of nonwhites can be accounted for by their lower income.[4] Still, the evidence suggests that differences in the quality of housing occupied by different races are almost wholly accounted for by income differences.[5]

The fiscal crisis of cities is intimately related to poverty. Largely because of rural to urban migration, increasing numbers of lower-income persons have come to be concentrated in large American cities. At the same time, city governments in our federal system have important functions in providing for the poor. Among these are the partial financing of so-called welfare payments, the provision of public elementary and secondary education, and supporting hospitals and health programs. City governments must, however, raise a substantial fraction of the funds spent for such purposes by taxes levied within their own boundaries. The growth in numbers of lower-income persons in cities has substantially increased the demands for what are essentially income redistributive expenditures and has probably reduced the yields of city taxes at given rates. The result has been rising taxes and fiscal stringency.

Employment is the principal income source for most persons in our society. Improving the employment opportunities of lower-income persons is thus a natural concern. Likewise, education is popularly viewed as one of the principal avenues for increasing one's income. To a large extent, much of the dissatisfaction with public education results from its apparent failure to facilitate the escape from poverty. If "Johnny can't read," people are concerned that he will miss out on a well-paying job, not on the joys of Shakespeare.

Because poverty is fundamental to urban problems, much of this book concentrates on issues related to poverty. Chapters 4 and 5 deal principally with housing problems of the poor and racial minorities. Chapters 7 through 9 deal with various aspects of labor markets, a knowledge of which is important for understanding why some incomes are low. Chapters 10 and 11 deal with programs and policies for raising the incomes

[4] Anthony H. Pascal, *The Economics of Housing Segregation* (Santa Monica, Calif.: The Rand Corporation, 1967), especially p. 178.
[5] Muth, op. cit.

of lower-income workers. The aim is not to decry problems or to incite the reader to storm the barricades of the Establishment. (Most citizens of this country are aware of the existence of poverty and are willing, if not anxious, to support measures to ameliorate it.) Rather this book concentrates on the reasons for problems and the shortcomings of previous attempts to deal with them, and it outlines more effective programs.

Minor problems

Though poverty and its consequences are our most crucial urban problem, quite different problems exist as well. Many are related to the failure to set appropriate prices, especially where production is undertaken or regulated by government. Among the more important of these are transportation and the control of air pollution. Other problems result from shortcomings in the structure of local government. This book is also concerned with economic aspects of these other problems, though they are treated less extensively than problems associated with poverty. Transportation and air pollution are discussed in Chapter 6, local governmental problems in Chapters 12 and 13.

Many urban problems are associated with the failure of governments to set appropriate prices for the use of scarce resources. Three of them were painfully obvious as I looked out the window of an office building not far from National Airport in Washington, D.C. First, over the entire area hung a pall of smoke and haze. Second, along the Shirely Highway traffic crawled into the district in the morning and, even more slowly, out in the evening. And third, shortly before 5 P.M. every afternoon, as many as ten or fifteen airplanes waited to take off at National Airport.

In all these cases, the charge borne by private users of a public facility are set too low. The fees charged airlines and private aircraft for using National Airport were minimal. Hence at peak periods, more planes tried to use the airport than it could handle, with resulting delays and wasting of aircraft hours, fuel, and, most important, the time of travelers. Though auto drivers pay for freeways and other highways in taxes on fuel and tires, no charge is imposed upon them for the delay they cause other drivers by using urban roads during rush hours. Thus, as at airports, rush-hour delays are encountered, and fuel and time are wasted. Though it costs something to build a factory smokestack or an automobile exhaust system, air polluters are not charged for the extra medical expenses and other costs their atmospheric waste disposal imposes upon others. Highway congestion and air pollution result not because the automobile is the work of the devil but because people respond rationally to irrationally low prices set by governments.

The declining use of public transit facilities is associated with faulty pricing of another kind. Many forms of transportation, of which intraurban rail systems are an excellent example, are characterized by what economists call economies of scale. By this is meant that the average cost of providing a particular service, say a passenger trip of some specific length, tends to decline over fairly wide ranges of output. When average costs are declining, the additional or marginal cost per passenger is less than the average cost. So long as the marginal costs per passenger are covered, the opportunity costs of resources used elsewhere in the economy are met. However, private, and indeed many public, enterprises are forced to recover the full costs of operation to remain in operation. If prices or fares charged cover average costs of providing the service, though, they exceed the opportunity costs of resources used elsewhere in the economy and the facility is underutilized. As with the overuse of highways, the appropriate remedy is through the pricing system—reduce fares to the point where marginal cost per passenger is covered and subsidize the producer, whether public or private, to make up the difference between average and marginal cost per passenger.

Finally, many of the problems associated with population concentrations are affected by the pricing of the output of local government. Although local governments sometimes impose fees or user charges (analogous to prices charged by private producers for the products they produce), in most cases residents are charged through taxes. These taxes may be viewed as representing a fee to the average taxpayer and user of municipal facilities, but some pay fees through taxes in excess of the services they use, and others pay much less. Such pricing arrangements inevitably lead to conflict between taxpayers who vote against bond issues and others who feel deprived of essential services such as better schools and hospitals. The most straightforward way out of such conflicts is to extend the range of services that are supported by fees and to narrow that supported by taxes. If fees were charged parents for sending their children to public schools, many of the difficulties in financing education could be avoided. The single biggest objection to such fees probably is that they would be oppressive to the poor. Such difficulties could, however, be obviated by increased payments to the poor through other programs.

Another set of problems is associated with the mismatch of local governments, especially central-city ones, to the job at hand. Local governments are mismatched in at least three important ways. Most important, probably, central-city governments are increasingly called upon to support what are essentially income redistributive programs, yet tax sources are increasingly found outside the central city. Second, central-city governments are too big for the provision of most local governmental functions and too small for others. Finally, local government is involved far too heavily in the production as opposed to the support of services such as education.

Earlier in this section attention was called to the increased demands for welfare, public education, housing, and health programs produced by migration of the poor to our central cities. While this migration has been occurring, higher-income families and business firms in increasing numbers have been locating outside the central city. To a great extent, the decentralization of population and production in our urban areas has resulted from improvements in transportation and from the growth of the size of these areas and has been going on throughout this century. It has been accentuated, however, by higher taxes levied by central-city governments to finance redistributive expenditures. For, by moving outside the central city, these higher taxes can be largely avoided, though at a cost.

It makes little sense to require central-city governments to continue to finance expenditures for welfare, schools, and other redistributive purposes out of taxes levied within their own boundaries. Doing so causes too much urban decentralization and hence a loss in potential output for the economy. When welfare and schools are supported by local governments, the level of benefits provided lower-income families differs from place to place. Though really solid evidence is lacking, there is reason to believe that lower-income families are attracted to places where benefit levels are high, increasing the burdens on the governments and taxpayers providing these benefits. On pure equity grounds, furthermore, there seem to be no sound reasons why the benefits received under government programs by persons otherwise identically situated should vary from place to place. The best way out of these difficulties is for the federal government to assume the support of programs that redistribute income and to levy the taxes that finance these programs.

The most important factors determining the best size of local governmental units are technical conditions of production, external effects, and scope for consumer choice. In police and fire protection and in public education, output is expanded principally by increasing the number of small producing units. In a few cases, however, such as water and sewage disposal systems and rail transit systems, average costs appear to decline over wide ranges of outputs. In other cases, especially control of commuter transportation and air pollution, external effects are areawide. Central-city governments are generally too large to allow for variation in the level of municipal services where conditions of production permit. At the same time, they are almost always too small to permit a truly areawide government for those functions requiring it.

There are good economic reasons why government should support or require libraries, garbage collection, and, most important of all, elementary and secondary education. At the same time, there is little reason for public production, as opposed to support, of education. An excellent example of an alternative form of support is provided by the educational benefits to ex-servicemen under the so-called G.I. Bill. The latter is the country's only large-scale experience with what are called educational vouchers and has been widely acclaimed. Educational vouchers would provide for increased efficiency in the production of education. Dissatisfied parents could switch their purchases of education for their children as they now do their purchase of medical care. The ability to select a school best fitting their needs would provide lower-income families the freedom of choice middle- and upper-income families now exercise by selecting a place of residence. Finally, the private production of education would remove much of the potential conflict over education from the political arena and almost certainly reduce the total amount of it.

Conditions

Before passing on to other matters, two aspects of cities are worth brief consideration: relatively dense concentrations of people and externalities. Many consider one or both of these to be the essence of urban problems. Unquestionably, concentration of people and externalities are characteristics of cities. Whether or not they are root causes of urban problems is a quite different matter, which now will be explored.

In a trivial sense, urban problems are the result of concentrations of people, for without such concentrations there would be no cities. It is also probably true that the greater the density of population, the greater the amount of commuter traffic and atmospheric waste disposal in a given area. Even if auto-clogged and smog-filled cities were to grow no bigger, however, these problems would still remain. Though more people intensify these problems, the problems themselves result from the failure to set appropriate prices for the use of urban highways and air masses. Much the same is the case as regards the fiscal problems of central-city governments. Increasing numbers of lower-income persons increase the demands for redistributive expenditure relative to the tax receipts of these governments. The solution to the problem, however, lies in assumption of income redistributive programs by the federal government, not in limiting the immigration of lower-income families to urban centers where their economic opportunity is greater.

Externalities, more specifically the failure to impose additional charges where external effects are present, are fundamental to the problems of urban commuter transport and air pollution. It is often claimed, in addition, that the condition of urban real estate is adversely affected by external effects in land use and the failure of local governments properly to regulate them. External effects in land use are an important feature of urban real estate markets and are discussed in some detail in Chapter 4. Again, it is a quite different matter to argue that the problem of poor-quality housing in urban areas is a result of externalities. The evidence strongly suggests that poor-quality housing results principally from the growth in the effective demand for it on the part of poor people; there is little evidence that housing quality is appreciably affected by faulty working of urban real estate markets.[6]

THE MEANING AND EXTENT OF POVERTY

Scott Fitzgerald is reputed to have remarked to Ernest Hemingway, "You know, Ernest, the rich are different than we are." "I know," Hemingway is alleged to have replied, "they have more money." Whether the phenomenon we call poverty means more than low incomes is an important question that has engaged the attention of many social scientists. Whatever the answer, it is distressingly clear that what we call poverty consists to an important degree of low income.

Measuring poverty

To many readers it will undoubtedly seem that being concerned with measuring poverty is the height of academic irrelevance. After all, many of you probably are thinking, we know poverty exists, why not just do something about it? One answer is simply that because other people measure poverty and talk and write about the numbers their measures produce it is useful to understand what their measures mean. A more satisfactory answer, though, is that measurement is important, even fundamental, in assessing any problem. By measuring it one comes to understand the extent of the problem, how its incidence varies among different groups in the population, and whether the problem is becoming more or less serious over time. Measurement furthers understanding, and understanding a problem is crucial in dealing with it.

In a wider sense, poverty is associated with a level of consumption that is low relative to the average for households

---

[6] Ibid.

in a particular society at a particular time. However, data on consumption expenditures of families are collected infrequently, and a family's consumption is closely related to its income. Therefore, poverty is generally measured in terms of income. Furthermore, where one sets the poverty cutoff line—that income level below which a family is counted as poor and above which nonpoor—is wholly arbitrary. Income distributions in the United States and most other countries have a single mode or value at which the density of families possessing a given level of income is greatest. They don't exhibit two or more peaks, which would suggest the mixture of two qualitatively different groups or populations. Below the modal income level, the lower the level of income, the poorer any family and the smaller the fraction of all families possessing it. Indeed, rather than characterizing a family as poor or nonpoor, it would be far more meaningful to characterize it by how far its income falls below some income cutoff level. The aggregate amount by which the incomes of a group of families falls below the cutoff level is usually called an income-gap measure of poverty.

Measures of the number of poor are usually based on an income cutoff level of $3000 per year in 1963 prices for an urban family of four. In today's dollars the cutoff could be somewhat over $4000 because of inflation, not because of any change in the level of real purchasing power associated with it, and any figure I might write down would be obsolete by the time you read it. This is the so-called official definition of the federal government; as such, however, it is more of a uniform standard for statistical reporting by federal agencies than a revelation of truth. This particular income cutoff level was initially selected because it was believed to be the point at which an urban family of four would spend enough to acquire a particular bundle of food. Called an "economy" food budget by the U.S. Department of Agriculture (USDA), it was characterized as being for "temporary or emergency use when funds are low."[7]

Though probably as good as any other such standard one might select, the official definition of poverty doesn't really

---

[7] Mollie Orskansky, "Counting the Poor: Another Look at the Poverty Profile," *Social Security Bulletin* 28 (January 1965), 3–29.

measure what it is supposed to. A careful examination of consumer expenditure data for 1960–1961 suggests that an urban family of four with an income of $2450 in 1963 prices spent an amount on food annually that was necessary to acquire the USDA's economy food bundle. However, to spend enough on food annually to acquire a food bundle the USDA considered a minimum for normal use, it would have been necessary for a family to exceed about $4000 per year in 1963 prices. Because the intensity of poverty varies inversely with the level of income, though, any such cutoff line is arbitrary. As a purely practical matter, whether one sets the cutoff line at $2450, $3000, or $4000 per year, the composition of the poor by factors such as farm vs. nonfarm residence and age of head remains pretty much the same.

Far more important than the cutoff line for an urban family of four itself is variation of the cutoff line by family type. For, although income is a good predictor of consumption, the relation between consumption and income as usually measured differs considerably for families of different kinds. This is the most obvious where families differ by size. The larger the family, the less the consumption per family member if income is the same. Most definitions of the poor reflect this fact in setting higher income cutoff levels for larger families.

Less obvious but of greater quantitative importance are variations associated with farm vs. urban residence and age of head. Partly because of food grown and consumed on the farm, the value of which is not counted in income as measured by the Census Bureau, a farm family consumes more food at any given census-measured income level than an urban one. Indeed, in 1955 a farm family of four whose measured income was just under $1800 per year consumed the same amount of food as a similar urban family whose income was $3000 (both in 1963 prices). Thus, a farm family is about as well off as an urban one whose income is two-thirds greater.[8]

---

[8] According to the latest information I can find, the cutoff level for farm families is currently 15 percent less than that for urban families, although 40 percent less was originally used. See Joseph A. Kershaw, *Government Against Poverty* (Chicago: Markham, 1970), pp. 8–9.

Similar problems exist in comparing the well-being of families whose heads are 65 or older with those of younger families. As families grow older they acquire more wealth in the form of net claims to durable consumer goods, the most important of which is equity in owner-occupied houses. The income from these is not directly received in the form of money and hence is not counted as income by the Census Bureau, yet it improves the well-being of its recipients in much the same way as money income does. Indicative of this fact, in 1960–1961 an urban family whose head was over 65 spent the same amount on food at an income level only 86 percent as great as a family whose head was 45 years old. Partly for this reason but mainly because they are smaller, a cutoff level of just over $2000 for the typical aged-head family in 1959 corresponded to the $3000 for an urban family of four.

Failure to choose different poverty cutoff levels for families of different types can lead to quite different perceptions of the nature of the poverty and its extent. Based on unadjusted cutoff levels of $3000 for a family in 1963 prices, there were almost 2.5 million poor nonfarm aged-head families and 1.5 million poor farm families in 1959. Using the adjusted cutoff levels just described, the corresponding numbers were 1.5 and 0.9 million, respectively.[9] There can be little doubt that poverty is more intense among farm and older families than among the rest of the population. But poor use of statistics makes the problems of farm and aged-head families seem much worse than they actually are.

Variations in poverty over time and space

It is widely believed that urban problems are becoming more severe over time. Many also feel that the poverty problem is becoming worse and that it is especially severe in cities. In fact, nothing could be more incorrect. In the post–World War II period, the fraction of recipients whose incomes fall below any given real purchasing-power level has declined greatly. In addition, the quality of housing has improved

---

[9] Calculated from U.S. Bureau of the Census, *U.S. Census of Population, 1960: Families,* Final Report PC(2)-4A (Washington, D.C.: U.S. Government Printing Office, 1963).

greatly, and the incidence of poverty and of poor housing quality are both substantially lower in urban than in rural areas.

Data on the incidence of poverty by location and by color are shown in Table 1.1. Incidence of poverty means the fraction of the persons in a particular group whose family incomes fall below the poverty cutoff line for that group. All entries are based upon the current official definitions already discussed. The most striking conclusion to be drawn from Table 1.1 is that the incidence of poverty has declined dramatically during the past decade. Whether one looks at the entries for the United States as a whole, for persons outside metropolitan areas, or for central-city blacks, the incidence of poverty fell by roughly 40 percent from 1959 to 1968. In the earlier year, more than one person out of five belonged to a poor family. At the end of the 1960s, however, only one in eight did.

Equally striking is the fact that in both years and both groups by race the incidence of poverty is about twice as great outside metropolitan areas as in them. Poverty seems uniquely urban to many simply because large numbers of the poor live in metropolitan areas. Indeed, in 1959 there were almost 22 million persons in poor families outside metropolitan areas, but in

TABLE 1.1
Incidence of poverty in the United States, 1959 and 1968[a]

| RACE | UNITED STATES | METROPOLITAN AREAS | | | OUTSIDE METROPOLITAN AREAS |
		Total	Central city	Suburbs	
All races					
1959	22.0%	15.3%	18.3%	12.2%	33.2%
1968	12.8	10.0	13.4	7.3	18.0
Negroes					
1959	55.1	42.8	40.8	50.9	77.7
1968	34.7	26.6	26.2	28.3	54.6

[a] Fraction of the particular group in families with incomes below a given level in dollars adjusted for price changes.
Source: *Statistical Abstract of the United States, 1970* (Washington, D.C.: U.S. Government Printing Office, 1970), table 502, p. 329.

1970 there were only slightly over 12 million. In metropolitan areas, the numbers for the two years were 17.0 and 13.4 million, respectively.[10] Thus, though poverty is worse outside cities, it is becoming increasingly concentrated in them. Table 1.1 also indicates that, although poverty is far from unique to the central cities of urban areas, central cities contain a higher proportion of the poor relative to their total population than do the suburbs. Interestingly enough, however, the incidence of poverty among suburban blacks is actually a little higher than for blacks in the central city. Suburbanization of blacks is not an obvious means of improving their position.

Much the same kind of picture emerges in Table 1.2, where data on dwelling-unit condition are shown. Substandard means dwellings that are dilapidated, in the sense of possessing specified exterior defects apparent to a census enumerator, or lacking certain plumbing facilities, such as separate toilets. Although aspects of what many would consider a satisfactory dwelling are not directly included in this measure, most of the omitted characteristics are probably related to those included, so that the data are highly reliable indicators of average housing quality.[11]

One sees from Table 1.2 that the frequency of substandard housing is over three times as great outside metropolitan areas

---

[10] *Statistical Abstract of the United States, 1972* (Washington, D.C.: U.S. Government Printing Office, 1973), table 544, p. 332. The data cited here use the farm cutoff level of 85 percent of the urban one.

[11] U.S. Bureau of the Census, *Quality of Housing: An Appraisal of Census Statistics and Methods,* Response Branch Report No. 66–16, Second Draft (Washington, D.C., April 1966), pp. III-8–III-10.

TABLE 1.2
Fraction of U.S. dwelling units substandard,
by location, 1950 and 1960[a]

YEAR	UNITED STATES	URBAN	RURAL
1950	36.9%	22.2%	63.6%
1960	18.2	10.5	36.0

[a] Dilapidated or lacking plumbing facilities.
Source: U.S. Bureau of the Census, *Census of Housing: 1950* (U.S. Government Printing Office, 1953), pt. 1, vol. I, table 7; and *1960 Census of Housing* (U.S. Government Printing Office, 1963), vol. I, pt. 1, table 9.

as within them. Whereas urban areas contained 60 percent of the nation's dwelling units in 1960, they contained only about 30 percent of the nation's substandard dwellings. Equally striking is the fact that the fraction of substandard dwellings fell by about half between 1950 and 1960, both for the United States as a whole and for its urban and rural portions separately. Data comparable to those in Table 1.2 were not collected in the 1970 census. If 1970 data on the number of units lacking plumbing facilities are compared with their closest 1960 counterparts, however, it appears that the fraction of substandard dwellings again fell by about half during the 1960s.

As average income levels in the U.S. economy continue to grow, there is little doubt that the incidence of poverty as currently measured will continue to decline and the average quality of urban housing will continue to improve. However, people's standards of what constitutes poverty undoubtedly will change. Certainly many of the American poor today have a standard of living that is nonpoor by the standards of the United States a half-century ago or by those of most underdeveloped countries today. In a relative sense the poor are always with us. Furthermore, even though past performance of the U.S. economy suggests rapid progress in the elimination of poverty in the absolute sense, there is no reason for complacency. A 10 percent incidence of poverty for the United States as a whole means roughly 20 million people with a standard of living that is meager by contemporary standards.

THE CONTRIBUTION OF ECONOMICS
TO UNDERSTANDING URBAN PROBLEMS

What economics
is about

Despite repeated attempts to convince them to the contrary, many people think "economist" is a synonym for "miser." However, there is a great distinction between miserliness and wise use of resources. And wise use of resources is what economics is all about.

Just as families do, all societies face the problem of allocating scarce means of production to satisfy alternative ends or human wants. In the study of economics, air and water once were the only cited examples of free goods—goods that exist in amounts sufficient to satisfy all demands for them. With the growing problems of air and water pollution, or perhaps only our growing awareness of these problems, even air and water seem scarce relative to our demands for them. Despite all that has been written about the affluent society and our having solved the problem of scarcity, the latter is as much a fact of the U.S. economy in the 1970s as the 1770s. I confidently predict that as the incomes of my readers increase as they grow older, scarcity of their own resources will seem as much a problem as ever.

Scarcity of the means of production would be a quite different problem, however, if there were only one use to which they might be put. If, say, bread were the only commodity produced using scarce resources, society's problem would merely be to produce bread as efficiently as possible. But if cheese and wine are also commodities that land, labor, and capital can cooperate in producing, then society must somehow choose how many of its scarce resources to devote to producing bread and how many to cheese and wine. It is the necessity of choice that distinguishes an economic problem from a purely technological one. Resources used to produce bread have an opportunity cost in terms of the cheese and wine foregone when additional amounts of bread are produced. The same may be said for programs for fighting poverty; resources used in community action programs have an opportunity cost in terms of other uses, including other antipoverty measures. As a teacher of mine once quite nicely summarized the fundamental principle of economics, "There is no such thing as a free lunch."

All societies face the problem of choice in allocating scarce resources among alternative uses, but the means they use may vary considerably. Yet comparative economic systems is but a small appendix to the main corpus of the discipline of economics. Traditionally, economics has been an English-language discipline, and today most economics is done in the United States. Economics is concerned primarily with the operation of economic systems like those of the United States today. Such systems are sometimes called capitalistic—a poor term, because all economic systems use capital. They are better characterized as market economies, better still as free, private enterprise economies. "Free" refers to freedom to enter into different occupations or industries. "Private" means that private individuals stand to benefit or lose directly in terms of the incomes they receive from the success or failure of the activities in which they engage.

In free, private enterprise economies, resource allocation is influenced by prices established on markets for final products and productive factors. If consumers in the aggregate want more wine as compared with bread, say, they spend more on wine and less on bread. Given the existing rates of output of wine and bread, the price of wine rises and that of bread falls. In the process the existing supplies are rationed among consumers, the rise in wine prices inducing consumers to make do with fewer bottles per month than they would otherwise buy. At the same time, growing wine grapes becomes more profitable, winemakers are given the incentive and the financial resources to plant more vineyards, and eventually the output of wine increases.

In market economies, prices also influence the techniques of production chosen and the size of the payments made to owners of productive factors. With a rise in the price of wine, winemakers offer more for wine grapes and for the land on which they are grown. With the rise in the rental value of vineyards, not only are more vineyards planted, but existing ones specially suited to growing wine grapes because of their soil and climate are cultivated more intensively. Those workers who by their skill and experience in grape cultivation and winemaking are in greater demand receive higher wages and devote a greater proportion of their time to specialized tasks as compared with wheat farmers and bakers.

Economics is largely the study of how prices in market economies influence the allocation of resources. This book reflects that fact. Chapters 3 and 4, in particular, inquire into how housing prices and residential land rentals affect spatial patterns of the production and consumption of housing in U.S. cities. Chapter 6 examines the role of prices in urban commuter transportation and air pollution. Chapters 7 to 10 consider what is perhaps the most crucial price for urban problems and poverty—the determination of wage rates for workers of various kinds. Chapters 12 and 13 deal with the role of taxes paid as the price of governmental production in influencing output decisions made in the public sector.

Poverty in a market economy

It is often asserted that poverty results from the faulty working of a market economy. Hence, as long as market economies have existed, reformers have argued for their elimination. This section will first inquire into the sources of poverty in a market economy, and then will mention the existing evidence on poverty in different types of economic systems and at different stages of economic development.

Some of the workings of a market economy are illustrated schematically in Figure 1.1. That the diagram resembles a computer flow chart is no accident, for a market economy may be thought of quite accurately as a large-scale analog computer for solving a society's problem of resource allocation. Households, business firms, and government, the economy's three basic kinds of decision-making units, are indicated by elongated diamond-shapes; inputs, outputs, and payments, which are the economy's processing operations, are represented by rectangles; small circles indicate the junction or separation points of flows; and arrows give the direction of flows. Unlike a computer flow chart, however, two distinct kinds of flows are shown—real flows of goods and services by solid lines and money payments by broken lines. Flows are arranged to the left if they occur in product markets and to the right if in factor markets. Finally, unlike a computer program, there is no start or stop, because the market economy is a "real-time" computer that operates continuously.

Most of what this book has to say about the economy's operation and poverty is said in later chapters. Figure 1.1 suggests, however, that there are two broad classes of reasons for a relatively low level of consumption, or poverty. Consumption is low because expenditures are low (the latter because in-

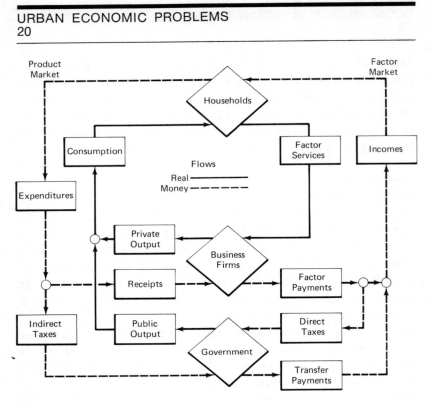

FIGURE 1.1
Schematic diagram of a market economy

comes flowing into certain households are small), or because somehow the expenditures some households make are diverted from consumption into other channels. In the late 1960s there was a spate of interest in whether the poor pay more for the commodities they receive from producers. Without going into the question deeply, it appears that they do and they do not. They do not appear to pay more for a given commodity in a given kind of store. Rather, they tend to buy primarily in kinds of stores that charge higher prices to everyone. Thus, the poor tend to buy smaller quantities at one time in smaller, widely scattered neighborhood retail outlets that frequently provide credit when other stores do not. The poor may also pay higher charges for financing durable-goods purchases, primarily because they are poorer credit risks.[12]

---

[12] For a summary of some of the evidence on this point, see Carolyn Shaw Bell, *The Economics of the Ghetto* (New York: Pegasus, 1970), chap. 6, especially pp. 138–147.

This book does not inquire very much into final product markets other than housing markets; pricing in housing markets is discussed mainly in Chapters 3 and 4. A given expenditure might also provide a lower level of consumption for the poor if, as is often alleged, a higher fraction of their expenditure were diverted by government as indirect—sales or property—taxes. Whether this is the case is examined briefly in Chapter 12.

A vastly more important source of the low consumption of the poor is the low incomes they receive. As the right-hand side of Figure 1.1 indicates, household incomes are composed both of factor payments made by business firms for services currently rendered in production and transfer payments made by government. (For simplicity, government as an employer of labor is not shown separately in Figure 1.1 but is treated as a business firm in this regard. This seems quite appropriate, however, for government differs from private firms principally in the distribution of its output and its receipts.) For the population as a whole, earnings from the sale of human labor are by far the biggest single source of income. Currently, almost exactly 80 percent of incomes received by households are in the form of wage and salary payments.[13] For this reason, Chapters 7 to 10, roughly one-third of this book, are devoted to matters related to the determinants of labor income.

For the poverty population, however, income from the sale of labor services is a much smaller fraction, slightly less than half in fact, of total income. The poor receive about two-fifths of their income as governmental transfer payments of two kinds—social security and public assistance.[14] Therefore, any study of urban problems should inquire into the nature of government transfer payments, and these are discussed in Chapter 11. In Chapter 11 it is also observed that direct or income-type taxes paid by the poor are of substantial size relative to the transfer payments they receive from government. It may surprise some readers that although incomes from property form a substantial part of the incomes of some persons, they are quite a small fraction of aggregate income in the United States.

---

[13] *Statistical Abstract of the United States, 1972,* table 546, p. 333.
[14] Ibid.

Because of the overwhelming importance of income from wages and salaries in the U.S. economy, a few additional comments are worth making at this point. The total income received from the sale of the services of human labor is usually called annual earnings. Annual earnings, in turn, are the product of hourly earnings, or the wage rate, and the number of hours worked per year. A person's annual earnings may be low either because his hourly rate is low or because he works few hours per year. The wage or hourly earnings rate corresponds most nearly to what is usually thought of as the price of labor services. Yet to a very great extent, hourly earnings rates vary among workers because of variations in productivity or in the amount of productive power per worker. Differences in annual earnings resulting from variation in hourly earnings for workers of given skill and experience are of much less importance. Babe Ruth was the highest-paid baseball player of his day because he hit the most home runs, not because he was paid a princely sum for each home run he hit!

It is widely believed that income inequality is characteristic of market economies and grows worse as they develop. Thus, it will probably infuriate many to read that precisely the reverse is the case. Yet this is what Nobel Prize-winning economist Simon Kuznets concluded in a massive review of the available evidence on the distribution of income.[15] Not only did he find the size distribution of income more unequal in less-developed than developed economies, but also that inequality in the latter has narrowed over time, at least during the twentieth century. Furthermore, among the four countries—Ceylon, El Salvador, Great Britain, and the United States, all around 1950—for which Kuznets shows data consumption per family was less unequally distributed for the United States than for any other.[16] This is not to deny that more inequality in economic well-being exists in the United States today than many of us would prefer. Much of this book is concerned with a discussion of programs that would

---

[15] "Quantitative Aspects of the Economic Growth of Nations: VII. Distribution of Income by Size," *Economic Development and Cultural Change* 11 (January 1963), especially pp. 67–69.
[16] Ibid., table 8, p. 28.

reduce the existing degree of inequality in consumption per family. Overthrowing the market economic system is not one of these programs, however. For the empirical evidence suggests that less, not more, inequality is associated with more highly developed market economies characterized by a smaller amount of government intervention.

Is economics a "dismal science"?

Over a hundred years ago, economics was tagged with the nickname "the dismal science." The belief has persisted, probably because people become very unhappy when told by economists that their pet reforms will not work. Probably because the subject matter of economics is somewhat familiar to non-economists, people seem much more willing to dispute the conclusions of economists than those of chemists. Because many readers may respond with disbelief to conclusions drawn later in this book, it seems useful to discuss briefly how economic conclusions are reached.

Is economics a science? Not if by science one means a discipline whose practitioners wear white coats and work with smelly mixtures. But if by science one means a method of solving problems, then economics qualifies. For economists, like physicists, build models to explain reality. Such models are abstractions that attempt to seize the essential features of an admittedly complicated reality to make the models manageable. As abstractions these models sometimes seem unrealistic. Such criticisms, though, are beside the point, for the usefulness of models depends upon the conclusions reached, not how they are reached.

What makes a model's conclusions useful? First, they must be logically correct; otherwise no confidence can be placed in them. Second, they should explain what they were designed to explain. Finally, and most important, they should yield new conclusions that are confirmed by experience in the real world. In general, the broader the range of phenomena with which a given model is consistent, the more useful it is. For if a single screwdriver will do ten jobs, one can do with fewer screwdrivers and not be concerned about which of ten screwdrivers to select for any particular job.

How does one decide how well a model works? In the laboratory sciences, models are tested by so-called controlled experiments. The essence of a controlled experiment is not that all factors affecting its outcome are controlled for. Rather, the impact of extraneous factors is eliminated by randomizing treatments to experimental material. Where one must rely on nonexperimental data produced by real-world experience, eliminating the effects of extraneous factors is much more difficult. In this regard, the methodological problems facing astronomers and meteorologists are essentially the same as those economists face. Like those in astronomy and meteorology, economic models are tested against real-world data using techniques of statistical inference. Models are tentatively accepted as verified if they correspond more closely with actual experience than alternative models.

Is economics an "exact" science? The question itself is meaningless. Physicists may "know" the velocity of light to more significant digits than economists know the velocity of money. But is 45 seconds a good time for a track event? It is a good time for the quarter-mile, unbelievably fast for the half-mile, but a snail's pace for the 220-yard dash. It is certainly true that considerable disagreement exists among economists on the diagnosis and best treatment of important economic ailments. But the same can be said of physicians regarding the causes and best means of treating that collection of diseases known as cancer.

Though patients infrequently object to a course of medical treatments because they find them unpleasant, many people do object to suggestions for improving economic matters. In similar fashion, a physician is rarely judged to be cruel and heartless if he prescribes radiation therapy, but economists are often so judged and assumed to be in league with "the interests" when recommending unpleasant courses of action. The best response to such charges is a quotation from Alfred Marshall, over a half-century old, regarding such charges made against the classical economists:

The fact is that nearly all the founders of modern economics were men of gentle and sympathetic temper, touched with the enthusiasm of humanity. . . . They were without exception devoted to the doc-

trine that the well being of the whole people should be the ultimate
goal of all private effort and public policy. But they were strong in
courage and caution; they appeared cold, because they would not
assume the responsibility of advocating rapid advances on untried
paths, for the safety of which the only guarantees offered were the
confident hopes of men whose imaginations were eager, but not
steadied by knowledge nor disciplined by hard thought.[17]

SUMMARY

Our most pressing urban problems result from the increasing
concentration of the poor in cities. As such, urban problems
are principally those that occur in urban areas rather than
problems that are uniquely urban in any meaningful sense.
Some problems, notably commuter transportation and air pollution, result mainly from the failure of governments to set
appropriately high prices for the use of certain facilities.
Larger concentrations of people make these problems worse
but are not the root of the difficulty. Central-city governments
are mismatched with the job at hand in that they, rather
than the federal government, raise taxes to finance expenditures for schools and welfare. They are too big for the effective
provision of police and fire protection, and too small to function as metropolitan-area governments where the latter are
needed.

Poverty means a low relative level of consumption. It is usually measured by the fraction of persons whose incomes fall
below some particular level. Where one draws the poverty
line, however, is arbitrary; the lower one's income level, the
poorer he is. Failure appropriately to adjust the line for different types of families, however, greatly exaggerates the extent
of poverty among rural and aged families. Over time the incidence of poverty has declined markedly. Poverty is less intense in urban areas than in rural areas and, among blacks,
slightly less intense in central cities than in suburbs.

Economics is concerned principally with how prices on markets allocate scarce means of production among alternative
uses. In market economies, income is received principally from
the sale of human labor services. Thus, the key to the causes

---

[17] Alfred Marshall, *Principles of Economics,* 8th ed. (New York: Macmillan,
1920), pp. 47–48.

of low income is to be found in examining how labor markets operate. Contrary to widespread belief, there is less income inequality in market economies than in undeveloped ones, and in this century inequality has decreased over time. Careful and systematic study of market economies frequently leads to unpopular conclusions. Yet men were once burned for claiming the earth is not the center of the universe.

CHAPTER 2

The growth of urban areas

WHY CITIES EXIST

An old dictionary defined a city as an important town, as "any cluster of houses recognized as a distinct place" or "any larger closely populated place." This definition reflects the fact that cities are most readily recognized as concentrations of housing, which is by far the most important user of urban land. One of the few available studies indicates that about three-quarters of privately developed urban land is devoted to residential use.[1] To be an important town, however, a city has to consist of something other than housing. The dictionary definition also recognizes the obvious but still interesting fact that cities differ in size.

Not surprisingly, though, the dictionary fails to capture the essential economic fact about cities: that they are relatively dense concentrations of labor and nonland capital (*relatively* dense because where one chooses to draw the line between a city and a town or village is rather arbitrary). Populated places, however, are largely manifestations of the fact that different kinds of economic activity differ in the relative importance of land as a factor of production. Of all the major categories of production, agriculture is certainly the most land-intensive; that is, it pays out the largest fraction of the value of its output in the form of payments to land.[2] What we call cities and towns are primarily spatial concentrations of nonagricultural production.

The notion of a city as a cluster of nonagricultural production corresponds most nearly with the urban or metropolitan area. In terms of available data, the urbanized area as defined by the Bureau of the Census is the nearest empirical counterpart to the idealized city. The urbanized area refers to a central city of 50,000 or more plus all the surrounding area built up

---

[1] Harland Bartholemew, *Land Uses in American Cities* (Cambridge, Mass.: Harvard University Press, 1955). Indeed land used for residences and for streets accounts for about two-thirds of developed urban land.

[2] In economics, a particular kind of production is said to be land- (labor or capital) intensive if relatively much of the factor is used compared with other kinds of production. Note, however, that in high school geography courses and elsewhere, certain kinds of agriculture (such as some fruit and vegetable crops in the United States and agriculture in western Europe) are said to be land-intensive if relatively little land is used. An economist would say that such land is used intensively.

to some minimum residential population density. The central city (or cities in some cases) is the largest political city or municipality of the urbanized area. Apart from matters relating to government, taxation, and local public expenditure, the boundaries of the central city have little economic significance in and of themselves. In what follows, the part of the urban area outside the central city will be called the suburbs. In this book the term "city," unless otherwise qualified, refers to the urban or metropolitan area as a whole—the Chicago area rather than the City of Chicago.

Urban-rural differentiation

Next to agriculture, housing is the most land-intensive major economic activity. Closely populated places are to an important degree clusters of houses and apartments surrounded by farms or other open space. For such clusters to exist they must have something to cluster around. Such a point may be called a market, a place or related set of places where goods and services are exchanged. Goods from elsewhere are shipped to this point, and the market may also serve as a collection point for the shipment of goods outside the area in question. Producers of various commodities, including housing, use land surrounding the market along with labor and other productive factors. The main purpose of this section is to determine why firms producing agricultural commodities and those producing housing tend to occupy disjoint areas surrounding the market. Later on in this section the reasons for the existence of the market will be explored.

Where a market exists, firms of all kinds may find it advantageous to locate close to it. A factory would find the delivered price of raw material higher if the latter had to be unloaded from freight cars into trucks and shipped over crowded city streets. Factories and farms, likewise, find that they realize more from the sale of their output the shorter the distance of shipment of their output to the rail head. Many stores find that they have a larger sales volume at a central location that minimizes the average distance a customer has to travel to shop. Many places of work are located close to the market. Therefore, sites adjacent to it are more desirable as places of residence, other things being the same, because workers have to travel shorter distances to their jobs. In consequence, workers offer more for a residence the closer it is to the market.

For most firms, then, locations close to the market would be more desirable if land costs were the same everywhere. For this reason the rental value of land must decline with distance from the market. If it did not, otherwise identical firms would earn higher incomes if located closer to the market. More distantly located firms would increase their incomes by offering higher rentals for sites closer to the market than its current occupants were paying. In the process, then, rentals of undeveloped land or land plus existing structures would rise close to the market and fall at more distant locations.

Thus, whether used for factories, housing, or farming, the rental value of land would decline with distance from the market. The rate at which rentals decline, however, will vary among industries. The more important transportation is, whether for raw materials or finished products, the greater the advantage to being close to the market and the more rapidly must rentals offered for land fall off with distance from it. In addition, the smaller the amount of land used in production per dollar's worth of output at any given rental value, the more rapidly must the rental offered for land decline with distance from the market to keep the earnings of firms producing a given product the same at all locations. Producers of office space, for whom land is relatively unimportant, will thus offer a greater premium for a location close to the market than will farmers. Though all firms might find central locations more desirable in an absolute sense, specialization depends upon comparative advantage, as everyone who has taken an elementary economics course will recall.

Given that the rates of decline in offers for land differ among firms in different industries, how are sites surrounding the market allocated among them? The answer is most readily seen diagrammatically, as in Figure 2.1. This figure shows the rentals offered for land by firms in two different industries, r_1 and r_2, as a function of distance from the market, u. (Though rentals may vary with direction as well, such considerations are postponed until the following chapter.) If the

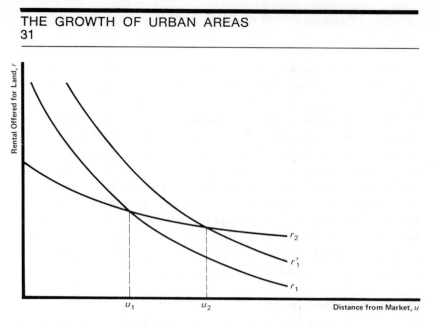

FIGURE 2.1
Rentals offered for land, by location and type of firm

rental functions of the two industries coincided everywhere, no clustering of firms of different kinds would take place. If one rental function, say that for the first industry, is steeper, for it to lie anywhere above the flatter rental-distance function it will do so closer to the market. As shown in Figure 2.1, when the first industry's rental function, sometimes called its bid-rent curve, is r_1, firms in the first industry will offer higher rentals for sites up to a distance u_1 from the market, whereas those in the second industry will locate at greater distances.

The principle just considered accounts for what is in broad outline a ringlike or annular structure of land uses in the vicinity of urban areas. Their downtown areas consist almost exclusively of nonresidential urban firms such as stores, office buildings, warehouses, and factories. Such firms use relatively little land per dollar's worth of output at given land costs per square foot and thus have the steepest rental-distance functions. Outside the downtown area residential uses predominate, whereas outside of what we think of as the city itself land is devoted primarily to agricultural uses. These statements should be interpreted only as tendencies, of course. A few persons live permanently in clubs or hotels in downtown areas; outside it many stores and factories exist.

Before passing on to the next topic it is worth stressing that the configuration of rent offers illustrated in Figure 2.1 is contingent upon general conditions of demand for products produced in the city. If the city were to grow (why cities grow will be taken up later), the rental-distance functions for urban users will shift upward, say from r_1 to r_1', yielding a new intersection with the agricultural rent offer curve at u_2. Land, previously farmland, at a distance from u_1 to u_2 will now yield higher rentals if developed for urban uses. Consequently the land area occupied by the city grows.

Breaks in transportation

Having considered why nonagricultural land users tend to cluster, it is now time to ask why focal points for such clusters exist. One answer, probably the least unsatisfactory one, is that markets or commercial nuclei tend to develop where a break in transportation occurs. Such breaks occur especially at the junction of land with water transportation, as at Chicago, or of one kind of water transportation with another, as at New Orleans. Indeed, of the seventeen U.S. cities that had attained a population of 100,000 or more before 1890, all were on sea or lake coasts or along navigable rivers. More striking is the fact that even in 1950, of the nineteen cities with populations of more than half a million, all were in such locations.[3]

To understand the importance of breaks in transportation, one must consider the structure of transport costs to producers of commodities. Not surprisingly, such costs consist of both fixed and variable components. Fixed costs are those incurred if a commodity is shipped any positive distance, independent of the distance shipped. Such costs, sometimes called terminal costs, are those associated with packing, loading, and insurance. Variable, or line-haul costs, tend to vary directly with distance shipped and with value per unit weight. (The latter is an interesting example of monopoly price discrimination,

---

[3] Otis Dudley Duncan et al., *Metropolis and Region* (Baltimore: Johns Hopkins Press, 1960), p. 24.

which arises for essentially the same reason that airlines charge businessmen higher fares than college students.) Line-haul costs, however, typically increase at a decreasing rate with distance shipped. Both for this reason and because terminal costs can be avoided, firms typically find it most profitable to locate either at a source of some raw material or at the point where their product is to be sold. For some commodities, said to be weight-gaining, transport costs are higher on the finished product, so production is market-oriented. Soft drinks, the syrup for which is generally shipped and water added at local bottling plants, are a good example of such commodities. Other commodities are weight-losing and are material-oriented, as in the case of the smelting of many metallic ores.

Where a break in transportation exists, however, additional fixed or transshipment costs must be incurred if freight is shipped past the breakpoint. In the case of iron ore, for example, ore boats must be unloaded regardless of where the blast furnace is located. If shipped past the breakpoint, though, the ore must be reloaded into railroad cars and unloaded again. Transshipment costs may be avoided entirely, however, if the blast furnace has its own harbor, as most do. Indeed, most factories and warehouses large enough to ship in carload lots are located adjacent to railroad lines. In cases where the variable costs on raw materials and final products are similar and costs of transshipment are relatively great, transshipment points are points of lowest transport costs.

Wholesale trade, which performs little actual physical transformation of commodities but primarily stores them and breaks large shipments up into smaller ones, is a good example of similarity of variable costs for its inputs and outputs. Closely associated with the physical act of wholesaling is its financing. It is thus no accident that the earliest port cities were principally commercial cities and that such cities developed prior to the industrial revolution. Even today, larger cities are more likely to be places of commerce and finance than of fabrication. As of the middle of this century there was no tendency for value added (essentially sales less the cost of purchased material inputs) by manufacture on a per capita basis to vary with city size in the United States. There were strong tendencies, however, for per capita wholesale sales, business service receipts, and demand deposits to increase steadily with city size for those with populations of 100,000 or more.[4]

Many have argued that cities arise because of economies of scale in the production of goods. This explanation seems unsatisfactory, however. If these economies were internal to a given firm, the firm would either expand its output until the economies were exhausted or until it was the only firm of its kind at that location. With the exception of a few kinds of production, of which electric power is a good example, there are few examples of single firms producing the whole of the output of some particular kind in any U.S. city. Further, the economies-of-scale hypothesis provides no explanation for the facts already cited in this section in support of the break-in-transportation hypothesis.

Others have argued that, in the absence of cost differences in space such as breaks in transportation produce, cities would arise because of economies in agglomeration (economies that are external to the output of any given firm and that depend on the total volume of production of all kinds). Greater flexibility in varying its level of employment in larger labor markets and the greater variety of firms selling specialized business services are examples of why a firm might find its costs of production lower in a larger city. Such cost advantages may well exist, though no one has ever provided any very convincing evidence of them. Like the internal-economies-of-scale hypothesis, moreover, the agglomerative-economies hypothesis provides no explanation of why larger cities are located adjacent to bodies of water. Nor does it account for the fact that larger cities are especially important as centers of commerce and finance but not of commodity fabrication.

Cities as central places

Many commodities are produced or sold only at points separated by significant distances. People in rural areas go to town to shop; those in cities and suburbs go downtown. The spatial

---

[4] Ibid., pp. 125 and 261ff.

separation of production of a given kind depends principally upon the balancing of the conflicting demands of economies of scale in production at the firm level, the frequency of purchase of the commodity per unit of land area, and costs of transport. Where economies of scale in production that are internal to the firm are slight relative to the density of demand for it and transport costs are relatively large, production of the commodity tends to take place on a relatively small scale in widely scattered locations. Conversely, when economies of scale are large relative to frequency of purchase and transport costs, production takes place on a relatively large scale but in relatively few places.

Grocery stores and elementary schools are good examples of the first type of commodity. Many consumers make several trips to the grocery store each week and children attend school five days a week for nine months of the year. Schools, moreover, grow larger primarily through the duplication of teachers and classrooms, and especially at the elementary level there are relatively few highly specialized, infrequently used pieces of equipment such as electron microscopes. Consequently, there is little to be gained by concentration of large numbers of students in a single location. Therefore, the neighborhood school makes good economic sense given conditions of demand and costs of production.

If steel mills were like grocery stores, something like Chairman Mao's idea for a steel mill for every backyard might be economically workable. In fact, steel production is one of the best examples of the opposite case. Particularly because of the savings on transport of the intermediate product made possible by the integrated steel mill, one in which blast furnaces, rolling mills, and other steps in the productive process are performed at the same location, economies of scale in steel production are relatively strong. For this reason, where production is organized on the basis of cost and demand considerations, steel production takes place at relatively few locations. Similarly, because most people attend few concerts or operas, such performances generally take place in large cities. Costs of transmission of television programs are probably quite low relative to their production costs. Thus, even if there is no particular advantage to concentration of the production of network programs in New York and Los Angeles, there is no economic barrier to such concentration.

Such considerations suggest that even the smallest clusters of nonagricultural activity—some have termed them hamlets—will contain certain types of production, such as grocery stores and drugstores that sell to the residents of the cluster and the surrounding agricultural "hinterland." Of course many types of retail and service activity, such as department stores, will not be found there. Larger clusters, however, do contain department stores, which sell their wares to the residents of that cluster and to those of surrounding smaller clusters. Similarly, production of a given kind becomes increasingly specialized with size of place. For example, very small clusters of population contain general practitioners, and cardiologists practice in somewhat larger areas, but heart-transplant operations are performed in only a few places in the United States. If the smallest economically viable market areas tend to fall into discrete classes, then a hierarchy of cities characterized by the kind of production that takes place would emerge. Many have argued that this is in fact true, and there is even a bit of empirical evidence that such is the case.[5]

The actual distribution of cities by size is consistent with the hierarchical notion in that the larger the size class of nonagricultural clusters, the fewer the clusters of that size. However, cities do not appear to come in discrete sizes as the hierarchical notion would suggest. Rather, they tend to be distributed more or less continuously by size. Indeed, in most regions the distribution of cities by size closely follows the so-called rank-size rule, which states that if ranks are assigned inversely by size, or the largest place is ranked first, the product of rank and size is constant. The notion of a hierarchy of cities by size can be squared with continuous variations in city sizes if randomness of the distribution of certain kinds of production is taken into account. Birmingham, Alabama, is probably as large as it is because of its steel production, which is a result of the fortuitous nearby occurrence of iron ore,

---

[5] See, for example, Brian J. L. Berry and William L. Garrison, "The Functional Bases of the Central Place Hierarchy," *Economic Geography* 34 (April 1958), 145–154.

coal, and limestone. Similarly, Washington, D.C., was selected as the nation's capital almost two centuries ago, while Norfolk, Virginia, happens to possess a particularly favorable harbor for naval operations. When random occurrences of this kind are superimposed upon an otherwise strictly hierarchical structure, the discrete size classes of cities tend to blur into one another.

WHY CITIES GROW
AT DIFFERENT RATES

The question of why clusters of nonagricultural activity exist and their interrelations with each other are fascinating. By and large, though, explanations of why cities exist provide little insight into questions of practical importance. Of these, the question of why cities grow at different rates is probably the most basic. Most questions of city planning and regulation and of providing for publicly produced goods and services depend critically upon expectations as to the future population of an area because many public investments, as in urban highways, tend to be long-lived and more or less indivisible. Later on in this section the question of the differential growth of cities will be explored. First, however, consideration will be given to the easier question of why cities or nonagricultural production tend to increase over time relative to the economy's rural sector.

The relative decline
of agriculture

It has long been observed that in most economies, growth and development are accompanied by a decline in the fraction of the economy's labor force that is employed in agriculture. This is probably the result of the fact that the quantity of farm products demanded is relatively unresponsive either to income or price changes. Empirically, most studies find price and income elasticities of demand that are substantially less than unity in numerical value. Thus, as incomes in the economy generally increase, the demand for farm products grows relatively less rapidly than the demand for nonagricultural output. Consequently, the demand for agricultural labor and farm earnings fall relative to those elsewhere in the economy, and workers migrate from rural to urban areas in search of better-paying jobs.

It is generally believed that mechanization in agriculture has forced workers off the farm. But mechanization has also occurred in many kinds of nonagricultural production as well. Improvements in farming have indeed occurred, but many of these are more or less neutral in their effect upon the agricultural demands for labor and machinery. Examples of such improvements are methods of crop rotation and the development of hybrid seeds and better fertilizers. With such changes, the same number of man-hours of labor combined with a given usage of machinery in plowing, seeding, cultivating, and harvesting yields a larger total output. Though fewer workers and machines are required to produce a given output, the marginal cost per unit of output, and thus price, falls. Because the price elasticity of farm product demand is less than unity, the resulting increased output is relatively smaller than the fall in price, and farm labor demand declines.[6]

Migration from farm to city has also occurred because returns to labor in the rural South have been persistently below those elsewhere in the economy since the Civil War, over a century ago. Such has been especially the case for blacks, as is pointed out in Chapter 7. Today, however, agricultural employment is so small—only 4.5 percent of the total as reported by the *Statistical Abstract* for April 1970—that a continuation of out-migration from agriculture will have much less of an effect on urban populations in the future.

Cities as open regions

In trying to answer the much more difficult question of why some cities grow more rapidly than others, most economists have constructed models similar to macroeconomic models of the economy as a whole. Like the macro models used in studying fluctuations and growth in national economic activity, regional macro models focus upon the interrelationships

---

[6] The effects of technological change upon the demand for labor are discussed in greater detail in Chapter 8.

among a few strategic aggregates. Whereas national macro models have been concerned principally with the determination of the national income or GNP, regional macro models pay greatest attention to employment as a measure of the level of activity. There are essentially two reasons for this difference. First, there is the fact that until recently few data on aggregate regional income were available, but employment data from census and other sources were readily obtainable. Second, total population is closely related to total employment, and, as already argued, the main purpose of the study of urban growth is predicting a city's total population for some future date.

A much more important difference between national and regional economic models arises from a crucial difference between the characteristics of the economic systems the models are meant to depict. National macro models are essentially models of a closed economy, for which the demand for final products and supplies of productive factors are generated internally. For this reason it is frequently sufficient to suppose that output consists of a single commodity. Likewise, it is assumed that factor supplies are fixed or, as in growth theory, that the stock of capital is given by past savings and the labor supply by outside forces.

Cities in the U.S. economy, however, are open regions. As the discussion of cities as central places suggests, the demands for certain commodities are generated internally; but most cities sell a substantial part of their products outside their borders. The demands for such commodities are thus determined primarily by forces outside the city itself. Therefore, in models of cities or other open regions it is usually desirable to distinguish between exports or exportable commodities and commodities that are consumed domestically.

The other important difference between models of the U.S. economy and those of cities is that for the latter movements of labor and capital into and out of the area take place to an important degree. For the nation as a whole the supply of labor is given primarily by the size and age distribution of a population. Population, in turn, grows principally because of an excess of births over deaths, immigration having been small throughout most of this century. As a result, the population of the United States as a whole has grown more or less regularly and slowly, at about 1 percent per year since 1920. For any given city, however, in-migration of population may occur from other cities or from rural areas. Differences in rates of migration among cities are relatively large and are the principal component of differential population growth rates of cities. Since 1900 the populations of U.S. urban areas have tended to grow at rates averaging 2 percent per year, but there have been wide variations among such growth rates. Some, among them Boston and Cincinnati, have grown at rates of 1 percent per year or less, whereas Los Angeles and a few others have grown at rates over 6 percent per year. Migration plays a critical role in all explanations of differential city growth, and its determinants will be considered more fully later in connection with these various explanations.

Just as labor may move from city to city, so may capital. For the nation as a whole the stock of capital assets depends upon levels of past savings. The latter appear to be essentially unrelated to variations in interest rates or other indicators of the returns to saving. Within the nation, however, capital is more or less free to move from areas where the demand for capital assets is growing slowly to those in which it is growing more rapidly. Though interest rates and the prices of machines may vary from place to place, so that the rental or use values of machines may vary, there is no particular reason to suppose that capital rental values in a particular city depend either upon the fraction of the nation's capital stock invested there or upon the rate at which this fraction is growing. In contrast, then, with the nation as a whole, for which the supply of capital assets tends to be perfectly inelastic, any city's supply of capital assets is probably highly elastic.

Before turning to specific explanations of differential city growth, two important aspects of regional economic development in the United States should be noted. The first is that in those parts of the country where population and employment are growing at above-average rates for the nation as a whole, employment also seems to grow at above-average rates for each particular industry. Thus, Florida, Texas, and

California have grown not so much because they have dispro-
portionate shares of their employment in aerospace and other
rapidly growing industries, but because all industries, regardless of their national rates of employment growth, have
tended to grow rapidly in those states.[7] Second, despite vast
amounts of internal migration, relative wage rates in different
states appear to have been remarkably constant over time.
From 1920 to 1950, for example, differentials in earnings per
worker both in agriculture and in nonagricultural employment
were remarkably constant. Differentials in per capita income,
especially as between the South and the rest of the country,
have narrowed markedly in the past hundred years. This appears to have occurred primarily because labor has shifted
out of agriculture, where earnings per worker are lower, more
rapidly in the South than elsewhere.[8]

The export-base theory

Almost everyone seems to believe that cities grow at different
rates because of differential increases in the demand for the
products produced there and sold outside their borders. As
a colleague once said, "After all, cities can't grow if everyone
merely takes in each other's washing." Yet this is precisely
what occurs in a closed economy, such as the United States,
or certainly the world as a whole. As Adam Smith observed,
with growth of the market, increased specialization and division of labor contribute to the growth in total output. Still,
it is an appealing notion that for cities, which are open regions
that sell a substantial part of their output as exports, differential growth results from differential shifts in export demand.
This notion might be characterized as the broad or strong
version of the export-base theory. However, there is little systematic empirical evidence to support it.
There is a weaker or narrower form of the export-base theory
with which little fault can be found. This is the idea that
employment in the production of goods sold locally depends
upon employment in the production of goods sold outside the
region or city in question. This form of the export-base theory

[7] See Harvey S. Perloff et al., *Regions, Resources and Economic Growth*
(Baltimore: Johns Hopkins Press, 1960), especially chap. 19.
[8] Ibid., chap. 28.

is thus a theory of local employment rather than total employment. Suppose, for example, the employment at the Boeing Company in the Seattle area were to increase because of an increase in its sales of 747s. With increased employment at Boeing, the demand in Seattle for groceries and health care would increase, as would the employment of grocery clerks and physicians. As usually stated, however, even this weaker version of export-base theory neglects an important factor influencing employment in domestic production—local wage rates. If Boeing were to increase wages, some grocery clerks might seek employment at Boeing, forcing grocery stores to increase the wages they pay clerks. The retail prices of groceries and other commodities produced and sold locally would rise, both absolutely and relative to the prices of imported commodities, and fewer workers would be hired by producers of domestic commodities. Thus, it is not enough to know the numbers of workers engaged in exportable and domestic production in cities of different sizes to predict domestic employment from a knowledge of total export employment.

There are at least two versions of the notion that differential shifts in the demand for exportable commodities produce differential changes in total employment and population among cities. In one, there is a general excess supply of labor in all local labor markets. Wage rates, however, are resistant to downward pressures, so that this excess is not eliminated. In Figure 2.2, for example, if the demand schedule for workers is D and the supply schedule S, employment is L_1 at the fixed wage $\bar{w}$ and $L_3 - L_1$ is the excess supply of labor. Under such conditions, an increase in labor supply from S to S' would not affect employment at all, but would merely add to the city's excess labor supply.

With an increase in demand to D', however, employment will increase to L_2 and the excess labor supply will decline to $L_3 - L_2$. The increased employment, in turn, will reduce the average period during which workers are unemployed, raising income per worker since wage rates are given. Workers from other labor markets may thus be induced to migrate to the city experiencing the increased demand for workers. When things have settled down again, the labor supply schedule is S', and the excess labor supply is $L_4 - L_2$, which may be much

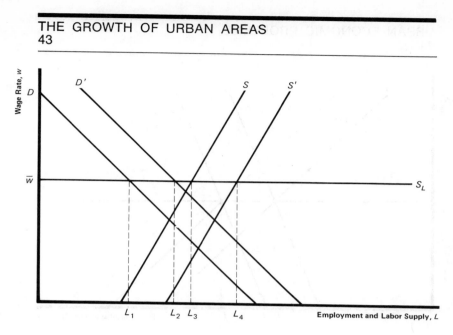

FIGURE 2.2
Local labor markets with rigid money wages

the same as it was initially, with employment and population having been redistributed among cities.

In the theory just sketched, migration is a movement that takes place in response to a redistribution of the locations of generally short job opportunities. It is a widely held theory and one with a certain intuitive appeal. It is consistent with the general constancy of relative earnings per worker in different parts of the country, and it may well be applicable for explaining relatively short-run changes in employment and unemployment. With recent cutbacks in employment at Boeing from over 100,000 to fewer than 50,000 workers, the unemployment rate in Seattle has risen to over 10 percent.

The theory is quite unsatisfactory on two counts, however. First, although wage rates may be unresponsive to downward pressures for short periods, the evidence cited in Chapter 8 suggests that wages are indeed flexible over longer periods of time. More important, in my own studies of differential growth in employment among U.S. cities in the postwar period, I find shifts in labor supply from migration, such as from S to S' in Figure 2.2, that are not induced by changes in the demand for labor and that lead to increases in employ-

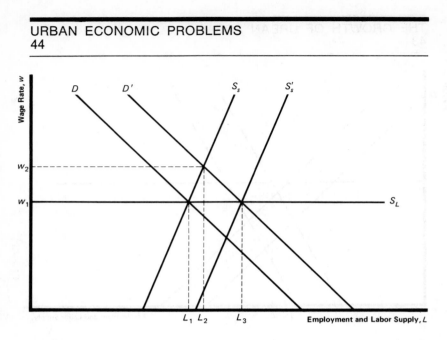

FIGURE 2.3

Local labor markets with highly elastic long-run labor supply schedules

ment that are about equal proportionally to initial employment relative to labor force. The theory behind Figure 2.2 however, implies that such shifts would have no effect upon employment.

Another version of the notion that differential growth in employment results from differential shifts in labor demand does not depend at all upon labor market disequilibrium. This version is illustrated in Figure 2.3. With an increase in demand from D to D', wages would rise from w_1 to w_2, and employment from L_1 to L_2, along a given short-run supply schedule of labor from a given population. These higher wage rates, rather than lower unemployment rates in Figure 2.2, induce migration of workers from other labor markets. The city's short-run labor supply schedule thus shifts from S_s to S_s' along the long-run supply schedule S_L. If the latter is highly elastic as drawn, wage rates are ultimately no higher than they would have been, but employment is larger.

This second version of the theory is also consistent with a relative constancy of earnings per worker in different parts of the country. However, few, if any, studies of migration have found any impact of wage rates at the migrants' destina-

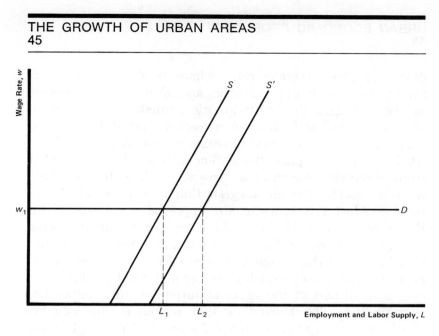

FIGURE 2.4
Local labor markets with highly elastic labor demand schedules

tion on the rate of in-migration. Furthermore, on the basis of either version of the shift-in-demand hypothesis, it is difficult to account for the fact that manufacturing employment of all kinds, most of which is for export, tends to grow at above-average rates for the specific industry in cities where total employment is growing at above-average rates.

An alternative explanation

An explanation of differential city growth that is much easier to sustain is that such growth arises from differential shifts in labor supply among cities. This is illustrated in Figure 2.4. Here the city's labor demand schedule is a highly elastic one. As will be argued in more detail in Chapter 10, horizontal shifts, or shifts in the number of workers employers wish to hire at given wage rates, have little or no effect if the demand schedule is highly elastic. The shifts in labor supply that in-migration would produce, such as from S to S' in Figure 2.4, would lead to increases in employment at more or less given wage rates. This explanation is consistent also with the relative constancy of earnings in different parts of the country. It is readily consistent with the fact that employment of all kinds, even in different manufacturing industries, has grown at above-average rates where total employment is rapidly growing. For all industries are affected by the increase in labor supply to the city in question. Finally, it is consistent with my empirical finding noted earlier that shifts in labor supply lead to proportional increases in employment.

At first glance, though, the notion of a highly elastic labor demand schedule for an urban area seems difficult to swallow. A little thought, though, suggests that it is not at all unreasonable. Most U.S. cities of any appreciable size have firms that produce and sell for national or world markets. Some firms, such as Boeing, Eastman Kodak, and Xerox, sell a substantial part of the output produced nationally. Others, however, perhaps firms producing lumber and wood products, sell only a small part of the national output of the commodities they produce. The demand for their output is thus a highly elastic one, much as is the demand schedule for a single, competitive firm. If the supply of capital to the city is also highly elastic, then under constant returns to scale in production—a condition that economists frequently assume exists in production—the wage rates such firms will pay are fixed and do not depend upon the level of employment in the city. Even though other firms in the aggregate, including producers for domestic consumption, have declining labor demand schedules, if labor is hired in the same market all firms must pay the fixed wage rate. The long-run effect of the decline in employment at Boeing would thus be merely to change the composition of Seattle's employment.

Even though one is willing to accept the notion of a highly elastic labor demand schedule for a city in the long run, there are still problems in accounting for differential city growth. These are mainly in explaining why migration rates have been higher into cities in the South and West than elsewhere. Economists are generally inclined to seek explanations in terms of differences in wage rates. Yet, as noted, there is little evidence that rates of net in-migration are much influenced by differences in wage rates. And, indeed, in most American cities wages paid workers of a given skill and training are probably pretty much the same. Many people undoubtedly find California's climate and topography alluring, but it is hard to accept this kind of explanation for the rapid growth of many cities in Texas. But, although there are still unsolved questions in explaining differential city growth rates, it is at least useful to know the right place to look for answers.

CONTROLLING URBAN GROWTH

Are some cities too large?

Currently there is a great deal of concern in many quarters over the growth of large urban areas. Such concern arises for a variety of reasons, but invariably it leads to demands for restricting the growth of larger areas and redirecting this growth to other places. As is the case with many questions dealt with in this book, there are indeed valid reasons for such concerns. Most of the commonly quoted ones are probably fallacious or at best incomplete. The valid ones, moreover, are rarely considered, even in professional discussion.

Probably the most prominent reasons for limiting the growth of large urban areas are beliefs that our present urban problems result largely from size or from past mistakes in the development of our cities. However, such beliefs are totally mistaken. I have already argued that poverty is our major problem and that it seems to be an urban problem mainly because it has become increasingly concentrated in urban areas. But the incidence of poverty, even among broadly defined population subgroups, is almost surely lower in urban areas. Bad as conditions for the poor may be in cities, they are worse outside them. It makes little sense to limit the already inadequate opportunities of lower-income persons by preventing them from moving to places where these opportunities are greatest for them.

Under current arrangements, the larger an urban area, the worse certain urban problems are, notably traffic congestion and air pollution. As mentioned before, transportation and environmental problems result principally from the failure of governments to set proper prices. The aggregate impact of such failures is worse in larger than in smaller places. The appropriate way to handle such failures, though, is not to throw out the baby with the bath water. Rather it is to impose taxes or other charges on users of urban transport systems and airsheds commensurate with the costs they impose on other members of society.

If such charges were imposed, the costs for any individual to live in larger urban places would rise relative to the costs of living in other locations. Individuals would thus view larger places as less attractive than smaller ones. Some potential migrants into areas such as Los Angeles undoubtedly would decide to locate elsewhere instead. And when changing jobs, some current residents of larger areas might be induced to move to smaller ones. Employers would also be induced to locate in smaller places for two reasons. First, they would be faced with higher nonlabor costs of doing business in larger places. Pollution charges or rules requiring the treatment of discharges into the air or water and higher freight rates to compensate carriers for the tolls they pay would raise production costs. And second, with employees paying more to commute to work, higher wages would be necessary to assemble the same size work force.

Closely related to this reasoning are arguments frequently heard on the West Coast that the growth of population, which leads to residential or other development of previously undeveloped land, adversely affects the natural beauty of the area. Indeed, the governor of Oregon recently urged people not to migrate into his state from elsewhere largely for this reason. In principle, however, congestion affects the enjoyment of natural beauty the same way it affects highways. Efficient use of the environment and other resources requires tolls or other charges that reflect the loss of utility experienced by other users. In this connection it is important to note that such charges should be imposed on existing residents of an area as well as upon new migrants. If by moving in migrants make a city a generally less desirable place to live, existing residents do exactly the same thing by remaining.

Related arguments concern differences among places with stable or even declining populations in contrast to growing ones. It is sometimes said that the former, which frequently are smaller and more remote from major urban areas, are desirable places for growth to occur because they already have streets, sewers, and schools, which are underutilized. In more rapidly growing places, though, new public facilities have to

be provided as population grows. The argument is partly fallacious in that the existence of certain facilities per se has no
particular bearing on the issue. Because the facilities already
exist, their opportunity cost to society is zero. Rather, they
are there whether used or not. The real problem in this respect
is that charges for the use of public facilities, whether paid
as fees or taxes, are generally fixed at the average cost of
providing the service in question. Where facilities are underutilized, marginal costs, or the costs per additional user, may
be below average. Similarly, in rapidly growing places where
public facilities are overutilized, marginal cost exceeds average
cost. Optimal use of resources requires pricing at marginal cost,
not average cost. If prices are set to reflect average cost, they
may exceed marginal cost in places with stable or declining
populations and fall short of marginal costs in others, thus
encouraging too rapid growth of already rapidly growing
places.

The final argument regarding growth policy relates to the
tax burdens lower-income migration places on higher-income
residents of urban areas. Not only are such arguments made
in connection with migration into a particular area, but they
are frequently offered as justification for opposition to public
housing projects in suburban municipalities. This whole matter will be discussed more fully in the final chapter. For now,
however, the major problem is in requiring municipalities to
finance expenditures for what are essentially income redistributive purposes by taxes levied within their own borders. If
expenditures for, say, welfare payments and public education
were to be made out of revenues provided by a higher level
of government, regardless of location within a metropolitan
area or the country as a whole, there would almost certainly
be less opposition to public housing in the suburbs.

Alternatives to large cities

The problems caused by the growth of larger urban areas
should be handled through the setting of proper prices for
publicly produced goods and services. It is desirable, however,
to point out some of the problems associated with redirecting
population growth away from existing centers. The discussion

is most easily organized around the two kinds of alternatives to larger urban areas: existing smaller places and so-called new towns.

The first type of alternative is sometimes described by the currently popular euphemism "growth center." The term reflects in part the realization provided by the considerations of cities as central places that not all can grow to be as large as New York. It also reflects the belief—perhaps "hope" would be a better word—that a given public expenditure would produce better results if concentrated in a few places rather than spread over many. Until recently, the Economic Development Administration (EDA) followed a policy of concentrating expenditures on what are thought to be underdeveloped regions in a set of such growth centers, many of which are located in or near the eastern mountains.

Such expenditures are made both for better public facilities such as water and sewer systems and for loans to private firms that establish new plants in these centers. The centers are located in broad regions characterized by above-average unemployment rates, below-average median family incomes, and high rates of out-migration. The expenditures made aim directly or indirectly at providing jobs for unemployed workers, thus raising incomes and stemming the flow of population from the area.

A variety of issues are raised by such programs. Most basic, perhaps, is why out-migration should be stemmed at all. Apart from the faulty setting of prices already noted in this section, the only really valid answer is that migration may be an especially costly alternative for some workers, especially older ones. One of the few facts clearly established by studies of migration is that migration rates are much higher among younger age groups than older ones. The best explanation for this is that the costs of migrating are probably lower for younger workers, who have fewer associations to break, who are better able to enter into new occupations, and who have longer working lives remaining over which to amortize the costs of moving to a new location. Such considerations might indeed justify temporary programs to ease the difficulties of older workers in such areas, but they by no means provide a rationale for permanent programs.

Programs of the types employed by EDA are likely to have

quite different results than those intended. Such programs are more appropriate to the conditions of excess labor supply characterized by Figure 2.2. The long-run problem in under-developed areas is more properly depicted by Figure 2.4, with a wage rate fixed by conditions of external product demand and supply of capital at a relatively low level. Investments in water or sewer systems or in better road systems, as in the Appalachian program, may indeed raise the wage rate paid by firms in the area by reducing other costs of production. Since the area's labor supply is likely to be relatively inelastic, however, better public facilities are not likely to increase employment to an appreciable degree. To the extent that firms are induced to set up plants in growth centers, however, the demand curve in Figure 2.4 is merely shifted horizontally along itself. What this means in more concrete terms, of course, is that workers employed in these new plants who are not brought in from outside the area are simply drawn away from other employers in the area.

A final consideration of importance regarding growth centers is that subsidizing capital costs of employers is, in general, the most costly way to increase the earnings of workers by any given amount. The cost to the economy as a whole of area development rather than out-migration is associated with the capital or machines used in the area in question rather than elsewhere in the economy. More specifically, the opportunity cost of area development is the divergence in earnings of capital invested elsewhere and in the underdeveloped area. It can readily be shown, though it requires advanced techniques, that increasing wages through a capital-cost subsidy diverts more capital from elsewhere in the economy than does either a price subsidy for the product or a direct-wage subsidy of the kind described in Chapter 10. The reason is that part of the effect of a subsidy to capital costs is dissipated in using more capital per worker than would otherwise be the case. Price subsidies are better in that they result in less capital per worker for a given wage paid; but direct-wage subsidies use the least capital per worker and so are best of all. It is ironic that governmental programs almost always involve subsidies to capital costs, sometimes involve price subsidies, but almost never include direct-wage subsidies.

The other alternative to existing large urban centers is to

build smaller clusters from scratch. These may be in the vicinity of existing large cities, as in Great Britain, or may be far removed, as in the case of the new capital city of Brazilia. The popular appeal of new towns is probably that by starting anew and avoiding past mistakes, our urban problems will be less severe in the future. But the present problems of our urban centers have little to do with unattractive architecture or poor city planning, so there is not much hope on this score. Indeed, when considering the results of public housing and urban renewal programs, there isn't much hope for government-supported new towns in any case.

One possible reason for government support of new towns is that although investment in them might be socially desirable, such developments would simply be too big for private firms to finance and undertake. A similar argument was made concerning federal support for development of the supersonic transport (SST) in the 1960s. Yet private firms found no particular difficulties in undertaking development of the 747 and other large commercial jet aircraft during the same time. (The difficulties of the Lockheed Company do not appear to have been uniquely associated with its jumbo jet, the L-1011, and Boeing and McDonald-Douglas did not experience similar difficulties with theirs.) The main problem with the SST appears to have been high costs relative to the demand for it under the current state of the art, yet government undertook its support and discontinued it quite reluctantly. New towns might face problems similar to so-called infant industries in international trade discussions. If nurtured by governmental support, such industries could conceivably become self-sustaining adults. All too often, in fact, they remain wards of the state well into senility, as the textile industry in the United States demonstrates.

The major problems of new towns are well illustrated by Reston, Virginia, not far from Washington's Dulles airport. Reston, privately developed, is beautifully laid out around a series of charming lakes and offers many attractive houses in a wide variety of sizes and architectural styles. About ten years ago, though, the cheapest houses were $40,000 to $45,000 and apartments started at $195 per month. Obviously, only relatively high-salaried workers could afford to live there, and there simply aren't enough jobs for such workers in many such complexes. Even the few Restons that could be supported in this way could not attract grocery clerks and other lower-income workers to provide a self-sustaining town. It was, therefore, no surprise that, because of financial difficulties, the major oil company that had supplied much of the financing for Reston assumed control of it. The last I heard of Reston was in a newspaper report over a controversy as to whether the bus taking some of its residents to and from their jobs in Washington could serve martinis on the homeward trip. Reston appears to have become as much a bedroom community for Washington as Westchester and southwestern Connecticut are for New York City.

SUMMARY

Like users of land tend to cluster together in broad annular areas surrounding focal points of economic activity. Those for whom land is least important as a productive factor offer the highest rentals for land adjacent to the focal point. Thus cities, which are relatively dense concentrations of labor and nonland capital in space, are formed. Such concentrations grow up around breakpoints in transportation, especially at the junction of water with some other kind of transportation. Larger cities are distinguished from other places primarily by a greater relative importance of trade and finance rather than the fabrication of goods. There is reason to believe that the group of cities in any region form a hierarchy by size. The larger the city, the greater the variety of goods and services produced there and the greater the degree of specialization of firms by function.

In this century, urban populations in the United States have grown at twice the rate, on the average, as the population of the country as a whole. The greater growth rate of cities reflects the declining relative demand for labor in agriculture with technological progress in it and with the growth in income levels in the economy. The demand for products produced in a city is determined to an important degree by forces outside the city, and labor and nonland capital are free to migrate from one place to another. Many believe that differential growth rates among cities are to be explained by differential growth in the demand for products exported from the city. A better explanation is provided by differential labor supply shifts resulting from differential rates of in-migration of people. However, there is no very satisfactory explanation for differential rates of population in-migration by city.

Much of the concern over city growth arises from the mistaken belief that our present urban problems are the result of past mistakes in city development or of growth itself. Though traffic congestion and air pollution are more severe in larger cities, these problems arise primarily because of the failure of government to set appropriate charges for rush-hour highway use and atmospheric waste disposal. Closely related to this, average cost-pricing for schools, sewers, and other public facilities results in underutilization of these facilities in smaller places and overutilization in larger ones. The fiscal problems of central cities result principally from the requirement that local governments finance income redistributive expenditures by taxes levied within their own borders. There is little rationale on economic grounds for seeking to prevent out-migration from rural or smaller urban areas, nor does there appear to be much rationale for the development of new towns.

CHAPTER 3

The internal structure of cities

NONRESIDENTIAL LAND USE

The foundations for the discussion of the internal structure of cities were laid early in the preceding chapter, where urban-rural differentiation was discussed. Most theories of city structure take the Central Business District (CBD) as the focal point about which urban economic activity is structured. Historically the CBD was close to intercity transport terminals, and it is still the part of the city where its intracity transport routes converge. Land surrounding the CBD is allocated to different users on the basis of who will pay the highest rental for it. Those users of land for whom the bid-rent curve is steepest tend to locate near the CBD, whereas those whose rent offers decline less rapidly with distance from the CBD are located farther away. Actually, though, little is known about the strategic factors affecting the rent offers of nonresidential users of land. This chapter thus pays greatest attention to housing, which is the largest single urban land user. But first a few of the more important considerations governing other land use will be discussed briefly.

Processing industries

Manufacturing and other firms engaged in significant alterations of the physical form of commodities purchased from other producers are affected to a greater or lesser degree by transport costs on commodities purchased from and sold to others. The considerations governing their location are, in large part, similar to those discussed in connection with breaks in transportation in Chapter 2. For such firms transport facilities of all kinds play roles that are similar to the point material sources and point markets described there. By selecting locations adjacent to rail or harbor facilities, many processors still may avoid substantial terminal and line-haul costs of moving commodities. Therefore they will tend to offer higher rentals for land adjacent to such facilities. Most other users of land, however, realize no particular advantage from such locations. And, indeed, most households would probably be willing to live next to the railroad tracks only if housing were cheaper for them there. Consequently, residential rent offers tend to be low along railroads, and separation of industrial and residential land areas would emerge even in the absence of zoning.

In discussing processing industries it is important to distinguish between so-called light and heavy manufacturing. The essence of the distinction is in whether shipments are received and made in less-than-carload lots or in carload lots. For a firm shipping in carload lots, a freight car can be delivered to a plant anywhere along a rail line for unloading. Similarly, a truckload of freight may be delivered anywhere in the city without first unloading, though some locations may be easier to reach than others. Consequently, location anywhere along a rail line or major highway may be equally advantageous to the carload shipper.

However, for light manufacturers and others, such as wholesalers, who ship in less-than-carload or truckload lots, shipments must be picked up at or delivered to a rail freight or truck terminal. The CBDs of cities originally grew up in the vicinity of rail terminals. Partly because many of their users were located near the CBD, when truck terminals were established later on they were located nearby as well. Consequently, the small shipper tends to minimize his costs of transfer by locating close to downtown. Though the development of highway transportation of freight opened up new location possibilities for the carload shipper, smaller shippers for whom transport costs are important may still find locations close to the CBD desirable.

Even so, the development of highway freight transportation has probably given a substantial impetus to the decentralization of manufacturing and other processing employment. Another frequently cited factor is the development of the assembly line. Techniques of production employing a continuous horizontal flow of goods from one point to another, at each of which a relatively small operation is performed, use relatively much land relative to other production techniques. Because land is relatively cheaper in outlying areas, so are assembly-line techniques. Though it is hard to quibble over the reasonableness of the association, causality is not clear. If firms found outlying locations preferable for other reasons, they still might be induced to adopt land-intensive production techniques in these locations.

Retail and
service business

Spatial structure of retail and service business within cities is governed by similar principles governing it between cities. Such firms as grocery stores, which produce frequently purchased commodities, which involve relatively high transport costs to the buyer for other reasons, and for whom economies of scale in production are small, tend to be widely scattered throughout the city. Others, perhaps shops carrying a wide variety of fine imported table wines, may be located only downtown. Similarly, lawyers in general practice may be found almost anywhere, but specialists such as corporation and labor lawyers may have offices only in the CBD. Indeed, there is reason to believe that a hierarchy of shopping centers, the CBD being the highest-order center, exists within a city in much the same way that a hierarchy of cities characterized by the range of commodities produced may be said to exist.[1]

Even prior to the development of the suburban shopping center in the post–World War II period or zoning regulations following World War I, retail and service establishments tended to cluster together at certain locations within the city. This clustering can probably be explained by the model of segregation described in Chapter 4. People typically visit more than one kind of store on a shopping trip, so sales are likely to be larger if a store is located in the vicinity of other retail or service establishments. Certain facilities such as parking lots can be shared. The sales of many kinds of establishments are all likely to be higher if located near the intersection of major intracity transport routes. At the same time, a house located between a grocery store and a restaurant is probably a less desirable place to live than one between two houses a block or two away. For these reasons, retail and service establishments, like many other types of economic activity, tend to cluster together.

The development of automobile transportation has probably led to the decentralization of retail and service business in two ways. First, it has brought about the suburbanization

[1] See Brian J. L. Berry, *Commercial Structure and Commercial Blight* (Chicago: Department of Geography, University of Chicago, 1963).

of residences, causing the sales potential for many kinds of businesses to rise in the suburbs. Second, it has almost certainly reduced the cost of circumferential vs. that of radial movement. Travel to downtown by bus or commuter railroad may still work reasonably well, but crosstown travel was especially time-consuming prior to the auto. The latter more readily permits travel to noncentral shopping centers. More important, perhaps, are the effects of increases in the population of urban areas. When a city is large enough to support only a single branch of a department store, the average distance customers travel is typically minimized by a downtown location. When several branches are economically viable in larger cities, however, the average distance customers travel is a minimum when all but the original branch are located away from the city center.

EQUILIBRIUM OF RESIDENTIAL LAND USE

The demand for residential land derives from the demand for housing. What is called housing is actually a bundle of consumer satisfactions that can be characterized in a variety of ways. Shelter from the elements, convenience, and social distinction are perhaps the ultimate wants satisfied in different degrees by the consumption of housing. Such things are provided by square feet of floor space, a variety of rooms, the attractiveness of decorations and furnishings, equipment for heating, cooking, and bathing, and so forth. In practice, however, and for good reason, larger houses generally contain more of all these features. As a first approximation, then, it is sufficient to think of housing as a one-dimensional quantity that, like food or clothing, may simultaneously satisfy more than one consumer desire. Further, although larger houses rent for more money, this is principally because they give a larger quantity of housing services. Thus, in the following discussion, the price of housing means the monthly rental value per unit, say per square foot of floor space, of houses or apartments. Therefore, the total rent paid is the household's expenditure on housing.

Housing is composed of a variety of elements in addition to land. Among these are the lumber, pipe and wire, and man-hours of construction labor embodied in the structure itself. Also important for many purposes are the fuel used for heat and light and expenditures made for repairs and maintenance. But, although the rental value or price per square foot of residential land varies greatly within a city, most other things are purchased at much the same prices everywhere. In consequence, it is a reasonable approximation to consider everything other than land itself as a single nonland input and to speak of housing as being produced by land and by nonland factors of production. Furthermore, the only difference in parcels of land in different places in the city to be considered is their location. Otherwise, for simplicity land is assumed to be homogeneous.

In considering the economics of residential land use, the willingness of people to purchase housing in different parts of the city will first be considered. Next the response of producers of housing to variations in the amounts consumers will pay per unit of housing will be explored. Finally, some of the implications of the fact that dwellings are used over a period of years will be discussed.

Household equilibrium

Though not all workers in a city are employed in or near the CBD, the latter is in most cases by far the most important place of employment per acre of land. Furthermore, in most U.S. cities persons working in the CBD are not clustered around it but tend to be scattered over much of the metropolitan area. Because households with one or more members employed in the CBD incur greater expenditures getting to and from work the farther from it they live, the price per unit paid for housing must decline with distance from the CBD. For if it did not, households living ten miles from the CBD could improve their well-being by moving closer and paying somewhat more for any given dwelling than its current occupants pay. Prices would thus rise closer to the CBD and fall farther from it.

Any given household faced with the choice of a residence can be thought of as balancing housing costs and transport costs in seeking the best location. For a household to be getting the most it can for its limited income it is first necessary that the additional satisfaction per dollar's worth of expenditure be the same for housing and for all other commodities. The additional satisfaction derived from housing relative to that from other commodities varies inversely with the consumption of housing relative to other things, declining as more housing is consumed. Consequently, households living farther from the CBD would tend to live in larger houses, other things being the same. The amount spent on housing, or the rental value per house, depends though, on the price elasticity of housing demand. Because the latter appears to be close to unity, one would expect households located at different distances from the CBD to spend the same amount on housing, given their income and preferences for housing and other commodities.

A second condition of household equilibrium is that the savings on the purchase of a given quantity of housing that could be realized by moving farther from the CBD and paying a lower price per unit of housing be exactly offset by the additional transportation expense incurred by members of the household working in the CBD. For if this second condition did not hold, the household could move, either closer to or farther from the CBD, consume precisely the same amount of housing as before, and have some income left over for expenditure on other things. Stated differently, the relative rate of decline in the price of housing is equal to the additional or marginal costs of transportation divided by the household's expenditure on housing. This follows from the fact that, where q is the quantity of housing purchased, p its unit price, p_u the change in price per mile, which is negative, and T_u the increase in transportation expenditure per mile, $-qp_u$ is the savings on housing costs so $-qp_u = T_u$ implies $-p_u/p = T_u/pq$.

The locational equilibrium of households is illustrated in Figure 3.1. The steeper curve, $-qp_u$, shows the saving on the purchase of a given quantity of housing that results from a short move farther from the CBD. The other curve, T_u, shows the additional transportation expense incurred by such a move. At distance u_1, the ordinate of the $-qp_u$ curve exceeds that of the T_u curve, indicating that a household can move farther

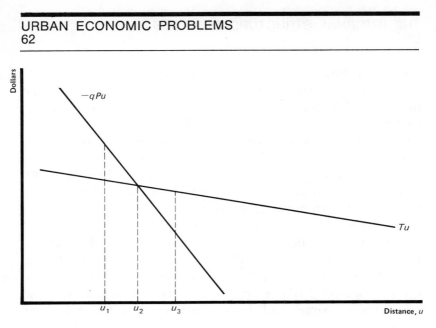

FIGURE 3.1
Gains and costs of varying residential location

from the CBD, consume the same amount of housing, and have income left over for spending on other things. Consequently, u_1 cannot be its equilibrium on best location. Similarly, at u_3 the household can move closer to the CBD and have more income left over, so u_3 cannot be its best location either. Only at u_2, as the figure is drawn, is the household unable to increase its well-being by changing its location.

For a location such as u_2 to be the best location, the price per unit of housing cannot decline too rapidly. Consider what would happen, for example, if the labels on the curves in the figure were reversed. At a point of intersection such as u_2, though a small move would not benefit the households, a larger one would. Indeed, if the curves were straight lines, a household would either try to move to the center of the city or as far away as possible. In the city of San Francisco, it could exhaust the possibilities for improving itself only by living in Union Square or in Alaska or Chile. The absurdity of such possibilities merely means that, of the two curves in Figure 3.1, the $-qp_u$ curve must be the steeper.

Given the pattern of housing prices in relation to distance from the CBD, each household has an equilibrium or best

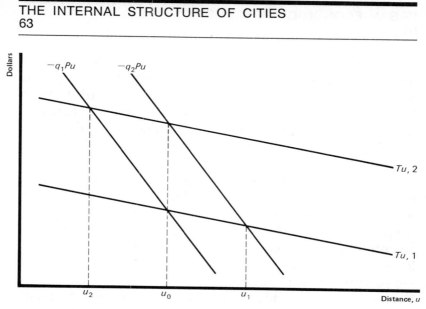

FIGURE 3.2
Variation in equilibrium location for different households

location, but these best locations differ from household to household. Several such possibilities are indicated in Figure 3.2. Consider, for example, two households for whom the marginal costs of transport are the same, as indicated by the curve $T_{u,1}$. Also, suppose that the second household has stronger preferences for housing relative to other items of consumption. Consequently, the savings in its housing expenditure as it moves farther from the CBD is given by the curve $-q_2 p_u$, as compared with $-q_1 p_u$ for the first household. The best location for the household with weaker preferences for housing is u_0. At that location, however, the second household consumes more housing and thus can increase its well-being by moving farther from the CBD. Its best location is at u_1, a greater distance from the CBD than u_0.

Similarly, households may differ in their marginal costs of transport. A good example is provided by a young married couple, both of whom have jobs downtown. Since both must travel to work, their marginal transport costs are higher than those for a similar couple one of whom teaches school outside the CBD, $T_{u,2}$ as compared with $T_{u,1}$. Consequently, the former couple will tend to live closer to the CBD, perhaps in a high-rise apartment building rather than in a walk-up or a rented town house. Conversely, retired couples make few trips to the CBD, so the marginal cost of transport for them are very low. The retired couple's best location, then, would be in the outer parts of the urban area. Thus it is not surprising that many older households continue to reside in the suburbs, even though their children are grown and have left home.

Most interesting and important of all, perhaps, is the effect of income differences upon a household's best location. Higher-income households, of course, consume more housing than lower-income ones. Consequently, the savings on housing expenditure they can achieve by any move are greater than for lower-income households, again as indicated by the curve $-q_2 p_u$ as contrasted with $-q_1 p_u$.

Higher-income households, however, incur greater marginal transport costs than do lower-income ones because transport costs include not only direct or out-of-pocket costs, such as bus fares and automobile operating costs, but also the indirect money costs of time spent in travel. As will be explained more fully in Chapter 7, the opportunity cost of time spent other than in working is the money income that might have been earned by working longer. Though it is by no means necessary that consumers value time at their wage rate, time costs are directly related to the wage rate earned. Members of higher-income households almost always earn higher hourly wages than members of lower-income ones—this is the primary reason their incomes are greater. Consequently, the curve showing marginal transport costs in Figure 3.2 is also displaced upward as income increases.

The impact of income differences, then, depends critically on how responsive housing expenditures and marginal transport costs are to income differences. Empirically, it would appear that housing expenditure increases faster than transport costs as income does. The best residential location for a higher-income family is thus farther from the CBD. The fact that in most U.S. cities higher-income families live farther out is also partly the result of the fact that higher-income families tend to live in newer dwellings. (Further consideration of this last point will be given at the end of this section.) Newer dwellings, of course, usually are located farther from the CBD than older ones.

Producer equilibrium

Given that the price per square foot, say, of housing tends to decline with distance from the CBD, land rentals per square foot must do so too. The reasons for this decline were spelled out early in the preceding chapter. Here it is appropriate to discuss the effect of variations in land rentals upon the intensity of housing output in different parts of the city.

Generally, when the price of a particular productive factor falls, more of it is used relative to other inputs in producing a given output of the final product. The production of housing is no exception to this tendency. The major way the input of land into the production of housing is varied is through varying the type of structure. High-rise or elevator apartment buildings typically predominate closer to the center of town, where residential land rentals are highest. Ranch or one-story houses on the outskirts of urban areas represent the other end of the spectrum. In between come walk-up apartments, row or town houses, and detached houses of three and two stories. Building additional stories onto a structure and squeezing structures together are ways of economizing on land. The less land used per dwelling, though, the greater the expenditure on structural features of dwellings. Frames must become increasingly more sturdy to bear the weight of more stories, and foundations must be more solid and dug deeper. Likewise, the greater the number of stories, the larger the fraction of potential floor space per floor that must be given over for stairs and/or elevators as well as for pipes and wiring.

Other forces produce much the same result. The more expensive land is, the less tendency there is to use it for off-street parking and the more likely it will be for a structure to have a parking garage in the basement and even in the lower floors. The top floors of high-rise structures may command premium rentals because of the views. Lower floors may well be rentable, however, only at lower prices per square foot than space in lower buildings surrounded by more open space. Regardless of the reason, any individual building owner undertakes the additional expenses of higher buildings only because land is more expensive. It should be kept in mind, though, that land is more expensive because of a stronger demand for housing. Ultimately, then, the intensity of housing output per unit of land is a reflection of the strength of housing demand on the price per square foot of floor space that buyers will pay.

Whether more is spent on land where land rentals are higher depends upon the degree of possibilities for substituting land for structures in producing housing. If these possibilities are limited enough, though fewer square feet of land may be used per square foot of floor space of housing produced, more will be spent on land relative to housing rentals. This is because the difference in land rentals is less than offset by the difference in square feet of land used. In such situations, the elasticity of substitution of land for structures in producing housing is said to be less than unity. Empirically, it appears that this is indeed the case. Thus, the fact that relatively more is spent for land closer to the CBD, where land costs per square foot are higher, in no way contradicts the fact of physical substitution of other factors for land.

In general, the smaller the fraction of housing rentals paid out as land rentals, the more elastic the supply of housing is. The supply of residential land need not be perfectly inelastic, if only because agricultural land is converted to urban land as the demand for the latter increases. Nonland inputs into housing production, though, can move freely, as between urban areas. Consequently their supply to any single area is highly elastic. It is thus easier to expand the output of housing in the outer parts of urban areas, where relatively less is spent on the factor land, whose supply is less elastic to the housing industry. The implications of this very important fact will be discussed further in the following section, which explores how the residential land-use pattern of cities changes over time.

Dynamics of residential land use

Before exploring changes over time in city form and structure, one other feature of urban housing markets should be considered. This is the fact of the durability of residential and other kinds of structures. Once built, structures are not only fixed in location but also tend to be fixed in terms of the services they currently render in production and consumption over considerable periods of time. This consideration has led many to conclude that the current state of cities is largely a reflection of their past development. However, this conclusion is almost surely too strong. The flow of housing services from a given structure depends to a degree upon current expenditures, reflecting how well it is supplied with heat and light and how well it is maintained when repairs are necessary. Interior renovation and modification are possible, so that the age of the exterior of a structure may be a poor guide to the age of the interior. Finally, dwellings tend to depreciate and/or obsolesce, effectively giving off a progressively smaller flow of housing services as they age.

Despite these considerations, it is a reasonable presumption that the parts of the city developed prior to 1920, following which automobile transport became widespread, are more densely built up than they would be if rebuilt today. As will be argued more fully in the following section, as intracity auto transport was introduced the marginal costs of traveling an additional mile to or from work declined. Earlier in this section it was argued that the relative rate of decline in housing prices would be smaller the smaller the marginal costs of transport. Consequently, if housing prices as a function of distance from the CBD looked like the curve p_1 in Figure 3.3 prior to the automobile, following its introduction and widespread use they would look like p_2. For distances greater than u_1, where p_1 and p_2 are equal, more intensive land use would have been called for following 1920. For distances up to u_1, however, reductions in the output of housing per acre of land would be called for because prices had fallen.

Empirically, though, there are not very strong tendencies for the value of housing produced per acre to be higher in older parts of the city once the effects of differences in location are taken into account. There are two possible reasons for this seemingly surprising result. First, since the introduction of automobile transport in 1920, the populations of most urban areas have grown greatly. At rates of growth of 2 per-

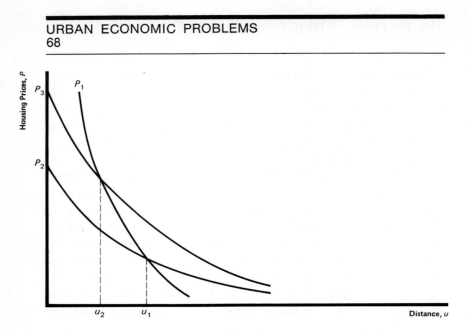

FIGURE 3.3
Changes over time in the spatial pattern of urban housing prices

cent per year, by 1950 populations would have grown by slightly over 80 percent. As will be discussed more fully, housing prices would tend to rise at all distances from the CBD with population growth, say from p_2 to p_3 in Figure 3.3. The effect of population growth then would overcome the effects of the automobile over the range u_2 to u_1 miles from the CBD. Another factor explaining the seeming discrepancy is that housing tends to depreciate over time. The rate of depreciation would seem to be about 2 percent per year as well.[2] At such a rate, the output of housing in 1950 from a given collection of structures would only be about 55 percent of the 1920 output. Thus, though structures may appear to be more densely built in the older parts of cities, the rate of flow of housing services need not be greater than in newer parts of the city.

The age of dwellings, however, appears to have a strong effect upon expenditures on housing per family for two reasons. First, as is mentioned in Chapter 4 in connection with the notion

---

[2] Leo Grebler, David M. Blank, and Louis Winnick, *Captial Formation in Residential Real Estate: Trends and Prospects* (Princeton, N.J.: Princeton University Press, 1956), Appendix E, especially pp. 377–382.

of filtering, there are strong tendencies in U.S. cities for the average incomes of families to vary inversely with the age of structures in which they live. Lower-income families, in turn, spend less on housing than higher-income families. And second, families at a given income level tend to spend less on housing the older it is. Both forces result, ultimately, from the durability of structures.

Structures and the dwellings they contain, which are the sources of housing consumption, do not tend to be more or less continuously replaced as are the foodstuffs that are the source of food consumption. Rather they tend to be held in the stock for a relatively long time, perhaps forty to fifty years, and then replaced. While retained in the housing stock, the rate of flow of housing services in physical terms declines more or less continually over time because of depreciation. At the same time, as incomes of consumers generally grow with time, the size dwelling unit families would most like to acquire tends to grow. This effect, as well, makes older dwellings smaller relative to consumer demand. Thus, the rental that households at a given income level will offer for a given dwelling tends to grow smaller with time.

Many have argued that because dwellings grow smaller over time, they will tend to be occupied by progressively lower and lower income groups in the populations. There are many examples, though, of central-city neighborhoods and older residential suburbs that have not undergone such filtering but have remained in occupancy of a given relative income group for a protracted period relative to the life of structures. More often, a neighborhood changes occupancy rather quickly from a higher- to a lower-income group. Such changes tend to occur in parts of the city that are spatially contiguous to previously lower-income neighborhoods along the lines described in Chapter 4. With an increase in the size, and hence in housing demand, on the part of the lower-income group, housing prices in its previous residential area rise, and private property owners convert housing from higher- to lower-income occupancy.

Typically there are many directions in which the lower-income neighborhood can expand. The specific dwelling units into which the lower-income neighborhood expands depend upon

which units are cheapest to convert into lower-income housing. Lower-income persons tend to consume less housing than
higher-income ones do. Because the effective size of dwellings
declines with their age, the older the dwelling, the higher the
rental a lower-income family will offer for it, generally, relative to the amounts higher-income families will offer. Consequently, the lower-income neighborhood tends to expand into
the areas where dwellings are oldest. Thus, income levels tend
to be highest in the newest dwellings.

CHANGES IN RESIDENTIAL
LAND USE OVER TIME

The discussion of the preceding section implies that housing
output per acre of land, either in physical or in value terms,
tends to decline with distance from the CBD. If the city were
continually being built anew, the consumption of housing in
physical terms would increase, but expenditures on housing
per family or per capita would be essentially constant. Taking
into account the fact that structures differ in age and that
older dwellings are located closer to the CBD, housing expenditures per capita also increase as one moves away from the
downtown area.

Now residential or nighttime population density, or population
per acre, is merely expenditure on housing per acre divided
by housing expenditure per person. These considerations thus
imply that population density declines with distance from
the CBD. Indeed, actual population densities tend to decline
at roughly constant relative rates with distance from the
CBD.[3] This section is concerned principally with the effects
on housing output and population densities over time as cities
grow and experience other changes.

Population and
income growth

A growth in either population or average income increases
the demand for housing in a city. In the former case the in-

---

[3] See Richard F. Muth, *Cities and Housing* (Chicago: University of Chicago
Press, 1969), chap. 7 and references cited there.

crease in demand results from the need to house a larger number of persons. In the latter, the amount of housing services the average person or family wishes to consume increases. In either case, the increase in demand leads to a rise in the price per unit of housing, and thus in the rental values of most, though not necessarily all, existing dwellings. In the short run, the increase in prices leads primarily to denser occupancy of the fixed housing stock. In the long run, though, the quantity of housing supplied rises, moderating the increase in housing prices. Because residential land rentals rise, land is converted from agricultural to urban uses. In addition, previously undeveloped parcels of land within the urban area are built upon. As older structures wear out they are replaced with newer, more densely built ones.

With an increase in income housing prices rise by a greater relative amount in the outer part of the city. The reader will recall from the preceding section that the relative rate of decline in housing prices with distance from the CBD at any given time must be equal to marginal transport costs divided by expenditures on housing per family. Because the price elasticity of housing demand appears to be about unity, the increase in housing prices itself leaves housing expenditures roughly unchanged. A growth in income, of course, leads to increased housing expenditures. Increased incomes, to the extent that they result from higher wage rates paid to CBD and other workers, tend to increase the value commuters place upon their time, so the marginal costs of transport rise as well. As was argued earlier in connection with the effect of income differences on the best location of households, increases in income appear to increase housing expenditures by a greater amount than marginal transport costs. Consequently, the relative rate of decline in housing prices is smaller following the increase in income, and housing prices increase more rapidly farther from the CBD.

Moreover, the general form of the city may be expected to change as population and average income grow because the output of housing is more responsive to price changes in the outer parts of cities, where land is a relatively less important input into housing production. Thus, with more or less the same relative increase in housing prices everywhere, the output of housing per acre expands at greater rates in the outer parts of the city. Unless something else occurs to cause consumption of housing per family to change differently, population will increase most rapidly in the outer parts of the city where the housing stock has increased most.

One would expect urban areas to become more decentralized as they grow in size and the average income of their inhabitants increases. Empirically, differences in size account for the largest fraction of differences among U.S. cities at a given time in the relative rate of decline in population densities.[4] An increase in urban populations of about 30 percent on the average during the fifties reduced the relative rate of decline in population density by about 15 percent and increased the land area occupied by the city by about 25 percent. According to my estimates, however, central-city populations would have grown only slightly less rapidly, about 27 percent, than the city as a whole because of population growth alone.

Transportation improvements

Transportation improvements, too, may be expected to produce urban decentralization or a greater relative growth in population in the outer parts of cities. To the extent that improvements in transport reduce either the time or the direct money costs of commuting an additional mile to the CBD, the relative rate of decline in housing prices must decline if households are to be in equilibrium. Note that what matters is marginal costs or costs per additional mile of travel. The frequent objection that people probably spend more in total on transportation today is beside the point. To a great extent, more is spent because incomes are greater, and urban populations are larger, too, so that the average person travels farther to a job in the CBD than previously. Quite apart from these factors, expenditures per family depend upon the price elasticity of demand for transport. If the latter is larger than unity, lower prices, or cost per mile, also result in greater expenditures.

[4] Ibid., especially pp. 180–183.

With the fall in the relative rate of decline in housing costs, prices rise in the parts of the city more distant from the CBD and fall in the older, more central parts. In response to these price changes, housing output falls in the core of the city and rises near its edges. Assuming consumption per family remains more or less unchanged, fewer people will live close to the CBD and more farther away. Thus, population densities will decline more slowly with distance from the CBD. Empirically, differences in marginal transport costs, as reflected in car registrations per capita, are the other major factors in addition to population differences leading to differences in the degree of population dispersion at a given time.[5] More important, though, the increase in car registrations per capita that took place in the fifties decreased the relative rate of decline in population densities by more than half. These same changes caused the land area occupied by cities to increase by about 45 percent, and central city populations fell by about 10 percent. Thus, there is good economic reason why the suburban parts of cities grew so rapidly during the 1950s.

Transport improvements not only lead to population decentralization generally but also to directional differences in population densities relative to the CBD. This is so because such improvements, as in the case with a freeway or a fixed-rail line, have a greater impact in areas adjacent to them than upon equally distant areas from the CBD but farther from the improvement itself. The greater the distance one lives from a freeway, the less the time saved in using the freeway as compared to the next best route because more time is spent getting to the freeway itself. A freeway or fixed-rail transit route thus tends to lower marginal transport costs along certain corridors as compared with other directions from the CBD. Housing prices, residential land rentals, and housing output per acre all tend to be higher at any given distance from the CBD in the sectors of the city served by these facilities, and all tend to decline less rapidly there.

The Chicago area provides an especially good example of such

---

[5] Ibid.

tendencies. Initially, suburban municipalities clustered along railroad lines that provided commuter service to the Loop area, Chicago's CBD. As automobile usage became more widespread, suburban areas grew up in the interstices between these rail lines. With the building of freeways to downtown Chicago around 1960, places convenient to these freeways experienced the most rapid urban development.

Suburbanization of employment

Along with the dispersal of residences within U.S. cities, many kinds of employment places have grown at faster rates in the outer parts of cities than in the downtown area. As a result, many have claimed that the CBD is dying as a focus of economic activity and that accessibility to the CBD no longer exerts much influence. Indeed, Los Angeles is frequently characterized as a city without a center because of the wide dispersal of employment places there. Yet population density declines with distance from the Los Angeles CBD as in other cities, though at one of the slowest rates among U.S. cities.[6] More generally, it does appear that the fraction of employment outside the central city exerts some, though not very much, influence upon the spatial distribution of population in urban areas. The fall in the central city's share in manufacturing employment from about 70 to 60 percent during the fifties reduced the population density gradient by about 7 percent and central city population by only about 4 percent.[7]

The main reason why the location of a substantial part of the employment places or their greater relative growth outside the CBD need not attenuate the effects of accessibility to the CBD is that such work places are usually widely scattered throughout the area of the city outside the CBD. This is in part the case because the existence of residential population results in a demand for grocery clerks, bank tellers, barbers, and schoolteachers in close proximity to them. Where the location of employment places depends very little upon the location of customers, moreover, there may be no single other

---

[6] Ibid., table 1 p. 142.
[7] Ibid., p. 181.

area of the city such as the CBD in which large numbers
of producers can find a locational advantage. To the extent
that non-CBD work places are widely dispersed, any worker
can live close to his place of employment without paying a
premium for housing. Consequently, there is no spatial struc-
turing of the housing and residential land markets about these
work places.

Workers employed in dispersed non-CBD work places do not
incur the costs of commuting to work that CBD workers
do. However, because of commuting costs to CBD workers,
the prices paid per unit of housing usually are lower at greater
distances from the CBD. In the absence of money wage differences, a non-CBD worker of a given skill level would always
be better off than a CBD worker and would be better off
the farther his place of employment from the CBD. For labor
market equilibrium to exist, or for workers to be content to
stay with their present employers, money wages would have
to adjust. In particular, workers of any given skill level would
have to receive higher money wages if employed in the CBD
than outside it. For employment places outside the CBD,
money wages paid would have to decline with distance from
the CBD to offset the decline in housing prices.

Of course, employment may be concentrated in large enough
numbers in certain places outside the CBD so that accessibility to these other centers has value. Good examples of such
concentrations are Oakland and San Jose, which are designated central cities by the Census Bureau in the San Francisco
Bay area. Where such concentrations exist along with enough
workers who care only about balancing off housing prices and
transport costs to make a housing market, housing prices, land
costs per square foot, and housing output per acre must decline with distance from the other employment centers as well.
Workers employed in the various centers will tend to inhabit
disjoint residential areas. For, if not, some workers can reduce
both the unit price of housing and their expenditures on commuting by moving toward their place of employment. With
a growth in employment in the non-CBD centers, money
wages, housing prices, and population densities near these
centers increase relative to those in areas adjacent to the
CBD.

PROBLEMS OF URBAN DEVELOPMENT

Popular discussions concentrate upon two particular problems of the internal development of cities: so-called urban blight and suburban sprawl. In many discussions the two are assumed to be related. In particular, it is frequently said that because of mistakes made in their previous development, the older, more central parts of cities have become blighted. The latter, in turn, is said to have caused people to flee to the suburbs. In fact, there is little empirical evidence for this view. As argued in Chapter 4, urban blight, to the extent that it is connected with poor-quality housing, is mainly the result of the poverty of large numbers of city residents. Earlier in this chapter it was pointed out that sprawl, or population decentralization, has come about principally because of population growth in cities as a whole and because of transportation improvements. Indeed, the process of urban decentralization has been going on for at least a century in U.S. cities, much before many of today's so-called blighted areas were even developed for urban uses.

Even though there are good economic reasons for urban decentralization, there may be problems associated with it. Some of these alleged problems are not really matters for concern at all. Those that are generally appear quite different when analyzed closely. This section, then, will analyze certain of these problems. Those associated with so-called suburban sprawl will be considered first, and then a few matters related to urban blight will be discussed.

Suburban sprawl

Even though there are solid economic reasons why the outer parts of cities have grown more rapidly than their inner zones, many arguments are advanced as to why too much decentralization has occurred. An old-time favorite is speculation. Speculators, who are handy villains in almost any discussion of economic problems, are said to buy up vast areas of land surrounding cities and withhold much of it from current development. Then, not only is too much land earmarked for future urban development, but those parcels developed for urban purposes at any given time tend to be located farther out than they would otherwise be.

It was probably easy to believe the argument that too much land had been platted for urban uses during the 1930s, when the depression led to an almost total halt to new construction of houses. Yet building during the 1950s went way beyond the unused areas of the 1930s. Undoubtedly certain areas are withheld from development in anticipation of still more lucrative development possibilities in the future. It is quite expensive for the economy as a whole, however, to tear down a block of single-family homes built ten years earlier to erect a garden apartment development or shopping center. Regardless of such considerations, the argument that too much speculation is carried on implies that speculators might have earned more by making other investments. The only good empirical study of the subject indicates that the rate of return on capital in holding of land that was later developed for residential and commercial purposes in the Philadelphia area was about the same as the return on common stocks.[8] No doubt more investment goes into land speculation because the income from it is taxed as a capital gain at lower rates than ordinary income. But it does not appear that too much land speculation goes on relative to other investments, such as common stocks, which are similarly affected by the tax laws.

Closely related to the argument just considered is that urban development imposes external effects upon others. For example, if I build a house on a half- or full-acre lot rather than a quarter-acre lot, others are forced to build their houses farther from downtown than they would otherwise. Consequently, I should be forced to pay a tax or charge equal to the additional travel costs I impose upon others. This argument is almost totally fallacious. Indeed, it provides an excellent example of the difference between an external effect and an external diseconomy. By so building I indeed force others to travel farther. But I have to buy the additional land at market prices to put my house on a larger lot. Thus, the

[8] F. Gerard Adams et al., "The Time Path of Undeveloped Land Prices During Urbanization: A Micro-Empirical Study over Time," *Review of Economics and Statistics* 50 (May 1968), 248–258.

price system already imposes the relevant charge for land so that I take into account the whole social costs of my actions.

This situation has more to it, however. Though I am charged the appropriate amount for land, I am not charged the appropriate amount for driving to work. This is because of congestion costs and my contribution to air pollution, discussed in Chapter 6. Consequently, if by some mechanism I am limited to a quarter-acre lot even if I am willing to buy a larger one, society does benefit to the extent that auto traffic is reduced as a result. The appropriate remedy for congestion and air pollution, however, is to charge me (and every other driver) an amount reflecting the social costs imposed on others by automobile commuters.

Perhaps of even greater concern on the part of young readers is the open space lost by converting agricultural or unused land to urban land. When a farmer sells his farm to a developer of tract houses, the sales price reflects the loss of agricultural output to society as a whole because the farmer sells the food and fiber he produces for a price. The farmer, however, does not sell the pleasant view afforded others and thus does not take this into account. As a purely practical matter, transportation improvements that produce sprawl have almost surely made open space more accessible to the average city dweller. Even though things are not necessarily becoming worse, they might be made even better by providing more open space. To the extent that open space is a public good, on which more is said in the final chapter, it can be publicly provided in the form of public parks and beaches. Furthermore, appropriate public bodies can subsidize cemeteries, golf courses, and other forms of open space. Finally, governments can buy up the development rights to farms, in effect providing the farmer with the difference between the value of his land in urban and agricultural uses. There is no reason why farmers, many of whom are poorer than the beneficiaries of the open space they provide, should pay for the enjoyment of city dwellers.

A final matter to be discussed is probably of greater practical significance than any other of the forces producing too much sprawl. This is the tax treatment of income from owner-occupied housing. As any reader who is both a homeowner and an income-tax payer realizes, there are strong tax advantages to homeownership. The homeowner in the United States is not required to report the implicit rental value of his home as income for tax purposes, yet he can take deductions for mortgage interest and property taxes paid. He is thus in the same position as a landlord would be if he paid a zero tax rate on any rental income he received from tenants. Interest on the value of a house and property taxes amount to roughly three-quarters of the cost of homeownership. A taxpayer paying a marginal or surtax rate of 20 percent thus pays only 85 cents per dollar's worth of housing purchased.

As a practical matter, homeownership means essentially single-family housing as opposed to apartment living. Single-family housing is land-intensive as compared with apartments, hence relatively cheaper in the outer parts of cities. In consequence, the tax advantage induces more people to live in the outer parts of cities than otherwise would. Indeed, about 17 percent more land is used for urban purposes than otherwise would be because of income tax and federal mortgage program advantages to homeownership.[9] Not only does the tax advantage result in too much sprawl, but it is an advantage whose value increases with income because homeownership and housing expenditure both increase with a family's income. It is clear enough that the tax advantage should be abolished.

Urban blight

For a long time, population and employment have been growing more rapidly in the outer parts of cities than in their inner zones. In the post–World War II period, this has even meant absolute declines in population and employment in some, though by no means in all, central cities. Such developments have led to concern whether our civilization isn't abandoning worn-out places of residence as nomadic tribes have done at other times and places. Concern over abandonment, in turn, has led to demands for government intervention in the renewal process.

---

[9] Muth, op. cit., pp. 319–322.

It may well be that because of improvements in transportation and for other reasons, any advantages enjoyed by the central city over suburban areas have declined for all kinds of production. For this reason, many foresee an eventual emptying out of vast areas of the central city, the so-called gray areas outside the CBD itself. Though the CBD itself appears to be quite robust as a location for office work—business and financial services and regulatory functions, whether public or private—few foresee private redevelopment of areas outside the CBD itself. The difficulty is that most people have not looked at the right things. After all, economic activity is structured in accordance with comparative, not absolute, advantage. Though a dentist may be more skillful in cleaning teeth than his hygienist, it pays for many dentists to concentrate on filling teeth, in which they are relatively even more skilled. (Matters here are quite similar to those regarding the differential advantages of automation, to be discussed in Chapter 8.)

Consider the influence of land costs on the location of employers, for example. In some lines of production, such as automobile assembly, the advantages to the horizontal flow of materials are very great. In others, perhaps the fabrication of women's garments, goods in process can probably be moved vertically almost as easily as horizontally. Similarly, firms with large work forces may well find cheap land for parking lots especially desirable. As firms of all kinds seek to locate where land is cheaper, land costs rise in outlying locations and fall in the central city. In the process, the cost saving from suburbanization declines, thus eliminating the advantages of suburbanization for firms whose land costs are small. Some firms, indeed, may even recentralize, or move closer to the CBD, as land costs change. Some firms will be dissuaded from suburbanization altogether if land costs fall far enough in the central city. At the same time, owners of land and other real estate in the central city undoubtedly would like to see the fall in property values prevented, hence the frequent support for government intervention in the form of so-called urban renewal from groups usually opposed to most other kinds of intervention.

At this time there is great concern over the problem of the abandonment of dwellings in the central city. Such abandonments are frequently pointed to as evidence of the gray-area problem. If one looks more closely, though, one can generally find good reasons for the examples cited in the press. New York City is everyone's favorite example. It has been repeatedly reported that over 100,000 dwellings have been abandoned there. New York, though, has had fairly strict rent controls since World War II. (Chapter 5 discusses the effects of rent controls on the profitability of maintaining rental property.) Another frequently cited example is Detroit, where something like 5000 dwellings upon which federally insured mortgages were made have been abandoned by their owners. Similar abandonments have occurred in other large cities. These mortgages were made on little equity and for long maturities under a federal program to increase homeownership among the poor. Laudable as its goals might be, the program fails to recognize the basic housing problem of lower-income families, which is their lack of income. The programs, though they reduced the capital costs of homeownership, did nothing to subsidize the current expenses for utilities, maintenance, and repair. When unexpectedly heavy expenditures for maintenance and repair were required, as frequently happens in older structures when, say, a furnace gives out, the owners of the house had little to lose by moving out and defaulting on their mortgages, and many did so. Essentially, it was the financial commitment, not the real estate, that was abandoned.[10]

Though there is good economic reason to anticipate private redevelopment of the central city, there are obstacles. One is the difficulty of land assembly. For private redevelopment to proceed it is frequently necessary to assemble a block of contiguous properties owned by many different persons. Any one of these, upon learning of the developers' plans, may seek to hold out for a higher price than he otherwise might expect.

---

[10] Government officials responsible for administering the program of homeownership subsidies for lower-income families and many newspaper writers have attributed these difficulties to fraud perpetrated by "speculators and other fast-buck artists." This strikes me as a convenient cop-out for the predictable failure of a poorly conceived program.

Redevelopment is thus delayed or perhaps not even undertaken. Hence, land assembly under eminent domain, where property owners are, ideally, forced to sell at fair market value for certain public purposes including urban renewal, may well be justified on economic grounds. If land assembly were the only problem, though, urban renewal projects would make money. In fact, they almost always lose substantial amounts.

Subsidy to renewal projects may well be justified, though, by external effects. (Externalities are considered at some length in Chapters 4 and 5, and the conclusion is that most commonly cited ones are either incorrect or unimportant.) A frequently mentioned example of the external effects of urban renewal is provided by the construction of a sports stadium in the renewal area. Though the owner of such a stadium receives the benefit of the revenue it produces directly, the sales of nearby restaurants may rise with attendance at stadium events. There is always the possibility, though, that restaurant sales elsewhere in the city will go down. If not, consumer expenditures for something else will decline, and with this decline the value of fixed physical assets used in production somewhere in the economy will fall. The matter of property taxes is similar. Though property taxes collected in the renewal area may well rise following renewal, the amount of capital formation for the economy as a whole is more or less fixed apart from short-run fluctuations. Thus, some property taxes that would have been collected elsewhere will not be because of urban renewal.

Even if there are not offsets elsewhere in the economy to the local external effects of urban renewal, there is no particular reason for federal as opposed to local subsidy of renewal projects. To the extent that the benefits of renewal are locally received, the subsidy to renewal can be paid out of taxes collected locally. There seem to be no moral grounds for residents of Atlanta to subsidize residents of Chicago. Indeed, since Atlanta has its urban renewal programs, too, it may well be that residents of rural areas of Georgia end up subsidizing both Atlanta and Chicago. The more carefully one looks at the current federal urban renewal program, the less desirable it appears from any point of view.

SUMMARY

Housing, like food and clothing, satisfies a variety of ultimate wants and is produced by using land and other productive factors. Households with a member who commutes to work in the CBD are spread throughout an urban area. Those who live farther away and thus incur greater costs in both money and time for getting to and from work are compensated by paying lower prices for housing than those living closer to work. Indeed, if no consumer can benefit from a change in his residential location, the relative rate of decline in housing prices is equal to the additional costs of commuter travel divided by housing expenditures. Because housing prices decline with distance from the CBD, residential land rentals do too. Producers of housing thus use more land relative to structures in producing housing where land rentals are lower. On the edge of the city single-family, detached homes may predominate, whereas close to the downtown areas of large cities dwellings may be primarily in high-rise apartment buildings.

As a city's population or its average income level grows, its demand for housing increases, and housing prices tend to rise everywhere. This leads to an expansion of the land area occupied by a city, as land is converted from agricultural to urban uses, and to a greater output of housing per unit of land. Housing output is increased most readily in the outer parts of cities, where expenditures on land are a smaller fraction of housing expenditure. Transportation improvements have also played a critical role in influencing the spread of urban population. Such improvements, by reducing the relative cost of commuting an extra mile, cause housing prices to decline relatively less rapidly with distance from the CBD. Housing prices fall and land is less intensively used than it otherwise would be close to downtown, whereas the reverse is the case in the outer part of the city. It is sometimes argued that decentralization of employment causes urban population dispersal, but empirical evidence suggests that this factor has had little effect.

Most arguments that too much urban decentralization has occurred are seriously deficient. If land speculation produced too much urban sprawl, speculators would lose money, yet it appears that the returns to holding land for future development are about as profitable as other investments. The market rental paid for residential land is the appropriate charge; if too much sprawl occurs it is because charges for commuting to work are not high enough. Though open space is lost when land is converted from agricultural to urban uses, there are a variety of means by which governments can maintain open space. With urban growth the returns to land and existing structures in the older parts of cities may well fall. As they do, however, new uses of them become profitable. The difficulties of land assembly may limit private renewal efforts, but it does not appear that publicly subsidized renewal has been economically desirable to date.

CHAPTER 4

Segregation and slums

EXTERNAL EFFECTS
ON URBAN PROPERTY VALUES

Most economists believe that urban property values are strongly affected by the type and quality of surrounding properties. Such effects are known in the economics business as external economies (if they are favorable) or diseconomies (if unfavorable), or more simply as externalities. External effects provide what is probably the major economic justification for governmental intervention in urban property markets or, for that matter, in private economic activity generally.

A now-classic illustration of what is meant by externalities is Robert Murray Haig's observation that a glue factory on Park Avenue would substantially reduce the values of surrounding properties. Thus, Haig argued, zoning and other forms of land-use controls by local governments are needed to prevent someone from setting up a glue factory there. To my knowledge, though, neither Haig nor more than a few economists since he wrote in the 1920s have ever asked why anyone should want to set up a glue factory on Park Avenue. To do so would almost certainly be more costly than at other locations. Ever since the New York Central tracks were put below street level, land on Park Avenue has been very valuable for apartment buildings, offices, and stores. This fact is but one example of a very general feature of urban property markets, namely that like uses often cluster together.

Almost everyone is familiar with the shopping center, clusters of tens to hundreds of retail stores and service establishments in the downtown areas of large cities, near the intersections of major streets, and isolated in the suburbs. By clustering, stores not only reduce the cost of facilities such as parking lots, but they take advantage of the fact that the customer's cost of a shopping trip is reduced by making several purchases on one trip. Most large cities have entertainment districts— North Beach in San Francisco and Rush Street in Chicago are two examples. Because people often like to bar-hop or combine dinner with the theater and perhaps have a drink afterwards, a tavern, say, is likely to have greater sales if located in the vicinity of other entertainment establishments. At the same time, people are likely to offer less for housing in the vicinity of night spots because of the noise associated with them late at night. To take still another example, since car buyers generally like to shop for a good deal, automobile sellers frequently cluster together along major streets.

In all these examples, none of which is so sensitive as to generate much emotion, one type of real estate user is willing to pay a premium to locate in the vicinity of others of the same or similar kind. In some (the entertainment district case, for example), other users will pay a premium to avoid them. The remainder of this section will examine the economic implications of such situations. Later on in the chapter these same notions will be applied to the more explosive examples of ghettos and slums.

A model of externalities

In analyzing the effects of externalities, I will suppose for simplicity that there are only two kinds of land users, A-types and B-types. A-types have either a preference for locating in the vicinity of other A-types or an aversion to locating near B-types. Further, their preferences are sufficiently strong that they are willing to pay a premium price for properties in the vicinity of other A-types. B-types may behave similarly to A-types, having preference for other B-types. Such is probably the case for Catholics and Protestants in Northern Ireland and for the many ethnic neighborhoods that used to exist in cities. B-types, however, may actually have a relative preference for living in the vicinity of A-types, as is probably the case with blacks and whites. If B-types prefer integration with A-types, however, it is assumed that they are willing to offer less of a premium to live among A-types than other A-types.

Suppose now that A- and B-types for some reason were initially scattered over properties at random. These properties are assumed for now to be identical, and both kinds of users are equally satisfied to occupy these existing properties. It is also assumed initially that the total number of both types of users is equal to the total number of properties. An initial random scattering of A- and B-types will produce some clustering—blocks or neighborhoods in which one type predominates, purely by chance. Few blocks or neighborhoods, though, will be exclusively occupied by one group.

Under these conditions, mutually profitable trades of properties between A- and B-types will exist. B-types in a predominately A neighborhood can sell their occupancy rights to an A-type user and receive a larger sum than is necessary to purchase equivalent rights in a predominately B neighborhood. It may be that users are slow to take advantage of such opportunities. Even so, households and business firms frequently move for other reasons. Firms are constantly growing and shrinking in size, some go out of business while other new ones are formed. Similarly, households grow and shrink in size, the principal breadwinner may change jobs, and so forth. Indeed, census data suggest that about one person in ten moves to a new house each year or that over a five-year period 45 percent of the population has changed residence.[1] When moves occur for other reasons, predominately A neighborhoods will come to be more so, as A-types outbid B's for vacancies that occur. Similarly, B-types will be able to acquire properties more cheaply in B neighborhoods and will tend to gravitate there.

The only equilibrium outcome of such a process is that in which A- and B-types occupy properties in disjoint neighborhoods. So long as any B-types live in predominately A neighborhoods, mutually profitable exchanges still exist. Landlords in predominately A neighborhoods will seek to fill vacancies with A-types both to retain their other A tenants and because a new A tenant will offer more than a B-type for the vacant space. For these reasons the landlord may even discourage B-types who might apply. Similarly, real estate agents would avoid showing B-types properties for sale in A neighborhoods. Mortgage lenders would be more reluctant to lend B-types funds to buy in A neighborhoods because under the conditions assumed here, a B-type is less likely to remain in the A neighborhood, and the costs of making the loan would be spread over a shorter period of time.

---

[1] The *1950 Census of Population* reported that in the city of Chicago, for example, about 90 percent of the population one year old or over had resided in the same house in 1949. In 1960, about 55 percent resided in the same house as in 1955.

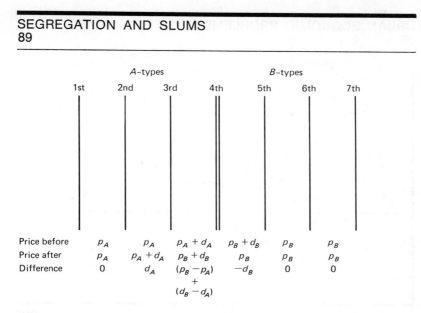

FIGURE 4.1
Contiguity effects on housing prices

Given that A- and B-type users occupy disjoint areas, external effects on property values will be manifested only along the boundary separating the two types of users. Again for simplicity, though empirical justification will be cited later, suppose that these external effects extend only one block and are uniform within that block. Within one block of the B neighborhood, rentals and sales prices of property occupied by A-types will be lower than in the A neighborhood's interior, which consists of all A-occupied properties more than one block from the B neighborhood. If B-types prefer segregation, properties within one block of the A neighborhood will likewise have lower prices than those in the interior of the B neighborhood. However, where B-types will pay a premium to live close to A-types, or prefer integration, B-occupied properties will be more highly priced within a block of the boundary.

This is all illustrated in Figure 4.1, a schematic diagram of the city from above, where the A neighborhood extends from 1st to 4th Streets, the B neighborhood from 4th to 7th Streets. The prices of properties in the interiors of the two neighborhoods are designated p_A and p_B, respectively. (Prices here may be interpreted either as sales prices or as rental values for some time period. It makes little difference which, provided the interpretation is consistently used.) Price dif-

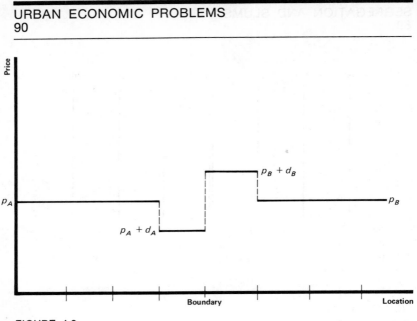

FIGURE 4.2
Equal interior prices

ferentials associated with contiguity to the other neighbor-hood are designated by d_A and d_B; thus, the B neighborhood price between 4th and 5th Streets is $p_B + d_B$. As Figures 4.2 and 4.3 are drawn, B-types prefer integration, for the B-neighborhood boundary price exceeds the interior price. In Figure 4.2 equality of interior prices for the two neighbor-hoods is assumed, which implies, of course, that boundary prices differ. Conversely, in Figure 4.3 it is assumed that boundary prices are equal. If so, the price in the interior of the A neighborhood must exceed that in the B interior.

Long-run equilibrium

Suppose, now, that conditions as depicted in Figure 4.2 exist, and recall that all properties are assumed the same and that A- and B-types do not differ with regard to the types of properties they wish to occupy. These conditions cannot persist indefinitely where properties are owned by many dif-ferent persons. The owners of occupancy rights to properties between 3rd and 4th Streets have the incentive to sell them to B-types. If they themselves occupy these properties, they can sell out to a B-type for the amount $p_B + d_B$ and purchase equivalent rights in the A interior for p_A, though the proper-

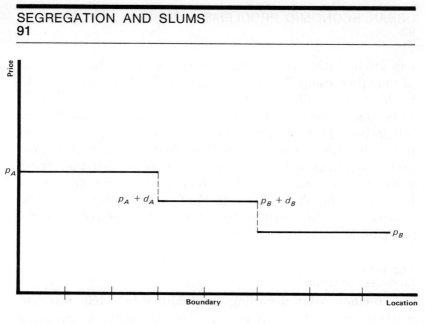

FIGURE 4.3
Equal boundary prices

ties they occupy are worth only $p_A + d_A$ to them. Alternatively, so-called absentee-landlords would find that as properties between 3rd and 4th Streets become vacant, A-types would offer only $p_A + d_A$ for them but B-types would pay $p_B + d_B$. Indeed, as the block changes, one could well find two different prices prevailing, with B-types offering or actually paying $p_B + d_B$ but with A-types paying at most p_A, contracted for on unexpired leases prior to the expansion of the B neighborhood to 4th Street. Over time, then, the B neighborhood would shift to 3rd Street, as would the price configuration shown in Figure 4.2.

Given stable populations and a growth of the B neighborhood relative to the A neighborhood, however, prices could not remain unchanged. Rather, to induce occupancy of a greater number of B-neighborhood properties by B-neighborhood types, the interior price p_B would have to fall. Similarly, with fewer A-neighborhood properties, the A-interior price would rise. So long as the B neighborhood expands, p_A will continue to rise and p_B to fall. Once price equality at the boundary is reached, as depicted in Figure 4.3, the process will stop. If boundary prices are equal, no property owner has an incentive to sell his occupancy rights to a member of the other group. The price configuration shown in Figure 4.3 is thus an equilibrium one, which when attained will tend to be maintained. If A-types prefer segregation and B-types integration, in this equilibrium A-types will pay a higher price for identical properties than B-types. If B-types also prefer segregation, however, one can only predict that prices along the boundary will be lower than in either interior in equilibrium. The relative level of interior prices will then depend upon the relative strengths of the preferences of the two groups.

The role of
land-use controls

One further point regarding externalities in urban property markets should be emphasized. Provided that the amounts persons are willing and allowed to pay for properties depend upon the inhabitants of surrounding properties, external effects on property prices will always be felt along the boundary separating two different groups of users. This fact is illustrated in Figure 4.1, where the levels of prices prevailing on the different blocks is indicated both before and after the boundary shifts from 4th to 3rd Street. Before the shift the A-neighborhood externality is experienced between 3rd and 4th Streets; after the boundary shift it shows up between 2nd and 3rd Streets. In like fashion, the B-neighborhood externality shifts with the boundary to the block between 3rd and 4th Streets. The net effect on the aggregate of all property values in the area is simply the difference in interior prices $p_B - p_A$, which is felt in the block bounded by 3rd and 4th Streets.

Thus, zoning and other land-use controls should not be aimed at preventing externalities. Externalities in land use will always manifest themselves along the boundary as differences between boundary and interior prices. Rather, zoning and other controls on land use should strive for equality of prices of identical properties in the interiors of different clustered uses. For if in Figure 4.1 the interior prices differ, say p_B exceeds p_A, then an expanson of the B neighborhood increases the aggregate value of existing resources. A necessary condition for optimal use of existing resources is that no shifts in use can increase their aggregative value, so if $p_B \neq p_A$ then resources are not being used as efficiently as possible. On the other hand, by equating boundary prices for two uses of identical properties, the private market may devote too many resources to one use at the expense of others. In the situation depicted in Figure 4.3, renewal or a shift of the boundary toward the B neighborhood would increase the aggregate value of existing properties because there p_A is greater than p_B.[2] The aim of governmental land use control, then, should be to regulate the relative sizes of different clusters of similar land uses, not to prevent externalities.

Evidence on boundary effects

Before considering two very important examples of clustering, segregation and slums, it would be appropriate to comment on the empirical relevance of the analysis of clustering just presented. There is a bit of evidence that external effects of the kind discussed do, in fact, occur. In a study of the effects of demographic characteristics on the sales prices of single-family dwellings in the Hyde Park area of Chicago, Martin Bailey found such effects associated both with race and dwelling condition.[3] More specifically, he found that both whites and non–slum dwellers pay less for houses in the vicinity of nonwhites and slum dwellers. Conversely, Bailey's results imply that nonwhites and slum dwellers both pay more when located in the vicinity of the other group. These effects were observed, however, only in special tabulations of census data for which the characteristics of residents on opposite (facing) sides of the same street were obtained. Such effects were absent when data for conventional blocks as defined by contiguous areas bounded by (usually four) streets were used. This fact suggests that externalities may be quite limited in their spatial extent and, like transuranic elements in physics, quite difficult to observe. A study by King and Mieszkowski of resi-

---

[2] The costs of renewal, however, might exceed the gains. If so, it would not be desirable on economic grounds.
[3] Martin Bailey, "Effects of Race and Demographic Factors on the Values of Single-Family Homes," *Land Economics* 42 (May 1966), 215–220.

dential rentals in New Haven found similar effects of racial characteristics on rentals.[4]

On the whole, though, the direct evidence for boundary effects is quite limited. The major reason why the analysis just presented is preferable to other explanations of clustering (some of which are discussed explicitly in the next section) is its generality and consistency with other explanations of economic phenomena. The examples of clustering cited at the start of this section, segregation by race or by income level, and many other examples are all quite consistent qualitatively with the analysis of this section. Other explanations offered for racial segregation in residences in the United States are almost invariably contrived to account for this particular phenomenon. Further, there is overwhelming evidence in support of the general proposition that in our society prices determined on markets influence economic activity.

GHETTOS: SEGREGATION BY RACE

The fact of residential segregation or spatial separation of residences, especially as regards whites and blacks, is a familiar one. Studies of this phenomenon suggest that it is very extensive, indeed, so much so that roughly 80 to 90 percent of the black population of U.S. cities would have to be moved to achieve racial equality in residential distribution over space. They also indicate that, if anything, such segregation is increasing over time and no more than half of it can be explained by income, occupational, and other differences associated with race.[5] Few Americans, though, understand the reasons for this segregation. They thus espouse measures that are of doubtful value in dealing with the problem.

Alternative explanations of segregation

Many feel that segregation results mainly from a unique aversion on the part of landlords and real estate agents to

---

[4] Thomas King and Peter Mieszkowski, "Racial Discrimination, Segregation, and the Price of Housing," *Journal of Political Economy*, 81 (May/June 1973), 590–606.

[5] Anthony H. Pascal, *The Economics of Housing Segregation* (Santa Monica, Calif.: The Rand Corporation, 1967).

dealing with blacks, which is not shared by the rest of the community. As a result, most action and legislation whose goal is to reduce the segregation of blacks is aimed at landlords and real estate agents. The former, by refusing to rent to blacks or by asking higher rentals from them, and the latter, by refusing to show blacks properties in all-white areas, are said to be responsible for the clustering of blacks. However, by refusing to rent to blacks, landlords experience a higher level of vacancies in their properties than they otherwise would. Real estate agents who fail to show properties to blacks make fewer sales than they otherwise would. Both could benefit by selling out to someone who does not share their aversion to dealing with blacks. In doing so, they could receive a larger value for their business than it is worth to them so long as they operate it. If businessmen as a group are as willing to undertake any activity in search of profit as is commonly believed, there would be no shortage of potential buyers. Even if there were, however, competitive forces would eliminate discriminating landlords and real estate agents. For, if competition among nondiscriminating landlords and agents eliminates excess profits for them, discriminators, whose costs are higher relative to revenues, would tend to lose money and be forced out of business.

It is also widely supposed that white sellers of single-family properties cause black segregation by refusing to sell their homes to black buyers, except perhaps at higher prices than they would charge whites. Whites might so behave simply because they dislike dealing with blacks. Or, though not prejudiced themselves, they may not wish to offend friends and former neighbors. Though various fair-housing groups have seemingly uncovered many instances of the alleged behavior, by itself it is not sufficient to account for black segregation. For, under the conditions postulated, other white buyers could profit by buying from white sellers and selling to black buyers. This does occur, of course, as so-called block-busting. But block-busting invariably leads to an expansion of the black residential area, not to integration, for reasons which will be discussed.

Another widespread explanation for the residential segregation of blacks is that landlords, real estate agents, mortgage lenders, and local governmental officials conspire to limit the availability of housing to blacks in order to profit from the resulting higher housing prices to them. Conspiracy is a popular explanation for all manner of economic, social, and political problems. It usually is suspect because it is too facile. Few people realize the difficulties in organizing and maintaining conspiracies involving large numbers of participants without active governmental intervention.

The failure of the several recent attempts by the National Farmers Union to raise prices by withholding farm products from the market provides an excellent example. Here, as would be the case in the urban housing market, such efforts are difficult to organize in the first place. Any one individual has the incentive not to join the conspiracy. By not doing so he avoids his share of the costs of the conspiracy, but, having a negligible effect on the outcome, shares in its benefits. If such a conspiracy were organized and succeeded for a time in raising prices, any of its members has the incentive to break the agreement and profit by selling a larger volume at a somewhat lower price. In the case of segregation, higher housing prices to blacks would provide the incentive for owners of white-occupied properties to rent or sell to blacks instead. There is no single instance in which a conspiracy of the magnitude that would be involved in urban housing markets has been demonstrably successful in raising prices without active government support in the form of legislation such as our farm programs. Thus, the conspiracy argument cannot be taken very seriously.

Now it is sometimes argued that government does indeed provide a strong degree of support to the residential segregation of blacks. Such support, it has been asserted, has been provided through the enforcement of deed restrictions prohibiting resale to blacks, through the refusal by the Federal Housing Administration (FHA) to insure loans in integrated neighborhoods, and through the restrictions imposed by suburban municipalities. However, over twenty years ago the U.S. Supreme Court held restrictive covenants regarding race to be unenforceable. Likewise, the FHA abandoned its practice about ten years ago. Yet it would appear that segregation has increased during the postwar period. Residents of some suburban municipalities might benefit in some ways from the exclusion of blacks, but higher housing prices to blacks is probably not one of them. Indeed, suburban enclaves of blacks have existed in the vicinity of many U.S. cities for many years with little tendency to grow. In a slightly different vein, violence or the threat of violence is often cited as a cause of racial segregation. Violence has indeed occurred in some instances when blacks have moved into previously white neighborhoods. But there are many more instances in which it has not.

Externalities and black segregation

Thus, most special explanations for the residential segregation of blacks are tenuous at best. The model discussed in the first section provides a much more natural explanation, and it poses no particular difficulty of its own. Applied to this specific case it states that whites have more of an aversion, in terms of the prices they would offer for housing, to living in the vicinity of blacks than do other blacks. If such were the case, landlords in largely white neighborhoods would be reluctant to rent to blacks because of the fear their white tenants would move out, and, perhaps, because they might expect a white tenant to offer a higher rental. Real estate agents would not wish to show properties to blacks for fear of the loss of future business of other white sellers. In neighborhoods in transition from white to black occupancy, prices paid by blacks would exceed those paid by whites. Mortgage lenders might avoid making loans in such neighborhoods because of greater uncertainty in these areas as to the future of property values.

It is frequently objected that the assumptions made by the model outlined in the preceding section are too restrictive when applied to the segregation of blacks and whites. No doubt, some whites are unwilling to pay the premium for segregation. Nonprejudiced whites, however, can always obtain housing more cheaply in the vicinity of the black residential area. Unless they are so numerous as to more than fill up the white boundary blocks, the analysis is not affected at all. And, in

long-run equilibrium, nonprejudiced whites can always obtain
housing still more cheaply in the interior of the black residential area. Few whites, however, buy into, let alone remain
in, predominantly black neighborhoods.

The analysis is likewise much the same if it is supposed only
that whites do not wish to be in the minority in their neighborhood. As the black population of a city grows, blacks would
tend to move into previously predominantly white neighborhoods. Once the black population reached a certain size in
these neighborhoods, whites would rent or buy homes there
only if they could do so more cheaply than in still largely
white areas. Consequently, all-black residential areas would
develop, though all-white ones might not. It is also objected
that some blacks prefer segregation to integration. Such
blacks, however, can always obtain housing more cheaply in
the interior of a black residential area. If only a minority
of blacks prefer integration, black-occupied properties on the
boundary of the white residential area will still command a
premium over those in the interior of the black area.

In most U.S. cities blacks are concentrated in the older, more
central parts of urban areas. The best explanation for this
is that given in Chapter 3 in regard to the effect of age
of dwellings on location by income level. As a lower-income
immigrant group into northern and western cities, blacks
would offer higher rentals than whites would for older and
smaller dwellings. Provided the lower-income population of
cities does not grow too rapidly, blacks and other lower-income
groups can acquire housing more cheaply in this way than
by living in newly built housing. Under these conditions,
blacks may occupy larger units than they otherwise would
and make greater rental payments, even though their rent
per square foot is smaller than whites pay. Note, however,
that in some southern cities, small pockets of black-occupied
housing are interspersed throughout white neighborhoods. In
these places blacks were part of the native population, and
the housing they occupy was originally built for their income
group.

The hypothesis of the first section provides a natural interpretation of block-busting. Block-busters purchase housing in
transition areas from white owners and resell to blacks at

higher prices. Note that block-busters and black buyers always have the incentive to buy white-occupied properties along the boundary of the white area rather than in its interior because prices are lower there. A little thought suggests, too, that blacks are by no means injured by block-busters. Blacks always have the opportunity to buy in the interior of the black area. Because of the proximity of the black area, whites, however, cannot sell at the white interior price, nor can they sell at the black boundary price unless they can be put in touch with potential black buyers. If established real estate agents were to handle transactions in changing neighborhoods, competition among them would bring white boundary sellers the black boundary price less normal commissions. With restrictions on competition among agents in transitional areas, however, block-busters may purchase from white boundary sellers at lower prices than otherwise.

If segregation by race occurs because of a greater aversion by whites to living among blacks, open-occupancy legislation and most other current efforts to end segregation are likely to be unsuccessful. Indeed, many places in the United States have had so-called fair-housing legislation for a number of years with little apparent effect. Such legislation can, of course, induce those who would otherwise not have done so to rent or sell to blacks. If enforced, such legislation might indeed result in a more rapid expansion of the black residential area as the black population grows. There is nothing in such legislation, however, to prevent whites in the boundary area from selling to blacks and moving out. Indeed, so long as the black area is growing relative to the white area, individual owners of white-occupied properties along the black-area boundary can profit by selling to blacks. Quota schemes seeking to limit the fraction of blacks in any neighborhood might, of course, be instituted. Such schemes, though, by limiting the expansion of the black residential area would make housing more expensive for blacks and more difficult for them to obtain. Schemes to foster integration by relocating blacks from the central cities would probably be frustrated in the long run by the development of suburban ghettos, many of which already exist. The best means for overcoming segregation would be to subsidize white residents to live in truly integrated areas by offering them housing for less than they would otherwise have to pay for equivalent housing. One can easily imagine the howls of anguish from all sides over such a suggestion, however.

Housing market discrimination against blacks?

The model discussed in the first section suggests that segregation by no means implies discrimination or higher housing prices to blacks for identical housing. Indeed, if whites prefer segregation and blacks integration, the model discussed earlier implies that if the black residential area is not expanding relative to the white area, blacks on the average pay less for housing of equivalent quality than whites. However, if the black area grows relative to the white area in response to greater black population growth, as has occurred in many cities, prices in the black area could exceed those in the white area. To settle the question of price differences by race, then, one must consult the empirical evidence.

It is widely believed that such evidence shows a clear-cut and large racial differential in housing prices—30 to 50 percent higher for nonwhites. Such beliefs are based principally upon census data but also on other survey data that show greater housing expenditures by nonwhites at any given income level. Expenditures, however, are the product of price per unit of housing, say per room or per square foot, and the number of units purchased. If the price elasticity of housing demand were unity, as I believe it to be, higher housing prices to nonwhites would not affect their expenditures. This is because the percentage reduction in quantity purchased would exactly offset the percentage increase in price. Expenditure differentials, then, would have to be accounted for by other differences between whites and nonwhites.

A variety of other evidence is now available regarding racial differentials in housing prices. Such evidence is by no means clear-cut, but it suggests that nonwhites may pay at most 5 to 10 percent more for housing of comparable quality than whites. I examined a variety of indicators of rates of physical consumption per household and production per unit of land area.[6] With but one exception, none of these gave any clear-cut indication on statistical grounds of a racial price differential in Chicago. Neither did these comparisons suggest that segregation confines nonwhites to areas of the worst housing, as is widely believed; rather they suggest that the poorer housing of nonwhites is the result of their lower incomes.

Most other studies are based upon a careful examination of rentals or sales prices controlling for differences in physical characteristics of dwellings. Martin Bailey's study of sales prices of single-family units in the Hyde Park area of Chicago suggests that prices in the interior of the nonwhite area were about 20 percent lower than in the white interior area.[7] A more recent study of Kain and Quigley suggests that nonwhites pay from 2 to 10 percent more than whites for rental housing in St. Louis, but revealed no clear-cut differences for owners.[8] King and Mieszkowski found that households headed by black males paid 7 percent higher rentals than whites in New Haven, Connecticut, as much as 13 percent more in all-black neighborhoods.[9] Dobson studied repeat sales prices of the same dwelling in University City, Missouri, a suburb adjacent to St. Louis into which substantial numbers of blacks moved during the sixties.[10] His results showed negligible differences between the black and white areas of the city, both before and after the change to black occupancy. In still another study, Victoria Lapham examined sales prices in Dallas, Texas, in 1960.[11] Like Kain and Quigley, Lapham found some component price differences in the housing bundle as between black and white areas. Neither the typical white-occupied home nor the typical black home, however, would have cost appreciably more in black prices than in white prices. The evidence is thus by no means unanimous, but it clearly fails to support wide-

[6] Richard F. Muth, *Cities and Housing* (Chicago, University of Chicago Press, 1969), especially pp. 238–240 and 299.
[7] Bailey, op. cit.
[8] John F. Kain and John M. Quigley, "Measuring the Value of Housing Quality," *Journal of the American Statistical Association* 65 (June 1970), 532–548.
[9] King and Mieszkowski, op. cit.
[10] Allen Dobson, "Price Changes of Single Family Dwelling Units in Racially Changing Neighborhoods," unpublished Ph.D. dissertation, Department of Economics, Washington University, 1970.
[11] Victoria Lapham, "Do Blacks Pay More for Housing?" *Journal of Political Economy* 79 (November/December 1971), 1244–1257.

spread beliefs that blacks pay markedly higher prices for housing of given quality than do whites.

SLUMS:
SEGREGATION BY INCOME LEVEL

In the real world segregation by race and slums, or areas of low-quality housing, tend to be associated because blacks have lower average incomes than whites and thus spend less on housing. In principle, however, separation by income level is distinct from separation by race. Separation by income level also involves at least one additional interesting feature, namely costs of converting properties from better to poorer housing. This section will consider alternative explanations for the existence of slums and the implications of the economics of clustering for the nature of slum areas. The following chapter is devoted to a discussion of public policy toward lower-income housing.

Deterioration and
"flight from blight"

Until quite recently dwelling-unit condition was widely regarded to be a characteristic of buildings rather than of its occupants. The existence and spread of slums was attributed to a variety of features that were believed to produce too much slum housing relative to the lower-income demand for it. The development of automobile transportation, for example, was said to have led to the deterioriation of older centrally located areas of cities by producing a decline in housing demand there. Others have argued that the ravages of time, the encroachment of nonresidential land uses into older residential neighborhoods, or failure of local governments properly to regulate or to supply older areas with municipal services has caused a decline in their attractiveness. Still others have asserted that local property taxes, provisions of federal tax law regarding depreciation for tax purposes, and capital market imperfections all have prevented owners of private property from making socially desirable expenditures on older dwellings.

Regardless of the reason, the deterioration of older central-city properties is usually cited as being responsible for urban decentralization or movement of middle- and upper-income families from the central city to the suburbs. With a decline in demand, owners of properties in the affected areas would tend to reduce their expenditures for maintenance and repair and allow their properties to deteriorate in quality. The future deterioration in quality would add impetus to the "flight from blight" by middle- and upper-income persons associated with the original decline in demand. At the same time, probably because they have less of an aversion to living in older housing in terms of the expenditures they make, lower-income households have come to inhabit the deteriorated areas of the central city. Thus, it is argued, governmental intervention is necessary to restore the physical condition of the central city and provide decent housing for lower-income persons.

The kind of forces just described may well have some empirical relevance, but they are seriously deficient. First of all they imply that too much slum housing exists relative to the lower-income demands for it. Yet, if anything, it is widely believed that slum housing is expensive in relation to its quality and highly profitable to its owners. Second, such arguments imply that by correcting the mistakes of the private market, urban renewal projects should make money. Yet such projects almost invariably require large public subsidies. Finally, most such arguments imply that the average housing quality should have declined in the postwar period. This is widely believed to be the case, of course. In fact, however, for the large U.S. cities I have studied, the fraction of dwellings that are substandard, that is, dilapidated in the sense of possessing exterior defects readily visible to census enumerators or lacking in certain plumbing facilities, declined from about 20 to 11 percent, or by almost half, on the average from 1950 to 1960.

Slum housing
and income

Statistical investigations using data both for different parts of the same city and for different cities at a given time have found little evidence that dwelling-unit condition is very much associated with any of the factors noted earlier in this section.[12] Rather, a close and quantitatively similar association

---

[12] Muth, op. cit., especially pp. 278–283.

of substandard fraction and income was found. And, indeed, quantitatively these findings are in close agreement with changes over time for the nation as a whole in average housing quality. Now it might be that the association within a single city could result from lower-income households being attracted to areas of the city where housing quality is poor for other reasons. But it is too much of a strain on the argument to attribute higher average incomes for certain cities than others or increasing income levels for the nation as a whole over time to differences in housing quality. And, by using appropriate statistical methods, it can be demonstrated that the association between using quality and income within a single city is due primarily to the latter's effect upon the former. A statistically significant effect of housing quality on the income level of the residents of a census tract seems to exist, but it is very small quantitatively. The effect of income on housing quality is strikingly large, however. This will be discussed more fully in the following chapter.

If income is the primary determinant of housing quality, the apparent decay of vast areas of our central cities is to be explained primarily by the growth in the absolute numbers of lower-income persons in our metropolitan areas. The growth in numbers, in turn, is the result partly of migration of lower-income persons (especially from the rural South) and partly from natural population growth. As the number of lower-income persons in a metropolitan area has grown, the area they occupy likewise has grown. In the process, some housing has deteriorated in absolute quality. Such deterioration is by no means inconsistent, though, with general quality improvement of central-city housing during the fifties. For, with rising income levels shared in by disadvantaged groups, the average quality of all housing has improved.

Slum- or poor-quality housing in this country is rarely newly produced as such, as it is in other countries. Rather it is produced primarily through converting better-quality housing. Such conversions take place partly through the actual physical dividing of larger units into several smaller ones. They also occur through property owners' reducing expenditures for maintenance and repair and thus allowing their properties to deteriorate in quality. In dividing larger into smaller units, resource costs associated with new walls, entrances, and cooking and sanitary facilities are incurred. Such investments, of course, are made at a cost.

At first glance, though, it might seem that failure to maintain properties provides additional revenues, not costs. Such is not the case, however. When passing to occupancy by lower-income groups who spend less for housing, rentals for units of a given size probably decline. This decline is offset by an owner's reduced investment in his dwelling only after a period of several years' reduced maintenance and repair expenditures. In the interim, the owner of the building sacrifices the return on the funds yet to be withdrawn from his building. This foregone return is a cost to the owner in precisely the same sense that the return foregone on funds invested in physically altering a dwelling is. Dwellings would be converted in either way by their owners only if they anticipated rental incomes to compensate for the foregone returns of either kind.

For a variety of reasons it seems logical to expect that higher-income persons would have more of an aversion to living among those of lower income than would other lower-income persons. The evidence provided by Bailey's study indicates that this is indeed the case. If so, the model in the first section of this chapter suggests that the two groups would tend to cluster into disjoint residential areas, as also seems to be the case. In applying the model of clustering, however, account must be taken of the fact that better- and poorer-quality housing units differ. Thus, one needs to take explicit account of quality differences and interpret housing prices as price, say, per room or per square foot of floor space for units of the two different housing qualities.

Second, and more important, one must take account of the costs of converting units from one quality level to another. Let c_{AB} be the cost of converting from A-type to B-type housing. (This cost is a capital sum if prices are interpreted as sales prices, interest on the capital sum if prices are thought of as rental values.) Then, the B area will grow only if its boundary price exceeds the A-area boundary price by more than c_{AB}. Conversely, when

$$p_A + d_A + c_{AB} = p_B + d_B$$

or

$$p_B - p_A = -(d_B - d_A) + c_{AB}$$

growth of the B area will cease. If as Bailey's evidence suggests, lower-income persons will pay a premium for proximity to higher-income residents, but the latter will live in the vicinity of the slum only if housing is cheaper for them there, the term $-(d_B - d_A)$ is negative. But c_{AB} is positive. Thus, even if the slum area has ceased to grow relative to the better-quality area, one cannot predict the relative levels of housing prices in the slum and non-slum areas.

With a growth in the numbers of lower-income persons in an urban area, housing prices in the slum area would rise. Growth in the number of higher-income families would also cause an initial rise in the prices of better-quality housing, but the stock of better-quality housing is added to by new construction, which tends to offset the rise in better-housing prices. As slum-housing prices rise, it thus becomes profitable to the owners of better-quality boundary housing to convert it. The specific dwellings converted depend upon their costs of conversion. Though there is no good evidence on the point, it seems likely that older buildings and multifamily ones would be less costly to convert by division and deterioration than others. Because of rising costs of conversion, it may be that increases in the size of the lower-income or slum area are accompanied by increases in the price of poorer-quality housing. If such is the case, the returns to owners of previously existing slum dwellings will increase and their buildings will be used more intensively. Differences in conversion costs among buildings in a given neighborhood may also mean that conversion is not uniformly profitable to all owners in a neighborhood. This last consideration may explain the hostility toward absentee-landlords and the existence of neighborhood improvement associations.

Other factors affecting urban housing quality

Other arguments relating to lower-income housing are worthy of mention before proceeding to a consideration of the effects of government housing programs in the next chapter. The first is the distinction between slums and blight, first made by Davis and Whinston.[13] Although recognizing slum housing as largely the private housing market's response to the provision of housing for lower-income families, Davis and Whinston point out that, in addition, because of a certain type of external effect on property values, too little may be spent on any one property. This is the case because expenditure on any one property not only increases its own rental value, but it may also increase the value of surrounding properties by making the neighborhood more attractive. Because the owner of the property on which expenditure is made cannot charge the owners of surrounding properties for his contribution to making the neighborhood more attractive, too little is invested in buildings generally. Davis and Whinston characterize this condition as blight.

Blight, as the term has been used by Davis and Whinston, may well be a factor of some importance in urban housing. Indeed, it seems reasonable to suppose that higher-income families are willing to spend more for pleasant surroundings than lower-income ones. If so, blight or neighborhood effects would be relatively more important in wealthier than in poorer neighborhoods. The potential for the effects of blight, however, are greatly attenuated by the fact of clustering of slum and non-slum dwellings in separate parts of the city. In addition, local building and occupancy codes, by setting certain minimum standards for the physical features of structures and their occupancy, may prevent manifestations of blight. The main difficulty with such codes, however, is that they may seek to impose middle-class standards on lower-income pocketbooks.

More important, however, is the fact that there are market means of preventing blight. To the extent that blight is important to middle- and upper-income groups, it pays for developers of residential subdivisions to take neighborhood effects into account when designing and constructing new developments. For, to the extent that developers do so, they earn higher income from the sale of the houses they build than they otherwise would. In similar fashion, if blight were an impor-

---

[13] Otto A. Davis and Andrew B. Whinston, "The Economics of Urban Renewal," *Law and Contemporary Problems* 26 (Winter 1961), 105–117.

tant feature in older neighborhoods, it would pay for insurance companies or others to buy contiguous parcels of properties, convert them to better structures, and resell them at a profit. That this rarely occurs suggests that blight may be relatively unimportant in older, lower-income areas. It might be argued, alternatively, that the difficulties of assembling a sufficiently large group of properties prevent otherwise desirable redevelopment to be privately undertaken. If such were the case, though, urban renewal projects, for which properties can be acquired through court action if necessary at fair market value, would make money. I have yet to hear of a federally supported urban renewal project that has made money in the sense that the proceeds from the sale of cleared land exceeded the costs of acquiring the properties demolished.

The other topic that should be mentioned here is the notion of "filtering," which refers to a more or less regular decline in the relative income level of the occupants of structures as they age. There are at least two reasons why this may occur. Depreciation of dwelling units as they age would mean that any given dwelling would become better suited to the circumstances of families with lower absolute incomes. Even if the size of any given dwelling were essentially fixed over time, however, but incomes were generally growing, families of a given absolute, hence progressively lower relative, income level would offer higher rentals for it and come to occupy it. Filtering is consistent with the tendency for lower-income families to live in older dwellings. It is often offered as a justification for government programs that stimulate the construction of better-quality housing for higher-income families. For, it is argued, the dwellings these high-income families would otherwise occupy are made available to those lower down the income scale.

As it is usually formulated, the notion of filtering is very much like "the emperor's new clothes." Like many other half-truths, the notion of filtering has become so well established in the literature that everyone who wishes to appear wise repeats it. Yet there are too many instances of central-city neighborhoods or older residential suburbs that have remained in middle- or upper-income occupancy to pass them off as exceptions to the general rule. At the same time, there are many instances of other blocks or neighborhoods that have passed from middle- or even upper-income occupancy to lower within the brief span of a year or two. The process should be characterized, rather, as one of "neighborhood succession." Lower-income immigrant groups in urban areas occupy older housing for reasons considered in Chapter 3. As they grow in number, the residential area they occupy tends to spread outward from the center to progressively new areas. For the reason described earlier in this chapter, namely the boundary price differential in higher-income occupancy, expansion of the lower-income residential area takes place along the boundary, and any given block changes quickly. At the same time, older areas remote from the lower-income area are more expensive to acquire, hence remain in higher-income occupancy.

SUMMARY

Segregation—the spatial separation of unlike uses or the clustering of like uses of urban land—is a common phenomenon. It is most satisfactorily explained by supposing that certain users of urban land will pay a premium to occupy sites adjacent to similar land users or remote from unlike users of land. Under such conditions, market forces produce spatial contiguity of a wide variety of different land uses. Equality of prices paid for land or for like parcels of real estate in the interiors of two different clusters of like use may mean a price differential on the boundary separating the two clusters. If so, the area whose boundary price is the higher will tend to expand, driving down prices of that type of land use and raising prices of the other until equality of prices at the boundary is reached. These considerations suggest that the proper role of zoning and other governmental land use controls is to regulate the size of different clusters of like uses so that equality of interior prices results. External effects will always be felt along the borders of these different land uses, and those experiencing the externalities are compensated by lower prices.

Many alternate explanations for residential segregation by race are offered, most of them ad hoc and seriously deficient.

Landlords and real estate agents who refuse to deal with blacks because of above-average prejudice would lose money and be driven out of business. It would be profitable to buy up houses from whites and resell to blacks if most white sellers refused to sell directly to blacks. Conspiracies to profit from higher housing prices to blacks would be short-lived if, indeed, they could ever be organized at all. If black segregation results from a greater preference by whites for segregation than blacks have for integration, most schemes for fostering integration would be defeated by whites moving out of integrated neighborhoods. Though evidence on housing prices paid by blacks relative to those paid by whites is mixed, there appears to be little housing market discrimination against blacks.

Slum areas are frequently attributed to factors increasing the relative supply of poor-quality housing, and urban decentralization is interpreted as a "flight from blight." If such were the case, however, slums would be unprofitable to their owners, urban renewal projects would make money, and average housing quality in central cities would be getting worse, none of which appears to be the case. Slum housing is primarily the market response to an increase in the relative demand for poor-quality housing on the part of lower-income urban immigrants. As the latter grow in number, slum areas grow along their previous boundaries. Better-quality dwellings are converted, at a cost, to poorer-quality ones, both through physical alteration and deferral of expenditures for maintenance and repair. Though the area occupied by lower-quality housing has grown, average housing quality has improved over time as lower-income families have experienced rising incomes along with other groups.

CHAPTER 5

Government low-income housing programs

$\mathcal{T}$he U.S. government first entered the low-income housing business in the 1930s with the establishment of the public housing program. Today it has so many housing or related programs that it takes a stack of looseleaf notebook pages over an inch thick to give brief descriptions of all of them. Despite the numerous programs, however, there is widespread and growing dissatisfaction with them. Congress is frequently blamed for our lack of progress in the low-income housing field by its failure to appropriate enough money.

However, the failure of Congress to make larger appropriations may indeed have been a blessing in disguise, for, until recently, government programs have almost certainly destroyed more lower-income housing than they have built. In 1968 the Douglas Commission estimated that governmental programs have led to the demolition of roughly a million dwellings, most of which were inhabited by lower-income persons.[1] About a third of these demolitions occurred under the federal highway programs, a third under the urban renewal program, and the balance under the public housing program. Only about two-thirds of a million units were built under the public housing program during its first thirty years. Contrasted with the record of government, the performance of the private housing market has been impressive indeed. During the 1950s alone, a net upgrading of 2 million dwellings from substandard to standard took place.[2]

Far from justifying the frequent assertion that the private market has failed in providing lower-income housing, the record clearly suggests that it has outperformed government. This chapter is concerned primarily with determining what went wrong with government programs and how they might be improved. The first section will discuss the effects of demolitions and other measures that reduce the stock of lower-income housing; the following one deals with housing subsidies. Other measures, especially rent control and the prospect

---

[1] National Commission on Urban Problems, *Building the American City* (Washington, D.C.: U.S. Government Printing Office, 1969), table 6, p. 82.

[2] Ibid., table 1, p. 70.

for lowering housing costs through factory-built housing, will be analyzed in the third section. The final section will consider whether a housing policy in addition to measures to raise the incomes of the poor is necessary at all.

TEARING DOWN
THE SLUMS

It is very difficult to understand why anyone should think that tearing down their homes would improve the lot of the poor. Yet most government housing programs consist of just this, or other measures that greatly limit the housing opportunities of the poor. Under certain conditions the building of federally supported public housing units has required the demolition of an equivalent number of slum units. Under the urban renewal program, slum housing has been demolished and replaced primarily with middle- or upper-income housing or with nonresidential structures. Dwellings demolished in cities under the federal highway program and for a variety of local public improvements are frequently slum dwellings. "Before" and "after" photos of such areas make for attractive slide shows and magazine layouts, but, by themselves, demolitions of slum dwellings can only harm the poor.

Short-run effects
of demolitions

The effects of demolitions of slum dwellings are illustrated in Figure 5.1. The demand curve for substandard housing is labeled D. Here, as in Chapter 3, the term "housing," when not qualified, means something more than the number of dwellings. It should be understood as aggregate potential for dwellings to satisfy consumer wants for shelter, comfort, and whatever else housing provides. For simplicity, though, it can be thought of as some one-dimensional quantity such as number of square feet of floor space or number of rooms of a given quality level.

Apart from the possible effect of relocation assistance, which will be discussed later, demolitions have no effect upon the lower-income demand curve for housing. Rather, demolitions shift the short-run supply curve of substandard housing from

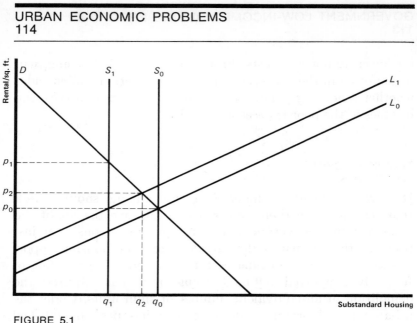

FIGURE 5.1
Demolition of substandard housing

S_0 to S_1. Here the short run is defined by a calendar time period so short that conversions of better- to poorer-quality housing or changes in the maintenance policy of slum landlords cannot take place. Consequently, the short-run supply schedule is essentially vertical.

As shown by Figure 5.1, demolitions reduce the stock of substandard housing from q_0 to q_1. Coupled with a fixed demand curve D, the rental per unit—per square foot or per room—of substandard housing must rise along the fixed demand curve from p_0 to p_1. When substandard housing becomes more difficult to obtain or its rentals rise relative to those of standard units, some lower-income families who would not otherwise have done so are induced to inhabit standard dwellings.

It might seem that those who do so are better off because their housing has been improved. Such a conclusion is extremely superficial. The process of demolition has done nothing to increase the availability of better housing to lower-income families; it has only induced them to take advantage of alternatives that were already open to them. That lower-income families did not take advantage of these opportunities, however, probably is due to the fact that standard housing costs more per unit than substandard housing. To inhabit better housing, lower-income families would have to reduce already meager expenditures for food, clothing, and medical care. Indeed, due to the added demand for standard housing resulting from the rise in price of substandard housing, the price of standard housing would rise with demolitions. Demolition thus makes it more expensive than before for lower-income families to upgrade their housing.

After demolitions, many, perhaps the majority, of lower-income families will remain in substandard housing but pay a higher price per unit for it. Due to the higher unit price, however, they will consume less housing per family. In part they will do so by doubling up into available units and thus will consume less space per person. It is likely, in addition, that families will occupy dwellings that are still more dilapidated than those they would otherwise have occupied. These last responses are probably overlooked entirely by most people in evaluating the effects of demolitions.

Long-run effects
of demolitions

In the short run, then, demolitions do reduce the fraction of the housing stock that consists of substandard units. Because of the rise in the rental of such units, though, the poor become worse off in the process. Because this fact has become so painfully obvious, at least to the poor, the short-run effects of demolitions have become more widely understood during the 1960s. What is still not well understood, though, are the long-run effects of demolition. By long run is meant a period of time long enough for property owners to adjust fully to the changes brought about by demolitions. The adjustments property owners make are of two kinds—conversions of better to poorer housing and increased expenditures on previously existing poorer housing—so that, in effect, any given substandard unit has greater power to provide shelter, comfort, and even a modicum of social distinction, to use Alfred Marshall's term.

The rise in the rental or price of substandard units from p_0

to p_1 that demolitions produce increases the profitability to private owners of converting better to poorer housing. If, prior to demolitions, the boundary price differentials between standard and substandard were just offset by the costs of converting units from standard to substandard housing, all of which were discussed in Chapter 4, after demolitions conversions will be privately profitable along the borders of the slum area. Thus the slum area will tend to grow outward in places other than where demolitions occurred. At the same time, owners of previously existing slum dwellings will find it profitable to increase their expenditures for maintenance and repair because of higher prices. The increase in such expenditures effectively increases the output of housing from a given number of slum units. These two effects are summarized by the long-run supply schedule labeled L_1 in Figure 5.1. This is the schedule obtained by shifting the predemolition long-run schedule, L_0, the same horizontal distance, $q_0 - q_1$, as the short-run schedules. Thus, in the long run, the rental per substandard unit is p_2, which is smaller than p_1, and the output of substandard housing is q_2, which is larger than the immediate post-demolition output, q_1.

The difference between the short-run and long-run effects of demolitions depends critically upon the elasticity of the long-run supply schedule of lower-income housing. Indeed, if, as most persons seem to believe, this schedule is very inelastic or nearly vertical, then the long-run effects of demolitions will not differ very much from the short-run ones. In my judgment, though, this is not the case. The greatest single mistake in our housing programs is our failure to realize that the private market's housing-supply schedule to lower-income persons is highly elastic. If the private market supply is highly elastic, however, demolitions will have little long-run impact on the lower-income housing market. The critics of urban renewal who assert that it merely relocates the slums would be essentially correct.

By now it is obvious to many that postwar growth in both lower-income urban populations and in demolitions has been associated with expansion of the area occupied by poorer-quality housing. This fact plus the rapidity of neighborhood change in many instances provides considerable evidence not only for elasticity of supply but for rapidity of its response. In a more systematic vein, between the 1950 Census and 1956 National Housing Inventory, which employed identical definitions of housing quality, the fraction of substandard dwellings declined about one-third, 90 percent of the decline occurring because of improvement in the quality of given dwellings.[3] The one-third decline is almost exactly what would be anticipated on the basis of changes in income and construction costs over the period and relationships that existed among census tracts of the same city or among different central cities in 1950. A 10 percent increase in income, say from $2000 to $2200 per year, would result in a decline in substandard fraction from roughly 40 to 27 percent.[4]

In a recent study, Warren Farb compared the ratio of rents in substandard and standard dwellings with the fraction of substandard dwellings in different cities.[5] Though his findings imply that the demand schedule for substandard housing is very inelastic, he estimated supply elasticities of the order of +10. This means that along a fixed supply curve a 1 percent increase in substandard rentals would produce a 10 percent increase in the fraction of substandard dwellings. Finally, there are theoretical reasons, much too complicated to describe here, for believing that when producing a rate of housing services markedly smaller than a structure was designed to produce, the flow of housing services per structure becomes highly responsive to price changes.[6]

Thus, despite common beliefs to the contrary, it is quite likely that the private market supply of housing to lower-income households is highly elastic. Many government housing programs have tried to shift the supply schedule horizontally, reducing it through demolitions and increasing it through building public housing units. For reasons that are quite anal-

---

[3] As analyzed in Beverly Duncan and Philip M. Hauser, *Housing a Metropolis—Chicago* (New York: Free Press, 1960).
[4] Richard F. Muth, *Cities and Housing* (Chicago: University of Chicago Press, 1969), especially pp. 279–280.
[5] Warren E. Farb, "An Estimate of the Relative Supply and Demand of Substandard Rental Housing in Major U.S. Cities," unpublished Ph.D. dissertation, Department of Economics, Washington University, 1970.
[6] Richard F. Muth, "Capital and Current Expenditures in the Production of Housing," Memo 123, Stanford University Center for Research in Economic Growth (October 1971), pp. 15–17.

ogous to the difficulties in job creation with a relatively elastic private demand for low-income workers described in Chapter 10, shifting a highly elastic supply schedule horizontally merely moves it along itself with little overall market impact. Demolition and building new units for lower-income families have important short-run effects, of course. In the long run, however, reactions in the private housing market seem likely largely to negate these effects.

Many supporters of urban renewal argue that the relocation assistance these programs require for displaced lower-income families overcomes the shortcomings of demolitions. In view of the considerations already outlined, their opinion seems quite naive, primarily because relocation assistance provides no new housing and affects housing demand only to the negligible extent of providing payment for moving expenses. Second, even if families displaced by demolitions are placed in standard housing, though at higher rentals, this housing may become substandard in the long run. Finally, the appropriate group for considering the effects of demolition is the whole of the lower-income population, not merely those displaced by the demolitions.

Taking the profit
out of slums

With a relatively elastic housing supply schedule, measures that shift the supply curve of housing vertically have more lasting effects, as illustrated by Figure 5.2. Many things done or advocated are adverse insofar as the lower-income population is concerned. Among these are more vigorous enforcement of building and occupancy codes, the rent strike, and public receivership of slum dwellings. Building codes are local regulations relating to structural characteristics of dwellings, occupancy codes rules regarding their use. They frequently require middle-income housing standards. They tend to be enforced primarily in neighborhoods actually or potentially in the process of transition to lower-income ones because of limitation in budget and staff for enforcement. The rent strike is a device whereby tenants either withhold the payment of rents until the landlord makes certain improvements, or they

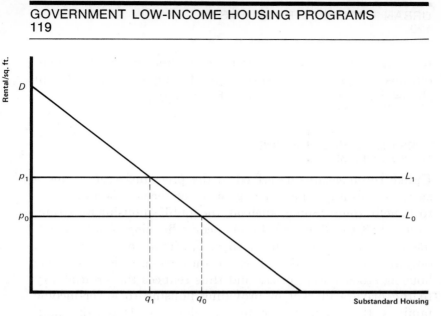

FIGURE 5.2
Code enforcement in slum areas

use their rental payments for this purpose themselves. Public receivership is quite similar to the rent strike. Under it, dwellings judged deficient with regard to standards set by building and occupancy codes are taken over by an agency of local government. This agency uses the rent payments of tenants to make expenditures for improvement to code standards and then returns the property to its owner.

Any of the measures just outlined may result in some improvement of the housing conditions of the poor in the short run while the number of lower-income units is fixed. However, such measures increase the costs of converting housing from higher- to lower-income units. In terms of the model of Chapter 4, it thus reduces the profitability of conversion and hence the rate of conversion.

In the long run, as the lower-income population grows, fewer units would be available to them than would otherwise have been the case. Some properties might even be reconverted to higher-income occupancy. The net effect would certainly be higher housing prices to the poor, even if the supply schedule were perfectly elastic, as shown in Figure 5.2. Though some persons apparently realize the shortcomings of horizontal shifts in the supply of lower-income housing through demolitions, few seem to realize that "taking the profit out of slums" has even more insidious effects on the poor.

SUBSIDIZING THE HOUSING OF POOR FAMILIES

Unlike the measures described in the preceding section, measures to subsidize the housing of lower-income families tend to benefit them. Some, such as the public housing program, which shift the short-run lower-income housing supply schedule horizontally, as from s_1 to s_0 in Figure 5.1, may do so only temporarily. This is because the increased lower-income housing stock lowers prices and thus reduces the profitability to the private market of providing housing to lower-income families. If the long-run supply is relatively elastic, the main long-run effect may be fewer privately supplied lower-income units on the private market. Even so, as explained further on, those families lucky enough to gain admission to public housing can consume more housing per family than in privately produced housing. Other housing programs, the rent supplement program, for example, in effect shift the long-run supply downward, as from L_1 to L_0 in Figure 5.2. These enable the lower-income family to purchase a greater amount of housing than it otherwise would, with none of the adverse or side effects of horizontal shifts.

Although housing subsidies are clearly superior to the measures previously described in improving the housing of lower-income families, those currently used suffer from a number of defects that greatly limit their benefits. By and large these are less obvious than the effects of demolitions. Many of the defects of housing subsidies can be illustrated by the public housing program, which is the only one to have had a substantial quantitative impact until the late 1960s.

Public housing

It is becoming increasingly fashionable in liberal and intellectual circles to be critical of the U.S. public housing program. Yet judged by the behavior of lower-income families, it must be deemed successful in providing better housing than is obtainable on the private market. Nationwide about two-thirds of a million units had been constructed by 1968. Waiting lists for admission into public housing were roughly as long as the total number of units, though, and might be even longer if people were not discouraged by long waits from applying. This huge excess demand clearly indicates to an economist that eligible families regard public housing as a superior alternative, considering rents charged for it and dwellings on the private market.

The excess demand for public housing is also indicative of one of its main failings. The two-thirds of a million units represents enough for only about 7 percent of all eligible families. At the same time, those gaining admission to public housing are substantially better housed than those not able to obtain such housing. It has been estimated that as of the middle 1960s, eligible families spent about $47 per month for housing, whether in public housing or on the private market, and had about the same average incomes.[7] It is estimated that the federal subsidy to public housing would permit Local Housing Authorities (LHAs), which construct and manage such projects, to cover their costs by receiving as little as 27 cents per dollar's worth of housing at market rentals.[8] Thus, if public housing projects were developed as cheaply as possible, given the form of the federal subsidy to them, those few lower-income families fortunate enough to gain admission would be able to increase their housing consumption by almost three times and to maintain their nonhousing expenditures.

For reasons discussed more fully in the last section of this chapter, however, an additional dollar's worth of housing at market prices need not be worth an additional dollar to its occupant if he cannot freely vary his housing consumption relative to his consumption of other commodities. Indeed, my estimate of the worth of the public housing subsidy to its occupants suggests the $130 additional housing at market prices provided by the program raises the well-being of ten-

---

[7] Edgar O. Olsen, *A Welfare Economic Evaluation of Public Housing* (Houston, Texas: Rice University, 1968), p. 84.

[8] Richard F. Muth, *Public Housing: An Economic Evaluation* (Washington, D.C.: American Enterprise Institute for Public Policy Research, 1973), p. 20.

ants by the same amount as a $71 per month increase in income would. The latter is equivalent to about a 30 percent increase in the average tenant's income. The difference between the market value of the additional housing provided and its value to the tenant is dissipated by reducing the marginal value placed on housing relative to other consumption by the tenant. The typical public-housing tenant in the mid-1960s probably valued a dollar's worth of housing in market prices at only about 37 cents.[9] Thus, the opportunity to live in public housing increased the tenant's well-being only by about half as much as an income subsidy that would cost the government the same amount.

Another defect of the program is that public housing has been very costly to build. Two features of the program account for the inefficiency in the production of public housing. First, almost three-eighths of the public housing units built during the 1950s were built up on cleared slum land. The costs of such land were about $1.12 per square foot, as contrasted with only about 9 cents per square foot for land used for other public housing units. Higher land costs lead to higher housing costs in two ways. The first is the direct effect upon expenditures for land. Second, as land becomes more expensive, builders tend to use fewer square feet per dwelling unit by limiting lot sizes and building multistory structures. The latter results in greater expenditures on structures per dwelling unit. Public housing built on cleared slum land during the fifties had over twice as many dwelling units per acre as others. Expenditures per unit of housing built on cleared slum land would have been an estimated 55 percent greater, given the costs cited.[10] Since about three-eighths of all dwellings built under the program in the fifties were built upon cleared slum land, the average public housing unit cost about 21 percent more than if all had been built on other land. In view of the effects of demolitions discussed in the first section, there would seem to be little rationale for building public housing on cleared slum land.

The other feature of the public housing program that raises its capital cost per unit is its method of financing. Public

[9] Ibid., p. 25.
[10] Richard F. Muth, "The Derived Demand for Urban Residential Land," Urban Studies, 8 (October 1971), 243–254.

housing projects are financed by bonds issued by LHAs. Interest paid on these bonds, like many other securities issued by agencies of local government, are exempt from federal personal income taxation. As a result, during the latter 1950s the interest rates on these bonds were roughly half those on home mortgages. At the same time, the federal government until recently paid 90 percent of the interest and amortization charges on LHA bonds. Consequently, the LHA bears only about 5 percent of the capital cost of public housing projects. LHAs must, however, cover all the expenditures for maintenance and operation out of the rentals they collect from tenants. The LHA thus has the incentive to make greater capital expenditures than it otherwise would, substituting these in part for current expenditures. In part, the additional capital expenditures may substitute directly for maintenance expenditures, as when more expensive but more durable materials are used in construction. However, the substitution may be partly indirect in that tenants are provided more structural features in lieu of current upkeep.

The additional capital expenditures made because of lower interest charges tend to be less productive of additional output in public housing than in the uses to which they would otherwise have been put. It is more difficult to appraise the effect of interest-rate subsidies on expenditure per dwelling than those of building on cleared slum land. The best estimate at the moment suggests that about 35 percent greater capital expenditures are made per public housing unit than if LHAs bore the full capital costs of building public housing.[11]

Building upon cleared slum land, combined with interest-rate subsidies to public housing projects, increases capital expenditures per public housing unit by about 63 percent ($[1.21 \times 1.35 - 1] \times 100$). Alternatively, in the absence of these factors, public housing built in the fifties would have cost about $8,300 instead of $13,500 per unit, or, for a given expenditure on the program, about 56,000 rather than 35,000 units per year could have been built. The public housing program thus not only wastes resources by using too much capital per dwelling, but is much less effective in serving the poor than it could be.

---

[11] Muth, "Capital and Current Expenditures in the Production of Housing," pp. 12–14.

Public housing has been criticized frequently for being provided in massive, high-rise concentrations. This is precisely the kind of outcome, though, that would be expected from building on cleared slum land and interest-rate subsidies. In this regard it is interesting to note that one such project of this kind, the Pruitt-Igoe project in St. Louis, now has a vacancy rate of over 50 percent, and part of it is being demolished. It is widely regarded as an example of the worst faults of the public housing program. Yet when designed and built in the early 1950s it won a prize for architectural excellence.

Other housing programs

Partly because of the obvious shortcomings in the production of housing under the public housing program, a variety of other housing programs were established by the federal government during the 1960s. Most of them, however, make use of interest-rate subsidies as a means of reducing housing costs to the poor. (This is a favorite technique of governments and is certainly not restricted to low-income housing programs. It is used, for example, for subsidizing higher-income housing under the FHA and VA mortgage loan programs, rural electricity, and loans to business firms that locate in parts of the country deemed to be underdeveloped.) These other programs thus can be faulted for the same shortcoming as the public housing program—encouraging too much capital expenditure for lower-income housing but doing nothing to increase expenditures for maintenance and operation of such housing once it is constructed.

This is also the case with two new wrinkles in public housing. Under the so-called turnkey program, private developers design and construct structures for the public housing program and sell the completed structures to the LHA. Under the program, however, the LHA has the same incentive, provided by the form of the federal subsidy, to purchase costly structures as it has to build them. Under another recent innovation, the leased-housing program, LHAs lease units on the private market for sublease to their tenants. However, tenants still bear the costs of utilities and other expenses of household

operation. Under each of these modifications of public housing, tenants are enabled to increase their housing consumption
but not their consumption of food, clothing, and other items.
Thus, as in the original public housing program, some of the
benefits the subsidy provides are dissipated in reducing the
value tenants place on additional housing.

The best way to avoid the wasteful effects of interest-rate
subsidies would be to subsidize the rental payments of lower-
income tenants directly because the financial incentive can
be provided the landlord to spend more on maintenance and
operation of the dwelling as well as to make greater capital
expenditures in new construction or in rehabilitation on existing dwellings. The only federal program under which rental
payments are subsidized is the Rent Supplement Program.
Under it, a lower-income tenant makes a rental payment equal
to 25 percent of his income, with the federal government paying the balance. To be eligible for the program a dwelling must
have been constructed by a nonprofit corporation, or one
whose dividends are limited to 6 percent of its owners' investment, and have been approved by the local government unit
having jurisdiction over the place where it is built.

So far, Congress has made but limited appropriations for the
Rent Supplement Program. However, the program suffers from
several crucial limitations that are likely severely to limit its
effectiveness. Most important, perhaps, is the limitation on
earnings of private developers of lower-income housing to 6
percent on their equity investment. Since most individuals
can earn about twice that on investment in common stocks,
it seems unlikely that much housing would be privately developed for the program. Second, private developers of housing
for the program are eligible for interest subsidies for building
lower-income housing, so that the same type of incentive to
use too much capital expenditure for lower-income housing
exists as under the public housing and other housing programs.
In addition, since a prospective tenant under the program
pays 25 percent of his income in rent, regardless of the unit
he occupies, he has every incentive to find the biggest eligible
unit possible. These two features imply that administrative
review and approval of prospective units would be required
to limit expenditures per unit under the program, with much

of the red tape associated with other housing programs. Finally, since local governmental approval is required, the same political pressures that can keep public housing units out of certain parts of central cities or out of suburban municipalities can also prevent the construction of units under the Rent Supplement Program.

A better housing subsidy

The best means to use for overcoming the difficulties of other government housing subsidies for lower-income families is what could be called a lump-sum rental certificate. Such a certificate could be used by lower-income families together with as much of their own funds as they wished to purchase housing on the private market, or from limited-dividend corporations or LHAs, in much the same way as food stamps are used. As is the case with food stamps, the seller of housing would redeem the certificate for cash. (The certificate device would be used, supposedly, to limit expenditure under the program to purchases of housing. This will be expanded in the last section of this chapter.) Unlike the food stamp program, under which the recipient of benefits receives a dollar's worth of purchasing power for, say, 30 cents, in this scheme the recipient would receive a certificate of fixed dollar value for the purchase of housing and pay dollar-for-dollar for any additional housing purchased. Tenants would thus have the incentive nonsubsidy recipients have to limit the size of the unit purchased, obviating the need for administrative limitation on the eligibility of units.

By allowing the certificate to be used for purchase of housing on the private market regardless of the earnings of property owners, more of these owners would be induced to supply housing to lower-income families than under the Rent Supplement Program, where earnings are limited. By making the certificates eligible for the purchase of "used" or existing housing as well as newly built housing on the private market, subsidy recipients would almost certainly be less concentrated spatially than in the public housing program. In addition, they would be less readily identifiable as subsidy recipients than when living in public housing or other projects built specifically for lower-income persons. Through the use of the certificate it would be far easier to give smaller subsidies per family to a larger number of families. Doing so would increase the value to the average lower-income family because less of the subsidy would be dissipated by reducing the value of additional housing.[12] Finally, the rent certificate would promote freedom of residence. It would be far more difficult for an alderman or a city council to exclude lower-income persons from a ward or suburb where these families rent housing available generally on the private market than where local government approval for construction of new units is required, as in other programs.

Probably the major reason why housing programs like the one just outlined have never been adopted is the fear that increased expenditures by lower-income families would merely serve to "line the pockets of landlords." On a naive level, it is sometimes asserted that private landlords would simply charge higher rentals for the same property under such a scheme. Though any single landlord might wish to do so if he could, competition among landlords would tend to prevent this. There are already available on the market better-quality units. If a single landlord tried to charge more for the same dwelling, a tenant could move to a better unit.

On a more sophisticated level, the objection asserts that the housing supply to lower-income families on the private market is a highly inelastic one. It was argued in the first section of this chapter that this belief is incorrect. It is precisely because the private market supply to low-income persons is a fairly elastic one that housing policy should aim at shifting the supply vertically downward or increasing the lower-income demand for housing. By making rent certificates eligible for the purchase of housing provided by semipublic bodies such as limited-dividend corporations or by LHAs, though, a built-in safeguard would be provided. For, if public bodies could cover the resource costs of providing housing to lower-income per-

---

[12] Under the public housing program, the average low-income family receives $0.07 \times \$71$ or about $5 per month in benefits. If the additional housing produced by the program were equally distributed among all low-income families, each would receive about $9.10 per month additional housing at market prices, the equivalent of an increase in income of $8.30 per month. See Muth, *Public Housing: An Economic Evaluation*, p. 27.

sons more effectively than the private market, they could do so under the certificate program. By providing the subsidy directly to the tenant in a manner designed to avoid the economic wastes of current programs, moreover, most of the administrative red tape involved in current housing programs could be avoided by local governmental bodies.

REDUCING THE COST
OF LOWER-INCOME HOUSING

It is becoming much more generally realized that the primary urban housing problem is the large expenditure required for the purchase of "decent" housing on the private market relative to the incomes of the poor. Housing subsidies of the type discussed in the preceding section are all attempts to overcome this problem by reducing the expenditure the poor must make to acquire housing deemed to be satisfactory. Measures to increase the incomes of the poor discussed later in the book are an alternative, whose merits will be considered in this chapter's final section. There are two other kinds of measures sometimes suggested for reducing the expenditure necessary for acquiring housing of any given quality: rent control and factory-built housing.

Rent control

Rent controls have existed in New York City since early in World War II, but they went out of existence with remarkably little fuss virtually everywhere else in the United States in the late 1940s and early 1950s. They have existed in some European countries since the beginning of World War I. With the inflation in the late sixties they have been advocated again, reinstituted in a few communities on a local basis, and imposed nationally during phases 1 and 2 of the Nixon Administration's price control program. Since there are few more insidiously harmful programs than rent control, a brief consideration of it seems appropriate.

Rent controls have usually been instituted by fixing money or dollar rentals at their existing levels early in a wartime period. As other prices rise with inflationary pressures, real rentals—dollar rentals relative to other prices—fall. In some

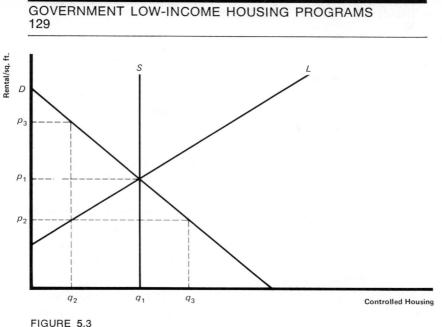

FIGURE 5.3
Rent control

instances, though, as was the case recently with the introduction of so-called rent stabilization of some previously uncontrolled rentals in New York City, controls are imposed that limit the extent to which dollar rentals can rise in any time period. And, indeed, under rent control proper some increases in dollar rentals are permitted as dollar prices generally rise. Despite the variety of real-world specifics, though, the net effects of controls are the same—to keep rentals below the levels they would reach in an uncontrolled market.

The effects of controls are illustrated in Figure 5.3. Here D is the demand curve for controlled housing, and S is the short-run and L the long-run supply schedule of such housing. The controlled level of rentals is p_2; the free-market equilibrium rental is p_1. At the controlled level p_2, purchasers of controlled housing would like to purchase q_3 of it, but even in the short-run only q_1 of its exists. Thus, even if the demand for controlled housing has not risen, as it may well have since the imposition of controls, rent control produces an excess demand for housing, or a housing shortage. Controlled housing is a good buy for those who can obtain it. Consequently it becomes difficult to obtain. People who might not otherwise do so, especially younger and aged persons, maintain separate households. Others, especially older families whose children have left home, maintain larger dwellings than they otherwise would. Vacancies that do occur are taken quickly. In Paris it is a common practice for apartment hunters to read the obituary pages early in the morning and rush to a deceased person's apartment in hopes of being able to bribe the concierge and obtain it. In 1968 it was observed that the waiting time in official queues for rent-controlled apartments in Greater Stockholm was about four to eight years. Only 20 to 25 percent moving into controlled apartments obtained these via the official queues, however; the usual way to obtain apartments appears to be through relatives, friends, employers, and even the black market.[13]

Inefficiency in the use of existing space is not the only factor contributing to a housing shortage. For in the long run the quantity of controlled housing declines from q_1 to q_2 in response to the lower real rental. Units may sometimes be removed from the controlled market by releasing them as furnished if they become vacant or by selling the ownership rights. Cooperative and condominium apartments are far more widespread in New York City, where some apartment rentals are controlled, than elsewhere in the country. The *New York Times* recently reported an interesting instance of the attempted removal of a building from controls. A church that owns what was characterized as "an elegant residence hotel" wished to sell it to its tenants as a cooperative. The chairman of a tenants' group was paying $421 a month rent plus $100 for maid and linen service. The purchase price for his unit would be $25,000, which might cost him $150 monthly; monthly maintenance was estimated at $366, maid service at $125. The *Times* quoted him as saying, "If this was a private firm you could understand them beating the other fellow if they could. But this is a church. When they do it, it's irreligious."[14]

[13] Assar Lindbeck, "Theories and Problems in Swedish Economic Policy in the Post-War Period," *American Economic Review* 58 (June 1968), pt. 2, 66–68.

[14] "Park Avenue Tenants Picket Against Cooperative," *New York Times*, 19, March 1973, p. 26.

In addition to the removal of existing units from the controlled stock, investors may build fewer new units of the type subject to controls out of fear of future imposition of controls on units not initially controlled. Such controls have been instituted recently under New York City's rent stabilization program. Finally, controls lead owners of affected units to spend less on them for maintenance and repair than they would if they could receive a higher rental. Units thus deteriorate in quality. In this regard it is interesting to note that from 1950 to 1956, New York City was the only one of six cities, data for which were gathered for the latter year by the National Housing Inventory, for which the fraction of substandard dwellings failed to decline markedly. Indeed, that fraction actually rose somewhat. The deterioration of controlled dwellings may become so bad that they are abandoned by their owners. There are estimates that over 100,000 units have been abandoned in New York City as compared with 5,000 to 10,000 for other large U.S. cities.

Despite the shortage of housing that rent control produces, it is frequently argued that controls are necessary to keep rentals at reasonable levels the poor are able to pay. It is not help to the poor, though, or even to a city's welfare budget, if housing cannot be found for the poor. Press reports have noted that welfare recipients in New York City have been housed, sometimes for three months or longer, in dilapidated hotels at a monthly cost of $700. Indeed, to the extent that the poor are new arrivals in disproportionate number or have more children per family, they may have particular difficulty in obtaining controlled housing. For it is easier for a landlord to refuse to rent to families with children when he faces an excess demand for the housing he owns. One recent study did find a tendency for the poor and for nonwhites to benefit somewhat from rent control in New York City.[15] This study's major finding, however, was that the benefits of reduced rentals under controls bore very little relation to the income and demographic characteristics of tenants of controlled dwellings.

---

[15] Edgar O. Olsen, "An Econometric Analysis of Rent Control," *Journal of Political Economy,* 80 (November–December 1972), 1081–1100.

A difficulty in rent control that is frequently overlooked is that the controlled rental may not be the appropriate measure of housing expenditure for tenants of controlled dwellings. Returning to Figure 5.3, given the demand curve D and stock q_2, tenants would offer as much as p_3 per unit for the available controlled stock. This price, which economists call the shadow price, exceeds the long-run free market equilibrium price p_1 if the supply schedule L does not coincide with S. Potential tenants may pay part of the difference between p_2 and p_3 as a bribe to obtain a controlled unit. Such bribes may take a variety of forms. Immediately following World War II, when controls were still in existence nationally, prospective tenants frequently paid "key money," that is, bought the key to an apartment for perhaps several hundred dollars. Or they might buy a few sticks of virtually worthless furniture from the departing tenant or landlord for a similar sum. Currently, there are agents in New York City who will find an available controlled apartment for a fairly steep fee. Thus, tenants need by no means benefit as much from controlled rentals as might appear on the surface.

Persons who have experienced the effects of rent control for any protracted period frequently realize the problems associated with controls. Those who are not economists, though, will almost invariably argue that rent controls cannot be removed so long as a shortage of housing exists. As pointed out, however, rent controls create a shortage in the sense of excess demand. As Milton Friedman once remarked in his *Newsweek* column, anyone advocating rent controls should be made to look for an apartment in New York City.

Reducing construction costs

Another set of programs for reducing housing costs relate to the search for new techniques to reduce construction costs. These are motivated in part by the high capital expenditures made on public housing projects, which were discussed in the previous section. The search for new techniques is stimulated, too, by perennial complaints that the residential construction industry is antiquated and hampered by restraints imposed by local building codes and trade unions. Interestingly enough, such complaints tend to be most vocal in inflationary periods such as the late 1940s and 1960s. Somewhat paradoxically, the wages of construction workers and union members generally tend to grow less rapidly in such periods than at other times.[16]

There is scanty empirical evidence on the effects of constraints on homebuilding given existing technology, but what there is indicates that these constraints increase construction costs by no more than 10 percent. Sherman J. Maisel calculated the effects of local building codes on the cost of a $10,000 house in the San Francisco Bay area in the early 1950s. The additional expenditure required by local codes over those in municipalities with a uniform national code averaged only about $100. Maisel also calculated that unions raised construction costs on such a house by only about $300. He further determined that large-scale tract builders had costs that were not more than 10 percent lower than those of the smallest builders.[17] A follow-up to Maisel's study indicated that the number and average size of large-tract builders ceased to grow in the middle fifties, suggesting that economies of scale in conventional house construction are fully exploited by a builder producing 500 to 800 units or so per year.[18] Despite the growth of the large-scale tract builder since World War II, though, many smaller builders continue to exist. Another study of factors affecting sales prices of new houses financed by FHA insured mortgages in different cities in 1966 and 1967 reached quite similar conclusions.[19]

It might plausibly be argued, though, that building codes and unions prevent the adoption of new and cheaper techniques of construction. There have been a variety of attempts at new methods since World War II. In the late forties prefabricated housing was widely hailed as a means of reducing con-

[16] Stephen P. Sobotka, "Union Influence on Wages: The Construction Industry," *Journal of Political Economy* 61 (April 1953), 127–143.
[17] Sherman J. Maisel, *Housebuilding in Transition* (Berkeley: University of California Press, 1952).
[18] John P. Herzog, *The Dynamics of Large Scale Housebuilding*, Research Report 22, Real Estate Research Program (Berkeley: University of California, 1963), pp. 25–28.
[19] Richard F. Muth and Elliot Wetzler, "Effects of Constraints on Single-Unit Housing Costs," Study S-322, Institute for Defense Analysis, Program Analysis Division, Arlington, Va. (September 1968).

struction costs. Such housing consisted of factory-built components, such as walls, floors, and so forth, that were assembled at the home site. It never proved very important and today is limited primarily to rural areas of the Midwest and South. In the early 1960s, when the effects of demolitions under urban renewal and expressway construction were becoming apparent, great emphasis in discussions of housing-problems was placed on using advanced techniques to rehabilitate the existing dwellings. Several experiments were made, particularly in New York City. I have never been able to find any detailed published results of these experiments—the military are not the only bureaucrats to classify their mistakes. Such experimental rehabilitations apparently were quite costly—$30,000 or more to renovate a New York brownstone. This is probably the situation because each individual structure presents unique problems in rehabilitation, hence standardization and large production runs are impossible.

The latest attempts at reducing construction costs are represented by the possibility of factory-built housing, The most recent manifestation of this idea is the program called Operation Breakthrough by the Department of Housing and Urban Development. Under such techniques, whole rooms or modules would be built and shipped to the construction site and fitted together. Such techniques, it is thought, would offer greater possibilities for reducing the use of highly skilled and expensive labor at the construction site than prefabricated homes. At the same time it adds problems of its own. Although it is less expensive to transport separate wall, floor, and ceiling components, when fitted together prior to shipment they become quite bulky and thus expensive to transport. There is little information on the cost of housing built from factory-assembled modules. The *Wall Street Journal* reported that Stirling Modular townhouses built for the Erie, Pennsylvania, housing authority were no less costly than conventional houses.[20] The cost at the factory for two or three bedrooms, living room, kitchen, and bath was about $12,000, but land and site development added $3,000, and transportation, erection, and finishing came to $7,000. The high transport costs

[20] "Instant Housing?," *Wall Street Journal*, 8 April 1971, p. 14.

of the finished product provide good economic reason why there is no General Motors in the residential construction industry.

ARE HOUSING SUBSIDIES NECESSARY AT ALL?

Superiority of income subsidies

My brother, who is also an economist, once remarked to me that "The first principle of welfare economics is to always give people money for their birthdays." Though he and I exchange neckties as often as money, his quip highlights an important point. People can always take the money you would have spent on a necktie and buy one themselves if that's what they feel they need most. But if they'd rather, they can use the money for socks instead.

Similarly, if given the opportunity to spend the money equivalent of providing, say, public housing, beneficiaries of the public housing program could always use it all to purchase housing on the private market. If anything, given the inefficiencies in the production of public housing discussed in the second section, they could purchase considerably more housing on the private market for what it costs government to provide public housing. If, however, beneficiaries choose instead to devote only a part of the subsidy to buying housing and they spent the rest on other things, even liquor, they do so presumably because they prefer the pattern of consumption they choose. Stated somewhat more technically, the reason for this is essentially as follows: Families and individuals, in selecting among alternative ways of spending their incomes, can make the best use of these incomes only if the additional satisfaction they receive per dollar spent is the same for all commodities actually purchased. If given an income subsidy, consumers can allocate their additional expenditure so as to preserve this balance. However, if they are required to spend the whole subsidy on one commodity, such as housing, then the additional satisfaction per dollar of expenditure is less for that commodity than for others generally. An additional dollar's expenditure on housing, however, requires the use of resources that could be used instead to produce other commodities that consumers would value at a dollar or more. It thus takes less than an additional dollar to compensate the consumer for the loss of a dollar's expenditure on housing. Housing subsidies, or any other specific subsidy program, such as food stamps, thus tend to provide the recipient less power to satisfy his wants than a general or income subsidy would.

Indirect benefits
of housing subsidies

Why, then, require lower-income families to spend an entire subsidy on housing? As a practical matter, it probably is largely a question of the popular mistake of identifying the most visible manifestation of poverty with its cause. In a somewhat deeper level, housing subsidies are preferred to income subsidies because of the widespread belief that the private market supply of housing to lower-income persons is very inelastic. The evidence for this belief was discussed in the first section. It is sufficient here to repeat that this view is mistaken. In addition, the proposition just enunciated on the efficiency of housing subsidies holds regardless of the elasticity of the lower-income housing supply. Economists, though, are quite ingenious at providing rationales for programs politicians wish to adopt anyway. It should come as no surprise, then, that several other reasons for housing subsidies as opposed to general income subsidies have been advanced.

As stated at the beginning of Chapter 4, externalities are probably the major justification for governmental intervention in the private housing market. As regards lower-income housing, there may be at least two distinct kinds of external effects associated with it. The first is that substandard or slum housing reduces the desirability of surrounding properties as places of residence or business and hence reduces their values. This kind of externality was dealt with at length in Chapter 4. To recall its conclusions, slum housing tends to be spatially separated from other uses of property, and its effects show up along its borders. Shifting the boundary separating slum and other areas merely shifts the location of external effects. Further, Bailey's study cited earlier suggests that the external effects of slums are quite limited in their spatial extent. It is probably for this reason that careful studies have found essentially no effects of demolition and redevelopment upon the values of surrounding properties.[21]

The second kind of external effect of slums is upon the expenditures local governments must make for police and fire protection and other municipal services. The greater incidence of crime, poorer health, and social disorders have long been thought by many to be the result of slum housing itself. Even if this were the case, no support for the demolition of slum dwellings would be provided. For, as argued in the first section, demolitions reduce the housing opportunities of the poor. To the extent that crime, poor health, and social disorders result from inadequate housing, demolitions by themselves only worsen these conditions. The association of social problems and slum areas, though, is no more convincing evidence of causation than the fact that big horses have big feet. Both may be manifestations of other factors, low incomes and associated conditions in the case of slum housing.

A fairly convincing a priori rationale can be developed to the effect that slum housing increases the costs of supplying a given level of fire protection. Most arguments regarding the causal impact of poor housing on crime, health, and social problems are quite tenuous, though. The types of public-health menaces associated with poor housing in underdeveloped nations today and in developed ones earlier in their development are largely absent in Europe and the United States today. Further, much of the disenchantment with public housing no doubt results from the fact that such housing obviously has failed to eliminate crime and social disorder. If anything, it has only served to concentrate it, and thus perhaps intensify it. A recent study of the effects of substandard housing on expenditures for local governmental services found them to show up principally in the expenditure for fire protection. These effects appear to be quite small. For example, the reduction in local expenditure resulting from Chicago's Hyde Park urban renewal project is negligible relative to the project's net

[21] Hugh O. Nourse, "The Effect of Public Housing on Property Values in St. Louis," *Land Economics* 39 (November 1963), 433–441, and Salvatore V. Ferrera, "The Effect of Urban Renewal and Public Housing on Neighborhood Property Values and Rents in Chicago," unpublished Ph.D. dissertation, Department of Economics, University of Chicago, 1969.

cost.[22] The only other careful analysis studied public-housing families paired at random with families who were privately housed but of otherwise similar characteristics. Although public-housing families were clearly better housed, in matters regarding health and social adjustment the differences between the two groups were minor.[23]

Housing subsidies, especially loans at low interest rates, are frequently justified by alleged imperfections in private capital markets. Private lenders, it is often argued, will make loans to lower-income families or in older areas of cities only at higher rates than for other kinds of investments. Such arguments lose much of their force when it is realized that interest rates of 3 percent or less are often charged under federal programs. And, if such imperfections in private lending were very widespread it would pay groups of life insurance companies and banks to buy up lower-income and older housing and rent it back to their previous occupants after improving the property. However, there are few instances of this.

Still another reason offered for housing subsidies as opposed to general income subsidies is another kind of externality, namely externalities in consumption. Middle- and higher-income persons, so the argument runs, feel better if lower-income families consume more housing then they otherwise would. Such an argument, though technically correct in a certain sense, shows the ridiculous extremes to which technique can be pushed. The aim of public policy toward the poor is to improve their lot, not to make the rich feel better about poverty. A closely related argument is pure paternalism, namely that the poor do not spend enough on housing in their own interest. The poor may indeed make mistakes in spending their incomes, as we all do. However, they have more intimate and detailed knowledge of their own situations, and, more important, must bear the consequences of their mistakes. This is not to assert that they are responsible in any meaningful sense for their own poverty. Quite the reverse. They are likely to make fewer mistakes than policy makers who needn't

---

[22] John C. Weicher, "Municipal Services and Urban Renewal," unpublished Ph.D. dissertation, Department of Economics, University of Chicago, 1968.
[23] Daniel N. Wilner et al., *The Housing Environment and Family Life* (Baltimore: Johns Hopkins Press, 1962).

bear the consequences of mistakes in directing other people how to lead their lives.

Thus, none of the arguments advanced for housing subsidies as opposed to general income subsidies make much sense. In fact, housing quality in the past has been highly responsive to improvements in income. Indeed, general income subsidies would have been no more costly during the 1950s per substandard dwelling eliminated than public housing was.[24] As argued at the start of this chapter, the private market has done considerably better in improving the housing of the poor than government has. What the private market cannot always do as effectively as society can do through government is to redistribute income to the poor. Given higher incomes, though, the case seems overwhelming that the private market can house people better.

SUMMARY

From 1937 to 1968 government programs demolished more lower-income housing than they built. In the short run, demolitions increase the price of housing to the poor. As a result, some lower-income families move into previously existing better housing but spend more for housing. Others may be induced to inhabit still smaller or poorer-quality dwellings than they would have in the absence of demolitions. In the long run, however, the rise in price of poor- relative to good-quality housing brought about by demolitions leads to conversions of good- to poor-quality housing by private landlords. Contrary to widespread opinion, it appears that the supply of poor-quality housing is highly elastic. If so, the principal long-run effect of demolitions is to relocate the slums. Stricter code enforcement or other measures that increase the cost of converting good- to poor-quality housing shift the supply schedule of housing to the poor upward, making housing more expensive for them.

Unlike demolitions and code enforcement, some housing subsidy measures benefit the poor directly, though by less than the same expenditure of resources might if better managed. The public housing program has allowed roughly 7 percent

---

[24] Muth, *Cities and Housing*, p. 334.

of the lower-income population to increase their housing consumption by about three times while maintaining their consumption of other items. Because the recipients of the housing
subsidy are not free to spend it as they wish, however, the
subsidy is worth only slightly more than half as much to
its recipients as the cost of providing it. Building public housing on cleared slum land and the federal subsidy to capital
costs alone have raised the cost of providing public housing
by more than half. Recent modifications to public housing
and other housing programs perpetuate many of the shortcomings of the public housing program. A program that gave
lower-income families a lump-sum to spend on any privately
or publicly produced housing as they choose would be much
superior to current programs.

Rent control attempts to reduce the amounts families must
spend for housing. By holding rentals below market equilibrium levels, however, it leads to excess demand for controlled
housing, or a housing shortage. Landlords may seek to remove
units from controls by leasing them furnished or by converting
them to owner-occupied housing. Fewer units of the type subject to controls may be built, and existing units are less well
maintained than they would otherwise be. Because tenants
may be willing to pay more than the market equilibrium
rental through bribery or other ways, rent controls make matters worse, not better. Various attempts to reduce housing
costs through factory building and rehabilitation of housing have also been attempted. These have generally proved
unsuccessful.

From the recipients' viewpoint, income subsidies are generally
superior to subsidies for specific items of consumption such
as housing. Many arguments have been advanced, though,
for housing subsidies based upon indirect benefits to persons
other than the subsidy recipient. In general, it does not appear
that the indirect benefits of housing subsidies are sufficiently
great to justify them. The experience of the post–World War
II period strongly suggests that, given increased incomes, the
private market can house people better.

CHAPTER 6

The urban environment

$\mathcal{I}$n a very broad sense Chapters 4 and 5, like this one, are concerned with the urban environment. Housing and other forms of urban land use are important aspects of the physical features that surround people in cities. Externalities are an important aspect of urban land use and are the very essence of urban transportation and air- and water-quality problems. The latter differ from housing problems, however, in that they entail assets of substantial quantitative importance that are privately used but not privately owned as houses are.

The absence of private ownership of urban roads and air masses has important economic implications. Indeed, urban transportation and air pollution are but two examples of a class of phenomena that is perhaps best characterized by the term "congestion." This chapter will first discuss general economic principles relevant to congestion phenomena and then apply these principles to transportation and to air pollution. Then some of the important features that are more or less peculiar to these important instances of urban congestion will be considered.

ECONOMICS OF CONGESTION

Crowding and congestion

The urban problem most obvious to the greatest number of people is probably rush-hour commuter transportation. Virtually every city dweller at one time or another has experienced delays in travel caused by the crowding of urban roads. To many it seems obvious that cities are strangling because of our attempts to move autos around in them. For this reason, in the minds of many the solution to the urban transportation problem is to eliminate the automobile. Yet by any objective standard the introduction of automobile transportation in the 1920s and the freeway in the 1950s has made it relatively cheaper to travel an additional mile to or from work than it was previously. The development of highway transportation has, by freeing resources for other uses, produced an increase in the economy's potential output. On economic grounds, there is no more reason to eliminate it than there is, say, to forbid farmers to use tractors because of the so-called surplus of farm products.

Furthermore, crowding is not uniquely a problem of highways, as the New York City subway system demonstrates, nor a problem of commuter transportation, as attested to by the landing and takeoff delays at city airports. Neither is crowding unique to transportation, as an attempt to buy tickets to a hit play on Broadway or to a professional football championship playoff game readily demonstrates. Finally, crowding is not even uniquely an urban problem, as trying to find a campsite in Yosemite National Park during the summer season reveals. Crowding arises in all such cases because of the failure to charge a high enough price for the use of some scarce resource or some output. Crowding is thus similar to the housing shortage that rent control produces, which was discussed in Chapter 5.

Crowding rarely occurs when resources are controlled by private individuals or firms. For, if the demand for some product exceeds the available stocks, private sellers have the incentive to raise prices. By raising prices sellers increase their incomes and at the same time, reduce the amounts buyers wish to buy. An interesting contrast in crowding under private and public ownership is provided by intercity transportation terminals. When significant numbers of people traveled by passenger train, delays in entering the railroad station were infrequent and of relatively short duration. The situation at bus terminals even today is similar. Rail depots and bus terminals are usually privately owned and operated, in contrast with airports, which typically are publicly owned. Because airports are publicly owned, no one stands to increase his earnings by raising charges imposed for takeoffs and landings when airports are crowded.

Congestion occurs only when facilities are crowded, but congestion is different from crowding. The difference between them is best illustrated by the sellout of a football game. So long as standers are not admitted, the fact that the stadium is sold out does little to detract from the enjoyment of watching the game. Indeed, the additional excitement generated by a capacity crowd may well heighten the enjoyment.

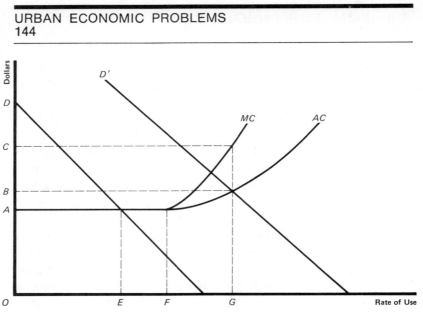

FIGURE 6.1
Unrestricted use of congested facilities

Congestion at airports occurs when arriving planes are stacked up waiting to land and departing planes queue up waiting to depart. For, unlike attendance at football games, any aircraft can enter the landing pattern or takeoff queue. .

When airport delays are experienced, an additional plane imposes further costs on the owners and occupants of other aircraft by adding to the delay of all planes behind it. The additional time spent in landing or taking off means more fuel is burned, and more aircraft hours are used in the flight, hence additional capital and maintenance costs per aircraft are incurred, and additional amounts are spent for flight-crew time. Less obvious, but even more important perhaps, is the additional time spent by passengers in completing their trips. Though each passenger may be delayed only a few minutes if an additional plane seeks to use the airport, many passengers are affected. Thus, the aggregate amount of time lost and hence the output foregone by the economy may be large.

The economic effects of congestion are illustrated in Figure 6.1. Here dollar amounts are shown on the vertical axis and the rate of use of a facility such as an airport on the horizontal axis. The average cost of using the facility, including fees

and landing charges, is represented by the average cost or
AC curve. Up to the rate of use, OF, which may be zero but
need not be and which is sometimes called capacity, the average cost to users of the facility is constant. Thus, if the demand for the facility is D, its rate of use is OE and no congestion occurs. If the demand curve is D', however, the facility
is used at the rate OG. Because average costs are rising in
the range of use, an additional user raises the cost borne by
all other users.

This last phenomenon, which is the essence of congestion,
is reflected in the marginal cost or MC curve. When the rate
of use is OG, the cost borne directly by each user is OB. In
the airport example, landing and takeoff delays cause airlines
to incur additional costs directly for fuel, aircraft, and crews
and indirectly in that passengers find the flight less attractive.
The additional costs borne by other users of the airport are
BC. When the demand curve is at D' the facility is overused
in the sense that the additional value received by any user
is OB but the additional cost borne by all users together is
OC. By reducing the rate of use of the facility, output worth
OB is foregone, but resources that would produce OC dollars
worth of output in other uses are released. The economy as
a whole gains BC dollars' worth of output by reducing the
rate of use of the facility.

The situation is quite similar in commuter travel in cities.
Through taxes on gasoline, tires, and other items, motorists
pay for the capital costs of the roads they use. In addition,
any motorist entering a highway bears the cost of his vehicle,
its operation, and his own time. At certain periods, principally
when large numbers of people are going to or coming from
work, when an individual enters a highway he reduces the
speed of all other cars on the road. Other motorists thus bear
additional vehicle operating costs and spend additional time
in travel. In Figure 6.1 the costs borne by the individual rush-
hour commuter are OB, those borne by other drivers BC. Freeways and other urban highways thus tend to be overused
during rush hours because each user individually is not
charged the full marginal cost, including the additional costs
borne by other users, which are incurred by his using his
auto.

Figure 6.1 also illustrates the problems of air and water pollution quite nicely. Provided the use placed upon it is not too great, that is, less than OF, an urban airshed or a body of water can dissipate waste materials emptied into it without harmful effects. Once the rate of use exceeds OF, however, additional waste is not wholly dispersed. Its accumulation may impose irritation or even health hazards to certain individuals. In addition it may impose additional costs, say for cleaning. These costs, represented by BC in Figure 6.1, are not borne by polluters, those who dispose of wastes into the atmosphere or water. The problem, however, is not one of eliminating all pollution. After all we all pollute the atmosphere by discharging carbon dioxide when we breathe. The ability of the atmosphere to dispose of wastes is a valuable resource in that it reduces the need for resources that might otherwise be required for disposal. The problem, rather, is overuse. When the rate of use is OG, the resources saved by the polluter are OB. However, OC dollars' worth of resources are used by all air or water users. On balance a net loss of resources of BC dollars is incurred by the economy as a whole for any additional pollution.

Congestion is a problem that occurs in a wide range of cases, many of which have little or nothing to do with urban areas as such. It is an important problem that occurs in the use of exhaustible natural resources. Many firms pumping oil from a common pool or fishing in a common body of water are excellent illustrations of congestion. Each firm incurs costs of pumping or fishing given by the AC curve in Figure 6.1 as a function of the rate of use. Any single firm pumping or fishing has a negligible effect on the amount of oil or number of fish in future years. Provided, however, that the current rate of fishing by all fishers is great enough so that the ability of the fish population to reproduce itself is reduced, all of them fishing together reduce the number of fish in future years and, hence, increase the costs of fishing at a later time. (In the oil-pumping case, point F in the figure coincides with O.) Each individual user bears the costs OB, but imposes costs of BC dollars on other users by using the common pool.

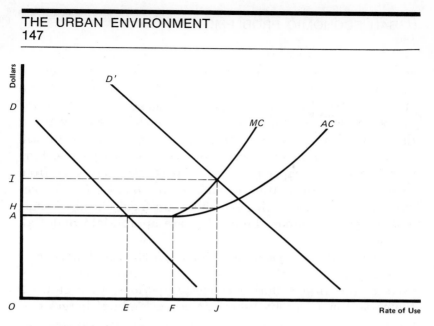

FIGURE 6.2
Best use of congested facilities

Optimal use
of congested resources

The optimum rate of use of a congested resource is illustrated in Figure 6.2. The demand and cost curves shown there are precisely the same as those in Figure 6.1. Suppose the demand curve for the use of the facility is D'. At a rate of use OJ, marginal cost of using the facility, including costs borne by all other users of it, is just equal to the price any users are willing to pay. This means that the value users place on the facility is just equal to the additional costs borne by the economy for use of it. At any lower rate of use, the value of using the facility exceeds the additional cost to the economy of using it, whereas at any greater rate of use the reverse is the case. Thus, output for the economy is made as large as possible if the facility is used at the rate OJ. At the optimum rate of use some congestion still occurs. Congestion is less, however, than when unrestricted use of the facility is permitted, as in Figure 6.1.

One response to the problem of airport congestion has been to impose limits on the number of takeoffs and landings in any time period at certain airports. Such measures, however, are likely to be inefficient, because the value to all users of the airport may not be the same. The opportunity to land at, say, O'Hare Field in Chicago is worth more to a 747 carrying 300 passengers than to a DC-9, which may carry fewer than 100. The opportunity to land or take off is worth still less to a private plane carrying only one or two people. Further, because the capacity of the airport, OF, may vary from time to time with weather conditions, the point OJ may likewise vary. Because airline schedules are fixed ahead of time, it is difficult to impose limits that are appropriate under all weather conditions.

A better regulatory system is to impose higher landing charges or fees that reflect the additional costs imposed upon other users of the airport during congested periods. In Figure 6.2 the costs now borne by users, including landing charges currently imposed, are OH at the optimal rate of use OJ. The imposition of an additional charge HI, reflecting the additional costs imposed upon other aircraft and their users, would equate private and social costs. This is the economic function of fishing licenses.

If such charges were imposed by airports, some aircraft would avoid congested airports. For example, a plane might avoid O'Hare and instead land at Midway Airport, Meggs Field on Chicago's lakefront, or even in Milwaukee. Given an appropriate fee, 747s might well be willing to pay it. Operators of DC-9s, however, might choose to land at Midway instead, since the opportunity to land at O'Hare is worth less to them, or to schedule the particular flight at some other time. Pilots of private planes would almost certainly avoid O'Hare during congested periods. It would be a relatively simple matter to vary the landing fee with weather conditions. Pilots could be informed of the current fee when requesting landing instructions.

Airports now impose landing charges, of course. Such charges, however, are merely sufficient at best to cover the costs of certain runway and traffic control facilities. (Hangers and terminal space are usually rented separately.) These fees are appropriate when demand is at D in Figure 6.2 and congestion does not occur. They are much too low, however, when demand is at D'. In the late 1960s landing fees were about

$25 for a 727 at National airport in Washington, D.C., for example. Yet from observing traffic during peak periods at that airport then, it seems not unreasonable that an additional takeoff or landing might delay ten airliners carrying an average of eighty people each by three minutes. Thus, forty man-hours of passenger time would be lost to the delay, each of which might have earned $6, for a total loss to the economy of $240.[1] Thus, the appropriate landing charge during congestion periods might well have been at least ten times the actual one.[2]

It should be stressed that in many instances, airports and urban roads being good examples, congestion is primarily a peak-period problem. In the airport case, congestion occurs principally in the early evening hours when the weather is good. At these times the demand for use of the facility is D' in Figure 6.2. At other times of the day fewer flights arrive and depart, and demand is at D. Thus, congestion tolls or higher landing charges would be appropriate only during the peak periods. At other times no congestion toll should be imposed.

So far the discussion has implicitly supposed that the capacity of the congested facility is fixed at OF. In the long run, however, the capacity of an airport can be expanded by building additional runways, hiring and training more air-traffic controllers, and installing more radar sets and other landing aids. In similar fashion, additional urban freeways can be built, existing ones widened, and curves straightened or banked better. A lake can be stocked with fish, and the capacity of a river to dispose of wastes can be increased by investing in water treatment facilities.

Whether it is desirable to expand the capacity of a congested resource depends upon the relationship of the benefits of doing so to the costs incurred for expansion. In Figure 6.2, at the optimal short-run rate of use OJ, use of the facility is worth

[1] For a discussion of the incomes and earnings of domestic air travelers and their valuation of their time in travel see Norman J. Asher et al., *Demand Analysis for Air Travel by Supersonic Transport*, Report R-118, Institute for Defense Analyses, Arlington, Va. (1966), Appendix C.
[2] A fuller discussion of appropriate airport landing fees is contained in Ross D. Eckert, *Airports and Congestion: A Problem of Misplaced Subsidies* (Washington, D.C.: American Enterprise Institute for Public Policy Research, 1972).

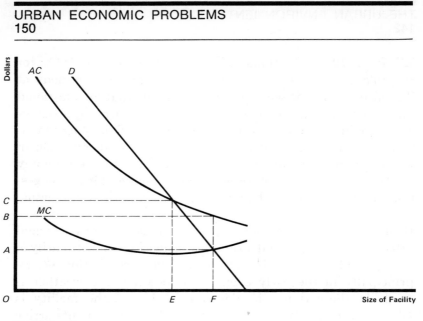

FIGURE 6.3
Best size of a congested facility

OI, whereas the user incurs direct costs equal to OH. Thus, the toll HI is a measure of the worth of additional capacity of the congested facility. If the average of the tolls collected over peak and nonpeak periods exceeds the cost of enlarging the facility so that additional use can be made of it at the same average cost to the user, it is desirable to enlarge it. This is the case because the value of additional use of the facility exceeds the cost to the economy of providing for additional use at a constant quality of the service it provides. Thus, in the long run, for a facility of optimum size the average toll over peak and nonpeak periods is just equal to the marginal cost of providing for additional use at a constant level of service quality.

This last point is illustrated in Figure 6.3, which shows average and marginal costs of providing output of the facility. The curve labeled D shows the optimal toll for a facility of varying size. It is derived from the peak and offpeak demand curves for using the facility shown in Figures 6.1 and 6.2 and cost curves for different size facilities similar to those shown for a single size. The larger the facility, the greater the rate of use (OF in Figure 6.1) at which congestion effects set in. Thus, given the position of the demand curve D', the larger the facility, the smaller the toll at the optimal rate of use (*HI* in Figure 6.2). The optimal size facility is *OF* in Figure 6.3, for which users pay tolls of *OA* averaged over peak and nonpeak periods. If average costs are declining as the size of the facility grows, as is the case where some indivisible or lumpy resource is involved, marginal costs are less than average costs. Consequently, the optimum toll charged is less than the average cost of the facility. To insure its best use, users of the facility would be subsidized by the amount *AB*, the difference between average and marginal costs. Though it seems likely that in many cases of interest—for example, airports, bridges, freeways, and subways—average costs are declining as in Figure 6.3, in others they may be increasing. If so, marginal cost would exceed average cost. Consequently, the optimal toll would exceed the average cost of the facility, and it would yield a surplus rather than incur a deficit.

Facilities that are publicly owned or regulated are rarely priced at marginal cost, however. Rather, as is discussed again in Chapter 13, they are typically priced at average cost so as to break even. In Figure 6.3, if average cost pricing is followed, the toll set is *OC*, and thus the size of the facility is *OE*. When average cost pricing is used and average costs are declining, the facility will be too small (this follows from the negative slope of the demand curve). The value to the user is *OC*, but the costs to the economy of expanding the facility while keeping quality of service to users constant is smaller. Thus, when average cost pricing is followed and average costs are declining, the facility is too small and more congestion is experienced during periods of peak demand than is economically desirable even if optimal short-run tolls are imposed. Congestion during peak periods is still worse if special peak-period tolls are not charged.

URBAN COMMUTER TRANSPORTATION

In this section certain peculiarities of urban commuter transportation will be discussed. Then the pricing of urban transportation will be explored and the desirability of urban rapid transit systems examined. The last section of this chapter will inquire into the regulation of waste disposal in urban areas.

The production
of commuter transportation

As is the case with all commodities, urban commuter trips are produced using land, reproducible capital, and labor. Transportation differs from many commodities, however, in that a significant portion of the inputs in its production are supplied by the user himself. In the case of a highway, for example, a public body determines its location, design, and the amount of maintenance it gets. Such decisions determine the amount of land to be used and much of the nonland capital to be invested in it. The user, in turn, determines the vehicle to be used. More important, though, the user supplies his own travel time, which is most of the labor used in the production of commuter transportation.

Land and nonland capital may be substituted for each other in the production of highways, rail transit, and other systems. With a greater amount of nonland capital investment, curves in a road may be reduced or eliminated, and elevated or double-decked freeways, which require more capital and less land per lane, may be built. The installation of automatic traffic signals, perhaps synchronized systems that permit a constant rate of travel without frequent stopping and starting, permits more vehicles to move along a given lane and requires less land for a given volume of traffic. Nonland capital may also be substituted for land in deciding upon the kind of public facility to build. In a rail transit system, such as the Bay Area Rapid Transit (BART) system in the San Francisco area, less land is used per passenger moved a given distance. But more nonland capital is invested in the system's roadbed, its rolling stock, control system, and stations.

Private users of transportation systems pay fees for the use of the public facilities on which they travel. In the case of so-called public transportation systems, for example, fares are charged. In the case of highway transportation, taxes on gasoline and tires are in effect user charges, the proceeds of which are used to defray the costs of building and maintaining highways. The users of public facilities supply their travel time in producing transportation. The labor supplied, as is dis-

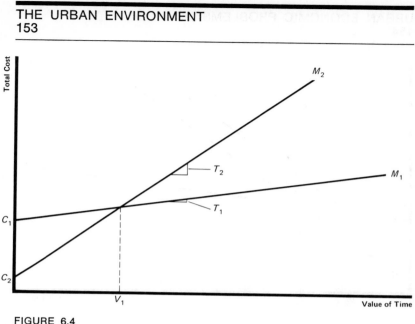

FIGURE 6.4
Choice of mode in transportation

cussed more fully in Chapter 7, has an opportunity cost that is related to the wages users may earn when working. Probably because time spent in commuter travel is not totally wasted but may be spent listening to a car radio or reading on a bus, and also because travel time is not taxed as work time is, commuters appear to value their travel time at substantially less than their wage rate. Most studies suggest that this value is of the order of two-fifths their wage or from three- to five-tenths of it.[3]

In traveling, a user of transit facilities may be expected to choose the means or mode of travel that is cheapest to him. Suppose that a commuter may choose between two modes of travel, his automobile, M_1, and public transit, M_2, in Figure 6.4. The total cost of a given trip by either mode is plotted on the vertical axis as a function of the value the traveler places on his time. The intercept of the cost curve on the vertical axis is the money cost of the trip, the fare paid for public transit, and the cost of owning and operating an automobile for auto travel. The slopes of the total cost curves are the times required for the trip by the particular mode.

---

[3] One of the best of these studies is M. E. Beesley, "The Value of Time Spent in Traveling: Some New Evidence," *Economica*, new series 32 (May 1965), 174–185.

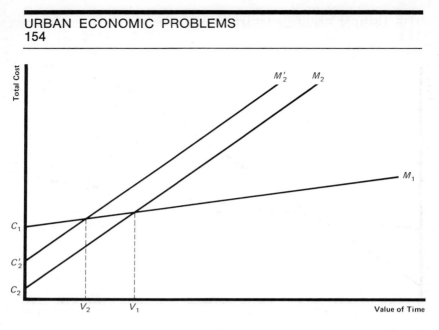

FIGURE 6.5
Effect of a rise in money costs on choice of mode

If the faster mode also requires less money cost, its total cost will be smaller regardless of the value of time for the traveler. Hence, if some travelers are to choose each of the two modes, the total cost curves must intersect as shown. Those travelers placing a value on their time less than V_1 minimize the cost of their trip by choosing public transit. Those with a value of time greater than V_1 will find commuting by private automobile cheaper.

A variety of conditions may change the relative advantage of public and private transit. An increase in public transit fares from C_2 to C_2' in Figure 6.5 shifts the M_2 curve in Figure 6.4 upward parallel to its old location. As a result, the largest value of time for which public transit is cheaper than auto commuting falls from V_1 to V_2. Consequently, the number of public transit users declines, and more people commute by auto. Similarly, a decrease in the frequency of bus service would increase the average amount of time spent in a given trip from T_2 to T_2'' in Figure 6.6, causing the M_2 curve to rotate about C_2 in a counterclockwise direction. This, too, would lead more commuters to use their autos instead of public transit.

On the other hand, the building of freeways and a dispersal

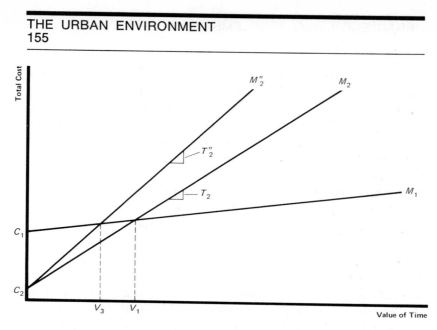

FIGURE 6.6
Effect of a rise in time costs on choice of mode

of residences and employment places stimulate auto travel by reducing the relative time it requires. Finally, if the average hourly earnings of people increase, and hence the value they place on their time, a larger fraction of commuters will choose auto travel over public transportation. (Partly for this same reason, the fraction of intercity passenger trips made by air as compared to train or bus has risen over time.) All the changes whose effects have just been described have probably occurred in U.S. cities since the end of World War II. All have contributed to increased auto commuting and the decline in public transit.

The money costs of using an automobile for commuting, especially when downtown parking charges are considered, are almost certainly higher than public transit fares. At the same time, those who travel by automobile generally have higher incomes and earnings than those using public transit. One infers, then, from Figure 6.4 that auto commuting must usually be quicker than public transit. Yet from observing freeway tie-ups and trains whizzing along their tracks most people are inclined to believe that rail transit must surely be the faster mode of travel. The apparent contradiction can be resolved when one notes that the line-haul part of the journey, that part spent on the freeway or on the train, is only one part of the journey. The other parts are generally called "residential collection" and "downtown distribution." These are the segments comparable to getting to and from the airport at the origin and destination of an intercity trip. As any air traveler knows, these parts of the journey may take more time than the flight itself.

The main advantage of auto travel is that the residential collection and downtown distribution parts of the journey to work are performed with the same vehicle as the line-haul segment of the journey. There are a variety of means of residential collection and downtown distribution in public transit, all of which require additional time of the traveler, if only in waiting for another vehicle. Feeder buses at either end of the line-haul portion may require additional fares. If one parks at the train station, one incurs much the same automobile cost of driving to work. If a wife drives her husband to the transit stop, there is the cost of the wife's time. Thus, public transit fares and line-haul trip times represent but a part of the cost of commuter travel by public transit. Meyer, Kain, and Wohl have argued that public transit suffers at least a ten-minute handicap as compared with the automobile because of the latter's superiority in collection and distribution.[4] With a ten-mile line-haul segment, transit would have to gain one minute per mile, or achieve an average line-haul velocity of thirty miles per hour if the auto's is twenty, in order to equalize total trip time of the two modes.

One of the main disadvantages of public transit is that relatively large vehicles are used. The average bus holds perhaps fifty persons, and many more are carried by a single subway or commuter railroad train. In consequence, to provide frequent service along a particular route, there must be a relatively large trip demand. On more lightly traveled routes, infrequent service imposes a higher time cost to the traveler. In a somewhat similar vein, 747s are fine for long-distance, heavily traveled intercity routes such as that from New York to Los Angeles. They cannot yet be profitably flown, however,

[4] J. R. Meyer, J. F. Kain, and M. Wohl, *The Urban Transportation Problem* (Cambridge, Mass.: Harvard University Press, 1965), pp. 104–105.

between San Francisco and Philadelphia and provide what travelers consider adequately frequent service. Consequently, airlines use 707s or DC-8s for nonstop flights between these cities.

Airline managers have an incentive to select suitable vehicles for different routes, for an airline's profits are increased by their doing so. In particular, air travelers may register their preferences for more frequent service through their purchase of tickets. Users of public transit generally cannot, however, for the managers of publicly operated facilities have no profit incentive to guide them in designing facilities for commuter travel. They are thus less aware of the time costs of users, who supply most of the labor used in commuter transportation, than are airline officials. For these reasons, probably, public transit officials have been less responsive to consumer desires than airline managers have.

The regulation of commuter transportation

Earlier in this chapter it was argued that the main problem with commuter transport is rush-hour congestion. Just as in airport congestion, an additional user of an urban freeway may impose additional vehicle operating and passenger time costs on other users when he enters the traffic stream by slowing it down. Just as in the case of airport congestion, the best means of regulating freeway and other forms of urban transportation is the imposition of congestion tolls.

Returning to Figure 6.2, during rush hours when demand is at D' rather than D, optimal use of commuter transit facilities could be achieved by an additional user charge equal to HI. This is the difference between marginal and average costs. With tolls on freeways and higher fares for public transit systems during rush hours, the rate of use of transit facilities would be reduced, though with optimal tolls congestion might not be eliminated. If rush-hour commuting were made more expensive, some shoppers would be induced to make trips at other times of the day. Higher costs of commuter transport would mean that employers in the CBD and certain other places would have to pay higher wages than others in order to induce people to work there. Some would thus have an incentive to relocate their businesses to places where their costs would be less, reducing the rate of use of congested facilities. Some employers would find it advantageous to adjust their business hours so that their employees would bear smaller costs in getting to and from work.

Freeway charges for rush-hour use would also reduce traffic in a variety of other ways. By charging tolls reflecting the additional burdens imposed on other motorists, C_1 in Figure 6.4 would shift upward, causing some drivers to shift to public transit instead. A fifty-seat bus adds little more to congestion than a single auto, so the toll per traveler would be far lower. Other drivers undoubtedly would be induced to form carpools. The comparison of single-passenger autos with carpools is qualitatively similar to that between public transit and private automobile. The vehicle money cost is lower for carpools but travel time is greater because of the larger amounts of time spent in residential collection and downtown distribution.

Congestion tolls are a relatively efficient means of regulating commuter traffic. They permit those transit users who could most easily make trips at other times to do so. Employers who could most easily change their locations or stagger their hours of work more cheaply would likewise be induced to do so in seeking to maximize their earnings. Those for whom it would be most costly to change their locations or stagger their hours would not be forced to. Those drivers who would find it least costly to switch to public transit or carpools would also have the incentive to do so.

Other means of regulating the use of urban roads exist of course. Lanes reserved for buses speed up bus travel and may lead some people to switch to it. But if unused much of the time, some vehicle-moving capacity of the urban road system is simply wasted. It is also possible to limit the number of vehicles entering freeways, as some cities have done experimentally. It is even possible to give buses or carpools priority, but imagine the fuss if a Cadillac, whose occupants almost certainly value their time more highly, were to be given priority over a Chevrolet. Yet Chevrolet drivers would probably find nonfreeway travel relatively cheaper than the drivers of Cadillacs.

It would be fairly easy, apart from the political repercussions, to charge higher rush-hour fares on commuter trains, subways, and buses. The biggest difficulty with congestion tolls on urban roads might be their costs of collection. Certainly, toll plazas, such as those on certain roads and many bridges, would slow down traffic. Electronic systems that would display and transmit the current freeway toll and register it on a device carried in the car are not only technically feasible but relatively inexpensive. By such devices, the freeway charge could even be made to vary from lane to lane, so that travelers who value their time more highly could pay a higher charge and travel faster.

However, many more modest devices might be employed to regulate commuter traffic. One example is a tax on downtown parking recently imposed by the City of San Francisco. Such a tax might be made higher or be limited to vehicles arriving at or departing from a parking facility during rush hours. Or vehicles might be required to display a sticker, similar to a city license or parking-lot sticker, in order to use certain designated roads during rush hours. The rush-hour toll would be collected as a fee for purchase of the sticker.

In some cases, however, charges currently imposed upon urban travelers are actually lower for rush-hour travel than for travel during off-peak periods. When I lived in Chicago ten years ago, parking in city parking garages was subsidized, hence especially cheap. As a result, the city parking garages were frequently full, and non-rush-hour commuters had to park in private garages or parking lots at higher rates. Most commuter railroads and some bus systems offer monthly tickets or passes at bargain rates. These tend to be purchased by peak-hour commuters; those who travel occasionally, usually during off-peak periods, buy single tickets at higher fares per ride. Such practices are easy enough to understand. Downtown parking is subsidized to attract more employment to the CBD, whereas transit system managers find commuter demand more responsive to price changes than the demands of the occasional transit rider. These practices, however, are perverse, in that they increase, not reduce, rush-hour congestion on urban transit facilities.

It was pointed out in the first section of this chapter that if the average cost of increasing the rate of use of a congested facility (while holding constant the quality of the service it provides) is declining, the sum of the tolls collected during peak and off-peak periods should be less than the total cost of providing the facility. Use of the facility would thus be subsidized. It is almost certainly true that average costs are declining for most rail transit systems. There is thus a good case on economic grounds for an appropriate subsidy to them, though not necessarily for any subsidy necessary to get them built. It is less obvious, but equally true, that bus systems should be subsidized. Additional vehicles and drivers can probably be provided at a constant average cost. However, if the number of buses provided is proportional to the number of trips, and the average wait for a bus is half the interval of time between buses, then the total time waited by all travelers is constant, regardless of how many travelers there are. Consequently, average costs, including waiting time of passengers, decline as the number of riders increases, and bus service should be subsidized.[5]

Note, however, that if rush-hour congestion tolls (and pollution charges) are imposed, freeways should probably be subsidized as well. Though a second freeway of given design probably can be built at the same total cost as the first, up to some point the cost per lane for a given freeway may decline as more lanes per freeway are built. Consequently, the average freeway cost per unit of vehicle carrying capacity would decline as capacity increases.

Many people argue that it would be desirable to subsidize public transit in order to draw commuters away from their autos. Whether such a view is correct depends upon whether appropriate congestion tolls are being levied upon commuters or highway use is otherwise limited to the optimal rate of use for the economy. In Figure 6.1, which illustrated the situation existing when congestion charges are not imposed, the value of using the freeway is OB, but the cost to the economy is OC. Thus, a net saving of BC dollars is realized for each

[5] For a fuller discussion of this point and some calculations of the appropriate subsidy level, see Herbert Mohring, "Optimization and Scale Economies in Urban Bus Transportation," *American Economic Review* 64 (September 1972), 591–604.

auto diverted from the highway by public transit subsidies
or by other means. In Figure 6.2, however, where appropriate
congestion tolls are imposed, no net benefit to the economy
results from the reduction of freeway use.

Is rapid transit
the answer?

It has just been argued that the appropriate answer to the
urban transportation problem is to charge users of urban roads
and other public facilities additional amounts during periods
of peak demand. Additional roads and other transit facilities
ought to be provided and subsidized if the charge averaged
over periods of peak and nonpeak demand exceed the costs
of providing additional transportation capacity. It would
seem, however, that virtually everyone believes that subways
and other rail transit systems are needed. To cite only one
example, the recent beginning of BART service in the San
Francisco Bay area has been widely heralded as providing
the opportunity to solve the problems of congested freeways.
The question should be raised as to whether so-called rapid
transit is indeed the appropriate solution to urban transportation problem. The answer, of course, depends upon the relative
costs of rapid-transit vs. other forms of urban transportation
in providing a given quality of service, principally total trip
time.

One important piece of information bearing on the desirability
of rapid transit was provided in a study by Moses and Williamson.[6] Using data on the time and money costs incurred,
they estimated the charges necessary to divert auto commuters to other travel modes in the Chicago area. These data
relate to the period around 1960 and were collected by the
Cook County Highway Department. Moses and Williamson
estimated that additional money costs of auto travel of about
$1.10 per day would be required to divert half the auto com-
muters to other travel modes, including the El and subway
system and commuter railroads. Alternatively, negative fares
would have been required on all modes of public transport
to achieve the same end if auto commuting costs were un-

[6] Leon N. Moses and Harold F. Williamson, Jr., "Value of Time, Choice
of Mode, and the Subsidy Issue in Urban Transportation," *Journal of Political
Economy* 71 (June 1963), 247–264.

changed. Those whose best alternative to the automobile would have been the El and subway would have had to be paid about $.90 per day on the average to reduce their cost for commuting to equality with that of auto travel. Thus it appears that even a very good urban rapid transit system is a poor alternative to automobile travel for the average commuter.

In another study, Meyer, Kain, and Wohl calculated the over-all cost per passenger, including residential collection and downtown distribution costs, of commuting between home and downtown by auto and by various forms of public transit for a given level of service.[7] They conclude that where hourly one-way traffic volumes along any corridor are 5,000 to 10,000 persons or fewer, as is the case in most U.S. cities, the automobile is as inexpensive as any urban transportation mode. Furthermore, their calculations indicate that for larger volumes of travel bus transit is as cheap as rail rapid transit in high-density residential areas and cheaper in low-density areas. The difference results from greater residential collection cost in low-density areas. Rail rapid transit is apparently justifiable only in the larger and older eastern and midwestern cities, many of which already have such systems.

An excellent illustration of how costly rail rapid transit is is provided by considering the case of BART. According to the latest estimates, the capital costs of the roadbed (including the tube underneath San Francisco Bay), stations, the train control system, and preoperating expenses will total about $1.3 billion.[8] Expenditures on these items will be defrayed through property and sales taxes in the counties in which BART operates and through toll receipts from San Francisco Bay bridges. Fares will be sufficient to defray only the capital cost of the system's rolling stock and its operating expenses. Since a dollar's capital investment earns about 12.5 cents in the private sector of the economy on the average, the opportunity cost of the capital invested in BART is about $160

---

[7] Meyer, Kain, and Wohl, op. cit., especially pp. 299–306, where their conclusions are summarized.
[8] Leonard Merewitz, "Public Transportation: Wish Fulfillment and Reality in the San Francisco Bay Area," *American Economic Review* 62 (May 1972), 78–86.

million per year. It is currently estimated that when the system is in full operation by 1975, it will have about 200,000 fares, or 100,000 riders, per day. Thus, the capital-cost subsidy to each BART commuter is at least $1600 per year, about the average capital cost of an automobile.

In traffic studies it is widely assumed that the average number of passengers per car is 1.6. If each commuter goes to work five days a week for fifty weeks a year, each auto is used for work trips 250 days per year. Thus, $1600 per commuter is somewhat more than $10 per auto per day. Furthermore, if, as has been argued, as many as half the BART riders would have ridden buses instead, the BART subsidy costs more than $20 per day for each auto removed from Bay Area roads. Adam Smith once remarked that by spending enough money very good grapes could be grown in Scotland. He also noted, however, that it was cheaper for the Scots to grow sheep and exchange the mutton and wool for wine. The situation regarding rapid transit appears to be quite similar. Though it will reduce auto travel, rapid transit is a very costly way for the economy to do so. In contrast, the study by Moses and Williamson suggests that auto commuting can be cut in half by imposing rather modest charges on it.

AIR POLLUTION

As was pointed out in the first section of this chapter, the problem of air and water pollution is very much like those of airport and freeway congestion. Once the waste-disposal capacities of air masses and bodies of water have been reached, additional waste disposal by any user imposes added costs on other users of air and water. As with airport and freeway congestion, the appropriate remedy is to limit disposal of wastes into the environment to such a degree that the value of such disposal is equal to the total cost of it to the economy, including the costs borne by individuals and firms other than the polluter. This section first will consider the effects of the failure properly to limit the amount of atmospheric waste disposal on urban land use patterns. Then alternative means of limiting waste disposal will be discussed and evaluated.

Air pollution
and urban structure

Because of both rush-hour congestion and air pollution, urban roads are underpriced and thus overused. As pointed out in the first section of this chapter, the use of congested facilities should be limited to the point where the marginal social cost of their use equals its marginal benefit. The marginal social cost includes not only the costs of vehicle ownership and operation and the traveler's time, which he himself bears, but the costs imposed upon others by his use of the road. In the case of air pollution these costs include additional cleaning expenses borne by everyone in the area because air is dirtier, the additional medical expenses incurred and earnings lost because of additional illness, and the decrease in satisfaction everyone experiences because the environment is less pleasant. These effects of air pollution are all too obvious. The failure properly to limit air pollution, however, has other economic effects that, though less obvious, might well be of even greater quantitative importance.

By failing to impose charges on automobile users equal to the additional costs they impose on others, the marginal private cost of traveling an additional mile to and from work is lower than it otherwise would be. The reader will recall from Chapter 3 that the spatial pattern of urban residential land use is strongly influenced by the costs of commuting an additional mile to and from the CBD. The lower this cost, the smaller the relative rate of decline of housing prices with distance from the CBD. The smaller the relative rate of decline in housing prices, in turn, the smaller is the rate of decline in population densities with distance from the CBD. Population densities tend to be smaller nearer the city center, and the city occupies more land. More land is thus withdrawn from agricultural production and other forms of open space, and more resources, including people's time, are devoted to commuter travel than would otherwise be the case.

The output sacrificed by devoting more resources to transportation and other urban uses is not a pure or complete loss, however. The land withdrawn from farming, for example, produces a return when used to produce housing and other nonagricultural commodities. When land is overused for urban purposes, however, the total return to all land in the vicinity of the city is smaller than it would otherwise be. If the charge for traveling an additional mile were set at the appropriately higher level, less land would be used by the city and more by agriculture. Urban land would be more intensively used and, on the average, yield a higher return per acre. Land that would otherwise have been used for urban purposes would yield an agricultural rental. With appropriate transportation charges, the higher rentals of more densely used urban land plus the agricultural rental of land otherwise used for urban purposes would more than compensate for the urban land rentals lost in reducing the city's land area.

Air pollution control methods resulting from the Clean Air Act of 1970 may well have some impact upon the structure of urban areas. Since three-fourths to four-fifths of air pollution results from automobile emissions, measures for restricting automobile travel are an important part of air quality improvement plans required by the Act. The latter part of this section considers the relative desirability of different methods of pollution control. Regardless of their relative efficiency, though, virtually any auto pollution regulatory scheme would increase the marginal cost of commuter travel in urban areas. If restrictions on automobile travel are instituted, families with a member working in the CBD would find it more desirable to live closer to work and to commute shorter distances than they otherwise would. Housing prices toward the city center would thus rise, whereas they would fall in the outer, suburban parts of the city.

The more rapid rate of decline of housing prices with distance from the CBD would lead, ultimately, to a more compact city. Even in the short run, higher housing prices would lead producers of housing to maintain their properties better or to improve them, perhaps by installing new cooking or sanitary facilities, repairing or redecorating more frequently, and even, perhaps, by adding additional rooms. Higher housing prices would lead any family to occupy smaller, poorer-quality quarters than it otherwise would. Since a greater output of housing would be produced in any given area and any family would tend to consume less of it, population densities would rise. In the long run, when centrally located sites are redeveloped they would be built upon more densely than they otherwise would have. Furthermore, as the city's population and average income levels grow, fewer farms would be replaced by tract houses. Thus, over time the city would come to occupy a smaller land area than it otherwise would have.

In addition to their effects on marginal commuting costs and thus on the intensity of residential land use, air pollution control measures may effect air quality differentially at different locations in the city. If so, the relative desirability of different residential sites and, hence, housing prices in these locations will be affected. Because of the concentration of auto traffic there, pollution from automobiles is especially severe in the vicinity of the CBD. In general, however, the precise spatial pattern of air pollution in any particular city can be a very complicated one. It depends in particular on the kinds and locations of industrial polluters and upon the prevailing wind direction and velocity.

To simplify matters, suppose a rail line runs in an east-west direction and that, for reasons already discussed in Chapter 3, factories are located along it. If the prevailing winds are from the south, the smoke these factories emit will be blown toward the north side of the city. The latter will thus be less desirable for residential purposes than the south side. Consequently, households will offer more for housing on the south side at any given distance from the downtown area. As argued in Chapter 3 in connection with the effects of accessibility to the CBD, land on the south side will be more highly priced and more densely built upon. Those households living on the wrong side of the tracks will be compensated for the additional pollution they experience by the lower prices they pay for housing.

Under the circumstances just described, too many of the economy's resources are all devoted to undoing the effects of smoke emitted from the factories. More nonland capital is used to produce housing on the city's south side than to produce what consumers consider to be equivalent housing on the north side. By shifting some of this capital from the south to the north side the total output of housing can be increased. At the same time, if the air were cleaner on the north side, fewer resources would be used in cleaning by northsiders and fewer in providing them medical care. Additional resources would be used in waste disposal by factories, perhaps by installing filters on their smokestacks. By reducing the amount of smoke belched forth to an appropriate degree, however, the savings in resources used to produce housing, cleaning, and medical care would exceed those used in reducing smoke.

Similarly, the rental offered for residential land on the south side of the city and for factory sites along the railroad would fall as smokestack filters were installed. Residential land rentals on the north side would rise, though, as smoke was reduced. At the appropriate rate of smoke reduction, the reduction of the former kind of land rentals would just be balanced by the increase in the latter, and the total rental value of city land would be maximized. If the reduction in factory smoke were carried too far, however, the additional savings in housing, cleaning, and medical costs of households would be less than the additional resource costs of smoke control. The net increase in residential land values resulting from further smoke reduction would then be less than the reduction of factory land rentals. Appropriate regulation of smoke emissions would result if regulators, as well as private landowners, would seek to maximize the rental value of this land.

The mention of filters for factory smokestacks suggests still another aspect of environmental quality. The discussion of congestion in the first section of the chapter indicated that if charges collected for use of a congested facility exceed the costs of expanding it, the facility should be made larger. Adding runways at airports and more lanes to urban highways are obvious examples of ways of providing for a greater rate of use of congested facilities while maintaining the quality of the service they render. In a similar fashion, smokestack filters and smog control devices for automobiles are ways of allowing more discharges into the atmosphere while maintaining a given concentration of waste matter in the air. Water purification plants are a means of allowing more wastes to be dumped into the water while maintaining its purity. Though greater waste discharges into a lake or stream may mean a larger fraction of its fish die in any period of time, the lake or stream may be stocked with additional fish. Devices such as these are all ways of maintaining environmental quality in the face of increased waste disposal.

Many proposals have been made for government subsidy for industrial pollution control equipment. Among these are tax credits, property-tax reductions, and low-interest loans. Whether such subsidies are desirable depends upon whether economies of scale exist in waste treatment. In the case of water purification and sewage treatment plants, there is strong reason to believe that average costs decline over a wide range of treatment capacity. There is thus a good case to be made for low-interest loans, such as the federal government has made to municipal governments for over a decade, for the construction of such facilities. In the case of smokestack filters, however, it is by no means clear that such economies of scale exist. If not, there are no economic grounds for subsidizing their installation.

Methods
of pollution control

The most common means of dealing with pollution of air and water is the imposition of what are called emission and effluent standards. These are merely limits set upon the amount of wastes any one polluter may dispose into the air or water during any time period. Their aim is to restrict the rate of waste disposal, hopefully to the best rate, which is OJ in Figure 6.2. Requiring all automobiles to install smog control devices or prohibiting the burning of high-sulfur coal would have much the same effect. The imposition and enforcement of such standards is rather like limiting the number of planes that may take off and land at a congested airport. Emission or effluent standards are likely to be inefficient, though with enough knowledge on the part of those developing them, they might work.

To see why this is the case consider Figure 6.7. This shows the marginal or additional costs to polluters of reducing their rate of waste disposal into the environment. Since it becomes progressively more difficult to remove a given small volume of wastes as more is removed, the marginal cost curves shown slope upward to the right. At the same time, the costs incurred by different polluters may differ for the same rate

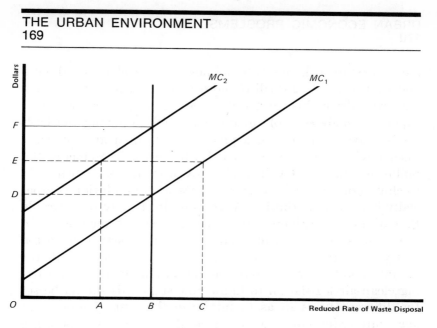

FIGURE 6.7
Best pattern of pollution reduction among different polluters

of waste elimination. If, for example, a smog control device
is designed as an integral part of a new automobile it would
probably be cheaper than if it were added to a five-year-old
car.

In Figure 6.7 the marginal cost for user 1 of meeting the
air quality standard OB is OD. That of the second user is
OF. By tightening the standard on user 1 and relaxing it for
user 2 so as to maintain the same total reduction in the rate
of waste disposal, a cost saving of DF can be achieved. Further tightening up on the first user and relaxing the standards
for the second polluter result in additional cost savings until
the marginal costs of the two polluters are the same. This occurs when the reduction is OC for user 1, OA for user 2, and
their common marginal cost is OE. Once this last situation
is reached, no further cost savings can be achieved so long
as the total reduction in pollution of the two waste disposers
is to be maintained.

An excellent example of the likely inefficiencies of emission
standards is provided by recent federal legislation requiring
a large reduction in atmospheric pollution by automobiles
built in 1976 or later years. It has been estimated that to

meet the standard, new automobiles will cost about $300 more and that gas mileage will be noticeably reduced. For a salesman who drives his car 25,000 miles or even more per year, expensive smog control devices may well be among the least costly ways of achieving a given reduction in air pollution. Such devices may be very costly, however, in reducing the pollution caused by a little old lady who drives her car only to church on Sunday. In certain areas where pollution is especially bad, such as the Los Angeles basin, it may be desirable that almost all drivers have such devices for their cars. In other areas, Montana, for example, such devices may be too costly given the increased air quality they provide for almost all automobiles. Yet it would be quite difficult for those writing clean-air legislation to know how standards should be set for different users so as to minimize the cost of any given aggregate reduction in waste disposal. And it might be quite difficult politically to impose the appropriate limits on different polluters.

For this reason, emission or effluent charges, analogous to higher airport landing fees and rush-hour freeway tolls, would be a more feasible means of minimizing the costs of achieving a given reduction in pollution. Examples of such charges are taxes on leaded gasoline or on high-sulfur coal. In Figure 6.7, for example, if a charge of OE dollars were imposed upon emissions, it would pay user 1 to reduce his rate of waste disposal all the way to OC. For any lower rate of waste disposal reduction the charge paid would exceed the marginal cost of reducing his waste disposal further. User 2, however, would reduce waste disposal only to OA. Any further reduction would be more costly than paying the tax. To return briefly to the automobile example, the salesman might well find it worthwhile to use expensive smog control devices, if by doing so he were able to avoid the tax on leaded gasoline, or to use unleaded gasoline. But the little old lady might well find it cheaper to pay the tax on the gas she buys for her weekly drive to church

Thus, emission or effluent charges would automatically result in each polluter's reducing his rate of environmental waste disposal to the point where the costs of doing so were the same for all other users. By making the charges high enough, any given aggregate reduction in pollution could be achieved. The level of tax on leaded gasoline, for example, could in principle be easily varied as between, say, Los Angeles and Montana. It could also be varied more readily over time in response to changed conditions than detailed air-quality standards. The main difficulty with emission or effluent charges is knowing the appropriate tax to set. The total amount by which waste disposal into the environment should be reduced is probably fairly easy to determine. However, without knowing how responsive polluters are to increased costs of waste disposal, the charge necessary to achieve the desired reduction would be difficult to determine.

A method similar to emission and effluent charges would be for the government to sell licenses to pollute or permits for environmental waste disposal. Though on first thought the sale of licenses to pollute is likely to strike one as unethical or worse, their function would be much the same as the sale of fishing licenses—to prevent overuse of a congested resource. If licenses to pollute were auctioned off to the highest bidder and made transferable, the highest prices would be offered by those for whom alternative methods of waste disposal were most costly. They would thus permit a reduction in pollution at the lowest cost to the economy. Licenses would have the advantage over emission and effluent charges in that in some instances those who desire clean air or water could buy them up and not use them. Because of the free-rider problem to be discussed in Chapter 13, however, in many important instances no one would have the incentive to buy up licenses to provide clean air.

The major advantage of licenses to pollute would be in overcoming uncertainty over the appropriate level of pollution charges. If the appropriate level of environmental waste disposal were known, licenses to dispose of this amount of waste could be sold. The bidding of waste disposers for the volume of licenses issued in any time period would then automatically determine the appropriate pollution charge. The licenses would be transferable, so if a successful bidder were to find other methods of waste disposal cheaper he could sell his licenses and make a lower bid in the next time period. It would not be necessary, therefore, to vary the pollution charge experimentally until the desired reduction in waste disposal was achieved.

SUMMARY

Any facility may be crowded or overused if too low a price is charged for its use. Facilities are congested if an additional user adds to the costs borne by other users or detracts from the benefits they receive. The use of congested facilities such as urban highways and air masses should be restricted to the point where the benefit received by any user is equal to the full additional cost of his using it, including the additional costs imposed upon other users. Perhaps the best way to regulate congested facilities is to impose tolls or charges equal in magnitude to the additional costs imposed upon other users. If the sum of the tolls so imposed exceeds the cost of adding to the facility's capacity, it should be enlarged. If the average cost of a facility declines as its capacity increases, the difference should be made up from funds collected from other sources, The rules just outlined would not necessarily eliminate all freeway congestion or air pollution, but they would promote efficiency in the use of scarce resources.

Urban commuter transportation is a product of land and movable capital, which are mostly applied by public bodies, and of labor, most of which is supplied by the traveler. Since commuters can convert time into money by working longer hours, time spent in commuter travel has an opportunity cost that is related to the commuter's hourly earnings rate. It is useful to think of commuters choosing between private (automobile) and public transit to minimize the costs in both time and money of making a given trip. Time costs of automobile commuting tend to be smaller than those of public transit primarily because of the smaller vehicle used. The latter permits trips to be made whenever it is most convenient for the commuter and reduces the time cost of residential collection and downtown distribution. Evidence suggests that relatively modest additional charges on automobile travel would induce shifts to public transit. Rail transit systems, such as BART, are very costly, and even in relatively densely populated areas they are no cheaper than bus transit when collection and distribution costs are included along with line-haul costs.

Air pollution is much like freeway congestion in that once the waste disposal capacity of an air mass is exceeded, additional atmospheric waste disposal increases the costs other air users bear. Failure to impose charges on auto commuters for their waste disposal reduces their costs of commuting an additional mile, causing the city to be more dispersed than it would be otherwise. Differential degrees of air pollution in different parts of a city affect the relative levels of housing prices throughout the city. On both counts, resources are used less efficiently in producing transport, housing, and other urban commodities than they might be. Air-quality standards, which reduce the amounts of waste anyone may discharge into the air in any time interval, are economically inefficient ways of controlling air pollution if the costs of reducing waste disposal differ among polluters. For this reason, many economists favor emission or effluent charges instead. Their main disadvantage, the difficulty of determining the appropriate level of these charges, can be overcome by selling licenses to pollute.

CHAPTER 7

WAGE RATES

The marginal-productivity theory
of distribution

The Holy Roman Empire is often said to have been inappropriately named, being neither holy, Roman, nor an empire. The term *marginal-productivity theory of distribution* is almost as misleading. To most people, distribution means what economists call the personal distribution of income. This is the amount of total income received by different consumer units—individuals, families, or households. The marginal-productivity theory, though, is a part of a theory of the functional distribution of income. The latter means the determination of wage rates and rental value of physical assets—in general the hire value of productive resources. In addition to the hire values or unit prices received for the resources they sell employers, the incomes of consumer units depend upon the amounts of various resources they own and sell. Indeed, it is almost certainly the case, as will become clearer later, that the annual earnings received by different consumer units each year differ much more because of differences in the quantities of resource services sold to employers than because of differences in prices per unit sold—wage rates or hourly earnings.

The term is also misleading insofar as it is applied to the functional distribution of income. As is the case for the determination of any price, economists find it convenient to analyze wage rates in terms of the demand for and supply of labor. Yet the marginal-productivity theory relates only to the demand. The supply of labor is governed by quite different considerations. Thus the theory might better be called the marginal-productivity theory of the demand for productive factors. The first two sections of this chapter deal mainly with forces affecting the demand for labor. The last is concerned with labor supply.

Many people, even some professional economists, feel there is something inherently cruel, heartless, and even incorrect in analyzing the determination of wage rates in the same manner as other prices. After all, it is so frequently said, human beings aren't machines. But this view is only half correct as far as economic analysis is concerned. Even though employers may be admirable persons, to the extent that they seek—and indeed are forced by competition—to earn as large incomes as they can, the demand for labor is determined in much the same way as that of any other factor of production. To the extent that labor is different from machines, it differs primarily on the supply side of the labor market.

There are two important differences between labor supply and the supply of other productive factors. Both are closely related to the absence of human slavery. First, unlike the owner of, say, a truck, the seller of labor must deliver it himself. The owner of a truck may care little about how a truck is used so long as he is compensated for any excessive wear and tear to which it is subjected. However, the worker himself experiences the conditions of his employment. Consequently, the wage he will accept in a particular kind of employment may be strongly influenced by the conditions of this employment. The other major difference between labor and physical assets is that the latter may be either bought or rented, but labor is only rented. For this reason, the individual worker cannot capitalize on his future earning potential the way the owner of a truck can. More important, purchase prices of trucks automatically take into account certain variations in rental values that don't reflect genuine price differences from a long-term point of view. As discussed toward the end of this section, though, interpretation of differences in hourly wage rates is frequently made difficult by factors that don't imply differences in earnings over a lifetime.

Having been put in proper perspective, the principle of the marginal-productivity theory of factor demand can now be stated. A necessary condition for producing a given rate of output at minimum cost under competition in factor markets is that productive factors be used in such a combination that the additional output per dollar spent is the same for all factors used in positive amounts. Not all producers use, say, whale oil; for those who don't, the additional or marginal product of whale oil per dollar spent on it is less than that for other factors no matter how little whale oil is used. Consequently, the firm reduces its total costs by not using any whale oil.

Similarly, for any other factor, if the additional output per dollar spent is less than for other factors, using less of the particular factor and more of others reduces the cost of production.

The common ratio of additional output per dollar spent for all factors actually used is equal to the inverse of marginal cost. The ratio of marginal product to factor price is additional units of output per additional dollar spent. Conversely, marginal cost is additional dollars spent on inputs per additional unit of output. In general, firms produce output up to the point where the added revenue from an additional unit of output, or marginal revenue, is equal to marginal cost. Thus, letting MP be marginal product, P the factor's price, i a subscript referring to a particular productive factor, MC marginal cost, and MR marginal revenue, $MP_i/P_i = 1/MC = 1/MR$ implies $MR \times MP_i = P_i$. Therefore, the principle of the marginal-productivity theory of factor demand states that where factor markets are competitive, firms hire factors up to the point where the added revenue per additional unit of the factor hired equals the factor's hire value or unit price.

The phrase "where factor markets are competitive"—the situation where producers and sellers of factor services take prices as given to them, unaffected by the amount they buy or sell—is an important qualification. For not only is the statement otherwise incorrect, but much of its significance for society as a whole is dependent upon the existence of competition in hiring. If each producer separately hires productive factors up to the point where the additional output is the same per dollar spent on every factor, no reallocation of inputs among producers can result in a larger output for the economy as a whole. Suppose, however, that in, say, steel production the marginal product per dollar spent on labor is less than that for machinery and that the converse is true in grocery stores. Then, by moving more labor into grocery stores and machinery into steel mills, the output of steel can be increased without reducing the output of grocery stores. For, under the conditions just assumed, it takes less than a dollar's worth of labor to replace a dollar's worth of machinery and keep grocery output constant. Likewise, less than a dollar's worth of machinery is required to replace a dollar's worth of labor and keep steel output the same. Consequently, not all of the dollar's worth of machinery transferred from grocery stores need be used in producing steel to keep output of the two industries constant.

Average wages for the economy as a whole

Forces influencing the additional output per man-hour of labor, that is, its marginal productivity, are many and varied. Some are more or less independent of the quality of human labor itself and depend primarily upon the amounts of other factors combined with human labor in production. The earnings of labor in southern agriculture are below those in agriculture elsewhere in the country and in urban areas for otherwise similar workers. In 1959, for example, nonwhite farm workers in the South with eight years of education who were between 35 and 44 years old earned about $1301 per year, compared with $4015 for similar nonfarm workers in the North and West.[1] Food prices are lower in rural areas, and income received in kind, such as food and lodging supplied, is much more important in the case of farm workers. Taking these differences into account, the real earnings for southern nonwhite farm workers were still no more than half those of nonwhites in nonfarm occupations outside the South. This is the case because farms are small, less machinery is used per man-hour, and, perhaps, farm land is less efficiently used.

Many of the forces affecting marginal productivity are associated with differences in human beings themselves, however. Even in southern agriculture, annual earnings per worker varied greatly with the worker's educational level. White workers 35 to 44 years old with less than an elementary school education earned about $1880 per year in 1959. Those with four or more years of college, though, had average annual earnings of $9890, about five times as much.[2]

Similarly, the demand for labor in the economy as a whole

---

[1] Calculated from data given in U.S. Bureau of the Census, *U.S. Census of Population, 1960: Occupation by Earnings and Education,* Final Report PC(2)-7B (Washington, D.C.: U.S. Government Printing Office, 1963).
[2] Ibid.

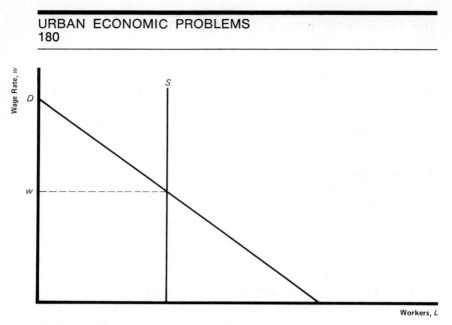

FIGURE 7.1
Demand and supply of labor for the economy as a whole

depends upon the quality of the human agent and upon other considerations. Among the latter are the economy's stock of land and other forms of physical productive agents and technology. Whatever the average quality of the labor force, the greater the number of workers for a given stock of physical capital the less the machinery used per worker in all kinds of production. Hence, the smaller the additional output per additional worker hired, the lower the wage employers will offer. Consequently, the labor demand schedule shown in Figure 7.1 slopes downward to the right. The quantity of labor supplied, however, is probably quite unresponsive to changes in average hourly earnings, as will be explored more fully toward the end of this chapter. The labor supply schedule for the whole economy, then, is essentially vertical. Shifts in the demand schedule, then, largely affect wages per worker but leave the number of workers unchanged.

Over time the supply of labor shifts to the right, from S S' in Figure 7.2, by perhaps 1 percent per year. A part of this shift is the result of population growth. More consumer units of all kinds mean more breadwinners, quite apart from changes in the composition of the population. Compositional changes may be quite important as well. The extent to which

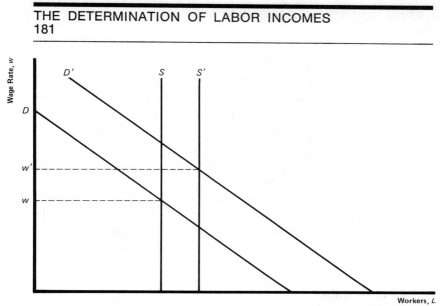

FIGURE 7.2
Changes over time in the economy's labor demand and supply

people seek employment largely depends upon their age. Teen-agers and younger adults seek work less frequently than those in the 25-to-54 age groups; still older workers also are less frequently at work or seeking work. Thus, an aging of the population may either increase or decrease the economy's labor supply, depending upon whether the population is rela-tively young or relatively old. Changes in social attitudes or conditions in the nonmarket sphere may also affect the labor supply. During the post–World War II period, as earlier in this century, there has been a substantial increase in the frac-tion of women employed, which is hard to account for solely on the basis of their higher hourly earnings.

The increase in the economy's labor supply by itself would tend to decrease hourly earnings per worker, yet wages have grown over time at rates of roughly 2.5 percent per year. Thus, the demand curve for labor in Figure 7.2 must have grown by more than enough to offset the increase in labor supply. Part of this increase is due to increases in the stocks of physi-cal capital of all kinds. The latter, in turn, are financed out of the past savings of consumers and of business firms. For some time, however, economists have believed that increases in the number of workers and in physical capital can account for only a relatively small part of the economy's increased output.[3] The remainder is sometimes ascribed to technological change—improvements in the amount of output obtainable from given inputs into production. Economists have come to realize, though, that much of the increased output has resulted from improvements in the human agent. Just as workers who are better educated receive higher wages, so increases in the average amount of education have led to greater marginal productivity, and thus higher wages, per worker. Jorgenson and Griliches have estimated that in the post–World War II period labor input of male workers has increased by about three-quarters of a percentage point per year because of increased education.[4]

Variation in wages among occupations

Differences in wage rates in different occupations may also be analyzed in terms of the demand and supply of labor. As in the case for the economy as a whole, the greater the number of workers in a given occupation, the less capital is used per worker on the average. Thus, the greater the number of workers, the lower the marginal product of workers in physical terms. In addition, however, given the demand for a product, say dental care, the greater the number of dentists and the output of dental care, the lower the price of an extraction. Consequently, the value of the marginal product is lower because of the lower value placed on the occupation's output. For both of these reasons, then, the demand for labor in a particular occupation slopes downward and to the right.

Though conditions of labor supply are important in influencing the course of average wages in the economy as a whole over time, supply conditions are of critical importance in determining wages in any given occupation. From the worker's point of view, the wage rate he receives is only one of the forces affecting the attractiveness of different occupations. In choosing an occupation a worker more or less commits himself

---

[3] See, for example, Moses Abramovitz, "Resources and Output Trends in the United States since 1870," *American Economic Review* 66 (May 1956), 5–23.
[4] D. W. Jorgenson and Z. Griliches, "The Explanation of Productivity Change," *Review of Economic Studies* 34 (July 1967), 249–283.

to a particular kind of employment for a substantial period of time. He is thus concerned not merely with wage rates at the time he makes his choice but with the probable course of wages per hour and the number of hours he is likely to work over many years in the future. In addition, since the worker must deliver his work in person, other conditions or terms of his employment may matter to him.

The annual earnings of workers in different occupations vary for many reasons other than variations in hourly wage rates. Traditionally, carpenters and other construction workers have worked fewer hours per year than manufacturing workers because of the restriction of construction work during cold weather. Consequently, carpenters must be paid higher hourly wages to make carpentry as attractive as employment in manufacturing. The employment of both construction and manufacturing production workers fluctuates to a much greater degree with short-run fluctuations in output for the economy as a whole than does the employment of clerical and sales workers. Though hourly earnings may be lower for the latter at any moment, fewer and shorter periods of unemployment may mean higher average annual earnings over a period of years. Finally, hourly wages and annual earnings may vary at different rates over the life span of any given worker. The starting salaries of engineering graduates are typically higher than for most other holders of bachelor's degrees. The annual salaries of engineers, however, generally increase less rapidly with work experience than those of graduates of business schools. For all of these reasons, then, variations in hourly wage rates may merely offset other forces affecting the income prospects associated with different occupations over a lifetime.

Nonmonetary considerations may also affect the attractiveness of different occupations. College teaching is probably more pleasant for many reasons than jobs that require punching a time clock. Hence, economists, chemists, mathematicians, and others on university faculties probably receive lower salaries on the average than their equally skilled counterparts employed in government or private industry. A pretty secretary, a key to the executive washroom, or in the case of government workers, a carpet on one's office floor are all partial substitutes for higher money earnings. For years, the armed forces have stressed travel and adventure as inducements to recruits. The opportunity to vary one's hours of work offered longshoremen and cab drivers may be a real inducement to some. Certain occupations such as grocery clerk or government worker may offer very much the same earnings to all who enter them. Others, perhaps professional baseball and acting, are like lotteries that offer a few large prizes and many relatively small ones.

All these considerations and many others, especially education (as will be discussed in Chapter 9), affect the level of wages in different occupations. The slope of the labor supply curve to different occupations depends, in addition, upon how different individuals view the various advantages and disadvantages of these occupations. Though some may prefer the freedom to vary one's hours of work that longshoremen and college professors have, and thus enter these occupations at relatively low wages as compared with the relevant alternatives, others may not. If so, to induce a larger number of workers into a given occupation, employers would have to offer higher wages. On balance, though, the supply curves of labor in different occupations are probably highly elastic in the long run, as shown in Figure 7.3. One would so infer on the basis of rather strong evidence that relative occupational wage rates have been very stable over most of this century.[5] If such is the case, then as shown in Figure 7.3, increases in demand as from D to D' will leave wages in the occupation more or less unchanged as compared to others, resulting mainly in greater employment in the occupation in question.

DISCRIMINATION IN EMPLOYMENT

An important source of earnings differences, of particular importance insofar as the poverty problem is concerned, is that associated with race or color. It is well known that the annual earnings of blacks and other nonwhites are typically lower than those of whites. This remains the case even when adjust-

---

[5] Paul Keat, "Long-Run Changes in Occupational Wage Structure, 1900–1956," *Journal of Political Economy* 68 (December 1960), 584–600.

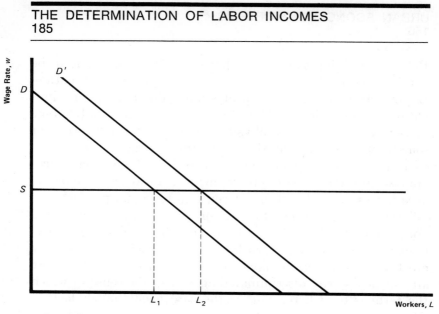

FIGURE 7.3
Demand and supply of labor in a particular occupation

ment is made for differences in age, education, sex, occupation, and other factors with which the annual earnings of either group separately are associated. Table 7.1 presents one illustration of this. At all educational levels, the annual earnings of nonwhites are less than those of whites, and the gap increases with the level of education. Such earnings variations are generally attributed to discrimination in employment.

TABLE 7.1
Annual earnings of experienced nonfarm male workers 35 to 44 years old, 1959, by color for selected levels of education (1959 dollars)[a]

EDUCATION	WHITE	NONWHITE
Elementary, 8 years	$ 5,227	$4,015
High School, 4 years	6,737	4,817
College, 4 years or more	11,162	7,123

[a] Excluding workers who have never had a job.
Source: U.S. Bureau of the Census, *United States Census of Population, 1960; Occupation by Earnings and Education*, Final Report PC(2)-7B (Washington, D.C: U.S. Government Printing Office, 1963).

Before examining the matter, however, it is important to be perfectly clear about what is meant here by discrimination. In popular, and even much professional, discussion, "discrimination" is used more or less synonymously with disadvantage of any kind. Just as a physicist uses the term "work" for something more specific than does the average person, however, discrimination has a narrower, technical meaning in economics. In the context of employment, it means a wage difference not associated with a difference in marginal productivity inherent in the worker himself or with a difference in the nonwage costs of employing him. Thus, if members of a particular class of workers earn lower hourly wages because they are less experienced or have higher job turnover rates, they are not necessarily discriminated against in the sense in which the term is used here. This is the case even though lack of experience or higher turnover rates are associated with general economic and social conditions beyond the employer's control, which impinge unfairly upon the lower wage group.

It is also important to distinguish clearly between discrimination and segregation in employment. The latter means a greater degree of separation of employment of members of two groups, say whites and blacks, than would occur on the basis of a random assignment of workers without regard to race or color. Discrimination and segregation may both be manifestations of prejudice or racism. However, in theory, either may occur without the other, or both may occur together.

Employer discrimination

Most people attribute discrimination in employment principally to employers. So-called fair employment practice legislation seems to be designed primarily to deal with employer discrimination. Yet employer discrimination is only one of several kinds of discrimination, and, indeed, it is probably the least important. Discrimination may result from the actions of employers themselves if they have a unique aversion not shared by the rest of the community to hiring members of a certain group, say blacks, women, or homosexuals. Such an aversion would mean that employers view the hire price of certain workers as higher than it would otherwise be, given the worker's market wage and other costs of employing him. Consequently, the employer would tend to hire fewer members of the group to which he is adverse.

In proceeding with the analysis it is important to distinguish whether members of the group in question and others are perfect substitutes in production. Perfect substitutes are factors whose relative marginal productivity is the same, regardless of the relative numbers employed. The fixed relative marginal productivity ratio, which need not be unity, then effectively governs relative wages in the absence of discrimination, and relative numbers have no influence wages. Examples of workers who are perfect substitutes in production are left- and right-handed chorus girls and blond and brunet baseball pitchers. For imperfect substitutes the relative marginal productivity varies inversely with the relative number employed.

Given an employer aversion to hiring one of two groups that are perfect substitutes in production, segregation in employment will result. Employers who have the least aversion to hiring, say, blacks, will employ only black workers. Those with the greatest aversion to hiring blacks would hire only whites. This follows from the fact that, though all employers view white workers as equally costly to hire, the greater an employer's aversion to hiring blacks, the higher he views the black worker's wage. Consequently, the least discriminating employer has a comparative advantage in hiring only black workers. If blacks and whites are imperfect substitutes, as they might well be because of differences in education and work experience, many employers could hire members of both groups simultaneously. The greater an employer's aversion to black workers, though, the fewer he would hire relative to whites at given wage rates. In either case, employer discrimination reduces the demand for black labor. Given the numbers of black and white workers, the wages of blacks would thus be lower and those of whites higher. The larger the number of black workers relative to whites, the lower the wages of black workers would be. In the case of perfect substitutes, for example, with an increase in the number of black workers, employers with greater aversions to hiring blacks would have to be induced by lower black wages to do so.

It is important to carry the analysis still further. For, regardless of whether blacks and whites are perfect substitutes or not, the costs of production are lower for employers who have less aversion to hiring blacks. If blacks and whites are perfect substitutes, for example, employers who hire only blacks would have lower wage costs than those hiring only whites. The earnings of firms employing black workers would thus be higher. Consequently, such firms have an incentive to expand output. Unless internal diseconomies of scale set in as output grows, the least discriminating employers producing any given product will tend to dominate the industry.

Even if existing firms cannot expand output indefinitely, other firms with less aversion to hiring blacks have a financial incentive to enter the labor market in question. This they may do by setting up new production facilities and hiring black workers away from other employers. Or, they may merely buy out employers with a greater aversion to dealing with black employees, for, employers with less aversion to dealing with blacks would have lower production costs and thus could offer more for firms than they are worth to the current owner. Given the willingness of employers as a group to search out opportunities for monetary gain claimed by the folklore of American capitalism, it can be expected that potential employers would always be available to eliminate most wage differentials resulting from employer discrimination. Therefore employer discrimination probably is not very important in the U.S. economy.

Employee discrimination

If discrimination in the narrower, technical meaning exists at all, a more likely source is suppliers of other productive factors or buyers of the final product. One form is employee discrimination. Employee discrimination may result if, say, whites will work with blacks only if they receive a higher wage than if they are employed by firms hiring only white workers. Under these conditions, the additional costs to employers of hiring black workers are not only the wages paid them directly but also the increased wages that must be paid white workers if the employer is to retain them. Consequently, employers, in adjusting to the additional costs per worker, would tend to hire fewer black workers.

Whether white employee prejudice is effective in reducing the wages of blacks depends upon the substitutability of black and white workers in production. If black and white workers are perfect substitutes, complete segregation in employment results. To see this, first note that an employer hiring only blacks is forced by competition to pay them their marginal product. A firm employing an integrated work force must thus pay black workers their marginal product. Otherwise blacks would seek employment in segregated black firms instead. The integrated employer, though, must pay white workers a higher wage than an employer who hires white workers only. Competition among employers with segregated white work crews forces them to pay white workers in such firms an amount equal to their marginal product. Integrated employers, then, must pay white workers more than their marginal product. Production costs thus are higher for integrated firms than for segregated firms, which hire only black or only white workers.

If blacks and whites are perfect substitutes in production, therefore, only segregated employment will be economically viable. Furthermore, competition among employers for labor will result in paying wages equal to marginal product in both black- and white-employing firms. Though segregation in employment would result, effective discrimination in the technical sense would not exist at all. An increase in the relative numbers of black workers would not affect the relative wages of blacks. If black and white workers were not perfect substitutes in production, however, integrated employment could result. The aversion of white workers to working with blacks would then result in lower wages of black workers, and an increase in the relative number of black workers would reduce their relative hourly earnings. It should be noted, finally, that if black and white workers are not perfect substitutes in production, the relative wages of blacks would vary inversely with those of whites even in the absence of prejudice on the part of white workers.

Before considering other forms of discrimination, the effects of so-called fair employment-practice laws when white employee prejudice exists ought to be noted. Such laws typically seek to prohibit employers from refusing to hire blacks or women or from paying differential wage rates to workers who are otherwise similar. When these laws exist, the cost to employers of hiring segregated white work forces is increased by an amount that varies directly both with the probability of enforcement action being taken against them and with the severity of the penalty imposed. These increased costs, in turn, will reduce the wage rates offered white workers in segregated white firms. Indeed, the cost of hiring a segregated white work force could be increased so much that hiring an integrated work force could become profitable to employers.

If this last is not the case, however, and enforcement action is not taken against all employers who hire segregated white work forces, fair employment-practice laws will be self-defeating because enforcement would increase the costs of employers against whom action is taken relative to those of other employers. Output and employment in firms against whom action is taken will then tend to decline. Indeed, in the long run such firms will tend to go out of business. Some, of course, may survive if they earned greater than normal returns prior to the enforcement action. Continued action against an ever-changing collection of firms would be required in any case. It is thus by no means evident that fair employment-practice laws would achieve integrated employment if not enforced sufficiently strongly. Furthermore, enforcement of such laws would merely lower the earnings of whites, not raise those of blacks.

Other types of discrimination

Discrimination against blacks or women may also result from the actions of suppliers of productive factors other than labor or from buyers of the final product. Among the former types is capital-market discrimination. Discrimination by white owners or suppliers of capital funds to business firms would result from their charging higher interest rates on loans to integrated or segregated black employment firms than to firms employing only white workers. Discrimination by consumers would result if they bought from firms hiring blacks or women only at lower prices than they would pay for products produced in firms employing only whites or men. The results of capital-market and consumer discrimination are similar. Since the former has certain more interesting aspects the discussion here will focus on it.

Probably because blacks historically have had lower incomes than whites, blacks own less capital in relation to their numbers than whites. In a totally segregated society, black workers would thus typically work with less capital than whites, so that their marginal product and wages received would be lower. At the same time, the returns to black-owned capital would be higher than the returns to white-owned capital because each black-owned machine would be working with more labor. Now, suppose that some white owners of capital supply funds to enterprises employing blacks. The latter will then use more machinery per worker, black wages will rise, and white wages will fall. If white capital owners continue to switch investments from white to black firms so long as capital earnings in black firms are higher, the wage differential between black and white workers will tend to be eliminated. However, should owners of white capital insist upon higher returns to lend to black firms, black wages will be lower than white wages. The differential, though, will be smaller than in a totally segregated society.

Given an aversion on the part of white owners of capital to lend to black firms, segregation in employment will result if blacks and whites are perfect substitutes. Those white owners of capital who have less aversion will lend to firms employing blacks. Those with a greater aversion will lend to firms employing segregated white work crews. The greater the relative number of black workers in a labor market, the more adverse the marginal white capital owner who lends to black employing firms must be. Returns to capital will then be higher in black firms. Less capital will be used relative to black labor, and the lower black wages will be relative to those received by white workers.

There are two interesting and much misunderstood points relating to capital market discrimination. The first relates to the effects of total segregation on the wages of black workers. Total segregation, or blacks employed only with black-owned capital, is frequently advocated by black and other groups. Yet if blacks own less capital per worker, as they surely do, then total segregation would only reduce the wages of black workers. Conversely, if black capitalism means anything at all it would presumably increase the hourly earnings of blacks by increasing the supply of capital of firms employing black workers. The other point to note is that capital-market discrimination reduces the earnings of white-owned capital. Thus, though white workers benefit from capital market discrimination, white capital owners, who presumably make up the Establishment, lose by it. The belief that the Establishment benefits financially from discrimination is largely without foundation.

Evidence regarding discrimination

There can be little doubt that blacks and women are disadvantaged in that their earnings are lower than those of whites or men. It is also equally clear that blacks and women tend disproportionately to be represented in the less-skilled and the lower-paying occupations. Many studies have analyzed the factors associated with such income differences. (These are summarized most clearly and succinctly in a book by Dale Hiestand.[6]) The typical study might find relative annual earnings of blacks that are 50 to 60 percent of those of whites. After adjustment for factors such as years of schooling, work experience as reflected in age, location, and occupation, the relative earnings of blacks are perhaps 70 to 80 percent those of whites. The remainder is typically attributed to discrimination.

Yet it is by no means obvious that differences that are unaccounted for are the result of discrimination in the narrower, economic sense. Whenever an unexplained residual is found, there is always the possibility that something else has been overlooked. More important, though, is the argument made by black and women's groups and their supporters that members of the disadvantaged group are essentially the same inso-

---

[6] *Discrimination in Employment: An Appraisal of the Research* (Ann Arbor, Mich.: Wayne State University, 1970), especially chap. 4.

far as factors pertinent to most kinds of employment are concerned. If so, blacks and whites and men and women would be perfect substitutes in production. This analysis implies, however, that prejudice would result in segregated employment under these conditions. Though some segregation in employment indeed occurs, by no means is it the rule.

Another study that has attempted to determine whether discrimination in employment in the narrower sense occurs is by Robert Weintraub.[7] Weintraub studied the earnings of men employed as production and maintenance workers in an International Harvester plant in Memphis, Tennessee, around 1950. This particular company even then had an announced policy of nondiscrimination in employment. Blacks in the plant earned about 9 percent less than whites—only 3 percent less if marginal positions were excluded and account taken of differences in education and other previous experience. Median incomes of blacks in Memphis in 1949, though, were only half those of whites. Though these findings are consistent with discrimination in employment, the plant through its employment policy may have been able to hire better black workers than average for the Memphis labor force.

Another, more recent study compared the relative earnings of nonwhite and white men and, separately, of women and men by occupation in various cities.[8] In neither comparison did the relative earnings in a particular occupation vary with the relative number of workers employed in that occupation. This result by itself is consistent with prejudice on the part of white or male workers for the case of perfect substitutes in production, though the general absence of segregation in employment is not. In the case of other forms of discrimination discussed previously, though, the relative earnings of two groups would vary inversely with their relative numbers. It is thus by no means clear that discrimination in the narrower sense exists to an important degree.

The study last cited did find, though, that the relative annual earnings of nonwhites and whites did vary appreciably with

---

[7] "Negro-White Earnings in a Southern Industrial Plant" (abstract), *Econometrica* 25 (April 1957), 368–369.
[8] Kenneth E. Galchus, "The Elasticity of Substitution of White for Nonwhite Labor," unpublished Ph.D. dissertation, Department of Economics, Washington University, 1970.

the relative number of nonwhites in a city's population, hence with its total labor force. This suggests that the unexplained income residual may be the result of social conditions generally, rather than discrimination in employment narrowly defined. One form such conditions might take is lower-quality education for blacks. Indeed, if an additional year's schooling resulted in less of an increment to earnings for blacks, the gap in earnings would tend to widen with years of schooling, as it appears to do in Table 7.1. It is not merely errant pedantry that leads to the conclusion that we need a better understanding of the reasons for the gap in black and white incomes. For if the fault does not lie in discrimination in employment, attacking the latter may do no good, as the discussion before of fair employment practice laws suggests.

ANNUAL HOURS WORKED

As was stressed at the opening of this chapter, annual earnings depend not only upon the hourly wage rate but also upon the number of hours worked per year. Yet all too often this fact is neglected and differences in annual earnings assumed to result solely from differences in hourly earnings. A study of the determinants of hours worked annually is important also for understanding the shape of the supply curve of labor from a population of given size. This section, then, concentrates on the nature of the supply of labor and its responsiveness to changes in wage rates and other conditions.

The supply of work and the demand for leisure

Human beings may use the time allotted to them in a variety of ways. Though what we call work certainly provides its own reward, at the margin between additional work and other uses of time the additional income earned from additional work is of critical importance. Most college professors, if freed from the necessity of earning a living, probably would like to do much the same research and teaching they now do. Chances are, though, that they would skip the paper grading and committee meetings, and they probably would be less inclined to undertake a particular piece of research merely because outside financial support is available for it. The additional income earned at the margin is used to purchase goods and services in the market to satisfy a wide variety of wants.

Time not spent at work may be used for the satisfaction of a variety of different purposes. To a great extent sleeping and eating maintain the human being as a producer and a consumer. A gourmet meal with a bottle of fine wine, though, is in a real sense a substitute for other forms of entertainment and relaxation. Washing the dishes or cutting the grass is, indeed, household or nonmarket production. Alternatively, family members could work longer hours and hire someone else to do the chores. To some extent, then, market and nonmarket uses of time are alternative means of satisfying the same ultimate end. Certain uses of nonmarket time—though surprisingly few—are leisure in the strict sense. Some forms of leisure, however, are more time consuming than others. Seeing a movie or an opera is a very close substitute for reading a book; the latter generally requires more time and less money. Though many uses of time spent not working are not leisure in the strict sense, economists generally find it convenient to speak of it that way.

Work and leisure in the broad sense can thus be considered as alternative means of satisfying human wants. Individuals or family members may be viewed as allocating their time between work and leisure to obtain as great an amount of satisfaction as possible. Each person is limited to a fixed total amount of time, say twenty-four hours a day. Thus, choosing to spend an additional half-hour per day at leisure is equivalent to choosing half an hour less at work. Consequently, the supply of work and the demand for leisure, or time not working, are but different sides of the same coin.

In addition to their preferences, the choice between work and leisure is influenced by the opportunities open to individuals. In discussions of the choice between the purchase of different commodities on the market, it is customary to think of a certain money income as being given to the consumer. When considering the choice between work and leisure, though, money income is an outcome of the choice. It is rather the chooser's nonwage income, the income he receives even though he does no work but spends twenty-four hours per day in leisure, that is the analog of income in the usual consumer choice problem. Such nonlabor income may be income from the ownership of property or from governmental transfer payments such as welfare payments. The rate at which leisure can be transformed into money income is given by the wage rate an individual can earn. In a very real sense, the price of leisure is the wage rate. Thus, the supply of work or labor and the demand for leisure depend upon the wage rate and upon nonlabor income in essentially the same way that the demand for a commodity purchased in the market depends upon its price and income.

A frequently heard objection to the foregoing formulation of the matter of labor supply is that hours of work are fixed by employers and not subject to the worker's choice. A little consideration, though, suggests that there is much more freedom in choosing hours of work than is immediately realized. Members of certain occupations, such as stevedores and insurance salesmen, determine their hours of work directly. If unable to work as many hours as they want in their regular occupation, some workers "moonlight," or take a second job. If one wants to work twenty hours a week on the average, one can do so by working forty hours per week half the weeks of the year, perhaps by changing jobs frequently and collecting unemployment compensation in the intervals between jobs.

Most important of all, however, is that employers have an incentive to set those hours of work preferred by their workers. In some instances, as in steel mills, it is feasible to have three eight-hour shifts or four six-hour shifts per day, though seven hours per day may be hard to arrange. But if airline pilots prefer to make fewer than two round trips per week from the West Coast to Hawaii, airlines can reduce their labor costs by hiring more pilots, each of whom is required to make three trips every two weeks. Hours of work are thus on very much the same footing as the kinds of automobiles sold: Though any one consumer chooses among a given array of autos built, the kinds of autos built depend upon the desires of all consumers in the aggregate.

An individual may be thought of as making two related choices regarding his hours of work. The first is whether to do any work at all. If at twenty-four hours per day of leisure the additional satisfaction achieved by spending an hour's pay exceeds the satisfaction from an additional hour of leisure, the individual will enter the labor force. The fraction of individuals from any group in the population so choosing is called the labor-force participation rate of the group. For some groups, "prime males," or men 25 to 54 years old, the labor-force participation is about 0.9 or more. (The term *prime male* is probably a holdover from the period of human slavery.) For others, such as married women and teenagers, rates are much lower, perhaps one-third.

Given that an individual chooses to enter the labor force, insofar as is possible he would seek to work that number of hours such that the additional satisfaction acquired by an hour's pay is equal to the additional satisfaction provided by an additional hour of leisure. For if he is not in such a situation, by working either more or less he can increase his total satisfaction. Alternatively stated, the hours of work of labor-force participants are so selected that the ratio of additional satisfaction from an hour's leisure relative to that of an hour's work is equal to the wage rate earned.

Income and substitution effects
of wage rate changes

Some readers are probably familiar with the income and substitution effects of a change in the money price of a commodity when the money income of a consumer is given. First, the fall in price makes the commodity in question cheaper relative to others. Consequently, the consumer tends to buy more of the commodity whose price has fallen and less of other commodities generally. Since the consumer substitutes the now cheaper commodity for others, this effect of a price change is called the substitution effect. However, when the money price of a commodity falls, the consumer could continue to buy the same amounts of all commodities as before and have additional money income to spend. He will thus tend to buy more not only of the commodity whose price has fallen but all others as well. This second effect upon his consumption is precisely the same as would result from supplying him with an appropriate amount of additional money income. Hence, it is termed an income effect.

Regarding the demand for leisure or the supply of work, a change in the money wage rate has the same two effects. A rise in the money wage rate makes leisure more expensive in relation to goods and services purchased in the market. The substitution effect of a change in money wages thus leads the individual to work longer hours, to consume less leisure, and to buy more commodities in the market. However, the rise in money wages means that if the worker continues to work the same number of hours as before he will have a larger money income but the same amount of leisure. The same effect could be produced by holding his wage rate constant but giving him additional nonlabor income. A rise in the money wage rate thus has an income effect, too. Since nonwork time encompasses a wide variety of activities, one would expect, in general, that the income effect of a money wage change would be to increase the amount of leisure chosen, thus to reduce the number of hours worked.

In the case of commodities, the income and substitution effects of price changes usually act in the same direction, each causing the consumer to buy more of the commodity whose price has fallen. It is thus almost impossible to think of instances in which the two effects operate in opposite directions, so perverse commodities are generally called Giffen goods, after one of the first to notice the phenomenon. In the case of hours of work, however, the two effects do act in opposite directions. The substitution effect alone causes longer hours to be worked, but the income effect leads to fewer hours of work. The net effect, then, is indeterminate on theoretical grounds and depends on whether the substitution effect or the income effect is stronger. This fact has caused considerable confusion in discussions of labor supply. Later on the responsiveness of hours of work to wage-rate changes will be discussed.

Labor-force participation rates may also change as a result of changes in the wage rate. However, the relevant income effect for the decision of whether or not to work at all is that evaluated at zero hours of work or twenty-four hours a day of leisure. Since the income earned by not working is zero regardless of the wage rate, the income effect is zero. Thus only the substitution effect operates, and a rise in the wage rate can only induce those who might otherwise have done no work to do some. That some studies have found small negative effects on labor-force participation of wage changes is probably due to the way labor-force participation is usually measured. A person is often counted as a labor-force participant if he works or is looking for work during a given calendar week, but a longer period, say a year, would be much more relevant. If some people reduce their annual hours worked by not working at all during some weeks of the year, labor-force participation as usually measured could appear to be inversely related to the wage rate.

Hours of work also depend upon the amount of nonlabor income an individual or a family receives. An increase in income from other sources increases the amount of money income a worker has if he works any given number of hours. It does nothing, however, to the rate at which an individual can exchange leisure for money income by working an additional amount of time. A change in other income, then, has an income effect but no substitution effect upon the number of hours worked. Since one would expect the income effect on the demand for leisure to be positive, an increase in income from other than earnings tends to reduce the number of hours worked per year.

Evidence
on labor supply

Many studies have been made of labor supply, especially of labor-force participation rates for which data are fairly easily obtainable. Not surprisingly, the results obtained differ from study to study, depending upon the data used and the kinds of comparisons made. Generally it appears that labor-force participation rates tend to increase with wages and to decline with income from sources other than earnings. For prime males, though, most of whom are heads of families and in the labor force, the variation is slight. Hours of work are usually found to show a very modest tendency to decline as wage rates rise. The overwhelming conclusion to be drawn from these studies is that annual hours of work are highly unresponsive to economic factors for the majority of workers and depend largely upon the age, sex, and family status of the worker.

One of the most careful and detailed studies of labor supply is a recent one by Michael J. Boskin.[9] Using a wealth of data provided by the Survey of Economic Opportunity of 1967, Boskin was able to make separate comparisons for persons defined by age, sex, race, and family status and for both labor-force participation and annual hours worked for participants. The data available permitted much better measures of the variables than is usually the case. To take an important example, it was possible to adjust wage rates and other income for taxes paid. Boskin found labor-supply curves that were essentially vertical for all males and for female heads of families. The latter, if in the labor force for six months or more, tended to work roughly 1500 hours per year as compared with 2000 or more for prime-age and elderly males. The only demographic groups showing labor supply elasticities of about 0.5 or more were white elderly and black wives and female teenagers. Nonearnings income generally was inversely associated with annual hours worked, though its elasticity was as large as 0.1 numerically only for white, prime-age husbands.

One of the few studies to reach substantially different conclusions is one by Kalacheck and Raines.[10] They limited their comparisons to relatively low-income persons ($8200 or less for a family of four). Their estimates of labor-supply elasticities were substantial, 0.5 or more for all groups. The difference may result from the fact that lower-income families are more responsive to wages and nonwage income than the population as a whole. Indeed, their study provides some evidence that labor-supply responses decline at higher income levels. However, by limiting their comparisons to individuals in consumer units of no more than modest income levels, some low-wage workers who work long hours are ignored. The relatively large

[9] Michael J. Boskin, "Economics of the Labor Supply," in G. G. Cain and H. W. Watts, eds., *Income Maintenance and Labor Supply* (Chicago: Rand McNally, 1973), pp. 163–181.
[10] E. Kalacheck and F. Raines, "Labor Supply of Lower Income Workers and the Negative Income Tax," in *Technical Reports of the President's Commission on Income Maintenance Programs* (Washington, D.C.: U.S. Government Printing Office, 1970).

labor supply responses Kalachek and Raines found may thus be overestimates of the true responses.

An important aspect of labor supply for the poverty problem is that lower-income family heads work much shorter hours than those of higher-income families. This is shown by the census data on labor-force participation and hours worked in Table 7.2. The table indicates that in families with incomes of $4000 or less, roughly only two-thirds as many family heads were in the labor force in the 1960 census week. Likewise, of those who are in the labor force, many fewer worked a full week or a full year. The differences between the lowest- and two higher-income classes are quite large relative to those between the two higher-income classes.

Part of the reason, probably, is that female heads, who typically work fewer hours annually than male heads, are a larger proportion of lower-income family heads. The aged and disabled are also disproportionately represented in the poverty population. Both liberals and conservatives have argued that the smaller quantity of labor supplied by the lower-income population results from low wage rates or the availability of income from other sources such as welfare payments. The preponderance of the evidence on labor-supply responses just

TABLE 7.2
Time worked by nonfarm family heads, United States, 1960, by income class[a]

1959 INCOME CLASS (THOUSANDS OF DOLLARS)	PERCENT OF HEADS IN LABOR FORCE, CENSUS WEEK, 1960	PERCENT OF HEADS IN LABOR FORCE WHO WORKED	
		35 hours or more in census week, 1960	50 weeks or more in 1959
4 or less	59.2%	76.7%	56.8%
4 to 8	91.6	91.5	79.6
8 or more	94.4	94.3	87.3
Total	85.2	90.1	78.8

[a] Strictly primary civilian families.
Source: U.S. Bureau of the Census, *U.S. Census of Population, 1960: Families*, Final Report PC(2)-4A (Washington, D.C.: U.S. Government Printing Office, 1963).

discussed indicates that this is not the case. The elasticity of labor-force participation rates with respect to wages for family heads is probably no greater than 0.1. Hence, a doubling of the wage rate lower-income family heads could earn would result in no more than about two-thirds of the family heads in the under-$4000 income class being in the labor force. If anything, the elasticity of hours worked with respect to wages is probably negative. Unless the finding of the Kalachek-Raines study that the lower-income labor-supply response is considerably greater than for the population as a whole is correct, one cannot attribute the relatively small quantity of labor supplied by the lower-income population to a lack of earnings opportunities.

SUMMARY

Employers hire the services of labor and other productive factors in such combinations that marginal product per additional dollar spent is the same for all productive factors used in positive amounts. For this reason marginal revenue times marginal product is equal to each factor's price when competition in factor markets prevails. The marginal product of a worker depends both upon the amounts of other productive factors combined with human labor in production and upon the quality of human labor itself. Over time, the accumulation of capital, or machines, and technological improvements have led to increases in average wage rates. Increases in the average amount of education per worker have also tended to increase marginal productivity and wages. Wage rates may vary among occupations both to compensate for lifetime earnings differences associated with given hourly earnings and for the nonmonetary attractiveness of different occupations. In the long run, however, occupational wage differences have been remarkably stable in the United States during this century.

Labor market discrimination means wage differences not associated with differences in marginal productivity or costs of employing different classes of workers. It should be carefully distinguished from segregation in employment—a greater degree of separation in employment than would occur on the basis of a random assignment of workers to firms—and from any sort of disadvantage that may result in income differences. Labor market discrimination is frequently attributed to an above-average prejudice on the part of employers but it is unlikely to result from this source. Discrimination by employees, customers of the firm, or suppliers of capital is much more likely. If white and black workers are perfect substitutes in production, however, and white workers will accept employment in firms employing blacks only at a higher wage than in firms employing only whites, segregated employment but not labor market discrimination would result. It is clear that the annual earnings of blacks and women are lower than those of white men even when account is taken of (some) factors producing differences in productivity. It is by no means evident, though, that the unexplained residual results from labor market discrimination narrowly defined.

Time spent in the market earning income and time spent in other ways are alternative means of providing for the satisfaction of human wants. The supply of labor is, for this reason, the mirror image of the demand for leisure. An increase in the hourly wage makes leisure more expensive relative to commodities purchased with money earned from the sale of labor. This effect of a wage change, known as the substitution effect, leads people to work more hours per year. By working the same number of hours as previously, however, a worker is enabled both to buy more market goods and to devote more time to leisure. This second effect of a wage increase is called the income effect and runs counter to the substitution effect. Most studies suggest that the labor supply schedules of prime males and other breadwinners are quite inelastic. If true, the fact that the heads of lower-income families work fewer hours annually than others cannot be accounted for by the lower wages they earn.

CHAPTER 8

Unemployment

MEANING AND TYPES
OF UNEMPLOYMENT

Subtle changes in wording can convey vast differences in meaning. One of the most famous of these was the muffled order of Chickamauga during the U.S. Civil War. The commanding general of the Union Army intended to direct a division in the center of his line to close up on the division on its left. His order, though, was interpreted as requiring a movement toward the left flank of the Union line. The division pulled out, leaving a gaping hole through which the Confederates poured, almost routing the Yankees. Almost equally drastic consequences follow from the widespread and equally mistaken translation of the word "unemployment" to the phrase "can't find a job."

Unemployment, rather than being like an industrial reserve army in the Marxian sense or a pool of chronically out-of-work persons, is more like water going over a dam. Though a certain volume of water is always falling, it is made up of a continually changing collection of water molecules. The rate of fall over the dam varies from time to time with the height of water in the reservoir behind it. The true nature of unemployment begins to emerge when one inquires into how data are obtained and when subsidiary data in addition to the overall total are examined. Such materials are considered in this section. In the following sections of this chapter, explanations for unemployment and the impact of declining labor demand will be offered.

How unemployment
is measured

The Bureau of the Census gathers data on the employment status of the population during the calendar week containing the nineteenth day of the month. These data are analyzed and published by the Bureau of Labor Statistics (BLS). The survey gathers information on individuals 16 years old or over in over 50,000 households. Though the sample comprises less than one household in a thousand, for most purposes it is quite large and provides very reliable estimates in the sense of being free from sampling error. For fine breakdowns of the population, say, black male teenagers, though, the sample is small. The resulting estimates of unemployment rates for such a group may fluctuate considerably from month to month.

In the survey, a moderately long series of questions is asked. The questions themselves relate to objective characteristics of the respondents—"were you registered for work with an employment service?" rather than "would you like to have a job?" Essentially, however, these questions may be reduced to two. First, "were you at work at any time during the preceding week or temporarily absent because of illness or vacation?" If the answer is yes, an individual is counted as employed. If the answer is no, a second question is asked—"were you actively seeking work at any time during the past four weeks?" (Note the question is not "could you find a job?") If the second question is answered yes, the individual is counted as unemployed. The employed plus the unemployed make up the measured labor force. Those answering no to the second question are counted as not in the labor force. Thus, to be counted as unemployed is not the same as to be not employed. All answering no to the first question are not employed, but only those answering yes to the second question are termed unemployed.

During 1970 the civilian labor force averaged about 82.7 million workers, or about 59 percent, of the noninstitutional population 16 years old or over.[1] In the same year, the unemployed averaged about 4.1 million persons, or 4.9 percent, of the civilian labor force. The last figure is roughly the average unemployment rate for the post–World War II period as a whole. Of these 4.1 million unemployed persons, 27.0 percent were 16 to 19 years of age and 21.1 percent 20 to 24. Thus, about half the total unemployed were younger workers. However, the unemployment rate for married men living with their wives, a good indicator of unemployment among breadwinners, was 2.6 percent, only about half that for the whole civilian labor force.

---

[1] Except if noted otherwise, all data on unemployment cited in this chapter may be obtained from *Statistical Abstract of the U.S., 1971* (Washington, D.C.: U.S. Government Printing Office, 1971), pp. 210 and 214.

Data on the duration of unemployment are also revealing. Of those unemployed during 1970, 52.3 percent, or more than half, were unemployed 4 weeks or less. Slightly more than three-fourths were unemployed for 10 weeks or less. Those unemployed for more than 26 weeks—the maximum duration of unemployment compensation—amounted to only 5.8 percent of the unemployed. The data on duration agree fairly closely with a constant probability of becoming employed if unemployed. Since the average duration of unemployment was about 8.8 weeks, the probability of becoming employed was about one-ninth per week.

These data on the duration of unemployment strongly suggest that unemployment is largely a temporary state. There appears to be little of what is commonly called "hard-core" unemployment. It would be consistent with these data, though, if large numbers of workers who were unable to find jobs had simply stopped looking for work or dropped out of the labor force. This number appears to be quite small, however. The Census Bureau made a special survey in 1967 of men 20 to 64 years old who had been reported as not in the labor force the preceding week.[2] Of these about three-fifths were sick or disabled and another 11 percent were retired. Of the remainder, half were again in the labor force. Only a small number, about 6 percent of the total surveyed, indicated they wanted a job but were not seeking one. These findings plus quarterly surveys made by the Census Bureau suggest that the number of "discouraged workers" or "hidden unemployed" is small. Among men their number is perhaps 10 percent of the total reported as unemployed.

Robert Hall has argued correctly that the problem lies rather among workers who are frequently unemployed.[3] In 1968, when the overall unemployment rate was 3.6 percent, about the average for post–World War II boom or cyclical peak years, about one-sixth of those unemployed at some time during the year were unemployed twice and another one-sixth

[2] Vera C. Penella and Edward J. O'Boyle, "Work Plans of Men Not in the Labor Force," *Monthly Labor Review* 91 (August 1968), 8–14.
[3] Robert E. Hall, "Why Is the Unemployment Rate so High at Full-Employment?" *Brookings Papers on Economic Activity,* 1970 (No. 3), 369–402.

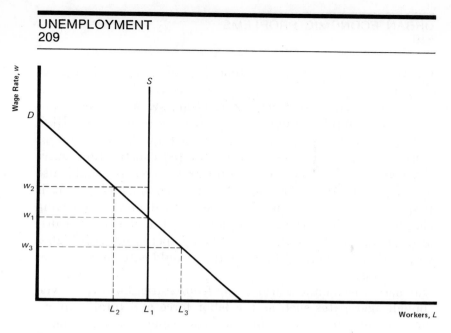

FIGURE 8.1
Labor market equilibrium and disequilibrium

three or more times. In total, those with two or more spells amounted to about 3 million workers. It may well be that, when employed, many of these workers hold jobs that are low-paying and offer poor prospects for advancement. The fact that they were employed part of the year strongly suggests that the problem is not an inability to find jobs, but low earnings opportunities, a very different matter.

Unemployment and labor-market equilibrium

The notion of "can't find a job" is most naturally associated with an imbalance in the labor market. Yet much of what is recorded as unemployment by the BLS is consistent with labor market equilibrium or balance. In Figure 8.1 the labor market is said to be in equilibrium when the quantity of labor demanded is equal to the quantity of labor supplied at the wage rate w_1. Imbalance or disequilibrium exists when quantity demanded is not equal to quantity supplied. Thus, at the wage rate w_2, quantity supplied, L_1, exceeds quantity demanded, L_2, or there is said to be an excess supply of labor.

Conversely, at a wage w_3 there is an excess demand of $L_3 - L_1$.

In a purely static or unchanging economic world there undoubtedly would be some unemployment recorded by BLS. Construction workers would spend part of the year out of work when severe winter weather limited construction activity. Cannery workers and migrant farm workers would also spend part of the year unemployed. Such unemployment is frequently termed seasonal. As was argued in the preceding chapter, though, workers unemployed part of the year because of seasonal factors would have to be compensated with higher wages when working. Otherwise, they would enter nonseasonal occupations.

Our actual economic world is far from static, however. Even though aggregates such as the labor force and total employment might remain constant, their components, like gas molecules, might be continually in motion. Much of this change would result from the nature of human life itself. Children grow into teenagers, who eventually become prime-age adults, who become older workers and retire. Female workers bear and nurture children. All of these events may be associated with entry into and exit from the labor force. Entry is usually associated with a period of looking for work. Superimposed on these changes are decreases in the demand for certain kinds of products and increases in the demand for others. Associated with such shifts in demand are layoffs of workers in some jobs and vacancies in others. Holt and David point out that the rate of separations (layoffs plus voluntary quits) is about 2 to 3 percent per month, so that in order to maintain a constant work force employers on the average must replace between 24 and 36 percent of their workers each year.[4] As workers move from one job to another, an interval is usually spent unemployed. For such reasons, some workers would be temporarily unemployed in a condition of labor market balance. Unemployment that is not seasonal is frequently called frictional.

---

[4] Charles C. Holt and Martin H. David, "The Concept of Job Vacancies in a Dynamic Theory of the Labor Market," *The Measurement and Interpretation of Job Vacancies* (New York: National Bureau of Economic Research, 1966), p. 80.

Seasonal and frictional unemployment are sometimes called voluntary unemployment. The term is quite misleading, however, to the extent that it arises from layoffs as opposed to voluntary quits and entries into the labor force. (The loss of income suffered by a laid-off worker is just as real when labor market equilibrium exists as when it does not.) The unemployment rate that would exist in conditions of labor market equilibrium is also called the natural rate of unemployment. Labor market equilibrium is also associated with the concept of full employment. This notion causes problems, though. For labor market equilibrium is a theoretical construct that, though analytically convenient, may never in fact be achieved. Thus, there are considerable discussion and difference of opinion about what measured unemployment rate constitutes full employment.

Conventional wisdom currently puts this rate at 4 or perhaps 4.5 percent of the labor force. Just after World War II, 5 percent was the more or less accepted rate. During World War II a condition of excess demand for labor almost surely existed. Wage controls were in existence, which limited, though by no means eliminated, wage increases. At the same time most defense contractors operated on cost-plus contracts. Firms were reimbursed for all wages paid as well as other expenses, within wide limits, and were paid a fee that was a fixed percentage of these costs. Such firms thus had the financial incentive to hire anyone they could, regardless of his productivity, and pay him the maximum wage allowed by controls and government auditors. Yet unemployment was 1.2 percent in 1944 and 1.9 percent in 1943 and 1945. In the post–World War II period unemployment has averaged about 3.7 percent in cyclical peak years, a little over 6 percent in recession years, and slightly under 5 percent on the average.

Additional insight into the level of unemployment rates can be gained by considering their components. Let u stand for the unemployment rate, pr the probability of an unemployed worker's taking a job in, say, a particular week, g the (gross) rate of entrants relative to the existing labor force, and s the (gross) rate of separations relative to employment. A little simple algebra then shows that for a constant unemployment rate, $u = g + s/pr + g + s$.[5] As pointed out earlier, in 1970 the probability of an unemployed worker's becoming employed was about one-ninth per week. The rate of separations, as noted, is about 2 to 3 percent per month, and this rate is more or less constant over the cycle. Little is known about g, though. If, however, $g + s = 0.006$ per week, the unemployment rate would equal 5 percent.

Excess supply of labor

Unemployment from frictional causes at full employment is not an unimportant matter. The time spent looking for a job has an opportunity cost both to the individual worker and to society as a whole. To the individual this cost is the wage income earned when working; to society it is the value of the worker's marginal product. (Given competition in the sale of products and the purchase of productive factors, the cost to the individual and the cost to society are equal.) If, as has been recently suggested, employment services were to be kept open at night so that a worker would not have to miss work to look for another job, the cost of changing jobs would be less and the national income greater. Historically, though, greatest concern has been shown for that unemployment associated with an excess supply of labor. The latter is often termed involuntary unemployment. What is called involuntary unemployment is illustrated in Figure 8.2.

Suppose that labor market equilibrium exists initially with the demand curve for labor D and the wage rate w_1 in Figure 8.2. Now let the demand curve for labor shift downward from D to D'. The new equilibrium wage rate is w_2. So long as the wage rate is w_1, however, the quantity of labor demanded is L_2, and an excess supply of labor equal to $L_1 - L_2$ exists. With the excess supply of labor the measured unemployment

---

[5] Letting U be total unemployment, E employment, L the labor force, u the unemployment rate, w the (gross) rate of labor force withdrawals, and $\triangle$ the change in the magnitude

$\Delta U = gL - (pr + w)U + sE$ and
$\Delta L = (g - w)L$

For a constant unemployment rate, $\Delta U = u\Delta L$, so

$g - (pr + w)u + s(1 - u) = u(g - w)$

Solving for u yields the expression in the text.

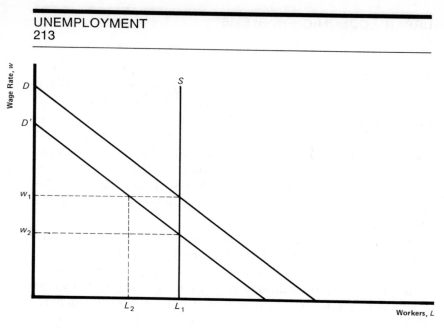

FIGURE 8.2
Declining labor demand and labor market disequilibrium

rate will typically rise, though employers may also reduce the average number of hours worked per week by their employees. If the decline in demand is of short duration and occurs for the economy as a whole, the increased unemployment is termed cyclical. When protracted and limited to certain industries, geographical areas, or special groups in the labor force such as unskilled workers, the additional unemployment is generally termed structural.

One might be tempted to think that unemployment associated with labor market disequilibrium differs from frictional unemployment in that it consists of a pool of workers chronically out of work. This does not appear to be the case, however. During 1969 unemployment averaged only 3.5 percent of the labor force. The fraction of those unemployed for more than 26 weeks was 4.7 percent, and the average duration of unemployment was 7.9 weeks. By April 1971 the unemployment rate had reached 5.7 percent. The fraction of those unemployed more than 26 weeks had risen to 11.0 percent. The last, however, was actually a little less than would be expected on the basis of the then average duration of unemployment of 12.6 weeks.

Rather than being a pool of chronically unemployed workers, so-called cyclical unemployment appears to be principally a reduction in the probability that an unemployed worker will take a job in any given week. Though the rate at which workers are laid off increases, voluntary quits decline so that the total separation rate from employment is more or less constant. Once separated from employment or upon newly entering the labor force, though, a worker searches for a job for a longer period of time. Thus at any moment, a larger number are unemployed.

The higher rate of unemployment will tend to persist until wage rates have adjusted to their new equilibrium level or until labor demand has increased once again to its initial level. The question of fluctuations in demand for the economy as a whole is a book in itself and will not be considered here. The adjustment of wages to their new equilibrium level is an important one for many of the issues here and will be considered briefly (briefly because, though empirically there is good reason to believe that money wage rates are rigid or sticky when labor demand declines, economists have yet to find a good explanation for their behavior).

The best period for revealing the downward rigidity of money wage rates is the onset of the Great Depression of the 1930s. Here the period of decline in demand was long enough so that the raw data themselves reveal the phenomenon rather clearly. As was pointed out over twenty years ago by Albert Rees, from the onset of the depression in 1929 until September 1931, when recovery seemed apparent to many both then and in retrospect, average hourly earnings in money terms in twenty-one manufacturing industries fell only about 5 percent.[6] During this same period money prices fell more, so that in real or in purchasing-power terms wages actually rose about 11 percent. Man-hours of employment fell 44 percent, however. Following 1931, though, money wage rates fell somewhat more. From 1929 to March 1933, the depth of the depression, average hourly earnings fell 22 percent. The fall was still not sufficient to catch up with the decline in prices, however, since

[6] "Wage Determination and Involuntary Unemployment," *Journal of Political Economy* 59 (April 1951), 143–153.

real earnings per man-hour rose 8 percent from 1929 to March 1933.

Though the resistance to downward pressures in money wages was clearly evident in this period, none of the ready explanations can account for it. The period preceded federal minimum wage legislation. Though unionism might have been an influence in some cases, Rees concludes that wage rigidity existed to a significant extent in nonunionized manufacturing industries as well. Worker resistance to cuts in their standard of living is not a very tenable explanation either, because real wages actually rose. The reason why money wage rates are rigid downward for moderately long periods is still very much a puzzle. It should be stressed, moreover, that the evidence of the 1930s is not at all consistent with the notion that money wages are rigid downward forever. For in somewhat less than four years money wages declined by almost one-fourth.

THE ECONOMICS OF SEARCH

The preceding discussion suggests that unemployment is a transient state characterized by searching for a job. As such it is perhaps the most fruitful application of a relatively new idea in economics, that of investment in the search for information. This section considers these ideas in some detail, with reference to investment in labor market information. Mostly for brevity, attention is focused primarily upon the behavior of unemployed workers. In a fuller treatment, however, quite similar considerations could be invoked to explain employer behavior in the face of job vacancies, which is the other side of the coin. An attempt is made to use this framework in explaining both variations in unemployment rates among different labor force groups at a given point in time and cyclical variations in overall unemployment rates.

Investment in information

Economists typically assume that buyers and sellers have complete information about market prices for various commodities and productive factors. Though never literally true in a purely descriptive sense, the assumption of perfect information is not a bad approximation in many instances. Most college freshmen are rather bewildered during orientation week, but by the time they leave for their first Christmas vacation they are pretty knowledgeable about how things are done at their school. In much the same way, consumers, in purchasing certain items repeatedly, quickly learn which stores are best for them and what prices are charged there. Similarly, businessmen work out arrangements with particular suppliers and customers that stand them in good stead so long as underlying conditions change slowly and regularly over time. Thus, though market participants do not literally know everything about prices and qualities of goods offered for sale, in many instances they have the information they themselves would want to make use of.

When conditions change quickly or an infrequently made decisions is to be taken, many of us take the time and expense of obtaining the necessary information. Most people shop for a time when buying a new car or dining-room furniture. Businessmen, too, may spend considerable sums on information when planning a new plant or retail outlet. Time and money spent in acquiring information are quite analogous to those spent for a physical asset itself. In each instance, funds and resources that might be used for current production are devoted to facilitating a larger output in the future. It is thus convenient to think of search as an investment process.

A worker who is unemployed either because he has just been separated from a job or because he has just entered the labor market is in much the same position as someone shopping for a new car. The car buyer has a general idea of the characteristics of different makes of autos and what accessories he would like. Though he may know roughly what car prices are, he probably doesn't know precisely what bundle of automobile components and which particular seller would represent the best deal for him. He thus shops or searches, making a purchase once he decides further time and money spent in searching are not worth the additional information he might unearth.

The unemployed worker, similarly, probably has a good idea of the skills he possesses and the average wage offered by

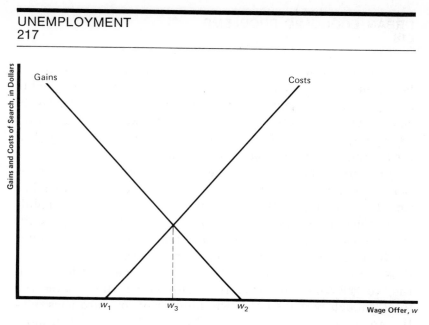

FIGURE 8.3
Gains and costs of job search in relation to wage offers

employers for workers of his particular skills. He doesn't know, however, which particular employers are hiring workers at the moment. Nor is he likely to know the particular skills these employers are trying to acquire, the wages they pay, or the other conditions of employment they offer. Information on possible job openings may be acquired from friends, newspaper advertisements, or employment services. The leads provided by such sources, however, must usually be checked out in person. In tracking down such leads, the worker incurs costs and gains information.

The gains and costs in dollars to a worker searching for a job in some particular day or week are illustrated in Figure 8.3.[7] The gains to searching further are the present worth of the additional future earnings the worker might expect to receive from this search. If a job is offered him, but must be taken before further search or the opportunity lost, the worker's best estimate of the wage paid would be the average wage for all workers of his own qualifications. In Figure 8.3 this is the wage offer shown as w_2, at which the gains to search

---

[7] For a more rigorous discussion see Dale T. Mortensen, "Job Search, the Duration of Unemployment, and the Phillips Curve," *American Economic Review* 60 (December 1970), 847–862.

become zero. For, if the worker receives an offer equal to w_2, he cannot on the average expect to receive a higher-paying offer. The curve showing the gains to search is negatively sloped. This is because the higher the best wage offer a worker has received, the less he can expect to improve upon it, given the average of all wage offers open to him.

The height of the gains-to-search curve in Figure 8.3 depends partly upon the probability that by searching out an additional job possibility the worker will find a job. This probability is most easily thought of as the fraction of all job possibilities for which the employer would make the worker an offer he would accept. It is larger the more skilled the worker, and thus the larger the fraction of current job openings for which the worker would qualify. It is also larger the greater the total, though perhaps unknown, number of job vacancies relative to the number of searchers. Finally, as discussed in more detail later, the probability of finding a job varies inversely with the minimum wage rate the worker would accept. The gains-to-search curve is higher, of course, the greater the probability of a worker's receiving a job offer he would accept.

In addition to the probability of finding a job, the height of the gains-to-search curve in Figure 8.3 also depends upon what economists would call the discount rate. This last depends both upon the rate at which the worker can borrow or lend and the length of time he expects to hold his job. The benefits from a higher wage offer are spread over the period of time the worker holds the job, yielding additional income in both the immediate and the more distant future. The larger sums available for consumption out of wage income earned in the future can be provided, alternatively, by consuming less now and incurring fewer debts or by withdrawing less from a savings account. The worth of future earnings thus depends upon how much can be earned in the future by consuming less now. The greater the rate of interest a worker receives on his savings or pays on debts he has incurred, the smaller the sacrifice in current consumption required to receive a given increase in consumption at some future date. Hence, the greater the rate of interest, the less the present worth of any given increase in future earnings. Similarly, the gains to further job search are greater the longer period of time the worker expects to hold the next job he takes.

The costs of search are the income foregone by searching for an additional job opening. They depend principally upon the income and consumption possibilities open to the worker while searching. These may come from a variety of sources, including help from friends or family and unemployment compensation payments made by government. The income a worker has at his disposal while unemployed is the amount w_1 in Figure 8.3. Provided the worker has received a job offer no greater than w_1, he loses nothing by continuing to search. The curve showing the costs of search slopes upward. This is because the higher the best wage offer yet received, the more he loses by continuing to search rather than accepting the offer.

The acceptance wage and the probability of finding a job

Having discussed the dollar gains and costs of job searching, let us now consider the best decision rule for a worker searching for a job to adopt. Returning to Figure 8.3, suppose first that the best wage offer so far received is less than w_3. The latter is the wage offer at which the gains and costs are equal. For a wage offer less than w_3, the benefits to continuing to look for work exceed the costs of doing so. A sensible worker would continue to search under these circumstances. For any wage offer greater than w_3, however, more would be given up searching for another job possibility than the worker could expect to gain. Consequently, a worker seeking to maximize the expected present worth of his earnings would accept any job offering a wage greater than w_3. The latter, then, is the lowest wage offer he would accept and is called the worker's acceptance wage.

The acceptance wage varies with the rate a worker discounts future earnings, the income available to him when unemployed, and his skills. The effects of varying the discount rate are illustrated in Figure 8.4. There it is assumed that the average wage rate, w_2, is the same for each of two unemployed workers, as is the income available while unemployed. The

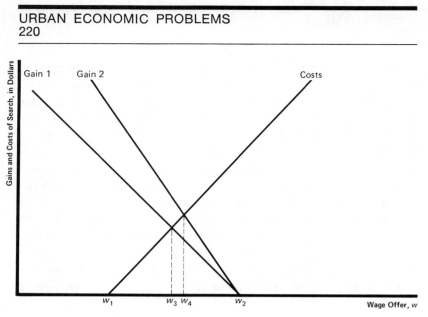

FIGURE 8.4

Duration of employment, gains from job search, and the acceptance wage

second worker, however, plans to retain the next job he takes for a longer period than the first. Consequently, for any wage offer less than w_2 the gains to further search are higher for worker 2 than worker 1, and 2's acceptance wage is higher—w_4 as compared with w_3. Indeed, since men typically hold a given job longer than women, the argument just made suggests that the average wage received by otherwise equally qualified men will exceed that of women. Similarly, of two otherwise identical workers, the one who is more highly skilled has the higher acceptance wage, as indicated by Figure 8.5. If worker 2 is more highly skilled than 1, the average wage for all job openings for which he qualifies is higher—w_4 instead of w_2. Thus, his acceptance wage is w_5. Finally, of two otherwise identical workers, the one whose income is higher when unemployed would have a higher acceptance wage. In Figure 8.6, the second worker's income when unemployed is w_4 and his acceptance wage w_5.

The probability that the worker will accept a job offer in any given week is closely related to his acceptance wage. This probability is the fraction of all job openings for which he qualifies less the fraction of such openings whose wage offer

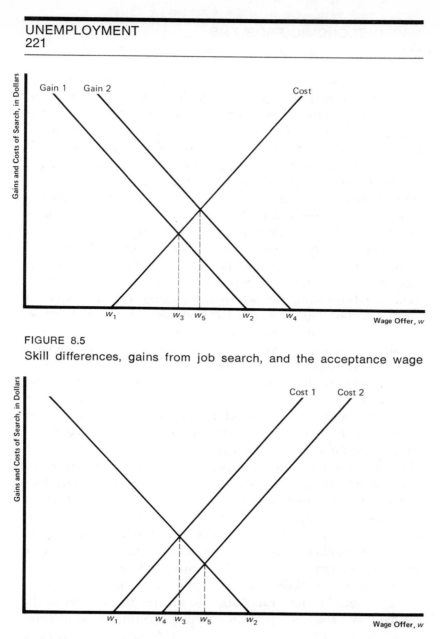

FIGURE 8.5

Skill differences, gains from job search, and the acceptance wage

FIGURE 8.6

Differences in income when unemployed, costs of job search, and the acceptance wage

is smaller than his acceptance wage. And, as was pointed out toward the close of the first section of this chapter, the unemployment rate varies inversely with the probability of finding a job. Because a lower discount rate increases the acceptance wage, a worker planning to retain his next job for a longer period has a smaller probability of accepting a job offer in any given week. This is because the fraction of jobs for which he is qualified and would accept is smaller. For essentially the same reason, the worker whose income when unemployed is higher has a smaller probability of taking a job.

The effect of differences in skill on the probability of finding a job is more complicated. The greater the worker's skills, the higher the average wage for all job offers open to him and, thus, his acceptance wage. This effect alone tends to reduce the probability of his taking a job. Unlike the first two cases considered, though, an increase in skill increases the fraction of job openings for which the employer would offer the worker a job. This second effect increases the probability of the worker's taking a job, running counter to the first. It can be shown, though, that if the worker's skill is low enough, the second effect predominates over the first.[8] For lower-skilled workers, then, an increase in skill raises the probability of taking a job and, hence, reduces the average duration of unemployment. For highly skilled workers the reverse may be true, and, indeed, may account for the phenomenon of the so-called overqualified worker.

Having considered the nature of the job-search process and some of its implications, it is perhaps proper to inquire how the theory of search might be used to account for observed variations in unemployment rates among different labor market groups. The reader will recall from the previous section that unemployment rates are greater the greater the rate of gross movements into the labor force and separations from employment, whether voluntary quits or involuntary separations. Unemployment rates are also greater the smaller is the probability of accepting a job within a given interval of time. One generally finds that in the real world unemployment rates are higher among lesser-skilled workers at any moment and higher for teenagers and workers in their early twenties than for older workers. They are also higher for women than men and for nonwhites than for whites.

[8] Ibid., 852–854.

Differences among labor-turnover rates undoubtedly play an important role in accounting for real-world differences in unemployment rates. Turnover rates are higher, usually, for production workers and less-skilled workers generally. In addition, Harry Gilman found that roughly half the difference in nonwhite and white unemployment rates in 1960 was associated with differences in the industrial composition of unemployment common to all workers.[9] Such industrial differences certainly reflect differences in turnover rates. Higher unemployment rates for women and for younger workers probably reflect more frequent entry into and exit from the labor force. Considerations of the kind just mentioned are probably of primary importance in accounting for unemployment-rate differences among population groups.

The search theory, however, is helpful in explaining certain differences. Lower unemployment rates among professional workers no doubt reflect the fact that they less frequently quit a job to look for another. A college professor, for example, probably will have accepted another position before resigning from his previous post. The theory of search implies that, among lesser-skilled workers, the probability of accepting a job varies directly with the worker's skill level. This implication helps account for the generally higher unemployment rates among less-skilled workers. Women and certainly younger workers may be less skilled than average because of a smaller amount of previous work experience, also contributing to their higher unemployment rates. Wives and younger workers may also have, in effect, greater incomes when unemployed because they share in the earnings of the family's principal breadwinner. The latter also implies higher unemployment rates for married women and younger workers. On the other hand, if women plan to be in the labor force for a shorter time than men they will search less.

The higher unemployment rates of nonwhites are frequently attributed to their being "last-hired and first-fired." However, there has been little careful analysis of why employers might wish to behave in the way required by this hypothesis. To the extent that labor market discrimination, as was discussed

---

[9] Harry J. Gilman, "Economic Discrimination and Unemployment," *American Economic Review* 55 (December 1965), 1077–1096.

in the preceding chapter, exists, the wages paid equally skilled blacks would be lower than those of whites. The theory of job search implies that among lower-skilled workers the lower their average wage, the lower the probability of accepting a job and the higher the unemployment rate. Unemployment rates might also be higher among blacks because they are less well educated on the average, hence less skilled. These educational differences could well result from blacks being disadvantaged but would not result from labor market discrimination in the narrow sense.

There has been little solid empirical study of the quantitative importance of the various factors just discussed. Qualitatively, however, the theory of job search would seem consistent with several important real-world differences in unemployment rates. In the judgment of many economists, the theory of job search is indeed a promising one.

Adjustments to changes in labor demand

The theory of job search may ultimately prove most useful in understanding market behavior when the demand for labor declines. Though such declines may occur for many reasons, so far as so-called business cycles are concerned, they result from declining demand for final products of various kinds.[10] Other sources of declining labor demand will be considered under the rubric of technological unemployment in the following section.

Perhaps the most fundamental consideration regarding general declines in demand for final products is that they are difficult to recognize as such. Even during normal periods the demands for certain products are declining, though these declines are offset by increasing demands elsewhere. Superimposed on these fluctuations in the components of aggregate demand are a whole host of erratic forces, such as the effects of a steel or dock strike, unanticipated changes in farm output and prices, and sudden changes in federal income tax withholding rates. Furthermore, important economic data become available only with a lag of one to three months. Their inter-

---

[10] See Edmund S. Phelps, "The New Microeconomics in Inflation and Employment Theory," *American Economic Review* 59 (May 1969), 147–160, for a fuller discussion of the notions discussed here.

pretation is made more difficult by problems associated with seasonal fluctuations. Small wonder, then, that it is frequently difficult to determine what is going on now, let alone to forecast what will happen six months to a year from now.

Though labor demand may decline by a substantial amount in six months to a year, week-to-week and even month-to-month changes are typically relatively small. Since labor turnover is substantial in normal times (of the order to 2 to 3 percent per month, as pointed out earlier), many reductions in employment may be achieved by not replacing separated workers. Furthermore, in the long run most employers have little control over the wage rates they pay their workers. Rather, they must pay the going market rate for workers of various skills. These considerations suggest the conjecture that a sensible reaction on the part of employers, given their lack of knowledge of the general decline in labor demand, is simply to maintain the wage rates they pay at previous levels and to reduce the number of new job offers made.

In similar fashion, individual workers who are searching for jobs are unaware, initially, that a general decline in demand for labor has taken place. They thus base their acceptance wages upon different conditions that existed in the past. As unemployed workers search for possible job openings, a smaller fraction of them receive job offers acceptable to them than before the decline in labor demand. Consequently, the unemployment rate rises.

One would expect that both employers and unemployed workers would gradually learn about the new conditions and adapt their behavior accordingly. Employers would observe fewer quits or voluntary separations by their employees. They would also observe a greater number of job seekers relative to the number of job openings they are trying to fill. Under these conditions it would be sensible for employers to reduce the level of wages offered to workers at different skill levels. It is frequently asserted that employers also raise their skill requirements, that is, systematically attempt to hire more highly skilled workers for given positions. The last assertion is consistent with the smaller cyclical variability of unemployment rates of more highly skilled workers. In any event, to seek to hire more highly skilled workers at a given wage rate is, in effect, a reduction in wage offers for a given level of skill.

Workers, too, may be expected to learn from their search for work and to adapt their behavior to changed conditions. Some may revise their acceptance wage downward rather quickly. Others, however, may do so only slowly. They may believe, for example, that the decline in labor demand is specific to particular industries, occupations, or localities, and thus search for jobs they might otherwise not have considered. Or, other workers might believe that the decline in demand and the wage offers of employers is only temporary. If so, they might plan to consume more leisure currently while its opportunity cost is low and less when it becomes more expensive in the future. In effect, then, the labor supply curve shifts to the left, employment falls, and real wages rise.

As time passes, however, both employers and workers obtain more complete information about changed labor market conditions. In particular, as workers learn that the reduction in the level of wages offered is neither specific to certain employers nor temporary, their estimates of the gains to job search are revised downward. Likewise, as unemployment compensation becomes exhausted and other sources of income while unemployed run out, the costs of job search increase. On both counts, the acceptance wage declines, a higher fraction of unemployed workers find acceptable offers, and the unemployment rate declines. Thus, although the initial impact of a decline in labor demand is likely to be a higher unemployment rate, the ultimate result is smaller employment and lower real wages in the class of jobs for which the decline in demand occurred.

IS HUMAN LABOR OBSOLETE?

Science fiction generally seems to be characterized by a plausible unreality—plausible because it is founded upon certain known principles of physical or natural science but unreal because it depicts events that haven't yet happened, to our knowledge at least. There is a similarity in books and articles that argue that because of recent technological advances, especially automation and the computer, sometime in the future many people won't be able to find any jobs at all, and those who can will work far fewer hours than today at very different jobs. It is further argued that such changes will require vast differences in our society's arrangements for directing economic activity and distributing income.[11] Though these assertions have a certain plausibility, the conditions predicted certainly haven't materialized yet. Indeed, these dire predictions date back at least to the start of the industrial revolution. Thus, it seems appropriate to refer to this literature as "social-science fiction."

The meaning
of technological change

In considering the matter of technological change and whether it produces unemployment, it is first necessary to distinguish between technological change and a mere change in the way of doing things. To an economist, not all differences in the way of doing things reflect different technologies. The term "technology" refers to the totality of known ways of doing things. Technological change itself means an increase in the collection of known ways. The fact that less land is used per unit of output in European than in American agriculture is not a difference in technology in this sense. Rather it is the use of a different technique of a given technology that results from the fact that land is more scarce, and thus more expensive, relative to other productive factors in Western Europe. To equate the marginal product of land to its higher rental there, less land must be used relative to labor and machinery. In much the same way, the use of a lot of labor and shovels may be a more appropriate technique in underdeveloped countries where wage rates are low relative to capital rental values, a fact frequently forgotten by advisors from countries where labor is relatively more expensive and bulldozers are used instead.

It is often difficult to tell whether any given change in technique results from an increase in knowledge or merely from the application of previously unused knowledge. It seems plausible that the discovery of nuclear fission was essentially exogenous to the economic system. On the other hand, its application to the production of electric power seems little

---

[11] This is argued, for example, in Robert Theobald, ed., *The Guaranteed Income* (Garden City, N.Y.: Doubleday, 1967).

different in principle from building an electric power plant. In either case resources that might otherwise have been used to produce commodities for current consumption instead are consciously used to increase consumption in the future. For example, the development of the supermarket and of frozen foods may be viewed as conscious attempts to reduce the use of increasingly expensive human labor. In writings on urban real estate it is often claimed that the development of the elevator made possible the construction of high-rise buildings. However, perhaps the elevator was developed to permit more output per unit of more expensive land.

There are a variety of ways to characterize technological change. For the present purpose the distinction between neutral and labor-saving technological change is critical. Neutral technological change itself may be defined in different ways, but for this discussion a neutral change is one that increases the output obtainable from given inputs of, say, labor and capital but does not affect their relative marginal productivity. A labor-saving technological change, in contrast, is one that reduces the marginal product of labor and increases that of capital for the inputs of labor and capital used prior to the change, but that leaves total output unchanged. (A capital-saving technological change, defined similarly, may be thought of as a negative labor-saving change.) As so defined, neutral and labor-saving technological changes are polar cases. Any actual change may well be some combination of the two.

A labor-saving technological change reduces the demand for labor in the kind of employment affected by the change. A neutral change may either increase or decrease the demand for labor, however, depending upon the circumstances. One good example of an essentially neutral change in technology is in the production of cameras and lenses. Prior to World War II the high-priced Leica and Contax were virtually the only quality cameras with f2 lenses. Today, cameras selling for a quarter to half the prewar dollar price, even less in real terms, have equally good or better f2 lenses, and much faster lenses are commonplace. These developments have resulted primarily from the use of better optical glass, lens coatings, and computer design of lenses. Essentially the same labor and machinery devoted to the grinding, polishing, and assembly of lenses produces better and cheaper lenses. Though it takes less labor and capital than previously to produce an optic comparable to a prewar one, more labor is used worldwide in the production of camera lenses.

Part of the answer to this seeming paradox is that incomes and, hence, the demand for cameras, have increased. Incomes are much lower in the Far East than in the United States, but one rarely sees a university student from the Far East who doesn't have a fairly expensive camera. Because many quality cameras are manufactured in Japan, where skilled labor—a vital input in the making of fine cameras—is relatively cheap as compared with the United States and Germany, fine cameras are about half as expensive in Japan. The demand for cameras appears to be highly responsive to their prices. With the reduction in costs of producing fine cameras, their relative prices have fallen. The resulting increase in quantity demanded has more than outweighed the direct effect upon the demand for labor, which results from the fact that fewer workers can produce a given number of cameras.

Thus, a change in technology may, but need not, reduce the demand for labor. It is frequently asserted, without any really solid empirical evidence, that the development of automation and the computer has reduced the demand for labor, especially unskilled. One of the principal applications of the computer has been in the "real-time" control of production. Though it may have reduced the demand for labor in, say, petroleum refining, it seems likely that space flights would never have been attempted without the reduction in the costs of control the computer permitted. To take another example, on balance the use of more automated fire control systems has probably increased the gunnery and related personnel on naval vessels. In both the latter cases the relative price effect of automation may well have increased the demand for labor. Similarly, the greater degree of automation in the direction of commercial air transport than in rail or bus travel may well have contributed to the lower relative cost and increasing popularity of air travel.

The greatest impact of the computer, however, has been in the field of data processing. It is almost certainly the case that fewer people are employed today in the factory part of the typical commercial bank, where checks are processed. On the other hand, because of the price effect far more people are employed in data processing in universities today than prior to the advent of the computer. Indeed, any self-respecting university probably employs more keypunch operators today than it previously had desk-calculator operators. Partly because of the computer, the average economist spends much more time working with numbers and less time searching through dusty library volumes. Yet, far more economists are employed in the United States relative to, say, historians than prior to World War II, and the average salaries of economists now rank along with those of physicists and mathematicians among the top in the academic world.

Economic adjustments to automation

The foregoing considerations, though admittedly casual, suggest that it is by no means clear that automation and the computer have reduced the demand for labor, perhaps even unskilled labor. For the sake of argument, though, suppose that they have. What economic adjustments might result? In particular, it is useful to inquire whether automation and the computer might result in higher unemployment rates.

The effects of a decline in labor demand were illustrated in Figure 8.2. With a decline in demand from D to D', at the old wage rate w_1 there is an excess supply of labor $L_2 - L_1$. As was described in the preceding section, with this excess demand, unemployment rates would rise initially since, with fewer job offers being made by employers, unemployed workers would spend a longer time searching for an acceptable job offer. Eventually, however, real wages would decline to w_2 and labor market equilibrium would be restored. If the decline in demand is limited to some segment of the economy, all that may be required for relative real wages to fall is for money wages to grow less rapidly in the affected segment. If experienced for the economy as a whole, monetary and fiscal measures could be employed by the central government to raise aggregate demand for final products. In the process the money prices of commodities would rise, reducing the real wage associated with a given money wage. Regardless, the experience of the 1930s cited toward the close of the first section of this chapter suggests that money wages, though temporarily resistant to downward pressures, do indeed decline after a time.

Thus, the ultimate impact of declining labor demand is likely to be lower real wages in the affected sectors. The situation is not unlike that of piston aircraft following the introduction of the commercial jet in the early sixties. Though many fewer were employed by the larger or trunk airlines in the United States, an active used-aircraft market exists. The piston aircraft replaced by jets were largely sold to other users, though often at greatly reduced prices. Around 1966 Constellations and DC-7s were selling for about $10,000 and Electras for about $350,000, as compared with $7 million for a new 707. Many used aircraft were sold to overseas buyers, others to private users in this country. At least one major-league baseball club once had its own DC-7, and private travel clubs using DC-7s existed in several large U.S. cities.

Now it is sometimes argued that new technological possibilities are so overwhelming that there will literally be no place for displaced workers to go. There are two shortcomings in this conclusion, even if its premise is correct. The first is that to be applied, automation and data-processing techniques must be embodied in new machinery or capital assets generally. During any interval of time the amount of new capital assets is limited by society's total savings. Second, even in the long run, allowing for sufficient amount of new investment, technological possibilities are applied only if it pays business firms to do so. It could certainly be that at the wage rates and capital rental values prevailing prior to automation, it would have paid all employers to use less labor and more machinery. Given society's limited stock of new machinery, capital rental values of new machines would rise. This, together with the fall in the values of older capital assets and wage rates, would mean some employers would find it advantageous not to automate. Among the latter would be those firms, perhaps grocery stores, for whom automation is less advantageous than for, say, petroleum refineries. For, as is stressed repeatedly in this book, what matters in economics is comparative, not absolute advantage.

At this point, the reader might well object that lower earnings rates, especially for unskilled workers, is no solution to the problem. After all, lower earnings rates, like higher unemployment rates, reduce the annual earnings of lower-income families. This is true. But it should be stressed that the problem posed by labor-saving technological change is lower earnings rates, not chronic unemployment. It is important to understand the true nature of the problem, though, if one wishes to combat it. Indeed, in Chapter 10 it is argued that many public policies are misdirected and likely to be of little value precisely because they seek to reduce chronic unemployment rather than to improve earnings opportunities.

Are unemployment rates increasing?

Shortly after 1957, unemployment rates rose and remained relatively high well into the early 1960s. At that time it was widely argued that the higher unemployment rates were due to structural factors such as the decline in demand for labor or for unskilled labor that automation and the computer were said to have produced. One heard such arguments much less frequently in the late 1960s, when vigorous aggregate demand brought unemployment rates to lower levels again. Indeed, today it has become fashionable to allege that structural changes in the economy have produced a tendency toward chronic inflation.

Many studies have examined the variation of unemployment rates for particular groups of the labor force overtime in the period following World War II.[12] With but one exception, there is virtually no evidence of any persistent increase in unemployment rates. Rather the rate for any particular group tends to fluctuate with the aggregate unemployment rate for the economy as a whole. Generally, the unemployment rates of less-skilled workers change more rapidly than the overall unemployment rate does. Likewise, the rates for younger work-

---

[12] For an excellent summary of this evidence see Robert M. Solow, *The Nature and Sources of Unemployment in the United States* (Stockholm: Almqvist & Wicksell, 1964).

ers, for men, and for nonwhites all fluctuate more widely than the overall rate does. Only for teenage workers, however, does the unemployment rate appear to have risen over time for a given level of the aggregate unemployment rate.

Furthermore, there is little reason to believe that the aggregate unemployment rate for the economy as a whole has risen. Comparing cyclical peak years, the unemployment rate was 3.8 percent in 1948, 2.9 percent in 1953, and 4.3 percent in 1957. In 1966 and 1969 the unemployment rates were 3.8 and 3.5 percent, respectively, which averaged out almost exactly the same as the years 1948, 1953, and 1957. There is thus little evidence that the long-run effect of automation and the computer has been to increase unemployment.

There is some evidence that real wage rates have risen less rapidly since 1957 than previously, but they have by no means declined. From 1929 to 1948 average hourly earnings in manufacturing, when adjusted for price changes, rose an average rate of 2.8 percent per year. From 1948 to 1957 the annual increase was slightly faster—3.1 percent per year. From 1957 to 1966, however, real average hourly earnings in manufacturing grew only 1.5 percent per year, whereas from 1966 to 1969 they rose even more slowly—only 1 percent per year.

During the 1950s the rate of growth of real annual earnings revealed by census data was generally smaller for less-skilled workers. During this period, the real annual earnings of professional and managerial workers grew at about 3.2 percent per year. For sales workers and for operatives, or semiskilled workers, the growth rate was 2.3 percent. For the least skilled, service workers and laborers, the rate of increase was only 1.3 percent per year.

The data just noted are consistent with a decline in the growth in demand for labor generally and for less-skilled labor in particular. Such declines could have resulted from automation and the computer. It seems clear, however, that the latter have not generally brought about increased unemployment. As the analysis earlier in this section suggests, the problem with technological change is not permanently higher unemployment. Rather, if anything, it is lower earning opportunities, especially among less-skilled workers. To the extent that the effects of technological change must be ameliorated, the principal way to do so is to seek ways of increasing the earnings opportunities of lower-income persons.

SUMMARY

Anyone at work or temporarily absent is considered to be employed, those not employed but actively seeking work to be unemployed. Unemployment is largely a transient state of relatively short duration; little of it is what is commonly thought of as hard-core unemployment. Seasonal and frictional unemployment may exist when labor markets are in equilibrium or overall balance. When an excess supply of labor exists at current wage rates, unemployment is greater as workers spend a longer average time in search of a job. Excess labor supply does not persist indefinitely, however, as money wage rates do adjust downward, though with a relatively long lag.

Unemployed workers may be thought of as searching for job information in much the same way as car buyers shop. The gains to such search are the higher hourly earnings received when employed, the costs the income foregone while searching. To maximize the present value of his future annual earnings, a worker would accept any wage offer at least as large as that which equates the gains and costs of search. The latter is called his acceptance wage. The probability that an unemployed worker will accept a job in any search period is given by the fraction of openings for which he qualifies less the fraction whose wage offers are below his acceptance wage. The theory of job search is consistent with some variations in unemployment rates among population groups, though differences in labor turnover rates are probably more important in accounting for such differences. It is also useful in understanding labor market behavior in the presence of a decline in labor demand.

Many differences in production techniques are the result of differences in economic conditions. Technological change means an increase in the totality of known techniques of production. A technological change that reduces the marginal productivity of labor relative to other productive factors reduces the demand for labor. Other changes, however, may increase the demand for labor because of the increase in output they induce, and have done so historically. If a change in technology leads to a decrease in labor demand, unemployment may rise temporarily, but a fall in real wages will restore labor market equilibrium. Even though the decline in demand may be a general one for the economy as a whole, reduced real wages and rental values of older capital assets would eliminate the inducement for some employers to automate. Except for teenage workers, there is no evidence of an upward trend in unemployment rates for any population group in the postwar period. There is some evidence, however, that real wages have grown less rapidly since the late 1950s and that the earnings of unskilled workers have grown less rapidly than those of skilled workers.

CHAPTER 9

Economics
of education

EDUCATION AS INVESTMENT
IN HUMAN CAPITAL

There are at least two aspects of education that are of interest
for urban problems. One is education as a productive enterprise. Organizations producing educational services hire labor,
buildings, and other inputs in factor markets in much the
same way business firms do. Some sell their services directly
to students, whereas others receive their revenues from taxes
levied by various governmental units. Matters relating to education as a productive enterprise, however, are reserved for
consideration in a later chapter. In this one attention is focused on a newer and exceptionally fruitful view of education
as a process of investment in human beings.[1]

The costs and returns
to education

Despite the fact that some readers may find it offensive, in
many respects education is perfectly analogous to investment
in machines. When a machine is constructed, labor, materials,
and other machines are withdrawn from other uses that might
have produced currently consumable output instead. The opportunity cost to the economy of constructing the machine
is the alternative output these resources might have produced.
At the same time, the person or firm purchasing the machine
must acquire funds to pay its producer for the resources used
in constructing it. These funds might have been borrowed
or might have come from the purchaser's accumulated savings.
The purchaser is willing to pay a certain sum for the machine
because of the expectation that using the machine in production will add at least a comparable sum to the present value
of his future output.

In very much the same fashion, persons acquiring education
incur costs and receive returns. From the point of view of
the student, the costs include tuition, the costs of books and

---

[1] An excellent, though more advanced, survey of many of the matters discussed
in this chapter is contained in Jacob Mincer, "The Distribution of Labor
Incomes: A Survey with Special Reference to the Human Capital Approach,"
Journal of Economic Literature 8 (March 1970), 1–26.

other supplies, and any additional living expenses. For public education, especially in elementary and secondary schools, these are generally quite small. Even in a private college or university such items are a relatively small part of the total cost of education to the student. The major cost to the individual is the opportunity cost of the time spent in acquiring education. Time spent in acquiring education could, alternatively, be used in working or in leisure. In Chapter 7 it was argued that so long as an individual freely varied his hours of work, time spent working and in nonwork or leisure would be valued at the wage rate the individual can earn by working additional hours. Thus, the opportunity cost of time spent in acquiring education is equal to the time spent multiplied by the wage the student can earn.

Similarly, by devoting time to education the student earns a return. These returns may take a variety of forms. One of the most obvious is the greater earnings opportunities open to better-educated workers. Indeed, economists have given their primary attention to returns in the form of higher earnings. Part of the greater earnings may accrue in nonmonetary terms in the form of more interesting or pleasant work. At the same time, education, to the extent that one develops an appreciation of Beethoven or Shakespeare, increases the future productivity of time spent in leisure. Finally, education may provide current enjoyment, as evidenced by the words of the Yale song, "bright college years, with pleasure rife."

Education is one activity in which the private costs and returns may differ significantly from the social costs and returns. Social costs include the resource costs of teachers, buildings, and books not borne directly by the student. These are large for public education, though capable of being estimated. The external returns, though, while possible to specify, are almost impossible to estimate. Society clearly benefits from a literate populace in a variety of ways. To name two, automobile traffic can be regulated much more easily if drivers can read road signs, and the ability to read and do simple calculations makes possible the personal income tax—our most efficient tax in that it is the cheapest per dollar of revenue raised to collect. One frequently hears the claim that a better-educated electorate means better public policies generally. However, this sometimes seems doubtful.

Finally, it is frequently argued that by acquiring additional education an individual not only earns a higher income himself but raises the earnings of other productive factors as well. This assertion, though, is largely mistaken. To the extent that competition prevails in labor markets, each individual is paid his marginal product, the increase in the revenue that results from a firm's hiring him. This is the case whether the additional output results from the worker's innate ability or from the time spent acquiring an education. Any individual worker thus receives the whole of the additional earnings generated by his investment in education. It is quite correct to state that the incomes of some other productive factors may increase if large numbers of workers become better educated, but incomes of other productive factors may likewise increase purely through an increase in the number of workers of a given educational level.

To formalize the relationships between the costs and returns to an individual acquiring education, let X be the earnings attributable to "raw" or uneducated labor, r the returns in dollars per dollar spent acquiring education, C the costs of education or dollars spent, and Y net earnings. The latter are total potential or gross earnings less the amount currently spent on education. Assuming, as is usually done for simplicity, that the only individual costs of education are foregone earnings, net earnings are what one usually thinks of as earnings—the amount the individual actually receives in dollars from working. Gross earnings, in turn, are the earnings of raw labor plus the returns to all previous investments. Thus, letting subscripts refer to time periods,

$$Y_t = X + (r_1C_1 + \cdot \cdot \cdot + r_{t-1}C_{t-1}) - C_t$$

The equation states that the earnings actually received by a worker in, say, 1970 equal the sum of (1) the return attributable to his raw or uneducated labor; and (2) the returns on all past investments from the time he began investing through 1969, each annual return being the product of the rate of return on that year's investment and the amount invested in that year; less (3) the amount invested in 1970. It is purely a definitional relationship, but it is a highly useful one when certain specific assumptions are made regarding its components, as will be done later.

Types of education

The equation just formulated turns out to be highly useful in distinguishing between two major kinds of education—schooling and on-the-job training. The commonsense distinction between the two types of education tends to break down in a surprising number of cases, one good example being medical education. The clinical period during the last two years of medical school is, by most outward appearances, virtually indistinguishable from internship; it is certainly more similar to internship than the first two years of medical school. Yet, in a real sense, the clinical period is schooling, and internship is on-the-job training.

A more precise distinction is provided by the size of net earnings. Schooling may be defined by $Y_t = 0$ (or ≤ 0 if costs include tuition as well as foregone earnings), on-the-job training by positive net earnings or $Y_t > 0$. Thus, during the schooling period

$$C_t = X + (r_1 C_1 + \cdots + r_{t-1} C_{t-1})$$

One sees, therefore, that the costs of education tend to increase with the length of the schooling period. Indeed, in the special case where education is wholly in the form of schooling for s periods of time and the returns per period are the same for all periods and equal to r, it is easy to show that, for $t > s$,

$$Y_t = X(1 + r)^s$$

More generally, in the postschooling period, since $Y_t > 0$,

$$C_t < X + (r_1 C_1 + \cdots + r_{t-1} C_{t-1})$$

Finally, if a point is reached when investment in education is no longer taking place, $C_t = 0$, so

$$Y_t = X + (r_1 C_1 + \cdots + r_{t-1} C_{t-1})$$

On-the-job training is most concretely thought of as work experience. In general, one may think of employers as both producing an output for sale to their customers and education to (some of) their employees. Such education or work experience, like schooling, may be thought of as increasing the worker's future productivity, hence his future earnings potential. The increase in the worker's future productivity, in turn, may increase his productivity to employers other than the one providing the training. In this case the training is said to be general. Alternatively, if training increases the worker's productivity only so long as he is employed by the firm providing the training, it is said to be specific. A good example of the distinction is provided by the training of military pilots. To the extent that a military pilot's training involves acquiring skills in manipulating an aircraft, navigation, and other things an airline pilot must know, the training is general. Since the employment of mercenary pilots is quite limited, training in techniques of attacking another aircraft or bombing is specific training.

The costs of on-the-job training may be borne by the worker through accepting a lower wage during the training period. They may also be borne by the employer if he pays the worker a wage that is higher than his marginal product while receiving training and a wage lower than his marginal product after the completion of his training. Having acquired general training, the worker can receive a wage equal to his now greater marginal product from employers other than the one providing the training. Private firms are generally unable to enforce contracts requiring a worker to remain in its employment. Unless there is some other limitation on the worker's ability to change jobs, the employer providing general training cannot recoup costs incurred for it by paying a wage less than the worker's marginal product when trained. Consequently, firms providing general training would usually not be willing to bear any of its costs.

To the extent that on-the-job training is specific, however, a worker can receive its benefits only by remaining with the firm providing the training. An employer would thus be willing to pay part of its costs. Indeed, unless the employer pays part of the costs, he has no incentive to retain the specifically trained worker. The worker would thus have no assurance of recouping the costs of specific training if he bore them all. But the employer would not pay the full costs of specific training, for if he did, the worker would have no incentive to remain in his employ. The sharing of training costs depends upon the employer's borrowing costs relative to the worker's. If the employer can borrow more cheaply than the worker, by paying higher wages earlier and lower wages later on, the employer could pay off a loan and have something left over.

An interesting exception to the foregoing is provided by the case of professional athletes bound to a particular club by the so-called reserve clause. Though some of a pro-football rookie's training is specific to a particular team in that it involves a particular system of nomenclature for designating plays, much of it is concerned with the mastery of skills and learning the techniques used by other teams and even individual players. Since a player is unable to negotiate with other teams as a free agent, salaries and bonuses much in excess of a player's value to his team during his rookie year have frequently been paid. The points made regarding training and earnings are also well illustrated by the difficulties experienced by the U.S. armed forces in retaining skilled personnel. Salaries and other benefits are determined by rank and length of service, with rank itself being dependent essentially on length of service. Traditionally, however, no distinction in military pay for skills acquired while in service was made. In consequence, to the extent that general training was provided members of the armed forces, they tended to be overpaid during the training period and underpaid thereafter. Therefore, it was difficult to retain men with salable civilian skills, even though persons receiving training were generally required to extend their period of service.

Time pattern
of investment

Two interesting aspects of investment in education are that it is generally spread over a period of many years and that it tends to be concentrated early in life. Both of these features are well illustrated by schooling and both are quite understandable when one considers the costs of and returns to education.

Chapter 7 discussed the notion of an individual allocating his time between work and leisure to equalize the marginal returns of time spent. When one considers education as a third use of time, the same principle applies. The twenty-four hours a day available to each individual will be divided up among work, leisure, and education to equalize returns to additional hours spent in each use. If, no matter how little time is spent in work or in education, the marginal returns are less than in other uses of time, no time will be devoted to that particular use.

The greater the number of hours devoted to education in any time period, the less is available for work and leisure. The less time, in turn, spent in work or leisure, the more valuable one would expect an additional hour devoted to leisure to become. Though one may "cram" for an exam or stay up all night to finish a term paper, one cannot devote this much time per day to education for very long. Thus, the opportunity cost of time spent in education rises as the amount of time devoted to it does, limiting the amount acquired in any day or year. Consequently, the period of investment in education tends to be spread over more than one year.

There are two principal reasons why the period of investment in education is concentrated early in life. First, the earlier in life one invests in education, the greater the number of years over which one can receive a return on it. Consequently, the returns to education are higher if attained early in life. Returns in the form of future earnings and consumption, however, are discounted or reduced in value to the size of the loan that can be repaid by the return when received. At any sensible rate of interest, say 10 percent per year, returns received more than twenty years in the future have a negligible current or present value. Thus, though this first consideration explains why few people go to school after age 45, it is not much help in explaining why even physicians have completed school by age 30 in most instances.

A more important reason for the concentration of education early in life is the rise of opportunity costs of education with time. Recall that gross earnings are

$$X + (r_1 C_1 + \cdots + r_{t-1} C_{t-1})$$

The larger t is, the larger gross earnings are, so long as r and C are positive. Thus, the greater the amount of schooling and on-the-job training, the higher one's hourly earnings will be and the greater the opportunity costs of devoting another hour to education. If 30-year-old males earn more than 20-year-old ones when working, then the costs of education are higher to them. With equal returns per hour at 20 and at 30 it would then pay an individual to invest more at 20 and to work more at 30.

DETERMINATION
OF THE AMOUNT INVESTED

Demand and supply
of investment in education

Having considered the nature of investment in education, let us now examine how the amount any one individual invests is determined. Later on in this section, variations among individuals and some questions of appropriate social policy toward education will be considered. As with many matters considered in this book, it is convenient to analyze investment in education in terms of demand and supply.

Demand for investment in education refers to those forces affecting the additional or marginal returns per additional dollar invested. These may be summarized by a curve or schedule CE as shown in Figure 9.1. For any given dollar amount of investment in education, say OA, the height of the curve, AD, is the maximum additional annual income that can be earned each year of the individual's working life. The gross earnings due to education are given by the area $OCDA$, and the average return to education for a dollar investment of OA is area $OCDA$ divided by OA.

Like most demand curves, CE slopes downward to the right because, after some point, additional investment in education combined with a fixed human capacity would be expected to yield diminishing marginal returns. The situation is analo-

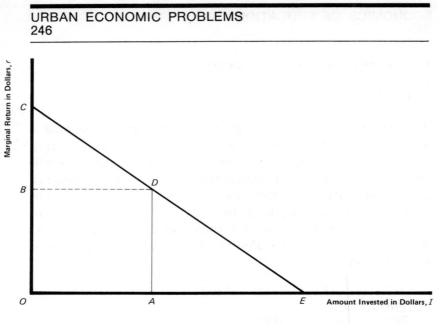

FIGURE 9.1
Demand for and returns to investment in education

gous to spending additional amounts in constructing a building upon a fixed plot of land. The height of the curve for
any given amount of investment, AD at OA, is determined
by the individual's capacities. These reflect not only his innate
abilities but the economic and social conditions that affect
his income earning opportunities. A technological change that
increases the demand for skilled labor would cause the curve
to shift upward, for example. Similarly, racial discrimination
in employment, as was discussed in Chapter 7, would lower
the curve for the group discriminated against and raise it
for others.

The actual amount invested by any one individual depends
upon conditions of supply as well as demand. The latter are
summarized by the curve labeled S in Figure 9.2. Conditions
of supply are those circumstances that affect the costs of funds
to finance education. The latter, of course, consist to a great
extent of earnings foregone while acquiring an education. A
reduction in earnings, other things being the same, means a
reduction in the current consumption of the consumer unit
to which the individual acquiring the education belongs. To
make up for a reduction in current consumption, however,

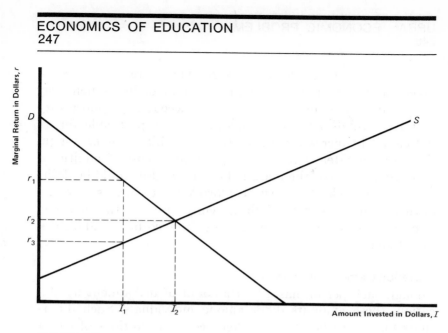

FIGURE 9.2
Determinants of dollar investment in education

individuals and families may borrow, either by incurring new debts or paying off old ones less rapidly. The costs of foregone earnings may thus be viewed as the interest payments made on the amount invested.

The height of the supply curve to any individual thus depends upon the interest rates applicable to him. To the extent that interest rates are lower for certain individuals or families than others, so is the supply curve for funds invested in education. For families with little savings and few assets, borrowing may mean an unsecured personal loan at interest rates of 18 to 24 percent or more per year. Alternatively, for a family with a moderate equity in their home, borrowing may merely mean inceasing the size of the mortgage. If so, the applicable interest rate may be 6 to 8 percent instead. For any family, however, additional investments may become increasingly costly to finance. Though many families may comfortably manage an undergraduate college education, medical school would be difficult for most. Thus, for most families the supply schedule of funds for investment in education slopes upward after a point.

Given the demand and supply curves in Figure 9.2, the optimal investment in education is I_2. The marginal return to investment is r_2. For any smaller amount of investment, say I_1, the marginal return is r_1, which exceeds the opportunity cost r_3 of funds invested. Thus at I_1, it is profitable for an individual to increase his investment. In like manner, for investments greater than I_2 the opportunity cost of additional investment exceeds the marginal return, and it would be desirable to cut back. As every beer drinker soon learns, one can have too much of a good thing. Only at I_2 do the marginal returns exactly balance off against the costs of additional investment.

Variations among individuals

Though each person has a best amount of investment in education, these amounts differ among individuals. Such differences may arise because of differences in conditions of either demand or supply. Those arising from differences in conditions of supply have somewhat different implications from those arising out of differences in demand. For this reason it is worthwhile to consider them carefully.

Perhaps the most obvious source of differences in the amounts invested by individuals is differences in supply. As suggested earlier, the opportunity cost of investment in education for children from poor families may be considerably greater than for children in families who are better off. Not only is the cost of borrowing likely to be higher, but the fraction of a poor family's potential earnings that a teenager might contribute may well be much larger. To take another example, it is probably the case that schools for black children, whether in large city ghettos or in the rural South, are inferior to those for white children generally. If so, it would take a larger amount of time, hence a greater investment, to obtain a given increment in earning power even in the absence of discrimination in employment. The net effect of this is to make investment in education more costly for black children.

For whatever reason, consider two individuals facing the same demand curve for investment in education. This is labeled D in Figure 9.3. However, let the supply curves differ, being S_1 for one individual and S_2 for a second. For the latter, the costs of investment are higher. If each of the two individuals

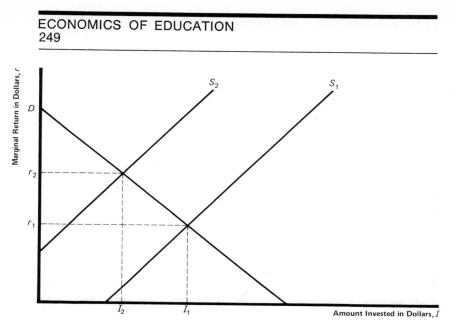

FIGURE 9.3

Effects of differences in the supply of funds for educational investment

makes the best amount of investment for him, given the conditions he faces, the first will invest I_1 and the second I_2. The marginal return for the second individual will be higher, r_2 as compared with r_1. The total returns to education, hence gross earnings assuming the same return to raw labor for each, will be larger for the first individual, however. The additional earnings of the first individual are given by the area lying under the demand curve D between I_2 and I_1.

Though the major source of differences in amounts invested may be due to differences in supply or opportunity, important differences due to differences in demand may exist as well. Education may have a greater impact upon earnings in some occupations than others, medicine being a good example. The average woman spends fewer years in the labor force than the average man. For this reason, the demand curve for education for women may lie below that for men. In addition, certain individuals, even though possessing no more ability to utilize education, may be more willing to undertake the study of Greek or calculus than others. Their demand curves would thus be higher.

Suppose that two individuals have different demand curves

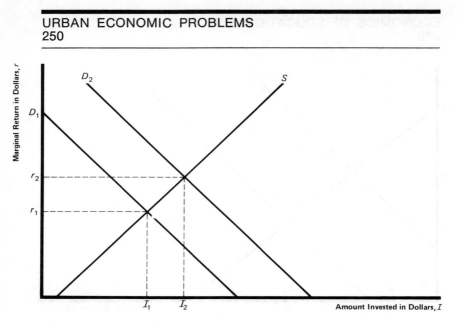

FIGURE 9.4
Effects of differences in demand for educational investment

for education, D_1 and D_2 in Figure 9.4, but the same supply curve. Each individual is presumed to invest the best amount for his own situation. The amount the second, whose demand curve is D_2, will invest is I_2, which exceeds the amount invested by the first. As with the case of differences in supply, the individual investing the larger amount will receive larger gross earnings. In Figure 9.4 the incremental earnings are represented by the area under the demand curve D_2 from I_1 to I_2 plus the area between the demand curves D_2 and D_1 from the origin to I_1. Contrary to the case of differences in supply, though, the individual investing the larger amount receives the higher marginal return if the supply curve slopes upward.

Higher gross earnings and incomes will thus be associated with greater investments in education. This is the case whether differences in the amount invested result from differences in demand or from differences in supply. The relation of marginal returns to amounts invested will differ, however. If differences in the amount invested result from differences in supply, larger investments will be associated with lower marginal returns. Differences in demand, however, would

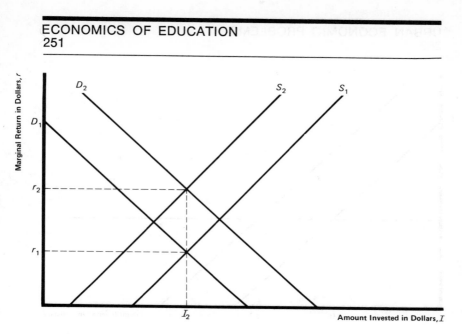

FIGURE 9.5
Equality of outcome in education

cause the marginal return to be higher the greater the amount
invested.

Social policy
toward education

Most Americans probably believe in equality of opportunity.
Insofar as this concept applies to education, it means identical
supply curves for investment in education. Equality of opportunity in this sense would eliminate differences in incomes
arising from differences in supply curves as shown in Figure
9.3. As Figure 9.4 shows, though, equality of opportunity
would not eliminate income differences associated with differences in demand for education.

Perhaps for this last reason, many people argue for what
might be characterized as equality of outcome instead. One
interpretation of this second notion of equality is that all
individuals should invest the same amount, regardless of their
demands for education. Equality of outcome on this first interpretation is pictured in Figure 9.5. To result in the same
amount of investment by individual 1 with the smaller demand for education, the supply schedule S_1 must lie below

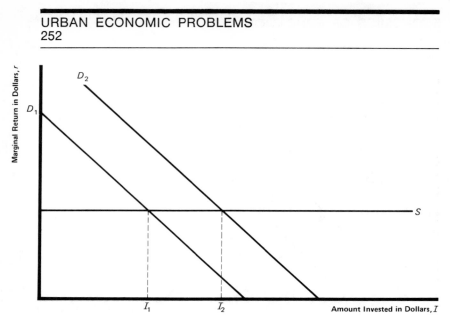

FIGURE 9.6
Equalized marginal returns to educational investment

that for individual 2. (If equality of outcome means identical
gross earnings, schedule S_1 would have to be lower still to
equalize the areas under the two demand curves. The following conclusions would apply even more strongly.) With equal
amounts invested, though, the marginal or additional income
generated by the second individual's investment, r_2, exceed
those of individual 1. If individual 2 were to offer individual
1 the amount 1 earns on his marginal investment and make
the additional expenditure himself, something would be left
over. Individuals 1 and 2 could thus both be made better
off by investing less in individual 1 and more in 2. As one
so often hears, not everyone should go to college.
Possibilities for mutual improvement always exist when individuals differ in their demand for education under equality
of opportunity if supply curves for education slope upward.
To utilize resources efficiently, supply curves for different individuals would not only have to be the same but would have
to be horizontal, as in Figure 9.6. It would be hard to think
of a terse, American-sounding phrase to characterize the world
illustrated in Figure 9.6. Essentially it means unlimited,
though not costless, opportunity. Indeed, for education to be

made truly costless to the individual, one would have to be paid a salary equal to one's gross earnings for going to school. (In this regard, Barney Poole, who played varsity football at the University of Mississippi both before and after World War II and at West Point during it, is alleged to have remarked during his second stint at Ole Miss, "I can't afford to turn pro.") Only by equalizing the marginal returns to education can one avoid the possibility of improvement by shuffling amounts invested. Of course, with differences in demand, the gross earnings of individual 2 in Figure 9.6 would exceed those of 1—indeed, by more than in Figure 9.4.

For this last reason, equalizing the marginal returns to education would seem undemocratic to most people. To the extent that public support for education is meant to redistribute income, however, there would seem to be no good reason to limit income redistribution to that achieved through education. As an alternative to college scholarships to ghetto youths, some might be offered loans to acquire nonhuman capital. Indeed, many youths, not only those from the ghetto, might benefit more from loans to set up auto repair businesses or photography studios. In view of the essentially identical characteristics of human and nonhuman capital formation, there is little distinction between labor and property on economic grounds. Almost surely more income inequality is associated with differences in the ownership of human than of nonhuman capital in the United States today.

Programs that come closest to achieving equality of marginal returns to investment in education are those for loans to college students. Two qualifications should be made, though. Most plans would allow students to borrow funds for tuition and living expenses at fixed interest rates. Such loans would be repaid out of earnings following graduation. However, in no such plan may students borrow annually up to their gross earnings as defined earlier. Even at private schools the major cost of education to the individual is the potential earnings he sacrifices. Second, in many plans, such as the widely heralded Yale plan, students would repay not a fixed amount per dollar borrowed but rather a fixed percentage of their net earnings for some period of time. The Yale plan would in effect make the supply schedule to individual 2 in Figure

9.6 higher than that to individual 1. The percentage repayment feature of the Yale plans is justified primarily by not wanting to discourage students from public service occupations, which are typically lower paid. As an alternative, though, society through government can make public service more attractive by offering higher salaries, perhaps through a subsidy scheme. As it stands, the Yale plan would induce too many to enter occupations such as teaching and the ministry, part of whose rewards are nonmonetary, or occupations in which more than an average investment in on-the-job training is made.

SOME IMPLICATIONS OF INVESTMENT IN HUMAN CAPITAL

Education and earnings distributions

One of the most useful insights provided by thinking of education as investment in human beings is that regarding the distribution of earnings received by different workers. A worker's earnings, of course, reflect his marginal productivity to employers in a market economy. Workers differ in their abilities and thus in the annual earnings they can achieve. Half a century ago it was correctly noted that ability tends to be more or less symmetrically distributed among human beings. This means that the fraction possessing, say, a given amount less than the average for the whole population is about equal to that possessing the same amount of above-average ability.

When one looks at earnings distributions, however, they are decidedly skewed in a positive direction. That is, the earnings distribution is stretched toward the right, or to larger values for annual earnings. Indeed, earnings would be distributed much more nearly symmetrically about their average when taking logarithms of earnings rather than their actual dollar values. In addition, many persons seem to believe that earnings vary more from worker to worker than might be justified on the basis of differences in ability.

Not surprisingly, there are many explanations for the variation in earnings among workers, some of which have already been discussed. One of the best, however, is provided by the point made in the first section: that actual earnings depend upon more than ability. It was argued that, neglecting differences in the timing of investment, earnings are given by

$$Y = X + r \cdot SC_- - C_c$$

where X is the return to raw labor, SC_- is total past investment in education, and C_c is current investment. Though the returns to raw labor might well be symmetrically distributed, the term $r \cdot SC_-$ introduces positive skewness into the distribution of Y provided r and SC_- are not too strongly negatively correlated.[2] The larger the component of earnings contributed by the returns to past investment, the more skewed one would expect earnings distributions to be. This expectation is confirmed by the fact that more-skilled occupations do indeed tend to have more highly skewed earnings distributions. Likewise, earnings distributions tend to be more skewed for older than for younger workers. For the latter, current investments, C_c, tend to be larger, reducing the impact of differences in returns to past investments.

Probably the best way to see the possible impact of returns to past investments on earnings is by numerical example. In Table 9.1, it is assumed that all investments are made by schooling. Thus, for s years, net earnings are zero, and for any $t > s$, gross earnings equal net earnings. As noted previously, assuming the same return r on all investments made, $Y = X(1 + r)^s$ for the postschooling period.

The first column of the table shows the ratio by which gross earnings would have to increase merely to cover the costs of previous investments. For a college graduate, postschool earnings would have to be somewhat more than six times those of a worker without any education. Annual earnings of $6.13 for every $1 return to raw labor would be necessary merely to cover the cost of past investments if the return were 12 percent per year. This magnitude will no doubt sur-

---

[2] Ibid., 9–10.

prise many readers. (For a really startling demonstration of the effects of compound interest, try calculating the present value of the $25 allegedly paid Indians for Manhattan Island several centuries ago!)

In the second column the entries in column one are shown as ratios to the first line. This is shown for comparison with actual annual earnings ratios in column three. The actual ratios are based on 1960 census data on annual earnings of experienced, white, male, nonfarm workers 35 to 44 years old living in the North and West, to remove the effects of other factors affecting annual earnings. One sees in comparing columns two and three that actual earnings do not vary nearly as much with education as one would expect on the basis of the hypothetical example. There are two reasons for this. First, the return assumed is that earned on college education. It appears, though, that marginal returns are higher for elementary and secondary education. Second, not all education is received as schooling. Though ultimately workers with more schooling may undertake more postschool investment as well, at younger ages less-schooled workers may have acquired more work experience. Regardless, the actual annual earnings differ-

TABLE 9.1
Influence of education on postschool earnings (r = 12 percent/year)

| YEARS OF SCHOOLING | $(1.12)^s$ | POSTSCHOOL EARNINGS RELATIVE TO 4 YEARS' SCHOOLING | |
		Expected (col. 1)	Actual[a]
Elementary, 1–7 (s = 4)	$1.57	$1.00	$1.00
8	2.48	1.57	1.11
Secondary, 12	3.90	2.48	1.43
College, 16	6.13	3.90	2.37

[a] Calculated from average annual earnings in 1959 of experienced, white, male, nonfarm workers 35 to 44 years old living in the North and West.
Source: U.S. Bureau of the Census, *United States Census of Population, 1960: Occupation by Earnings and Education*, Final Report PC(2)-7B (Washington, D.C.: U.S. Government Printing Office, 1963).

ence between college graduates and grade-school dropouts is large relative to other sources of earnings differences already cited in Chapter 7.

Mainly because it is difficult to determine how much human capital investment different individuals have made, it is difficult to state confidently how much earnings inequality is due to such differences. The number of years spent in school can be counted, as the Census Bureau does, but differences in the quality of schooling are difficult to determine. More important, perhaps, there is almost no information available on the extent of investment in the form of on-the-job training. Some very ingenious ways of surmounting these difficulties have been employed recently by Jacob Mincer.[3] His estimates suggest that half to four-fifths of the variation of annual earnings in 1959 of white, nonfarm males was attributable to differences in human capital.

Age-earnings profiles

In most of the earnings comparisons presented heretofore in this book, the age of workers has been held constant because it has long been recognized that earnings vary with age of a worker. Typically, annual earnings increase with age. The rate of increase slows down after a time, reaching a peak in the age range of 40 to 50 years. The increase in earnings at earlier ages has long been attributed to greater experience. The notion of education as investment in human capital provides a somewhat more precise explanation of age-earning profiles.

Recall from section one that net earnings are given by

$$Y_t = X + (r_1 C_1 + \cdots + r_{t-1} C_{t-1}) - C_t$$

where the subscripts refer to time periods when investments are made and returns are received. Net earnings at any age in relation to those received a year earlier are

$$Y_t - Y_{t-1} = r_{t-1} C_{t-1} + (C_{t-1} - C_t)$$

[3] Jacob Mincer, *Schooling, Experience, and Earnings* (unpublished, February 1973).

In words, the difference in net earnings has two components. The first is simply earnings on last year's investment. This first component, of course, cannot be negative. The second component is last year's investment minus this year's. If the amount invested declines over time, the second component will be positive as well. For both reasons, then, net or observed earnings will tend to increase with age.

The equation above also suggests that the greater the investments made in human capital, or the greater the Cs, the more important will be the influence of age on earnings. In particular, the receipt of returns on greater investments will generally mean that, once positive, earnings will increase more rapidly. Empirically, it does appear to be true that age-earnings profiles become steeper for workers who have acquired more schooling. The profiles of workers with more schooling also tend to reach a peak at later ages. The latter would result from larger investments being spread out over a longer time period. Finally, the fact that earnings increase at faster rates for more highly educated workers implies that variability of earnings for workers of a given age increases with the age of the group.

Specific training and unemployment rates

Investment in human capital also provides an explanation for some variations in the degree to which the unemployment rates of different groups in the labor force fluctuate with changes in the average unemployment rate for the labor force as a whole. Typically, unemployment rates fluctuate less for more highly skilled workers, for older workers than for younger ones, and for white than for nonwhite workers. Though there are many specific factors that might influence the amplitude of fluctuations in unemployment rates, the notion of specific on-the-job training provides a more or less unified explanation.

Specific training, as stressed earlier, raises a worker's productivity only so long as he is employed by the employer providing the training. An employer providing specific training would be willing to pay part of the costs of this training.

At the same time, when workers are to be laid off, the greater the amount an employer has invested in a worker, the more he stands to lose by laying him off. This is because the worker may well find another job before the employer seeks to rehire him. To replace him with a new worker would require new expenditure on specific training. Consequently the more specific training invested in a worker, the less likely he will be laid off.

At the same time, workers in whom investments in specific training have been made have less incentive to leave a job voluntarily in search of another. The more invested in specific training, the higher the earnings a worker can expect from the employer providing the training. Such is the case because employers pay only a part of the costs of training, or else the specifically trained worker has no incentive to remain. For both reasons then, separations from employment are typically less frequent for more highly skilled workers.

One might expect the typical managerial employee to have more specific training than the average clerical worker. Similarly, foremen and skilled craftsmen probably have more invested in themselves than the average laborer. Older workers, too, probably have a greater average duration of employment in their present jobs, as do white as compared with nonwhite workers. The major exception to the probable association between amplitude of fluctuation of unemployment rates and length of experience with a given employer is provided by the comparison of men and women workers. That the unemployment rates of women workers fluctuate less than those of men at the same age is probably due to their concentration in less cyclically sensitive employment and to the fact that, if laid off, women who are secondary earners may drop out of the labor force.

Recognition of training costs requires explicit discussion of another matter neglected until now. This is that wages paid are not the only component of the cost of hiring workers. Though for many purposes training costs may be neglected in comparing wage rates, account must be taken of them for others. For these purposes it is useful to think of employers as hiring workers up to the point where the total cost of employing them is equal to the marginal product. In addition to wages, the total costs include specific training and any fixed costs associated with hiring and separation of workers. These include the costs of arranging for and terminating the payment of wages, deductions for payroll taxes and personal income tax withholding, and participation in fringe-benefit programs. Also included in turnover costs are the extra expenses an employer bears because of absenteeism and low worker morale.

The lower the degree of labor turnover an employer experiences, the lower will tend to be the nonwage cost of employment he bears. Turnover may be influenced favorably in a variety of ways, for example, bowling teams, Christmas parties, and longer coffee-breaks. The most important, probably, is paying higher wages. One would thus expect employers for whom training and other cost of employing labor are relatively important to offer higher wages to workers of a given skill level in order to reduce the nonwage employment costs they bear. Those for whom labor turnover is less costly would pay lower wages. Workers who prefer steady employment will tend to be attracted to higher-paying firms. At the same time, those who prefer casual employment may be required to accept lower-paying jobs to obtain it.

EVIDENCE ON THE RETURN
TO INVESTMENT IN EDUCATION

In the United States education has long been viewed as the means of achieving a better life. Partly for this reason, great emphasis has been placed upon educational programs as means of eliminating poverty. An appraisal of the results of educational programs should seek to determine the returns to education in the form of increased earnings in relation to the costs of education. This section examines some of this evidence.

Estimates of the rate of return
to investment in schooling

A variety of estimates of the rate of return to investment in schooling have been made. This rate is the increase in annual earnings in dollars per dollar invested in schooling. Esti-

mates of this kind are useful in judging whether too few resources are being devoted to investment in schooling as compared with other investments and with production for current
consumption. For, if an added dollar spent on schooling produces an income stream of, say, 20 cents per year, while an
added dollar spent on constructing buildings or machinery
produces 14 cents, the output for the economy as a whole
is increased by reducing investment in nonhuman capital and
increasing that in schooling. Alternatively, if a certain kind
of school investment were to return only 5 cents per dollar
invested, the recipient of the 5 cents per year could be made
better off by giving him a claim on the income earned from
a dollar invested in machinery instead.

The rate of return on investment in schooling cannot be observed directly. Rather it is usually estimated on the basis
of data relating to actual annual earnings of persons who have
received different numbers of years of schooling. The resulting
estimates are subject to many severe problems. Probably the
most serious limitation is the positive correlation between
ability and the amount of schooling individuals actually obtain. As shown by Figure 9.4, more able individuals will have
higher demands for education and will make greater investments in themselves. Greater investments mean more years
of schooling. In addition, if supply curves for investment are
upward-sloping as in Figure 9.4, higher marginal returns will
be earned by more able individuals.

A variety of other limitations exist, however. Higher earnings
are not the only private return to education. Some returns
take the form of current consumption during the schooling
period; others are nonpecuniary returns associated with subsequent leisure or with more pleasant employment of the kind
discussed in Chapter 7. In addition, a year's schooling need
not be of the same quality for all groups, grade levels, or
places.

Among the first estimates were those of investment in college
education made by Gary Becker.[4] Becker suggested that the
private return net of income taxes for urban white males was

---

[4] Gary S. Becker, "Underinvestment in College Education?" *American Economic Review* 50 (May 1960), 347–348.

about 12.5 percent in 1940 and 10 percent in 1950. The lower figure for the latter year was almost wholly due to higher personal income taxes paid. For both years, the before-tax return on all costs, not merely private ones, was about 9 percent. For nonwhites the rate of return was about two percentage points smaller. Becker concluded that the rate of return to college education is roughly the same as that to physical capital used by business firms. Thus, there appeared to be little reason to believe that too few resources are devoted to investment in college education.

Later, more detailed estimates using 1959 earnings data from the 1960 census were published by Giora Hanoch.[5] These estimates were based on estimates of age-earnings profiles of the kind discussed in the previous section for individuals with different years of schooling. The effects of a variety of other factors associated with earnings differences were removed statistically from the raw data. Private rates of return before the payment of taxes were then calculated from the age-earnings profiles. In general the estimates suggest that the rate of return declines with years of schooling. For whites in the North, the return was about 22 percent for eight as opposed to five to seven years, 16 percent for twelve vs. nine to eleven years, and 12 percent for sixteen against thirteen to fifteen years. The latter agrees closely with Becker's estimate. Though of questionable reliability at higher levels of education, Hanoch's results generally suggest lower rates of return for nonwhites at all levels of schooling.

The fact that the returns estimated for nonwhites appear to be below those for whites may have important implications. Earlier it was pointed out that the supply of funds for investment in education is probably smaller for blacks than for whites. If this factor alone were at work, however, along with smaller investments one should also find that the marginal returns to investment should be higher, not lower, than those for whites. To explain the observed results, the demand for investment by blacks would have to be lower than for whites. A lower demand for black education could result from labor market discrimination, which becomes progressively more

---

[5] Giora Hanoch, "An Economic Analysis of Earnings and Schooling," *Journal of Human Resources* 2 (Summer 1967), 310–321.

severe at higher skill levels. It could also result from other economic and social conditions that limit the ability of blacks to capitalize on education, though innate differences in ability are also consistent with these estimates.

Citing more recent data from the 1966 Survey of Economic Opportunity, Finis Welch suggests that because of recent increases in the relative quality of black schooling, the returns to black education have risen.[6] Welch's findings indicate, though, that the returns to black schooling in the middle sixties were still below those of whites. Another recent study suggests, in contrast, that in 1967 the returns to black schooling were about the same as those for whites.[7] The study also found, contrary to what many believe, that blacks educated in rural areas or small towns in the South had not received poorer-quality schooling than other blacks insofar as school quality is reflected in earnings.

Even if the returns to black schooling were equal to those of whites, however, the economic evidence gives little confidence in better education as a means of equalizing the earnings of blacks and whites, for blacks still obtain fewer years of schooling than whites, which suggests that their demands for education are lower. With lower demands and equal marginal returns, black earnings would fall short of those obtained by whites. Thus, even though one wishes to support improved opportunities for blacks, programs other than improving black schooling may be better suited to the task.

Special education programs

Closely related to the last remark is evidence related to differences in expenditures on schooling and earnings. In recent years there has been a variety of attempts to improve educational performance by making greater public expenditures on schools or by adopting unconventional kinds of programs. In general, it is quite difficult to appraise the returns to such expenditures. The available evidence, however, fails to offer much assurance that greater expenditures on special educa-

[6] Finis Welch, "Black-White Differences in Returns to Schooling" unpublished paper presented at Conference on Discrimination in Labor Markets, Princeton University (October 1971).
[7] Leonard Weiss and Jeffrey G. Williamson, "Black Education, Earnings, and Interregional Migration: Some New Evidence," *American Economic Review* 62 (June 1972), 372–383.

tional programs offer returns sufficient to offset the opportunity costs of the resources used in such programs.

There are several reasons why it is hard to appraise the returns to special educational programs. Foremost, perhaps, is the fact that it is hard to get any systematic, useful information about them. Although one frequently reads isolated reports of apparently successful programs, one has a right to wonder whether other, less favorable appraisals simply go unnoticed or are deliberately buried. There are but few instances in which students exposed to special programs are randomly selected along with a control group not exposed to the program and before and after measurements of the performances of both groups made. Instead, most cases of above-average school expenditures occur in areas where students are from higher economic and social backgrounds, which are known to be associated with better performance on conventional measures of educational attainment. Perhaps most important, it is quite a problem to convert increased measured IQs or reading levels into greater future earning power. Yet it is the latter that is important in appraising better education as an antipoverty device.

By far the most complete and thorough evaluation of special educational programs is a study by Ribich.[8] This study attempts to determine the increased earning potential in relation to program costs of a variety of special educational programs. The only such program to show much promise is really not a school program at all but rather worker retraining. Worker retraining programs will be discussed in the following chapter. Ribich's appraisal, however, suggests that preschool programs, compensatory education, and greater-than-average per pupil expenditures in conventional schools all result in a smaller increment to earnings than the opportunity cost of resources used by the programs.

The preschool program Ribich analyzes is one that took place in selected Harlem schools in the early 1960s for preschool slum children.[9] Those volunteered for the program, consisting of intensive nursery school and enriched kindergarten classes,

---

[8] Thomas I. Ribich, *Education and Poverty* (Washington, D.C.: The Brookings Institution, 1968).
[9] Ibid., pp. 79–80.

were divided at random among experimental and control groups. The group receiving the special education showed a greater average gain of six IQ points, roughly comparable to 0.7 year additional schooling completed. The additional schooling, at average returns for the population as a whole, would result in increased earnings of about $1400 when discounted at a relatively low rate back to the start of the program. Yet the added costs were $2400 per pupil. In this connection it should be noted that the returns to preschool education are long delayed, twelve years supposing the education is received at age 4 and earnings begin at age 16. At rates of return of 12 percent per year, a dollar received twelve years from now is worth only about 25 cents today.

Ribich also reports on a compensatory education type of program, Higher Horizons in New York, and on estimates of greater earnings associated with Project Talent. Regarding the former he finds differences among experimental and control groups small and of uncertain direction. He estimates that the benefits of the program are at most 60 to 90 percent of their costs.[10] The Project Talent data consisted of sample data on American high school students gathered during the sixties. From these, attempts to infer the effects of greater per pupil expenditures on performance in conventional schooling may be made. Such inferences are difficult, however, because of the lack of experimental selection of treatment and control groups. Ribich's calculations imply benefits of only about $60 in increased present value of earnings of disadvantaged youths per $100 additional expenditure per student year.[11] Evidence such as this gives little basis for supposing that increased educational expenditure is an advantageous route to the elimination of poverty.

Education and poverty

Finally, a careful look at data on the incidence of poverty by years of schooling completed made possible by 1960 census data suggests that poverty is but little reduced by additional schooling beyond the elementary level. These data are presented in Table 9.2.

[10] Ibid., pp. 63–72.
[11] Ibid., p. 95.

In 1959 the incidence of poverty, as defined by the now famous "$3000 per year for an urban family of four in 1963 prices" standard, was perhaps 17.5 percent for the nation as a whole. Among husband-and-wife families in central cities whose head had less than eight years of elementary education, the figure was about the same. As the first column of Table 9.2 shows, completion of elementary school cuts the incidence of poverty about in half. Successive increases in educational attainment reduce the incidence of poverty further, but by progressively smaller amounts. Indeed, the poverty rates for high school dropouts seem but little higher than those of graduates, whereas going to college makes for even less of a difference over completing high school. In view of the great amount of public attention given to going to college, to say nothing

TABLE 9.2
Influence of education on poverty, 1959[a]

	PERCENTAGE OF FAMILIES POOR,[b] IN		
EDUCATION OF FAMILY HEAD	Central cities	Urban fringe	Rural farm areas
Elementary			
<8 years	17.2%	10.9%	40.9%
8 years	9.0	5.6	23.6
High school			
1–3 years	6.8	3.7	18.5
4 years	4.3	2.4	14.0
College			
1–3 years	3.9	2.5	11.1
≥4 years	3.0	2.0	6.5
Total	7.7	4.0	24.7

[a] Among husband-and-wife families with head 25 to 64 years old.
[b] Calculated using the following poverty lines based on adjustment for size and location of family: central city $2760, Urban fringe $2810, and rural farm $1780. These correspond closely to the $3000 for an urban family of four in 1963 prices standard but use a lower cutoff for farm families than the "official" definition. Source: Calculated from data in U.S. Bureau of the Census, *U.S. Census of Population: 1960, Sources and Structure of Family Income*, Final Report PC(2)-4C (Washington, D.C.: U.S. Government Printing Office, 1964), table 3.

of completing high school, Table 9.2 is quite revealing. Indeed, it suggests that a high school dropout in a farm area has far more to gain by moving to the city than by completing high school and staying put.

A study by Weisbrod suggests, indeed, that it is not worth the effort to try to get dropouts to finish high school.[12] Weisbrod studied the experience of a program in St. Louis from 1960 to 1962. The earnings of dropouts who returned to school were not known, so these were calculated on the basis of average earnings from the 1960 census for those completing and not completing high school. Even at the low discount rate of 5 percent per year used, the present value of increased earnings of rescued dropouts would have been about $3400. Yet, because the program achieved very little success in inducing dropouts to return to school, it cost about $8200 per rescued dropout.

SUMMARY

Education can be viewed as investment in human beings. The private returns to education include increased earnings in future years, and the earnings foregone while obtaining additional education constitute the most important component of private cost. Education is schooling if net earnings are zero or negative, on-the-job training if net earnings are positive. The latter may be either general or specific; general on-the-job training increases a worker's productivity to firms other than the one providing the training, but specific training does not. Employers pay part of the costs of specific training, but a worker bears the whole cost of general training. Education tends to be received early in life primarily because its opportunity cost rises with age.

The total number of dollars a worker invests in himself through education depends on forces affecting the marginal returns, or demand, and the marginal cost, or supply, of funds for investment. Greater investments are always associated with greater annual earnings. If differences in education result

[12] Burton A. Weisbrod, "Preventing High School Dropouts," in Robert Dorfman, ed., *Measuring Benefits of Government Investments* (Washington, D.C.: The Brookings Institution, 1965), pp. 117–149.

from differences in supply, larger investments are associated with lower marginal returns. But if due to differences in demand, those obtaining more education receive higher marginal returns. Equality of opportunity in education would eliminate earnings differences associated with differences in supply but not those arising out of differences in demand. Equality of outcome would result in differences in marginal returns if differences in demand exist, implying that a change in the pattern of investment by different individuals could make everyone better off.

A substantial part of annual earnings differences among individuals, perhaps one-half to four-fifths, is associated with differences in educational investments. The tendency for annual earnings to increase with the age of a worker may be explained by investments made in on-the-job training. Workers who are more highly skilled generally have more invested in them in the form of specific training by their employers. Since the employer would risk losing his investment if he laid them off, unemployment rates fluctuate less for more highly skilled workers. The marginal returns to college education appear to be about the same as the marginal returns to investment in machines, the marginal returns to less amounts of investment being greater. Economic evidence suggests that the marginal returns to educational investment in blacks are no greater than for whites, even though blacks obtain less of it. To date it appears that the returns to investment in most special educational programs are less than the opportunity costs of the funds spent.

CHAPTER 10

Programs for raising labor incomes

The preceding three chapters have discussed the important determinants of labor income in a market economy. Though some comments have been offered on methods for increasing the earnings of the poor, the principal focus has been on the way the economy operates. Particularly in view of the main conclusion of Chapter 9 that better education is not the panacea for eliminating poverty that it is widely believed to be, the time has now come to examine a variety of other questions related to the earnings of lower-income workers and proposals for raising them. The programs discussed in this chapter are what might be called labor market policies. Methods of raising the incomes of the poor through governmental transfer payments will be considered in Chapter 11.

MINIMUM WAGES

One of the oldest and most widely supported programs for raising the earnings of lower-income workers is minimum wage legislation. Such legislation establishes lower limits to the wages private employers may pay in certain kinds of employment, generally termed covered employment. Minimum wage legislation was first established on a nationwide basis by the Fair Labor Standards Act of 1938. Legal minimums have since been raised upon seven occasions, the latest being 1974, and their coverage expanded, particularly in 1961 and 1966. The legal minimum has tended to be low and it has shown little trend in the postwar period relative to average wage rates. It was 54 percent of average hourly earnings both in 1950 and 1968.

Even more than in the case of other matters considered in this book, public discussion of minimum wages is characterized by a great deal of heat relative to the light thrown on the subject. Thus, a careful analysis of the economic effects of minimum wages seems desirable.

Short-run effects

Consider a labor market as depicted in Figure 10.1. Initially the market is in equilibrium at the wage rate w_1 with L_1 workers hired at any moment. Now let a minimum wage of w_m

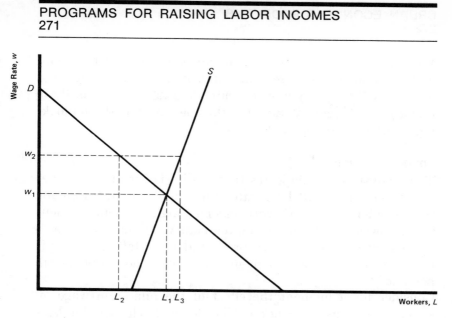

FIGURE 10.1
Short-run effects of minimum wages

be set. If w_m is less than or equal to w_1, employers will find it advantageous to pay wages at least as high as the minimum. Consequently the minimum will have no direct effect at all.

On the other hand, suppose the legal minimum is established at some rate above w_1, say w_2. Employers will no longer wish to employ L_1 workers. Rather, as indicated by the demand schedule D, the maximum number of workers employers will seek to hire is L_2. The reduction in employment may take many forms. Some firms faced with higher wage costs may shut down entirely. Others will use more machinery and more skilled labor relative to less-skilled workers affected by the minimum wage. All remaining in business will tend to produce smaller outputs because their costs have risen, hence they will seek to hire fewer workers. At the same time, additional workers may seek employment because of the higher wage rates paid those employed. The quantity of workers supplied rises to L_3. An excess supply of workers, $L_3 - L_2$, thus develops.

As was indicated in Chapter 8, with an excess supply of workers the fraction unemployed at any moment will tend to rise.

Workers who voluntarily quit or are laid off by certain employers following the general cutback in employment from L_1 to L_2 will generally have to search longer than previously to find a job. A larger fraction will thus be out of a job and looking for one at any moment.

Long-run effects

The analysis so far indicates that the initial impact of higher minimum wages will be greater unemployment rates among the affected groups of workers. The higher unemployment rates, however, will tend to be temporary. Though wage rates in covered employment are prevented from falling to eliminate the higher unemployment rates, other adjustments are possible.

Consider for a moment the effect of the minimum wage on average earnings per worker. The demand schedule for less-skilled workers affected by the minimum in the long run is almost surely elastic. (This last point is discussed more fully in the fourth section of this chapter.) Consequently, raising the wage rate from w_1 to w_2 reduces the aggregate amount paid out in the form of wages. At the same time the number of workers seeking employment may have increased. Thus, although the wage rate paid per employed worker per hour has risen, average annual earnings per worker will tend to fall. The average worker affected by the new minimum will thus find covered employment less attractive relative to alternative jobs than before the minimum was instituted.

The consequence of this is that some workers who otherwise would have sought jobs in the range of employments covered by minimum wages will seek them elsewhere instead. Retail trade was not covered by minimum wage legislation prior to 1961, and the 1966 amendments to the Fair Labor Standards Act first extended coverage to large establishments in certain service industries and to large farms. Most of agriculture has been exempt since the inception of federal legislation, as are household workers. Self-employed workers likewise are not covered; indeed, it is difficult to imagine how the self-employed could be subject to minimum wage legislation.

The increase in the supply of labor in uncovered occupations leads to a decline in wages in these occupations. Traditionally

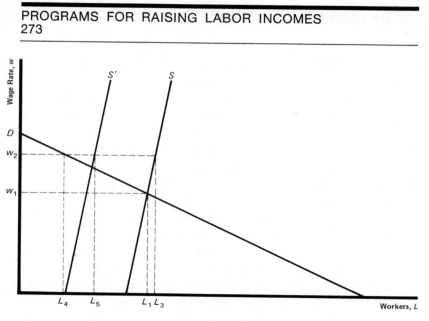

FIGURE 10.2
Long-run effects of minimum wages

in the United States earnings in uncovered occupations have been below average for the economy as a whole. At the same time, as indicated in Figure 10.2, the supply of labor to covered employments declines from S to S'. As it does, the excess supply of labor declines, as do unemployment rates.

Unemployment rates in covered employments may remain higher than they were prior to the minimum wage, however. When employed, workers in jobs covered by the minimum wage earn higher hourly rates than the same class of workers in uncovered employments. To equalize the net advantages of covered and uncovered employment, therefore, average hours worked per year would have to be smaller in covered than in uncovered employments. The shorter hours worked in covered employment may show up partly in more time spent searching for jobs, hence in higher unemployment rates. The labor supply shift from S to S' in Figure 10.2 may thus not eliminate the excess supply of labor entirely.

There is thus a strong presumption that minimum wage legislation harms the group it is designed to help. Though the initial impact is higher unemployment rates, its ultimate effect is less employment for the affected class of workers in covered employment and lower annual earnings for the group in both covered and uncovered employment.

At this point the reader may ask whether anyone benefits from the imposition of minimum wage rates. The answer is yes—workers initially earning more than the minimum. To illustrate why, suppose there are just two classes of workers, skilled and unskilled, and let a minimum wage greater than the earnings of the unskilled but less than skilled wage rates be instituted. If skilled and unskilled workers are perfect substitutes in production and firms covered by the legislation hire some of each group after the legislation becomes effective, the hourly earnings of skilled workers must rise in the same proportion as those of unskilled workers in covered employment. More generally, since skilled workers are certainly good substitutes for unskilled workers, the imposition of the minimum wage tends to increase the demand for skilled labor. Because of the reduction in the number of unskilled workers hired, however, the marginal productivity of skilled workers may rise less rapidly than that of unskilled workers actually employed once the minimum wage becomes effective. In any event, it is no surprise that labor unions, most of whose members are of above-average skill for the labor force as a whole, are among the strongest supporters of minimum wage legislation.

Empirical evidence on the effects of minimum wage legislation

Though the analysis just presented is standard and not at all subtle, many persons argue that special circumstances of one sort or another render it inapplicable. Thus good empirical evidence on the effects of minimum wages is certainly welcome. Yet such evidence is difficult to find.

Part of the problem is that much of the discussion about minimum wages focuses on unemployment. The foregoing analysis indicates, however, that increased unemployment rates of affected workers in covered employment are largely temporary. The principal lasting effect is a reduction in employment. Yet in our economy, employment changes take place for a variety of reasons unrelated to changes in minimum wages. Further, as noted earlier, the minimum wage has traditionally been low relative to average hourly earnings in manufacturing. Consequently, many kinds of covered employment are not directly affected by the minimum wage at all. The employment effects of minimum wages will show up principally in low-wages industries or areas. Finally, the demand for, and thus employment of, workers earning more than the minimum wage probably rises because of the legislation. Thus, some kinds of employment may actually increase.

Politicians supporting minimum wage legislation are usually quick to point out that unemployment rates for the economy as a whole have generally fallen when minimum wage rates have been raised. Overall this is correct but beside the point. Shortly after the 1949 increase the United States entered the Korean War. In 1956, 1961, and 1967 the economy was in a cyclical upswing each time a new minimum became effective. Consequently in each case one would have to look closely indeed to pick up the effects of the new minima on unemployment rates. After all, one cannot see a virus through a magnifying glass.

The effects of minimum wage legislation have become more pronounced in the 1960s as the coverage has been extended. Actual or relative employment effects have been discovered by many studies of different periods, industries, and areas. An excellent summary of this evidence on the employment effects of minimum wages is contained in a recent book by John M. Peterson and Charles Steward, Jr.[1] They conclude that "the impression created in most government studies that no significant adverse employment effects occur is erroneous," and add that academic research demonstrates adverse relative employment effects that are directly related to the relative wage impact of minimum wages.[2]

Probably the most dramatic bit of evidence on the effects of minimum wages is the experience in Puerto Rico when the Fair Labor Standards Act first became effective there at the same time as on the U.S. mainland. Indeed, the Puerto

---

[1] John M. Peterson and Charles T. Steward, Jr., *Employment Effects of Minimum Wage Rates* (Washington, D.C.: American Enterprise Institute for Public Policy Research, 1969).
[2] Ibid., pp. 153–154.

Rico experience represents a critical or dramatic "experiment" of the kind rarely found in matters relating to economic affairs. The initial federal minimum wage of 25 cents an hour was only 40 percent of average hourly earnings in manufacturing in the United States, but it was twice the level of average factory wages in Puerto Rico. To quote Peterson and Stewart,

The immediate effects were disastrous. Some employers refused to comply with the new law and many others shut down temporarily. In the island's major industry, home needlework, which had been paying wages as low as three to four cents an hour, employment and output dropped to a small fraction of its former level within a year's time.[3]

As a result, even Congress got the message, and in 1940 the Fair Labor Standards Act was amended insofar as it applied to Puerto Rico.

A recent study by Kosters and Welch has provided almost as clear evidence on the impact of minimum wages for the U.S. economy as a whole.[4] They find that higher minimum wages have reduced the shares of teenage workers, who are less experienced and lower-paid, in normal employment and increased those of adult workers. On balance, then, the evidence fairly strongly supports the conclusion that minimum wage legislation has adverse, not favorable, consequences for the incomes of workers paid lower wage rates. Minimum wages as a policy for raising the earnings of lower-wage workers is rather like taking heroin to kick a methadone addiction.

CENTRAL CITY GHETTOS AND SUBURBAN JOBS

Most readers are aware of the tendency for urban areas to grow more rapidly in their outer parts since the end of World War II. This has been true for employment of most kinds as well as for population. Yet blacks and other minority per-

---

[3] Ibid., p. 123.
[4] Marvin Kosters and Finis Welch, "The Effects of Minimum Wages on the Distribution of Changes in Aggregate Employment," *American Economic Review* 62 (June 1972), 323–332.

sons have tended to remain in the central city. Especially in the early 1960s, when unemployment rates were above the postwar average for most groups in the labor force, it was fashionable to argue that the high unemployment rates of blacks were due to the suburbanization of jobs. Thus, special transportation systems, relocation of central-city minority persons to suburban areas, and a variety of other proposals for improving access to suburban jobs have been made.

This section will inquire into the probable effects of suburbanization of employment on central-city residents. First, the theoretical case for higher minority group unemployment rates will be examined. Then what little empirical material there is bearing on the question will be discussed.

Theoretical basis

Probably the strongest reason for believing that the suburbanization of employment had adverse employment effects on black and other minority central-city residents is the matter of transport costs. A shift of the location of plants or stores from the central city to the suburbs would increase the time and other costs central-city residents incur in getting to and from work. This is the case because relatively few may own automobiles, and suburban jobs, being widely dispersed, are difficult to reach by bus or other means of public transportation.

One may readily grant that the suburbanization of employment places would increase the costs of transport to work for many central-city residents. An increase in transport costs to work, given the gross daily wage paid by employers, reduces the net daily wage the worker receives after his travel expenses are deducted. However, as was seen in Chapter 7, labor-force participation rates of primary workers tend to be highly unresponsive to wage rates received. For such workers, the principal effect of suburbanization of employment would be a reduction in net earnings, not employment. Working wives and teenage workers might withdraw from the labor force in significant numbers in response to a fall in the wage net of transport costs they might earn. Such withdrawals would represent an increase in the number not employed. But they would increase unemployment mainly to the extent that such

workers tended to enter and leave the labor force more frequently than before.

One response to a fall in the net earnings of central-city workers whose job locations shifted to the suburbs would be to
move their residences closer to their jobs. It is widely argued,
though, that nonwhites are "excluded" in some sense from
the suburbs. This is mistaken. Though most nonwhites are
central-city residents, virtually every major U.S. city has suburban black enclaves. With a suburbanization of jobs, blacks
would offer more for housing in suburban ghettos than in
central-city ones relative to what they would have offered
prior to the change in job locations. Suburban ghettos would
thus tend to grow and central-city ones to contract. There
is little reason to believe this last has happened, however.
The few instances of expansion of blacks into suburban areas
seem more like a spilling-over of the central-city black residential area into the suburbs rather than an expansion of
suburban black areas.

Still another reaction to lower earnings of central-city residents would be for firms to set up stores or plants in ghetto
areas. For if the net earnings of black workers had fallen because of the suburbanization of their jobs, other employers,
especially those for whom labor costs are of particular importance, would find ghetto locations more attractive. There apparently has been little tendency for new plants or stores to
be set up in ghetto areas in recent years. If anything, the
trend seems to be the other way.

It can be concluded that a shift of jobs to suburban locations
would reduce net earnings rather than employment. Lower
net earnings of a particular group would not be expected to
produce higher unemployment rates as such. However, it
might be argued that central-city blacks spend more time
searching for jobs as some jobs shift to suburban locations.
Many hints as to where to look for jobs come from friends
or neighbors. If few of them are employed in suburban jobs,
central-city blacks may learn of few suburban job openings.
In addition it may take longer to search any given opening
if it is in a suburban area. In Chapter 8, though, it was pointed
out that an increase in the costs of search reduces the acceptance wage and thus increases the fraction of job openings

a worker of given skills would accept. Consequently, the number of jobs searched would decline, counteracting the greater amount of time required to search a given job. Though the effect on the average duration of job search is not clear without knowledge of the relevant numerical magnitudes, it is widely believed by economists that increasing the costs of search increases its duration.

Empirical considerations

There is little good empirical evidence on the impact of the suburbanization of jobs on the employment and earnings of central-city blacks. This is the case partly because until the 1960 census there was little systematic data on the distribution of total employment within urban areas. There is, however, some evidence bearing indirectly upon the matter. Most important, perhaps, is the fact that places of residence as well as employment have been becoming more decentralized in urban areas. Coupled with the fact that historically central cities have generally contained a larger fraction of an urban area's jobs than of its residents, it is by no means clear that persons remaining in the central city have been adversely affected by recent suburbanization of employment.

Data have been collected on both manufacturing employment and populations of forty-six central cities and the standard metropolitan statistical areas (SMSAs) of which they are a part.[5] (The SMSA is a combination of contiguous counties containing a central city of 50,000 or more persons and its suburban areas.) These forty-six include most of the larger U.S. cities as well as some smaller ones, omitting only those such as New York and the San Francisco Bay area, which have more than one central city. From 1947 to 1958 the fraction of the SMSA's manufacturing production workers employed in the central city declined in thirty-eight of the forty-six urban areas. This, of course, is consistent with common observation. However, during essentially the same period, 1950 to 1960, the fraction of an area's population residing in the central city likewise declined, but at a slightly greater

---

[5] Richard F. Muth, *Cities and Housing* (Chicago: University of Chicago Press, 1969).

rate. In all but four of the forty-six areas the central city's population share was smaller in 1960 than in 1950. In 1950, only ten of the central cities had a larger population share than their share in employment of manufacturing production workers.

By 1960, however, only six did. At the end of the decade there was but one area in which the central city's share of production worker employment had fallen below its population share. There were five areas, however, in which the central city's share of production worker employment rose above its population share during the decade. The vast majority of central cities had larger shares of production worker employment than of population both at the beginning and the end of the fifties. On balance, however, the central city's share of employment tended to rise relative to its population share rather than the reverse.

A recent study by Kalachek and Goering concluded that central cities typically had a higher proportion of jobs than residents in 1960 in the categories of employment most relevant to central-city blacks.[6] In 1960, 52 percent of all blue-collar workers lived in the central city but 59 percent worked there. Both for semiskilled and unskilled blue-collar workers, 54 percent lived in the central city and 57 percent worked there. Of workers with annual earnings under $3000 per year, 52 percent lived in the central city in 1960 and 56 percent worked there. On balance, then, even in the job categories most relevant for the employment prospects of ghetto dwellers, central cities in 1960 were net importers of workers from suburban areas.

Another bit of evidence regarding the suburbanization-of-jobs argument for the unemployment rates of central-city blacks is the behavior of unemployment rates over time. If accessibility of jobs to members of central-city minority groups was declining over time and higher black unemployment rates were the result, one would expect to discern trends in black unemployment rates nationally. It was pointed out in Chapter

---

[6] Edward D. Kalachek and John M. Goering, eds., *Transportation and Central City Unemployment,* a report submitted to the U.S. Department of Housing and Urban Development, Washington University, St. Louis, Mo. (March 1970), p. 3.

8, though, that once differences resulting from varying aggregate unemployment rates nationally are removed, there is little evidence of an upward trend in unemployment rates for less-skilled workers or for nonwhites. Indeed, one finds such trends only for teenage workers. Teenage unemployment rates tend to be rising over time for whites and nonwhites, males and females, and for youths attending and not attending school. It is thus difficult to make any kind of case for trends in black unemployment rates.

One of the strongest pieces of evidence regarding the suburbanization of job hypothesis is the Tempo Northwest experiment in St. Louis in the late sixties. Tempo Northwest operated sixteen fifty-seat buses from the heart of the St. Louis ghetto to the Hazelwood industrial area of St. Louis County, approximately twenty miles away, which contains some of the largest employers in the St. Louis area, including the McDonald-Douglas aircraft plant. Sizable sums were spent through a St. Louis advertising agency to promote the transport facility among ghetto residents. The special bus route considerably reduced the time necessary to make the trip.

Yet the experiment was a flat failure. As Kalachek and Goering report, Tempo Northwest led to relatively few jobs for ghetto workers.[7] Indeed, they state that "the goal of formal cost-benefit evaluation was abandoned when early results indicated that the costs of Tempo Northwest would greatly exceed any recognizable benefits."[8] Whatever the reasons for the problems of ghetto workers, it surely seems that transportation to suburban jobs is not one of them.

A more recent study by Bennett Harrison presents data on average weekly earnings and on unemployment rates for urban males in March 1966, classified by residential location.[9] For whites there is a clear tendency for improvement when comparing first central-city poverty areas with the rest of the central city and then the latter with suburban areas. Weekly earnings rise progressively and unemployment rates fall, espe-

---

[7] Ibid., pp. 7–8.
[8] Ibid., p. vi.
[9] Bennett Harrison, "Education and Underemployment in the Urban Ghetto," *American Economic Review* 62 (December 1972), 796–812.

cially with the first step in the comparisons. There is little difference in weekly earnings or unemployment rates for non-whites, however. Though average weekly earnings of nonwhite suburban males exceeded those in central-city poverty areas, they were actually a little smaller than those in the rest of the central city. Furthermore, the mean unemployment rate of nonwhite suburban males was 8.8 percent as compared to 10.4 percent for the corresponding group in central-city poverty areas. There was no statistically significant difference between the two rates. From these comparisons it is by no means clear that central-city residence reduces the earnings of blacks.

JOB TRAINING
AND RETRAINING

Unlike many programs discussed so far, some job training programs appear to produce benefits for lower-income workers that exceed the opportunity cost to the economy of providing them. The rationale for such programs is poorly understood, and the nature of the genuine benefits they provide often is overlooked. This section concentrates on the rationale for worker training, the benefits of such training, and evidence regarding program effectiveness.

Rationale
for training programs

Most arguments for training programs are based upon a crude and woefully inadequate view of labor markets. Most proponents of these programs appear to believe that a fixed number of jobs of various kinds are available. If the number of workers seeking a particular type of job exceed the number available, some of these workers must remain unemployed. In similar fashion, if the number of workers seeking jobs of another kind fall short of the number available, unfilled vacancies must remain. In this view, the task of training programs is to convert workers seeking jobs existing in inadequate number to workers seeking jobs with unfilled vacancies. Indeed, the situation is viewed as requiring the conversion of desk-calculator operators into keypunch operators, or unemployed aerospace engineers into pollution control specialists.

The view just described may well characterize a labor market as it exists at one moment, but it is exceedingly myopic. Such imbalances do exist at any moment, as indicated by the discussion of excess supply of labor and unemployment in Chapter 8. But the market economy has built-in corrective mechanisms. The number of jobs of a given kind is a decreasing function of the wage rate paid in such jobs relative to the employer's cost of other jobs and nonhuman productive factors. The number of workers seeking jobs of a particular kind is an increasing function of the wage rate such jobs pay. An excess of job seekers means that the wage currently being paid for a particular job exceeds the market equilibrium wage.

Apart from minimum wage laws, union-enforced wage rates, and similar forces, wage rates tend to adjust downward if an excess supply of labor exists. Though this adjustment may be protracted, the evidence from the early thirties, cited in Chapter 8, clearly indicates that such adjustments do in fact take place. In addition, when wage rates are generally rising due to inflation or technological improvement, which raise the demand for labor, downward adjustment of relative wage rates may merely require that money rates rise less rapidly over time than they otherwise would. Even where forces such as minimum wage legislation impede the adjustment of wages, as was seen earlier in this chapter, a movement of job seekers to other locations or kinds of jobs will tend to eliminate the imbalance.

In the longer run, then, a decline in the demand for aerospace engineers and scientists in California—to take a recent extreme example—will result in lower annual earnings for such workers in the particular location. Suppose that when making their career decisions, some aerospace engineers viewed this occupation as being as attractive as certain alternatives. Then if an unanticipated decline in demand, and hence earnings, of aerospace engineers occurs, these alternative occupations will become relatively more attractive in terms of their prospective earnings and other conditions of employment.

Though few aerospace engineers can be considered poverty-stricken, the same principles apply to lower-income workers. As was argued in the last section of Chapter 8, the lasting impact of reductions in the demand for unskilled labor has not been higher unemployment for them. Rather, it is in a reduction of their earnings rates relative to earnings in more highly skilled occupations. Even though breadwinners in lower-income families may have initially secured appropriate schooling and on-the-job training, changed labor market conditions may mean that additional investments in human capital are now called for. Worker training might also yield returns in excess of those on other investments if some workers, because of the high cost of funds for investment in education, initially obtained less education than they would have had it been no more costly to them than to the average worker.

Of course, one might reasonably ask at this point whether, if such investments are privately profitable, private individuals will undertake them on their own initiative. To some extent they will, no doubt. At the same time, the failure of some individuals to undertake further human capital investment reflects its unprofitability relative to other uses of their time. However, the costs of retraining may be large in some cases, requiring the sacrifice of a considerable part of an individual's potential earnings for a year or two. In the absence of borrowing, training would require a severe cutback in a family's level of current consumption. Borrowing amounts anything like the sacrifice of one's current earning potential on the private market might only be done at very high rates of interest. Essentially, the supply schedule of funds for investment in themselves, as discussed in the second section of Chapter 9, may be very steep after some point, particularly for the older worker who is his family's principal breadwinner. Through training programs, society as a whole can provide funds for investment in human beings at lower rates—rates more nearly equal to the opportunity cost of such funds elsewhere in the economy. Probably the main reason why individuals cannot secure such funds for themselves is the difficulties private lenders face in insuring their repayment.

Benefits and costs of training

Much discussion seems to suggest that the major benefit of training is that a trained individual can obtain any kind of job. Indeed, many evaluations of training programs merely count the number of workers who were unemployed at the time they started training and who found a job at the completion of it. This kind of evaluation, however, would be appropriate only if the myopic labor market view were correct.

A more appropriate view is to see the present value of the increased lifetime earnings that result from training. Unemployment is one factor affecting differences in lifetime earnings produced by training but probably not the main one. As stressed in Chapter 8, unemployment is far less a permanent or chronic condition than it is a transient one. The labor force is in a constant state of flux, with workers constantly entering and leaving it. The greater the rate of job turnover in a particular occupation, the more frequently will the average worker in it be seeking a new job and the greater the amount of time he is unemployed. If, as a result of training, a worker switches to a kind of job in which unemployment rates are lower, his annual earnings will rise on the average.

In the U.S. economy, however, there is a strong negative relation between wage rates and unemployment rates, with higher-paying jobs also carrying less frequent periods of unemployment. (The association is not perfect, however; some occupations pay higher hourly earnings to compensate for more frequent periods of unemployment.) The major result of obtaining a more skilled job is the higher hourly earnings associated with it. To take a hypothetical example, suppose that occupation A has average unemployment rates of 10 percent and a wage rate of $2 per hour and occupation B an unemployment rate of 5 percent and hourly wages of $4. Then average annual earnings in occupation A, assuming a full year's work is 2000 hours, are $3600, whereas in B they are $7600. All but $400, or 90 percent, of the difference, however, is due to higher hourly earnings. This illustrates the fact that the major benefit to worker retraining is the higher hourly earnings such training allows.

In calculating the benefits of training, it is necessary to take into account the fact that a dollar received a year from now is not worth the same as a dollar now. Rather a dollar received sometime in the future is worth the amount of a loan a dollar will pay off at that time. At an interest rate of 10 percent per year, a dollar five years from now is worth roughly $.61, a dollar ten years from now $.37, and so forth. Similarly, a dollar each year forever is worth $10, a dollar every year for twenty years about $8.64.[10] Thus, the returns to training depend to some extent upon the age at which it is received. The effect is not substantial, however, if the training is received even at what to most readers will seem the advanced age of forty-five.

The present value of a dollar a year forever, however, depends very much upon the rate at which one discounts future earnings. At 5 percent per year a dollar per year in perpetuity is worth $20, whereas at 12.5 percent per year it is worth $8. The returns to training depend very much upon the rate at which future earnings are discounted. There is considerable difference of opinion among economists as to what is the appropriate rate. More nonsense appears in professional discussions of the question than any other topic. Five percent or so is commonly used as a measure of the opportunity cost to the economy of funds used for governmental programs. However, 12.5 percent is much closer to the mark.[11]

The costs of worker training programs, of course, include the direct costs of teachers, equipment, and resources. As stressed in Chapter 9, though, these are probably a minor part of the total. The biggest is earnings foregone during the training period. It is felt by some that if unemployed workers are taken into training programs that the foregone earnings are zero. As was argued in Chapter 8, though, unemployment tends to be a temporary rather than a permanent state. Although high unemployment among the class of worker being trained may mean that on the average foregone earnings per worker tend to be smaller than otherwise, on the average income is sacrificed in obtaining training.

Evidence on the benefits and costs of worker retraining

Though many types of worker training programs were instituted during the 1960s, there have been relatively few careful

---

[10] For those readers wishing to check my arithmetic, the numbers in the text were calculated for continuous compounding with interest at the stated rate of payments made at the annual rate of $1.

[11] The one really good discussion of the issue is Arnold C. Harberger, "On Measuring the Social Opportunity Cost of Public Funds," *IDA Economic Papers,* Arlington, Va. (May 1971).

evaluations of them. Indeed, as most programs seem to be motivated by the myopic view of the labor market, most attempts at evaluation merely state the number of previously unemployed workers who find jobs at the completion of the program. Ribich, however, in the work cited in the preceding chapter, discusses the results of three evaluations of retraining programs.[12]

The three studies, all of which presumably relate to older workers rather than to youths, reported vastly different estimates of benefits in relation to costs. All three, however, showed benefits substantially in excess of costs. Ribich discusses differences among them and revises the estimates for comparability and for converting them to the most economically justifiable basis. Adjustment considerably reduces the difference in benefits in relation to costs and lowers them. Even after his adjustments, though, benefits exceed costs by a factor of three times. Though Ribich uses a 5 percent discount rate, where 12.5 percent would seem a more appropriate figure, the training programs certainly appear to be economically more efficient than purely redistributive measures for raising the incomes of certain lower-income workers.

In a more recent study, Harden and Barus evaluated the results of a variety of Manpower Development and Training Act (MDTA) program in Michigan in the early 1960s.[13] Among other things, they estimated the gains in annual earnings attributable to training and the costs of this training. The latter included foregone earnings, expenses during the class, and costs of instruction and administration. For short programs, those involving 60 to 200 hours of training, the increase in annual earnings was almost three times the total costs of the program, suggesting very high rates of return indeed. For longer programs, however, annual earnings of trainees were actually lower in the year following training than estimated earnings in the absence of training. This may have been because workers enrolling in longer programs received more on-the-job training from their employers once

---

[12] Thomas I. Ribich, *Education and Poverty* (Washington, D.C.: The Brookings Institution, 1968), pp. 38–50.
[13] Einar Harden and Michael E. Barus, *The Economic Benefits and Costs of Retraining* (Lexington, Mass.: Heath, 1971).

their training was terminated. It also suggests, however, that some types of training may be inappropriate. Though good empirical evidence on worker training programs is scanty because annual earnings for a protracted period following training are especially difficult to determine, the evidence suggests that such programs may yield benefits substantially in excess of their costs. Considerable research is needed, however, to determine which kinds of programs are beneficial.

AN EMPLOYER
OF LAST RESORT?

Particularly during presidential election years one frequently hears the assertion that the federal government should become an employer of last resort. This means that it should stand ready to offer jobs to workers who are unable to find them on the private market. The underlying rationale for such a suggestion is similar to the naive argument for worker training programs, namely that a more or less permanent excess of job seekers over jobs available exists for some groups of workers. Though this notion is mistaken except for relatively short periods, a case may be made for programs to increase the demand for workers with below-average earnings opportunities.

Direct hiring

Most proposals for increasing the demand for lower-paid workers involve the hiring of workers by the federal government, either directly or under federally sponsored programs. Many such programs suppose that hiring will be done for public service employment, as in hospitals, but the purpose for which workers are hired is largely irrelevant to an appraisal of their labor market impacts. In analyzing the effects of direct hiring, suppose that prevailing market wage rates are paid, as is customary in government hiring. If higher than market rates are paid, of course, the government would become an employer of first resort. Either it would employ all workers of a particular class, or it would limit the benefits of the program to a favored group.

The effects of government hiring programs are to increase the demand for the particular group of workers at whom the

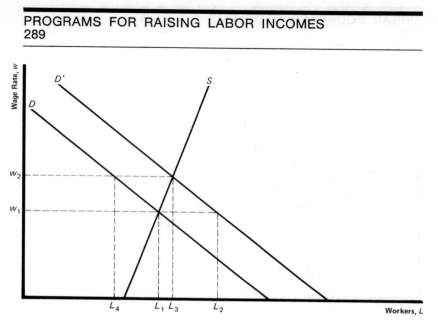

FIGURE 10.3
Effects of direct hiring programs for low-income workers

program is aimed. Consider Figure 10.3, where, for the particular group, demand is D and supply S. The market equilibrium wage initially is thus w_1, and L_1 workers are employed at any particular moment. Though some degree of labor turnover will probably exist, and thus some unemployment, at the wage w_1 no excess supply or demand for workers exists. Now, let the government seek to hire $L_2 - L_1$ workers at prevailing market wage rates, so that the demand for the particular group of workers rises from D to D'.

The increase in demand will lead to a rise of wages for the group from w_1 to w_2 in the new equilibrium and an increase in employment from L_1 to L_3. The extent to which employment increases depends, of course, on the elasticity of the supply curve of workers of the particular group. As was argued in Chapter 7, empirical evidence mainly suggests that labor force participation rates of primary workers or heads of families tend to be very unresponsive to earnings rates. Thus, the increase in demand would do little to increase the employment of breadwinners. Rather, it would largely increase their annual earnings. Direct hiring might, however, tend noticeably to increase the employment of wives and teenagers.

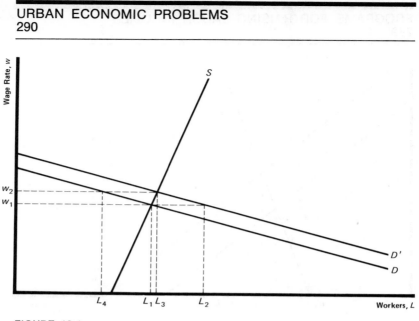

FIGURE 10.4
Labor demand elasticity and direct hiring programs

In Figure 10.3 one sees that the increase in employment is less than the number of workers hired under the federal program. The difference is made up in a reduction of workers hired by conventional employers—private employers and various levels of government besides the direct hiring program. The number of workers displaced from conventional employment is $L_1 - L_4$. The flatter or more elastic the labor demand curve at w_1, the greater will be the displacement of workers from conventional employment and the less will the wage rate tend to rise. This last point is illustrated by a comparison of Figures 10.3 and 10.4. In Figure 10.4 everything is the same as in Figure 10.3 except that the demand curves are flatter. One sees from Figure 10.4 that conventional employment declines more and the market wage rises less than in Figure 10.3. Indeed, in the limit as D and D' become perfectly elastic, D' coincides with D and the market wage remains unchanged.

In Figures 10.3 and 10.4 the expenditures made by the federal government, either directly or indirectly to support the hiring program, are equal to $(L_3 - L_4)$ times w_2. The increase in income per worker is $(w_2 - w_1)$, and the total benefits essentially $(w_2 - w_1)$ times L_1 since the supply curve is probably a very inelastic one. In comparing the figures one sees that expenditures under the program are larger relative to the benefits of the program the flatter or more elastic are the demand curves D and D'. Thus, the benefit-cost ratio for government hiring programs depends critically upon the private market demand elasticity for lower-wage workers.

Though little direct evidence on demand elasticities for less-skilled workers exists, direct hiring is likely to be a relatively unattractive labor market strategy. Even if the demand for less-skilled workers is no more elastic than for all labor in the economy, direct hiring is likely to be much more costly than other measures for raising the incomes of lower-income persons.[14] The basic reason is that the increase in earnings depends upon the vertical shift in the demand curve. Direct hiring shifts the demand curve horizontally, however, and the more elastic the conventional demand curve for labor, D, the smaller is the vertical shift for any given horizontal shift.

Wage subsidies

One of the simplest and most direct means of vertically shifting the demand curve for less-skilled labor is through paying a wage subsidy. Such a subsidy could probably be implemented most easily by paying conventional employers a bonus for hiring such workers. Employers would then receive not only the worker's marginal contribution to the revenues of the firm but also the bonuses. Competition among employers for workers of the group being subsidized would then bid up the wage conventional employers would offer them.

The effects of a wage subsidy are illustrated in Figure 10.5. In it, the same underlying conditions of labor demand and supply depicted in Figure 10.4 are shown. Rather than hiring less-skilled workers, however, the government pays employers an amount $w_2 - w_1$ for each such worker he hires. The conventional demand curve for less-skilled labor thus shifts vertically by the amount of the subsidy. For L_1 workers employers in

[14] Richard F. Muth, "The Evaluation of Selected Present and Potential Poverty Programs," Study S-244, Institute for Economic Analysis, Economic and Political Studies Division, Arlington, Va. (January 1966).

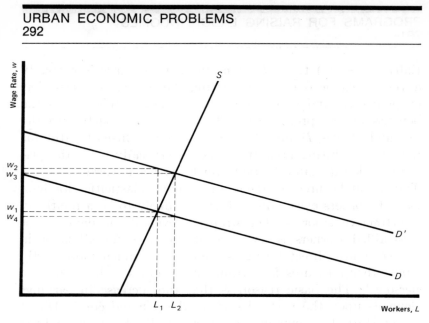

FIGURE 10.5
Effects of wage subsidies for low-income workers

the aggregate would be willing to pay a wage of w_2, w_1 of which reflects the worker's marginal product and $w_2 - w_1$ the subsidy. Given that L_1 workers are employed, if any worker were paid a wage less than w_2, some other employer could add more to his revenues than to his costs by hiring the worker at a wage higher than the current employer pays.

The new equilibrium position when the wage subsidy is being paid is L_2 workers employed at a wage of w_3. How much L_2 exceeds L_1 and w_3 falls below w_2 depends principally upon the elasticity of the labor supply curve. If the subsidy were paid only in certain kinds of employment—say in schools, hospitals, and other "public service" jobs—the relevant labor supply schedule would probably be a highly elastic one. In this case, L_2 would be large relative to L_1, w_3 close to w_1. The net impact of the subsidy would be to shift less-skilled workers out of other employments into public service, with little increase in earnings per worker.

If, however, the subsidy were paid to employers generally for hiring less-skilled workers, the labor supply schedule probably would be a relatively inelastic one, as shown in Figure 10.5. The rise in relative wage undoubtedly would induce some workers who would have secured more training and entered more highly skilled occupations to enter less-skilled positions instead. If payment of the subsidy were restricted to workers earning less than \$4 per hour, say, this effect probably would be relatively small though. The new equilibrium level of employment would be L_2, close to L_1, and the new equilibrium wage w_3, close to w_2.

It would be a relatively easy matter to vary the subsidy inversely with the wage that the worker would receive net of the subsidy, which is w_4 in Figure 10.5. The government would merely offer a bonus equal to some fraction, perhaps half, of the difference between, say, \$4 per hour and the wage he is actually paid. Consider a worker, for example, who would be paid \$2 per hour in the absence of the subsidy. The new equilibrium wage for such a worker would be \$2.67. For each hour the worker is hired the employed would receive \$2 worth of output and half of \$1.33. At any lower wage rate, \$2.40 per hour, his employer would receive \$2.80 for each hour he hires the worker, so the worker's wage would be bid up by competition among employers. On the other hand, a worker receiving \$3 per hour in the absence of the subsidy would receive \$3.33 per hour after the subsidy were instituted, a smaller absolute and relative increment than the first worker receives.

A wage subsidy for less-skilled workers would attack directly the principal employment problem facing the poor, which is not the inability to find a job, but the meager rate of pay for jobs open to less-skilled workers. To the extent, however, that minimum wages or other factors limit the availability of certain kinds of jobs, a wage subsidy would tend to undo the effects of such wage floors. For, if the minimum wage were less than w_3 but higher than w_1 in Figure 10.5, the wage subsidy would negate its effects. Also, the wage subsidy scheme would overcome objections to income maintenance programs based on the so-called Protestant ethic. ("Political ethic" would be a better term.) For, a person would have to be employed to collect the bonus. Mainly, however, wage subsidies would seem a preferable alternative to most other labor market strategies for dealing with poverty because they are suited to the probable conditions of demand and supply of less-skilled workers in the U.S. economy.

There are many practical problems associated with the payment of such a subsidy, only some of which will be discussed here. Perhaps the principal one insofar as the general public is concerned is how the subsidy would be paid and especially to whom. To an economist, how the subsidy would be paid is a minor question because, as discussed more fully in the following chapter, it has long been known that the economic effects, and thus the incidence, of a tax or subsidy do not depend upon who collects it. One way to pay the subsidy would be for the Internal Revenue Service to send a supplementary paycheck to the eligible worker upon receipt of verification of wages paid and hours worked in some particular period. In Figure 10.5 an employee would receive a check of $w_3 - w_4$ from the Internal Revenue Service and a check of w_4 per unit of time from his employer. It would be needlessly costly, though, to send weekly or even monthly checks to several million workers.

A cheaper alternative would be to send a single check to each employer of eligible workers at less frequent intervals. The use of special checks could be avoided largely by granting each employer a tax credit based upon its wage payments to eligible workers. I say *largely* because to be fully effective a check might still be sent to those whose credit exceeds its tax liability otherwise. The use of tax credits would be preferable because they would reduce the resource cost of paying the subsidy. (It must be admitted, though, that tax credits are frequently viewed as loopholes that allow wealthy firms to avoid the payment of taxes. There is always the danger that some latter-day candidate for high office would seek to have the program eliminated on these grounds.) In any event, if payments were made directly to firms, eligible workers would receive payments of w_3 per unit of time from the employers.

Another set of questions is concerned with which workers would be eligible for subsidy payments. Presumably those whose wages one would want to subsidize are those whose earnings would be relatively low in the absence of the subsidy. It could be quite difficult to determine the last directly. Given that the labor market conditions are like those depicted in Figure 10.5, an excellent guide would be wage rates paid inclusive of the subsidy. Thus, as hinted earlier, payments could be made, say, to workers who earn $4 per hour or less inclusive of the subsidy.

Somewhat more important is the fact that one would probably want the subsidy paid primarily to workers from poverty families. It is probably the case, though, that a substantial fraction of those workers earning relatively low hourly earnings are secondary workers from families whose incomes are above the poverty line. Payment of the subsidy might thus be restricted to heads of or primary workers in families and certain unrelated individuals. It would be no more difficult for a worker to claim such status than to check an appropriate box on a tax-withholding form. Payment of the subsidy to secondary workers might conflict, indeed, with other antipoverty methods. For example, raising the wage rates of teenagers via a wage subsidy increases the private, though not the social, cost of education to them and would lead to their securing less education than otherwise.

This last remark suggests another question, namely whether wage subsidies are to be preferred to worker training programs. Actually, one is not faced with an either/or choice. To the extent that training programs yield benefits that exceed their cost when future earnings are properly discounted, they should be instituted. Though many less-skilled workers might benefit from training programs, others might not. If one's aim is to eliminate poverty, there seems to be little reason for seeking to eliminate the poverty only of those workers who benefit from training. If anything, though, payment of wage subsidies would facilitate on-the-job training by private employers. The costs of general training, in particular, are borne by the worker himself in the form of reduced earnings during the training period. Subsidies to lower-wage workers would thus increase the number of workers in jobs in which on-the-job training is important.

SUMMARY

Minimum wage legislation is frequently advocated as a means of reducing poverty. Such legislation is almost certain to increase poverty. Though such legislation may increase the wage rate received by workers previously earning less than the minimum when they are employed, it reduces the number of man-hours of such workers employed. Since the demand for less-skilled workers is almost surely an elastic one, minimum wages also reduce the total wage bill paid affected workers in covered employment. Though in the short run unemployment rates may rise for affected workers, the principal long-run effect is to increase the supply of less-skilled labor to uncovered occupations. These may include self-employment or forms of ghetto employment not usually recognized as such. Regardless, however, annual earnings in uncovered employments have been even lower than in covered employment.

Many also believe that the suburbanization of employment in the postwar period has resulted in greater unemployment rates for workers living in central-city ghettos. On theoretical grounds one would expect the effects, if any, to be lower annual earnings net of transport costs and, in addition, lower hours worked annually for secondary workers. Empirically, however, there is not much reason to believe that central-city residents have been harmed by the suburbanization of jobs. Though manufacturing employment has indeed grown more rapidly in suburban parts of cities, residential population has suburbanized even faster. Central cities are still net importers of workers from their suburban areas, even in the job categories most important to ghetto dwellers. Recent comparisons suggest that earnings and unemployment rates of black, urban males do not differ very much with their residential location.

Unlike many of the measures considered earlier, worker training programs appear to offer some promise for raising the incomes of less-skilled workers. By far the most important benefit of such programs is the increase in annual earnings they result in, not the matching of excess workers in some occupations with vacancies in others. Direct hiring of less-skilled workers through government programs is not likely to increase very much the total of such workers who are employed. And since the demand for less-skilled workers is probably an elastic one, direct hiring would do little to raise wage rates. Wage subsidies to breadwinners of poor families, however, would shift labor demand curves vertically and thus raise the hourly earnings of their recipients.

CHAPTER 11

Governmental transfer payments

he preceding four chapters have considered how incomes from the sale of human labor are determined in a market economy, and problems related to earnings of the lower-income population were discussed. As was pointed out in Chapter 1, labor incomes are by far the most important source of before-tax incomes for the population as a whole, amounting to roughly four-fifths of such income received by consumers. The poor, however, received a much smaller fraction of their spendable incomes from earnings. For them, income received in the form of governmental transfers under programs commonly called welfare, social security, and the like is of substantial importance. This chapter examines the existing system of transfer payment programs and some proposed changes in this system, primarily attempting to assess them as antipoverty devices.

CURRENT FEDERAL PROGRAMS

Transfer payments are usually defined as payments that are not made for the current sale of factors of production on the market. Some, so-called welfare payments and gifts from family members or friends, are not associated with any sale of productive factors at all. Others, such as retirement pay for former members of the armed forces and private retirement programs, are deferred compensation for services rendered in the past. Transfer payments may be made either by private individuals and firms or by governmental units.

Governmental transfer payments may take many forms. In many cases, social security for example, the payment is in the form of cash, which may be spent for any purpose. In others, say the food stamp program, the payment is made in what has best been characterized as "funny money," either in cash or certificates, which may be spent only on a limited range of items. In still others, such as the public housing and school lunch programs, the payment is made in terms of commodities themselves, or "in kind." Payments made in funny money or in kind have, in principle, an equivalent cash value, though admittedly it may be difficult to make a good estimate of what this is. Regardless of the method of payment, governmental transfer payments seek, among other things, to increase the spendable income of their recipients.

This section concentrates on the effects of transfer payment programs of the federal government. Expenditures under federal programs are probably more important quantitatively than those made by all other levels of government. Most suggestions for new programs relate to the federal government. Indeed it will be argued in Chapter 13 that there are strong economic reasons for the federal government's assumption of programs for redistributing income that are currently the responsibility of local governments. There is also a pragmatic reason to concentrate on federal programs here—information about them is much more readily obtainable.

Federal transfers and the poor

Most readers will probably be surprised by two aspects of federal transfer payment programs—their size and the small fraction of the benefits of such programs that are received by poor families. Table 11.1 summarizes some of the findings of one of the most comprehensive studies of federal transfer programs. In 1960 federal transfer programs provided aggregate benefits estimated at about $28.6 billion in 1960 prices. Aggregate benefits were estimated to be $41.5 billion in 1966. Yet only about three-eighths of the aggregate benefits, or about $11.0 billion, was received by families with incomes under $3000 per year.[1] The latter figure was somewhat greater than the so-called official poverty line for 1960. The fraction of benefits going to the poor varies widely from program to program—100 percent for public assistance programs, about half for social security, and only one-eighth for farm price supports.

Though it can be tedious to describe such magnitudes precisely, $11 billion was perhaps two-thirds of the income of poor families from other sources. At the same time, the $17.6 billion in benefits of income transfer programs received by the nonpoor is roughly the same as the total amount by which

---

[1] On the basis measured by the Bureau of the Census, of which more is said later.

the incomes of the poor, including the transfers they receive, fell below the poverty line. Federal transfer payments clearly make a substantial contribution to the spendable incomes of lower-income families. At the same time, a redirection of spending under current programs could substantially increase the well-being of the poor.

The programs included in the totals in Table 11.1 include all those on which expenditures of over $100 million were budgeted for the fiscal year 1966. Federal programs only are included. Excluded, for example, are the effects of matching expenditures by state and local governments on public assistance programs. The study included all programs for which

TABLE 11.1
Estimated poor families' share of welfare and income-maintenance program economic benefits, 1960

PROGRAM	TOTAL ECONOMIC BENEFITS (MILLIONS OF 1960 DOLLARS)[a]	ESTIMATED BENEFITS TO FAMILIES WITH INCOMES LESS THAN $3,000 (PERCENT)
Public assistance	$ 1,922.7	100.0%
Old-age assistance	1,112.6	100.0
Other[b]	810.1	100.0
Trust funds and pensions	19,140.7	39.2
OASDI	10,797.9	51.4
Veteran's	3,312.4	20.8
Unemployment insurance	2,366.2	23.6
Other[c]	2,664.2	26.7
Other programs	7,532.8	20.8
Agricultural price supports	6,000.0	12.3
Other[d]	1,532.8	54.2
Total, all programs	28,596.2	38.5

[a] As provided by expenditures by federal government only.
[b] Aid to Dependent Children, to the Blind, and to Permanent and Total Disabled.
[c] Railroad, Civil Service, and Military Retirement and Railroad Unemployment Compensation.
[d] Primarily Public Housing, Rural Electrification and School Lunch Programs.
Source: Neil S. Weiner, *The Distribution of Gross Benefits of Present Federal Welfare and Income Maintenance Programs*, Institute for Defense Analysis, Economic and Political Studies Division, Arlington, Va. (February 1966).

increasing someone's spendable income is an important goal of the program. Public assistance and social security clearly belong in this category. Others, such as civil service and military retirement pay, which totaled about $1.5 billion, might more appropriately be considered primarily as deferred compensation. Requiring members of the armed forces to take a substantial part of their pay as deferred compensation, like social security, is frequently justified as preventing impoverishment in later years, however. Rural electrification, one of the other programs, may be justified as increasing the efficiency of resource allocation. Those buying electricity produced under the program are clearly better off, though, to the extent that they pay less than they otherwise would per kilowatt hour. Thus, the inclusion of certain items in Table 11.1 may be questionable, but all have a significant impact on the well-being of their beneficiaries.

It should be stressed that Table 11.1 shows benefits received under the programs rather than federal expenditures on them. Expenditures were somewhat smaller in the aggregate in 1960, $24 billion as compared with benefits of $28.6 billion. In most cases, benefits are equal to expenditures, since the latter are made in cash payments to beneficiaries of the program. In some, however, there are important differences. Under farm-price support programs, for example, expenditures are made to purchase farm products. Such purchases produce benefits in the form of increased farm incomes. To take another example, expenditures on the public housing program are payments made for interest and amortization of bonds issued to construct public housing units. The benefits relate to the difference between market rentals and the payments actually made by public-housing tenants.

One of the striking facts about Table 11.1 is that almost three-fifths of the benefits of federal expenditures are provided by two programs, social security and agricultural price supports. Alternatively, almost 70 percent of the benefits of federal transfers in 1960 were received by adults of age 65 or more or by nonaged farmers.[2] This is illustrative of the fact that

---

[2] Neil S. Weiner, *The Distribution of Gross Benefits of Present Federal Welfare and Income Maintenance Programs,* Institute for Defense Analysis, Economic and Political Studies Division, Arlington, Va. (February 1966), table 2b, p. 9.

federal programs tend to be categorical. Their beneficiaries are determined by factors such as age and farm residence, rather than by income from other sources alone. The social security and price support programs are also excellent examples of the fact that federal programs have side effects. As is the case with many medicines that have direct benefits, these side effects may themselves be quite adverse.

Social security—Old Age, Survivors, and Disability Insurance (OASDI)—is frequently compared with private insurance. It is widely believed that the program is actuarially sound in that the present value of the expected benefits to a particular covered individual are equal to the present value of his expected payments. Actually, actuarial soundness is nothing more than a myth. It may be that for current tax and benefit schedules, future receipts equal future payments for the program as a whole when both are discounted at the federal borrowing rate. Even the Social Security Administration admits, however, that for any individual the correspondence between payments made and benefits received is weak.[3] Calculations presented recently by Campbell suggest that persons now retired receive far more in benefits than the cumulated value of their social security payments.[4] Under social security provisions existing in the late 1960s, however, younger workers would receive less in benefits when they retire than they paid into the system while working. Social security is in fact a combination of categorical assistance programs and two of the most regressive taxes in the United States.

Social security payments are financed by payroll taxes. These taxes are levied at the rate of 5.5 percent both on the worker and his employers on earnings up to about $12,000 per year. Earnings beyond this level are not subject to the tax. Payroll taxes are much larger, then, in relation to the earnings of lower-paid workers. Furthermore, that employers pay half the tax is a myth that is even more erroneous than that of actu-

---

[3] U.S. Social Security Administration, *Social Security Program in the United States* (Washington, D.C.: U.S. Governmental Printing Office, 1965), pp. 12–16.

[4] Colin D. Campbell, "Social Insurance in the United States: A Program in Search of an Explanation," *Journal of Law and Economics* 12 (October 1969), 251–256. On p. 257 Campbell also argues that, if viewed as insurance, the social security reserve fund is much too small.

arial soundness. It is more correct to state that half the tax
is collected from the employer.

Who collects the tax, however, need bear little relation to
who pays the tax. To see why this is so, consider Figures
11.1(a) and 11.1(b), which differ only in the relative steepness
of the demand and supply schedules. In each figure, the market is initially in equilibrium at the price p_1, and a tax equal
to $p_2 - p_3$ is then levied on the sale of the thing in question.
After the imposition of the tax, the price paid by the buyer
is p_2, which is the sum of the price received by the seller,
p_3, and the tax. If the demand curve is relatively inelastic
and/or the supply curve is relatively elastic as in Figure
11.1(a), the effect of the tax is principally to raise the price
of the thing exchanged to the buyer relative to the price received by the producer. Figure 11.1(a) more or less reflects
the situation in regard to sales and excise taxes on the purchase of final products by consumers. If it reflected labor market conditions, the worker's share of the payroll tax would
in fact be paid by employers.

Labor market conditions, however, are more accurately reflected by Figure 11.1(b). The evidence discussed in Chapter
7 strongly suggests that insofar as primary workers are concerned, the supply of labor is highly inelastic with respect
to changes in the wage a worker receives. If supply is highly
inelastic as reflected in Figure 11.1(b), the principal effect
of a tax is to reduce the price received by the seller net of
the tax. The price paid by the buyer remains essentially unchanged. Figure 11.1(b) shows the short-run effect of real
property taxes, to be discussed in Chapter 12. It also reflects
the effect of payroll taxes on the earnings of primary workers.
Regardless of the fraction of the tax collected from the employer, $p_4 - p_3/p_2 - p_3$, where p_4 may be anywhere between
p_2 and p_3, the worker pays the tax because he receives a wage
that is lower by the amount of the tax than it otherwise would
be.

The effective payroll tax rate is thus 11 percent, as compared
with a first-bracket income tax rate of 14 percent, on earnings
up to $12,000 and zero on any additional earnings. Payroll
taxes now provide twice as much revenue as the corporate
income tax and two-thirds as much as the personal income

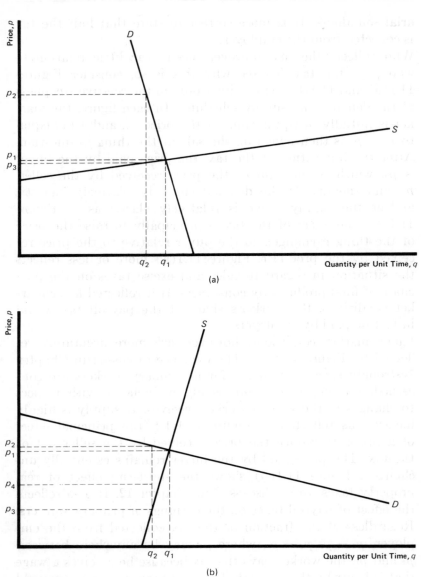

FIGURE 11.1
Tax incidence

tax. They are thus of far greater quantitative importance than many of the so-called loopholes that enable the wealthy to pay lower marginal tax rates. Any agenda for tax reform ought to include elimination of the payroll tax as its first item.

The social security system imposes much higher taxes upon the recipients of social security benefits. An older worker who earns more than $140 per month loses $1 in social security payments for every $2 of additional earnings. He is thus in precisely the same position as he would be if the size of his social security check did not depend upon his earnings but he paid federal personal income taxes at the rate of $.50 on every additional dollar earned. Relatively few taxpayers pay such a high marginal rate; indeed, 50 percent is now the maximum income-tax rate on earnings. This feature of social security reflects another feature of most governmental transfer payment programs, of which more will be said later. Though categorical, government transfer payments are income- or earnings-conditioned. Eligibility for benefits does not, in general, depend upon income from other sources, but the size of the benefit received varies inversely in most cases with income earned from the sale of labor.

Federal farm programs provide another interesting example of side effects of transfer payment programs. In some public discussion much is made of the fact that some large farms receive large payments from the government. The effects of price support and other farm programs, however, are largely independent of who receives these payments. Under our farm programs, an attempt is made to raise farm incomes by raising farm prices. Farm prices are raised primarily by government purchases of so-called surplus farm products. The increase in the gross receipts of farmers, in turn, depends upon the size of their outputs, regardless of from whom the purchases are made. Farmers who produce above-average outputs would receive above-average benefits, even though actual purchases of farm products are made wholly from small farmers.

The increase in the gross receipts of farmers is only the beginning of the matter, though. This increase tends to increase the demand for land, buildings, machinery, and labor used in the production of farm products. The supply of buildings and machinery is probably highly elastic, so that the increase in factor demand results in more tractors rather than higher earnings per tractor. The supply of farmland, though, is probably relatively inelastic. Price support programs would thus result in higher annual rentals and thus sales value of farmland. Only a part of the benefits of price support programs flow to labor used in agriculture in the form of higher earnings. Yet our greatest farm surplus has been one of farm labor.

Partly because of the size of federal expenditures made to purchase farm products and thus keep farm prices up, various measures have been adopted to limit the purchases necessary to maintain farm prices at any given level. Among these are acreage allotments, which limit the number of acres of land a farmer might plant in certain crops, and the so-called soil bank. Under the latter the federal government essentially leases land from farmers and allows it to remain unused. The soil bank thus increases the demand for farmland directly and drives up the incomes of the owners of farmland. Land resources are literally wasted by acreage allotments and the soil bank. At the same time, by withdrawing land from agricultural production, the marginal productivity, and thus the demand for farm labor, is reduced. The problem of low labor earnings in agriculture is thus intensified. At the same time, since lower-income families spend higher fractions of their incomes on food than richer families, higher farm prices impose a heavier relative burden on the poor.

Variation of transfer and taxes with income

As indicated in connection with the variation of social security benefits with earnings, the size of federal transfer payments depends upon the level of earnings and income. Indeed, governmental transfer payments are merely negative taxes. As a family's income increases, not only may the size of the transfer payments it receives decline, but the amount of positive taxes paid increases. For these reasons any appraisal of the impact of government on the incomes of the poor must consider the size of the taxes paid and the variation of taxes and transfer payments with income as well as the size of transfer payments made.

The best data available for such an appraisal are those obtained by the 1961 Survey of Consumer Expenditures made by the Bureau of Labor Statistics and the U.S. Department of Agriculture (BLS-USDA). These data, which enable one to determine the amounts of certain transfer payments received and taxes paid by income class in 1961, are shown in Table 11.2 for the lower-income classes.[5] Included among the total transfers shown in column three are public assistance, pension benefits—particularly those under OASDI programs—and unemployment insurance. Transfer payments received as benefits from agricultural programs, public housing, and many others, however, are not included. Taxes shown include OASDI payroll taxes and personal taxes, but do not include any allowance for other taxes such as sales taxes paid. In line with the previous discussion of the incidence of payroll taxes, the employer's share of payroll taxes has been included in before-tax/transfer income and in total taxes.

[5] Richard F. Muth, *Federal Poverty Programs, Assessment and Recommendations,* Institute for Defense Analysis, Economic and Political Studies Division, Arlington, Va. (January 1966).

TABLE 11.2
Effects of current tax and transfer-payment programs on the income of low-income U.S. families (1961 data)

AVERAGE PER FAMILY, $[a]

INCOME CLASS (AFTER TAXES AND TRANSFERS)	THOU-SANDS OF FAMI-LIES[a]	Income before taxes and trans-fers[b]	Total trans-fers[c]	Before-tax after transfer income[b]	Total taxes[b,d]	Income after taxes and trans-fers
Under $2,000	8,003	$ 608.7	$690.4	$1,299.1	$ 58.2	$1,241.0
2,000–2,999	6,187	1,933.7	728.4	2,662.1	191.1	2,471.0
3,000–3,999	6,449	3,242.4	562.6	3,805.0	376.6	3,428.4
4,000–4,999	7,098	4,750.1	295.4	5,045.5	682.1	4,363.4

[a] Including single persons.
[b] Employers' contribution to public OASDI programs, assumed equal to employee's contribution, has been included in before-tax-transfer income and in total taxes.
[c] Includes pension benefits, mainly OASDI, unemployment compensation, and public assistance.
[d] OASDI contributions and other personal taxes.
Source: Richard F. Muth, *Federal Poverty Programs, Assessment and Recommendations,* Institute for Defense Analysis, Economic and Political Studies Division, Arlington, Va. (January 1966), p. 58.

Somewhat surprising is the fact that average transfer payments received are actually a little larger in the second-lowest
than in the lowest income class. This is the case even though
before-tax/transfer income, shown in the second column, was
only about one-third as large in the lowest income class. Thus,
not only do less than half the benefits of federal governmental
transfer payments accrue to the poor, but the poorest of the
poor tend to receive a smaller average share of these benefits.
Despite this fact, though, income inclusive of transfer payments but exclusive of taxes paid is markedly greater for the
poor. Income after transfers but before taxes, as shown in
the fourth column, is essentially the definition of income used
by the Census Bureau, upon which the "official" data on poverty are based.

The latter two columns of Table 11.2 indicate, however, that
there is considerably more to the effect of government on the
spendable incomes of the poor. Total taxes in column five
rise rapidly with income class and are certainly of significant
quantitative importance for the poor. Though receiving somewhat more than $700 per family in transfer payments on the
average, families and individuals in the $2000 to $3000 income
class paid taxes averaging $200 per family. OASDI payroll
and personal taxes were of roughly equal importance in influencing the behavior of total taxes paid. Because lower-income
families pay taxes as well as receive transfers, the average
spendable incomes shown in the final column of Table 11.2
were only slightly larger than incomes before taxes and transfers in the income class just above the poverty line.

Table 11.3, based upon the same data as Table 11.2, shows
both the average and marginal impact of the federal government on income over the entire range of income classes for
which the BLS-USDA survey tabulated data. The first two
columns show average per family before-tax/transfer income
and net taxes (taxes paid less transfer payments received).
The first two columns seemingly suggest that matters operate
pretty much as one would like. Average net taxes paid rise
more rapidly than before-tax incomes. Stated differently, the
poor pay lower average taxes than others.

The latter three columns, however, tell a quite different story.
Columns three and four show incremental, additional, or

marginal before-tax income and net taxes as one moves from one income class to the next. Even in terms of absolute or dollar amounts the poor pay very large additional taxes as compared with the middle-income groups. As Table 11.2 indicates, part of the increase in net taxes results from an increase in positive taxes paid and part from a decrease in transfer payments received. The impact of additional taxes paid is even more dramatic when expressed as a fraction of additional income, as in the last column. The marginal, or surtax, rate paid by the poor is much higher than that paid by most taxpayers. At a time when the first-bracket federal personal income tax rate was 20 percent, the rate averaged about 20 percent for all above $5000 per year except for the highest

TABLE 11.3
Average adjusted income and taxes, incremental taxes, and marginal tax rates[a]

INCOME CLASS (AFTER TAXES AND TRANSFERS)	AVERAGE PER FAMILY		INCREMENTAL[b]		
	Adjusted income before taxes and transfers	Adjusted net taxes	Adjusted income before taxes	Adjusted net taxes	MARGINAL TAX RATE[b]
Under $2,000	$ 608.7	$ −632.3	$ 1,325.0	$ 95.0	7.2%
2,000–2,999	1,933.7	−537.3	1,308.7	351.3	26.8
3,000–3,999	3,242.4	−186.0	1,507.7	572.7	38.0
4,000–4,999	4,750.1	386.7	1,153.4	194.4	16.9
5,000–5,999	5,903.5	581.1	1,516.4	316.4	20.9
6,000–7,499	7,419.9	897.5	2,279.4	482.2	21.2
7,500–9,999	9,699.3	1,379.7	3,860.4	721.9	18.7
10,000–14,999	13,559.7	2,101.6	14,923.4	4,509.9	30.2
15,000 and over	28,483.1	6,611.5			
Average for all classes	6,013.9	560.0			

[a] Adding Employer's OASDI Contribution (assumed equal to employee's contribution) to before-tax income and to net taxes.
[b] Incremental and marginal data refer to the difference between averages for adjacent income classes.
Source: Richard F. Muth, *Federal Poverty Programs, Assessment and Recommendations*, Institute for Defense Analysis, Economic and Political Studies Division, Arlington, Va. (January 1966), p. 62.

income class. Yet the rate applicable just above the poverty line actually exceeded the rate between the two highest income classes.

The data in Table 11.3 reflect the fact that in our society the poor pay very high additional taxes on additional income. These data, however, hide large variations in marginal tax rates paid by the poor. Some not receiving benefits from transfer payment programs may have paid no more than the payroll tax rate, considerably below the 11 percent rate in 1960. Others receiving welfare benefits, say, under aid to families with dependent children (AFDC), in effect paid 100 percent marginal taxes. For in 1960 welfare payments generally declined dollar for dollar with earnings.

This point is important enough to be illustrated with another example from more current conditions. Consider a family living in public housing and buying food stamps. Tenants of public housing pay a fixed fraction of their income as rent. This fraction may vary from time to time or project to project but cannot exceed 25 percent. Many currently pay the maximum fraction. Under the food stamp program, a family of four was entitled to buy $106 worth of stamps monthly, paying amounts varying with their incomes less certain fixed expenses. Payments for stamps rise by 30 cents per dollar of net earnings, at least over the lower range of payments.[6]

Suppose now a family member earns an additional dollar. In fact, he would have earned $1.055 had not the employer been required to make a OASDI payroll tax contribution for him. Deducting his own contribution to social security, the family member has only $.945 left as take-home pay, even if not paying a federal personal income tax. The family must now pay, say, 25 percent of this for its public housing dwelling and 30 percent to receive its $106 monthly allotment of food stamps. The family thus has about $.425 left for additional expenditure over what it was spending before. Its earnings have thus been taxed almost at the rate of 60 percent.

Matters are far worse if the family is also on welfare, that is, receiving payments under the AFDC program. It is re-

[6] U.S. Office of Economic Opportunity, *The Food Stamp Program and How It Works,* OEO Pamphlet 61324 (Washington, D.C., February 1971), p. 68.

quired by statute that AFDC payments be reduced by $2 for every $3 of earnings. (In practice the actual reduction may be different because of discretion exercised by caseworkers in determining the payment to which a family is entitled.) In the foregoing example, then, when earning more than $30 per month, the family's welfare payment might be reduced by as much as $.63 for each additional dollar earned. Out of the $.315 left over as additional income, the family would pay about $.17 more for its public housing dwelling and its food stamp allotment. It would thus be left with $.145, or 13.5 percent of its additional earnings.

People's first reaction upon seeing figures such as these is usually to think of the disincentive the federal tax system has for earning additional income. The incentive effect of taxes and transfer payments is an important question and will be considered in the latter part of this chapter. Regardless of these effects it is clearly inequitable to impose such stiff taxes on the poor. Because of the high marginal tax rates they pay, the poor find it very difficult to escape from poverty by their own efforts. If they are trapped in poverty, as is so often asserted in public discussion, it is in large part because of the structure of governmental programs.

ALTERNATIVE INCOME TRANSFER PROGRAMS

Currently almost everybody is dissatisfied with the so-called welfare program, if not with the whole system of governmental taxes and transfers. Some feel that governmental expenditures are too large, others that the benefits provided are too small. It is thus quite natural that a great variety of substitute programs has been suggested. In this section certain common features of these programs will be pointed out. Next certain of the alternative proposals will be described and contrasted. In the last section, certain of their economic effects will be considered.

Characterizing income transfers

Proposals for new programs carry names such as negative income tax, guaranteed income, and family allowance. These names sound different enough for one to believe that they must be quite different. Actually, they contain many features in common, so much so that it is more sensible to think of them as different breeds of cats rather than as elephants and donkeys.

One common feature of new programs is that they are paid in real money rather than in funny money or in kind. That is, they would provide generalized purchasing power rather than currency that could be spent only for a limited range of commodities. A second important feature of most proposals is that a particular consumer's unit qualification for benefits depends upon its income rather than whether one is aged or a farmer. These proposals are frequently called income maintenance programs to distinguish them from categorical assistance programs.

To see some other common features, consider for a moment the relation of after-tax income A to before-tax income B. In most instances of personal taxes, positive taxes are paid at some marginal rate t for before-tax incomes in excess of a zero tax level Z. Thus,

$$A = B - t(B - Z)$$
$$= tZ + (1 - t)B \quad \text{for} \quad B \geq Z$$

and

$$A = B \quad \text{for} \quad B \leq Z$$

In 1971, for example, a taxpayer could deduct \$675 times the number of exemptions claimed from his total income. Neglecting deductions, the difference (called taxable income) was taxed at a first-bracket rate of 14 percent. Thus for a family of four, supposing none were 65 or older or blind, $A = 378 + 0.86B$ in the first tax bracket.

Income maintenance proposals would extend the positive tax part of the foregoing formula to the range of before-tax incomes less than the zero tax level. For $B < Z$, a family would receive a payment, in principle not very different from a refund of taxes overwithheld, from the government. Such proposals are thus frequently called negative tax proposals,

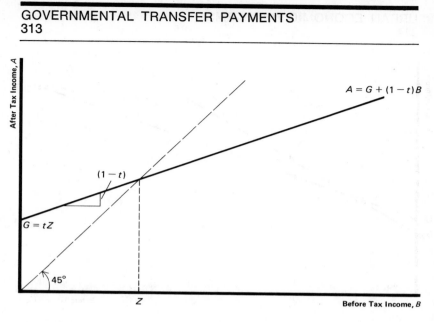

FIGURE 11.2
Common features of income maintenance programs

though by now the reader realizes that any subsidy is nothing but a negative tax.

Figure 11.2 diagrams the relation of after-tax to before-tax income under an income maintenance or negative tax program. The only oversimplification is that the marginal tax rate t is assumed to be constant, though it would not be under many proposals. With a constant marginal tax rate the graph of after-tax income is a strictly linear function of before-tax income. The intersection of this graph with a 45° line through the origin is at the zero tax level of income, Z. The slope of the graph is 1 minus the marginal tax rate. Up to the before-tax income level Z a family's tax payment is a negative one, so after-tax income exceeds before-tax income. Beyond Z a positive tax payment is made, and after-tax income is less than before-tax income. Because after-tax income exceeds before-tax income when the latter is less than the zero tax level, A is positive for $B = 0$ (provided t and Z are positive). Thus, any such scheme has a guaranteed minimum spendable income level, G. With a constant marginal tax rate, $G = tZ$.

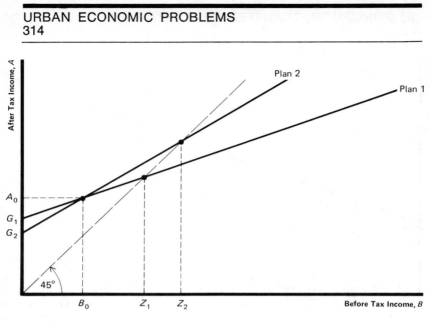

FIGURE 11.3
Variation of marginal tax rate with guaranteed income

Any income maintenance program has associated with it a zero tax level, a marginal tax rate, and a guaranteed income G such that $A \geq G$. If the graph is linear, however, any two of these three characteristics describe the plan, since the third follows from the other two. This fact is illustrated by Figure 11.3, which portrays two alternative schemes, called Plan 1 and Plan 2. Both plans would provide an after-tax income of A_0 to a family whose before tax income is B_0. Plan 1 carries a higher marginal tax rate and thus a higher guaranteed income level, G_1, even though its zero tax level is lower.

Figure 11.3 illustrates an unavoidable feature of income maintenance programs. Higher income guarantees are invariably associated with higher marginal tax rates. This is true even if the marginal tax rate is made to vary with before-tax income. In order to provide a higher income guarantee it is necessary to make it more difficult for a family to increase its spendable income. Alternatively, the easier one makes it for a family to improve its condition by lowering the marginal tax rate, the lower the income guarantee. The only way out of the dilemma is to raise the zero tax level, but by so doing,

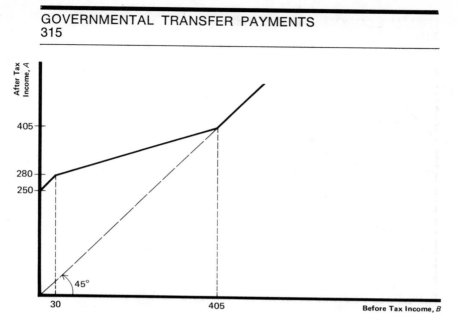

FIGURE 11.4
Typical AFDC program viewed as an income maintenance program

part of the benefits of the program accrue to the less needy.

Before discussing new proposals it is useful to point out that the current welfare program may be viewed as an income maintenance or negative tax program. It is represented graphically in Figure 11.4. As was noted earlier, under the current AFDC program a family may earn up to $30 per month with no reduction in its benefits. If its earnings are greater its payment is reduced by as much as $2 for every $3 earned. Maximum payments vary considerably from state to state, recently having been about $800 per year in Mississippi and almost $4200 in New Jersey. Most of the industrial states in the North and East paid $3000 per year or more, so $250 per month is taken as the maximum payment for purposes of illustration. The graph of after-tax income is parallel to the 45° line up to a before-tax income level of $30 per month, at which point the marginal tax rate rises to two-thirds. Once earnings have risen by $375 more, the welfare payment is reduced to zero, so $Z = \$405$. For greater earnings the marginal tax rate is zero under the welfare program considered in

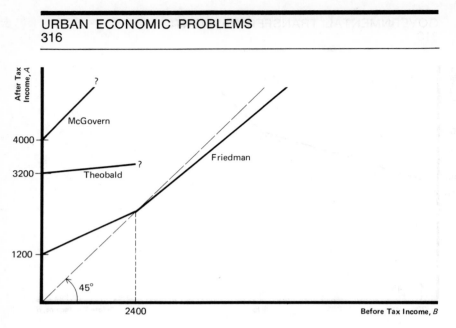

FIGURE 11.5
Some income maintenance proposals contrasted

isolation, so the graph of after-tax income coincides with the
45° line.

Proposed programs contrasted

The negative income tax proposal proper is generally associated with the name of Milton Friedman.[7] Friedman suggested
that a family would begin by figuring its personal income
tax in much the same way as it does now. If its total income
were to exceed its exemptions and deductions, it would pay
the same positive personal income tax it would normally pay.
However, if its income were smaller it would receive a payment through the Internal Revenue Service equal to half the
difference between the sum of its exemptions and deductions
on the one hand and its total income on the other.
When Friedman wrote, each exemption amounted to $600.
Thus for a family of four none of whom were aged or blind,
and neglecting deductions for simplicity, the zero tax level
under the Friedman proposal would have been $2400, as illus-
trated in Figure 11.5. For incomes below this level the marginal tax rate would have been 50 percent, whereas for larger

---

[7] It is explicitly discussed in Milton Friedman, *Capitalism and Freedom*
(Chicago: The University of Chicago Press, 1962), pp. 191–194.

incomes it would have been the same as the existing positive tax rate, which was then roughly 20 percent effectively. For a family with no before-tax income, the negative tax payment would have been half of $2400 or $1200. The latter is the lowest after-tax income possible under the Friedman plan. Though called the negative income tax, one of its features is a guaranteed minimum income.

The proposal for a guaranteed income is generally associated with the name of Robert Theobald.[8] His proposal suggested annual payments of $1000 per adult and $600 for every child. A typical family of four would thus receive $3200 per year as a guaranteed minimum income. More or less as an after-thought, Theobald suggested that a family be allowed to re-tain a premium of 10 percent of its private income. Conse-quently, though called the guaranteed income, the Theobald plan has implicit in it a marginal tax rate of 90 percent. Theobald was not explicit as to whether the payments under the plan would be taxable and at what rates. By itself, though, it has a zero tax level of about $3556.

Still another type of proposal is the family allowance scheme. Under the family allowance proper, a family would receive a payment of some stipulated amount for each child in a cer-tain age range. There would be no explicit provision for a reduction in the amount of this payment as the family's in-come from other sources increased. Presumably, though, greater taxes would have to be levied upon some individuals to provide the funds for the allowance. Quite similar is Sena-tor George McGovern's pre-1972 nomination proposal for a payment of $1000 to "every man, woman and child." As illus-trated in Figure 11.5, it would provide by itself a guaranteed minimum income of $4000 per year and a zero marginal tax rate.

The three recent proposals just described differ considerably among themselves. All carry different guaranteed minimum incomes, though of the three Friedman was quite explicit in noting that the level of payments under his proposal would depend principally upon how much in the way of income

---

[8] His original proposal is elaborated upon in Robert Theobald, ed., *The Guaranteed Income* (Garden City, N.Y.: Anchor Book, 1967), Appendix.

transfers society wished to provide. More significantly, the marginal tax rates vary considerably, Theobald's requiring a higher marginal tax rate than current welfare programs. Also important is the fact that only Friedman's plan is explicit about the zero tax level and the marginal tax rate above this level.

Most important of all, perhaps, only Friedman has been explicit about the relationship of his income maintenance proposal to existing transfer payment programs. One of the major advantages of his program as he saw it was that it would replace existing transfer payment programs. It would almost certainly be cheaper in terms of resources used to implement a negative income tax through the federal personal income tax than through the current set of transfer payment programs. More important, if a Friedman-type plan were to replace the current collection of transfer payment programs, a far higher fraction of the benefits of such programs would accrue to lower-income families. Most important of all, perhaps, is that the true nature of a system of taxes and transfer payments may be quite different than the nature of a single income maintenance proposal viewed by itself.

This last point is well illustrated by the Family Assistance Program (FAP) of the Nixon Administration. As proposed in 1970, FAP would be very similar to the Friedman proposal. A family of four would be provided a guaranteed income of $1600 per year. It could earn up to $60 a month, or $720 per year, with no reduction in its FAP payment. Beyond this level, its payment would be reduced by $1 for every $2 of earnings until its payment reached zero. FAP thus provides for a guaranteed minimum after-tax income of $1600, a marginal tax rate of zero up to an earnings level of $720 per year, and a marginal tax of 50 percent from $720 to $3920 of earnings, the last figure being the zero tax level.

As Friedman pointed out in his *Newsweek* column, however, in conjunction with other tax and transfer payment programs FAP looks quite different.[9] The food stamp program was restored and states were required to make supplemental public assistance payments where their current public assistance

---

[9] May 18, 1970. Figure 11.6 is based upon calculations presented in Friedman's column.

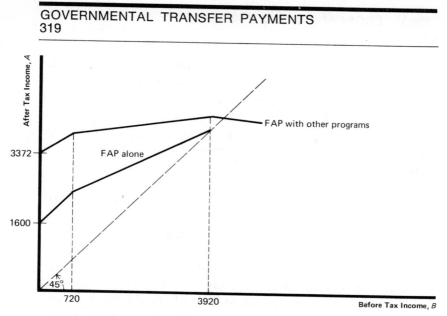

FIGURE 11.6

The family assistance program

Source: Based on data from Milton Friedman, "Welfare: Back to the Drawing Board," *Newsweek*, May 18, 1970, p. 89. Used by permission. Newsweek-Walter Bensi.

benefits exceed those under the original FAP proposal. In addition, workers would pay social security and federal personal income tax as they now do. The net effect of these additional features is shown in Figure 11.6. The lower graph shows the FAP program alone, the upper graph the program in conjunction with these others. Viewed in isolation, FAP is very similar to the Friedman proposal. In conjunction with other programs it is very much like the current AFDC program it is intended to replace. Indeed, it is worse. Modified FAP imposes higher marginal tax rates throughout its range than AFDC.

Figure 11.6 pretty clearly shows how a good idea can get fouled-up. It is difficult to say what guaranteed income and set of marginal tax rates would be best. It seems clear, however, that the poor pay high marginal tax rates now and that correcting this requires eliminating the regressive features of current tax and income transfer programs.

Effects
of transfer payments

The first question that almost everyone asks regarding a proposed income maintenance program is "how much will it cost?" Almost anyone asking this question, including some professional economists who ought to know better, really mean "how large would governmental expenditures be under the program?" The two are quite different questions. The cost to the economy of an income maintenance program is the output foregone because of it. Governmental expenditures, though, relate to the amount of transfers or negative taxes under the program. These are cause for concern to some because they need to be balanced by positive taxes on others. But the amount of positive and negative taxes under the program may well be quite different than the cost of the program.

The distinction between costs and transfers may be well illustrated by a program of more immediate concern to most readers of this book—the draft. Perhaps the critical objection to the idea of a volunteer army is that it would "cost more," that is, that federal military expenditures would be higher than with a draft. But it would surely cost the economy less. The manpower cost of any army is the civilian output sacrificed because of its existence. This is the marginal product of soldiers in civilian occupations, which is equal to their earnings. Under random conscription, if numbers in the bowl are properly mixed, the average potential civilian earnings of inductees is the average civilian earnings of the group liable for conscription. Under a volunteer army, those with the lowest civilian earnings tend to volunteer. The draft actually imposes a tax on each inductee equal to the difference between his civilian earnings and his military pay. It is because inductees pay this tax implicitly that federal expenditures—and thus taxes on the majority of us—are lower with a draft.

Under a system of transfer payments, the cost to the economy is the output lost as a result of the positive and negative taxes imposed. Though there are a variety of positive tax combinations that might be imposed to pay for income maintenance programs, higher personal income taxes for some people would almost certainly be part of any package. Though there is little really good direct empirical evidence on the matter, positive income taxes probably have little effect upon the economy's output. An increase in a positive income tax reduces the taxpayer's wage rate net of taxes. The reduction in the worker's take-home wage resulting from the positive tax leads him to work fewer hours annually because of the substitution effect discussed in Chapter 7. But a positive tax reduces a taxpayer's disposable income if he works the same number of hours as he would have otherwise. A positive tax thus has a negative income effect on the demand for leisure. The latter increases hours worked and tends to counteract the substitution effect of the tax.

It is sometimes said that since a positive tax has no effect upon hours worked, neither would a negative tax. This is wholly incorrect, though. Like a positive tax, a negative tax reduces the after-tax wage if the marginal tax rate is positive. The substitution effect of a negative tax is very much the same as that of a positive tax. But a negative tax has a positive income effect, which, after all, is its purpose. Unlike a positive tax, a negative tax increases after-tax income for one of its beneficiaries if the latter works the same number of hours as prior to the imposition of the negative tax. The income effect of a negative tax is thus to reduce hours worked. Unlike the case of a positive tax, for which the income effect runs counter to the substitution effect, the income effect of a negative tax reinforces the substitution effect. Both cause the recipient of the negative tax to consume more leisure than he would in the absence of the tax or to work fewer hours. On a priori grounds, then, one would expect a negative income tax to reduce the supply of labor from the group of families who receive benefits under it.

There have been relatively few studies of the impact of income transfers on the supply of labor. Brehm and Saving, using data for the early sixties, estimated the effect of increases in the level of public assistance payments on the number of recipients of such benefits.[10] They found that an increase of public assistance payments of $30 per month results in an increase in the number of recipients equal to about 1 percent of a place's population. Since their comparisons were made for data relating to different places at a given time, part of the observed effect may have been migration from places

---

[10] C. T. Brehm and T. R. Saving, "The Demand for General Assistance Payments," *American Economic Review* 54 (December 1964), 1002–1018.

where benefit levels are lower to places where they are higher.

By translating the Brehm-Saving result into a specific example, the practical significance of this result is more readily understood. Around 1970 about one person out of seven, or 1.1 million persons, received welfare payments in New York City. Benefit levels were $3600 to $4000 per year as compared with a more or less typical value of $3000 in the Northeast. The Brehm-Saving finding thus implies that there were 150,000 to 225,000 more welfare recipients in New York City because of its higher benefit levels than there would have been had benefits averaged the same as elsewhere in the Northeast. Higher benefit levels account for a part of the welfare roles, but only a part. Little support is provided by these findings for the two most common views of welfare recipients—that they are lazy or that welfare is their only alternative. Rather, it appears that welfare recipients respond to economic incentives, as we all do.

Several indirect estimates of the labor supply response to income maintenance programs have been made. These are based upon estimates of the response of the population to changes in earnings opportunities and income from sources other than earnings of the type discussed toward the close of Chapter 7. The most complete set of estimates has been provided by Michael J. Boskin, based upon his own estimates of individual labor supply functions cited earlier.[11] Boskin provides estimates of responses of various labor supply groups as defined by age, sex, color, and family status.

Boskin's estimates suggest that negative income tax programs of the kind currently discussed would result in substantial reductions in the supply of labor from lower-income groups. The estimates suppose that an individual can earn $1 an hour and that his family has $500 of other income after all other taxes. Guaranteed income levels examined range from $1600

---

[11] Michael J. Boskin, "Income Maintenance Policy, Labor Supply, and Income Redistribution," Memo 111, Stanford University Research Center in Economic Growth (May 1971); Edward Kalachek and Fredric A. Raines, "Labor Supply and the Negative Income Tax" (unpublished), reach similar conclusions but present less-detailed estimates.

to $3200 for a family of four, and marginal tax rates from one-third to two-thirds. His estimated effects vary from group to group. The labor supply of white, prime-age husbands would decline by about 30 to 60 percent, depending upon the guaranteed income levels. Those of all other husbands would fall considerably less, from 10 to 20 percent. Except for white, prime-age wives, the labor supply of wives would fall considerably more, whereas the labor supply of female family heads would be virtually unaffected by negative income taxes.

Boskin has also estimated the labor supply impact of family allowance schemes or McGovern-type proposals for allowances to a family of four, which vary from $1000 to $3000. Such schemes, of course, have a zero marginal tax rate. His estimates suggest the reduction in labor supply under McGovern-type plans would be quite similar to those of negative income tax plans. This plus the observation that Boskin's labor supply impacts are essentially independent of the level of a positive marginal tax rate suggests that the labor supply impact of income maintenance programs would depend primarily upon the level of the income guarantee. The estimated impacts depend very little upon how large the marginal tax rate is.

Currently there are several income maintenance experiments under way.[12] These, which are supported by the Office of Economic Opportunity, should provide additional, direct evidence upon the labor supply impact of income maintenance programs. In the experiments a randomly drawn sample of households are given money payments similar to those that would be made under an actual program. Regular information regarding their economic behavior is obtained from them and from a control group receiving no payments. When it becomes available, such information should be very valuable for appraising the effects of income maintenance programs. For now, though, the evidence available suggests that income maintenance programs produce fairly great reductions in the labor supply of the benefit population.

---

[12] The best known, the New Jersey experiment, is described in some detail in Harold W. Watts, "Graduated Work Incentives: An Experiment in Negative Taxation," *American Economic Review* 59 (May 1969), 463–472.

Undoubtedly many persons would object to income maintenance programs because of the reduction in labor supply they produce. Partly this is because of a dislike for paying taxes to support "loafers," partly because of a very important mistake in equating leisure or time not working with loafing. As was stressed earlier, time spent working and time not working are alternative means of producing consumer satisfaction. In some cases, much the same kind of satisfaction, say prepared food or entertainment, may be alternatively bought in the market or produced at home. Nonwork uses of time such as these, rearing children, and investing in schooling or in labor market information have value.

If income maintenance programs present problems, it is not because they lead people to use time in ways that have no value (which is presumably what loafing means). Rather, they give people a distorted impression as to what their time is worth. A labor force participant receiving benefits adjusts his allocation of time between work and leisure in such a way that he values his leisure at a rate equal to his wages net of taxes. Yet by working he adds output to that produced in the marketplace at a rate equal to his gross wage or wage inclusive of the tax. If his time allocation is essentially unaffected by the income maintenance program, as would appear to be the case for female family heads, the economy foregoes no output. However, if white, prime-age husbands work fewer hours a week, the market output foregone is more valuable, at the margin, than the nonmarket output that replaces it. In effect, time is wasted, and more market and nonmarket output together could be obtained if the worker were to reduce his nonmarket time and increase his market time.

For this last reason, alternative means of increasing the income of the poor would seem desirable. Income maintenance programs might be limited to families with female heads or families whose heads are not likely to work because of illness or physical disability. One might be tempted to add aged heads as well, but Boskin's estimates suggest that their labor supply is more responsive than might have been expected. The incomes of families with male heads could be raised through a program of wage subsidies, as discussed in the preceding chapter. Boskin has also calculated the impact of wage subsidies on the labor supply of the various groups.[13] His results imply that the labor supply of family heads, both male and female, would be very little affected by such subsidies because the substitution effect of a wage subsidy leads the worker to work longer hours on the average, offsetting the income effect of the subsidy. In this sense a wage subsidy is essentially the opposite of a positive income tax, more so than is a negative income tax.

Wage subsidies and income maintenance plans share two important advantages over current transfer payment programs. If designed to reach low-wage workers or low-income families, a higher proportion of the benefits of such programs would be paid to the poor than under current categorical transfer payment programs. Also important is the fact that wage subsidies and/or income maintenance plans would be much less costly to administer than current programs. Eligibility based upon wage rates or income would be relatively easy to determine, involving no more, certainly, than the information required by the short form of the federal personal income tax return. Under many current programs, AFDC and public housing for example, large amounts of labor are devoted to determining a person's or family's eligibility for benefits, reviewing plans for new housing projects, and so forth. By eliminating most of their paper work, the time of social workers could be put to better uses, such as counseling their clients.

SUMMARY

Federal transfer payment programs provide benefits to lower-income families that add up to perhaps two-thirds of their income from other sources. Yet only about three-eighths of the benefits of federal programs are received by poor families. Eligibility for benefits is determined primarily by whether a family's head is aged or a farmer, not by whether or not the family is poor. The size of benefits received under many programs, however, is income conditioned—that is, it varies inversely with earnings from other sources. Programs such as

---

[13] Boskin, op. cit.

social security and welfare thus impose very high marginal tax rates on families who receive benefits under them.

As contrasted with current categorical assistance programs, income maintenance programs would pay benefits to families in amounts depending upon their incomes from other sources. These benefits would be paid in generalized purchasing power, not in funny money or in kind. All such programs provide for a guaranteed minimum income and a marginal tax rate. In general, higher guaranteed minima are associated with higher marginal tax rates. Programs popularly called negative income tax, guaranteed income, and family allowance differ primarily in the levels of the guaranteed minima and tax rates they imply. When combined with existing federal programs, the net effect of any one of these on the poor could be quite different than its appearance in isolation.

One characteristic of a best kind of antipoverty program is that it have as small an economic cost as possible. Economic cost is the output, both market and nonmarket, that is foregone in the process of transferring income to the poor. To the extent that a program produces no changes in economic behavior, no output is foregone. It appears that increasing positive income taxes to pay for negative taxes or wage subsidies would not affect the labor supply of family heads appreciably. The same can be said of wage subsidies to lower-income family heads and income maintenance programs insofar as female family heads are concerned. Antipoverty or redistributive measures consisting of the elements just enumerated would probably have as small an economic cost as any measures that could be practically implemented. How much income should be redistributed, however, is not a question that economics as such can answer.

CHAPTER 12

Local taxation

$\mathcal{L}$ocal governments raise revenues in many ways. As the demands placed upon them increase, so do the number of ways in which they seek to raise revenue. Table 12.1 shows the major revenue sources of local governments in the United States, their relative importance, and their rates of growth over roughly the past fifteen years. The property tax is the largest single revenue source. It produced roughly two-thirds of local tax receipts and one-third of general revenues in 1969–1970, even though over the past decade and a half property taxes have grown more slowly than any other local revenue source shown in Table 12.1. In this chapter, attention is thus focused first on the economic effects of property taxes. Later on, sales taxes and the simultaneous determination of local taxes and local expenditures will be considered. Some

TABLE 12.1
General revenue of U.S. local governments, 1956 and 1969–1970, by source (millions of dollars)

SOURCE	1956	1969–1970	PERCENT OF INCREASE
Taxes	$5,447	$13,647	150%
Property	3,986	9,127	129
Sales and gross receipts	833	2,422	191
Other[a]	627	2,098	235
Charges and Misc.	1,429	5,068	255
Current	821	3,113	279
Other[b]	608	1,955	222
Intergovernmental grants	1,566	7,906	405
From state	1,346	6,173	359
From federal and other local	220	1,733	688
Total	8,442	26,621	215

[a] Including licenses.
[b] Includes special assessments, interest earnings, and receipts from the sale of property.
Source: U.S. Bureau of the Census, *City Government Finances in 1958* (Washington, D.C.: U.S. Government Printing Office, 1959), table 1; and *City Government Finances in 1970–1971* (Washington, D.C.: U.S. Government Printing Office, 1972), table 1.

attention is paid to user charges and to intergovernmental grants in the following chapter.

THE PROPERTY TAX

Despite its importance, the property tax has received relatively little attention from economists, most of whom seem to be primarily interested in national rather than local problems. Consequently, its effects are not very well understood. Before turning to an analysis of these effects, however, some preliminary matters should be settled. The property tax is generally levied as some percentage of the value at which a piece of property is assessed for tax purposes. However, the relation of assessed to market values of physical assets subject to the tax may vary widely. For analytical purposes it is convenient to suppose that all tax rates are converted to rates relative to the market value of taxable assets. Whether assessment practices themselves introduce problems is an issue that will be considered in the last part of this section.

Another point to consider is that property taxes are primarily taxes on real, as opposed to personal, property. The distinction is one that law students spend a considerable amount of time studying, but for our purposes it is sufficient to characterize real property as nonmovable. Somewhat more concretely, land and buildings are everywhere subject to property taxation, except for certain parcels, which are specifically exempted. In most states, the machinery, equipment, fixtures, and inventories of business firms are also subject to the property tax.[1] Some states also levy taxes on the personal property of households, though such taxes are principally taxes on newer automobiles. In practice, most furniture and other personal possessions are not subject to the tax.

Most important of all, it is impossible to speak of the effects of the property tax in isolation. Local governments never levy property taxes and impound the receipts in Swiss bank accounts. Rather, an increase in the property tax is usually an

[1] C. Lowell Harriss, "Property Tax: Who Pays?" *Tax Review* 33 (April 1972), 14.

alternative to raising some other tax or is accompanied by an increase in local governmental expenditures for, say schools or street lights. In this section it will be supposed, again for analytical convenience, that an increase in the property tax rate is accompanied by a decrease in a personal income tax of such an amount that the total receipts and expenditures of local governments remain unchanged. (The precise form of the personal income tax does not make much difference, for reasons to be discussed immediately.) Other alternatives will be considered in later sections of the chapter.

Short-run effects

With an increase in the real property tax the spendable incomes of persons liable for payment of property taxes fall. Though in Britain tenants are usually liable for paying the "rates," as property taxes are called there, in the United States owners are generally liable for them. At the same time, as income tax rates are cut, the spendable incomes of income tax payers rise. In most states that have state income taxes, all income earned by residents is taxed, and generally income earned in the state by residents of other states is taxed as well. Thus, the expenditures of property tax payers tend to fall and those of income tax payers tend to rise. It is not at all clear, however, that these changes will have any appreciable effect upon the demand for taxable assets at all.

To a great extent property and income tax payers are the same persons. Therefore, the effects of the tax change on spendable incomes largely cancel each other out. There are at least two reasons, though, why some spendable incomes may change. First, the ownership of taxable property may be distributed differently among individuals than income is. It is widely believed that the ownership of real property is disproportionately concentrated at the upper end of the income distribution. Most people fail to realize, though, that income from real property is a relatively large proportion to total income at the lower end of the income distribution, being of below average importance only in the middle.[2] Fur-

---

[2] See D. Gale Johnson, "Rent Control and the Distribution of Income," *American Economic Review* 41 (May 1951), 569–582.

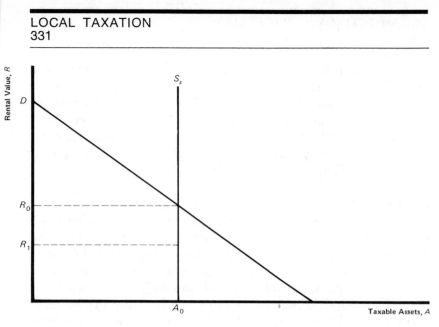

FIGURE 12.1
Short-run effects of a property tax increase

thermore, changes in the distribution of spendable income produce changes in the demand for final products, and thus in
the assets used to produce them, only if the relation of expenditure to disposable income is nonlinear. For these reasons,
there is no very strong presumption that the change in taxes
will alter the demands for various taxable assets. Likewise,
the change in taxes might have differential effects because
of differences in the location of property and income tax payers. In general, however, it is quite difficult to anticipate what
these effects might be.

The natural conclusion to draw from these considerations is
that the substitution of property taxes for income taxes has
no effect upon the demand curves for various taxable assets.
Thus in Figure 12.1 the demand curve for these assets is D,
both before and after the property tax increase. In the short
run there is a given stock of assets subject to property taxation. This stock is represented by the vertical supply curve
S_s. With a given demand curve and a fixed quantity of assets,
A_0, supplied, the rental value of assets inclusive of property
taxes is unchanged at R_0. Thus, with the imposition of a property tax of $R_0 - R_1$, the rental value of property exclusive

of the tax falls from R_0 to R_1. The only short-run effect, then, of imposing a property tax and reducing the income tax is to reduce the spendable incomes of property owners relative to those of income tax payers. Statements to the contrary are nonsense. When landlords say they are raising rents because property taxes have gone up, they are merely giving excuses for what they would have done anyway.

Long-run effects

The long-run effects of a property tax increase, allowing reactions to take place within the economic system, are quite different, however. For, though initially the stock of assets subject to taxation is fixed, it need not be in the long run. In analyzing the long-run effects of property taxes it is important to consider the size of the area in which the tax increase takes place. Two cases will be distinguished here. The first is a differential increase in a single municipality, or even urban area, over the level of rates in the remainder of the economy. Quite different effects follow in the second case, in which the increase is uniform throughout the economy as a whole.

Consider the former instance, in which the property tax substitutes for an income tax in a single municipality. As Figure 12.1 shows, the rental income of taxable assets falls initially by the amount of the tax. If, prior to the imposition of the tax, the rental return per dollar of asset value were the same in the given municipality as elsewhere in the economy, the return after tax is now lower there than elsewhere. Investment in housing, factory buildings, and other taxed assets in the municipality is now less profitable than in other parts of the economy. In consequence, fewer new houses and other assets will be built in the community in question and less will be spent on maintaining and improving existing taxed assets. Rather, more will be invested in assets located in other communities. As a consequence, as is illustrated in Figure 12.2, the stock of taxed assets will fall from A_0 to A_1 in the community where taxes are raised. Where the long-run supply schedule of assets is S_L, the rental value of taxed assets inclusive of the tax, the price paid by users of the assets, rises from R_0 to R_2. The rental value exclusive of the tax, the return

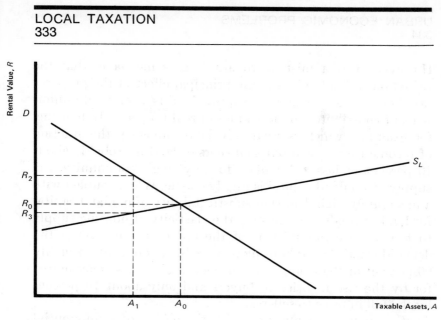

FIGURE 12.2
Long-run effects of a property tax increase

received by owners of the taxed assets, falls from R_0 to R_3. In the new long-run equilibrium, the net rental value in the taxing community, R_3, is the same as elsewhere in the economy. The gross (of the tax) rental value, R_2, is higher than elsewhere.

The extent to which R_2 rises above R_0, and R_3 falls below it, depends principally on the elasticity of the long-run supply schedule, S_L. As has been stressed earlier in this book, housing and other real property are produced using both land and nonland capital. The supply of land has, essentially, a zero elasticity insofar as any region of the globe is concerned. Consequently, as less nonland capital is invested than would have been in the absence of the property tax increase, the marginal productivity of land tends to fall in the taxing community. Hence, its rental value inclusive of the tax falls as well. A part of this lower rental value is now paid out to local government in property taxes, so the returns per acre of land fall with the imposition of the property tax. Thus, the differential property tax tends to reduce the incomes of landowners in the taxing community, and the market value of an acre of land falls.

However, it is a mistake to argue, as some have, that the reduction in land values is the principal effect of the property tax. For, though inelastic in supply, land is a relatively unimportant contributor to most kinds of real property. In housing, for example, which is relatively land-intensive, the fraction of income that is paid out to owners of land is probably about 10 percent or less.[3] Moreover, for any single community, the supply of nonland capital is highly elastic. When coupled with a moderately high degree of substitutability of nonland capital for land in producing housing, the elasticity of housing supply to the taxed community is of the order of +10.[4] Since the demand elasticity for housing is probably about unity, roughly 90 percent of the change in housing rental values is accounted for by the rise in price to buyers and only about 10 percent by the fall in price to sellers.

Another point in connection with the effects of a differential increase in property taxes in a single community needs special stress. The rental values received by owners of real property fall not only in the taxing community but throughout the whole economy. When the tax is imposed, less nonland capital is invested in the taxing community, and is invested elsewhere in the economy instead. As more nonland capital is used in the production of real property elsewhere in the economy relative to the amount of land used and to the demand for real property elsewhere, the rental value of nonland capital falls in these other parts of the economy too. Correspondingly, the rental values to buyers of real property fall because a greater quantity of nonland capital and the same amount of land are used in its production outside the taxing municipality. The rental values received by the owners of land outside the taxing community rise.

When one aggregates over groups throughout the economy as a whole, both inside and outside the taxing community, the effects upon renters of real property and owners of land tend to cancel. Inside the taxing community, the prices paid for the use of real assets rise; outside it they decline. Similarly, the rental values received by owners of land fall in the taxing

[3] Richard F. Muth, "The Derived Demand for Urban Residential Land," *Urban Studies* 8 (October 1971) especially 246 and 251.
[4] Ibid., 246–248.

community but rise outside it. Both inside and outside the taxing community, though, the owners of nonland capital receive lower net returns after payment of taxes. In this last sense, then, it may be said that capital owners in the economy as a whole bear the incidence of the property tax.

Quantitatively, a tax in any single community has a relatively small impact for the economy as a whole. However, the impact upon buyers of the services of real property in the taxing community is far from unimportant. A differential property tax is, in effect, an excise tax on commodities produced in the taxing community. Housing is affected in a particularly important way, both because housing accounts for a large part of taxed property in most communities and because real property accounts for a much larger fraction of the costs of producing housing than virtually any other commodity. A property tax at above-average rates in some particular community is to a great extent an excise tax on housing in that community. But the property tax has adverse effects on all groups within the taxing community. Not only are housing prices higher relative to those in the absence of the property tax, but the rental values of land and nonland capital net of the tax are lower in the taxing community as a result of the property tax. Outside the taxing community, while the returns to nonland capital are lower, housing prices are lower and the rental values of land higher than they would otherwise be. In this sense, then, the incidence of the property tax is on the taxing community itself.

The long-run effect of a property tax is quite different when levied at uniform rates throughout the economy as a whole. The rise in real property rental values that occurs when a single community raises its tax while others do not occurs because some nonland capital is invested elsewhere in the economy instead of in the taxing community. When taxes increase throughout the whole economy, however, escape routes are greatly limited. There are two minor and one major escape route. The minor ones are investment outside the United States or investment in nontaxed assets such as furniture and phonograph records. Though some such escapes undoubtedly occur, these possibilities are quite limited. The only really quantitatively important escape route is not to become capital at all.

For an economy such as the United States, the supply of capital is essentially the supply of its own past domestic savings. The level of income at any moment is an important determinant of the rate of saving at that time. The rate of saving may also depend upon the returns to saving, as reflected in interest rates. There have been a large number of studies that have attempted to determine the effect of changes in the rate of interest upon the rate of saving. The one rather overwhelming conclusion of these studies is that changes in the returns to saving have no appreciable effect upon the amount of saving.[5]

The reason is essentially the same as why the quantity of labor supplied by primary workers is highly inelastic with respect to wage rates. As was described in detail in Chapter 7, a rise in wage rates has both substitution and income effects; these work in opposite directions and offset each other. In similar fashion, a fall in interest rates has both substitution and income effects. The rate of interest is, in effect, the price of present as opposed to future consumption. With a rate of interest of 5 percent per year, a dollar loaned today returns $1.05 a year from today, whereas at 10 percent per year it yields $1.10. A fall in the rate of interest thus reduces the amount of consumption one sacrifices a year from today from an additional dollar's worth of consumption today. A fall in the price of consumption today might be expected to increase its amount, thus to reduce today's saving, which is the difference between today's income and today's consumption. This is the substitution effect of a change in the returns to saving.

But like a fall in the money price of a commodity or in the wage rate, a fall in the interest rate has an income effect as well. If the rate of interest falls from 10 percent to 5 percent per year and if I save the same amount today, I will receive a smaller income in the future and thus have less to consume

---

[5] In recent years the stability of private saving as a ratio to income has come to be called "Denison's Law" after Edward F. Denison—"A Note on Private Saving," *Review of Economics and Statistics* 40 (August 1958), 261–267—who argued that the gross private savings ratio has been remarkably stable since World War II. This same stability had been noted much earlier for other than depression or wartime periods in pre–World War II data, however.

a year from today. In effect, the fall in the rate of interest has reduced my wealth. A reduction in my wealth, in turn, would lead me to consume less both today and a year from today. The reduction in today's consumption is, of course, an increase in saving with income being given. Thus, the income or wealth effect of a fall in the rate of interest is to increase saving. The latter effect runs counter to the substitution or incentive-to-save effect. It is because the two effects work in opposite directions that on balance there is little effect of changes in the return to saving on the rate of saving.

Since the rate of saving at any moment appears to be largely independent of the returns to saving, so is the economy's stock of capital at any moment. If the economy's capital stock as well as its stock of land is the same, irrespective of the rate of property taxes, the rental values inclusive of these taxes are invariant. Consequently, the only effect of a property tax at uniform average rates nationally is to reduce the income to capital, both land and other assets. Housing, in particular, is no more expensive than if the revenues raised by the property tax were raised by an income tax instead.

All communities levy property taxes. In consequence, the only differential effect of these taxes depends upon differences in the rates at which they are levied. In communities where the property tax is levied at about-average rates, housing prices are high and land values low relative to what they would be if the revenue due to the differentially high property tax were raised by an income tax instead. The reverse is true where property taxes are levied at rates below the national average. Nationally property tax rates average perhaps 2.5 percent per year. Only where local rates differ from 2.5 percent are differential effects felt.

Is the property tax regressive?

A persistent and largely mistaken notion is that the burden of property taxes falls especially heavily upon the poor. In part, this results from a failure to distinguish between the long-run effects of differential property taxes and those levied at uniform rates throughout the economy. The most common belief, probably, is that the burden of property taxes falls on consumers of housing, but this is correct only in the case of a differentially high property tax. In part, shortcomings in the common view of the incidence of the property tax result from an incomplete understanding of the relationship between spending for current consumption and income. Though these two matters are most important, probably, other considerations apply as well. These will be taken up in the following section and in the next chapter.

As has just been stressed, the property tax reduces the returns to capital throughout the whole of the economy. Not only are after-tax returns to real property in the taxing community reduced, but the returns received by property owners outside the taxing community fall, as more of the economy's capital is invested outside. Furthermore, the net of tax returns fall on untaxed as well as taxed assets everywhere in the economy. For this reason, the incidence of property taxation among different income groups depends principally upon the ownership of capital in the different income groups.

Almost any data on the distribution of income from property or the ownership of wealth by income class show a relatively greater concentration at the upper end of the income distribution than elsewhere. Such data may be somewhat misleading, though, for they generally include things such as ownership of real estate, stocks and bonds, and bank deposits, which are relatively easy to measure. Assets such as furniture and other personal possessions and the equity value of owner-occupied housing are more difficult to measure and harder to include in measures of wealth. Capital invested in human beings through education, to say nothing of other ways such as health and migration, is also an important part of the economy's capital stock but is rarely included in measures of wealth. These typically omitted items, though probably larger in absolute amount for higher-income groups, may well be of greater relative importance in the lower part of the income distribution. Regardless, it is almost certainly not the case that lower-income families receive larger fractions of their income from capital than higher-income ones. Consequently, the incidence of the property tax does not fall disproportionately upon lower-income persons.

It is widely believed, however, that lower-income families

spend greater fractions of their income on housing than higher-income ones. If this were the case, the higher housing prices in communities with above-average property tax rates would impose an extra heavy burden on the poor. It is becoming increasingly apparent, however, that the common view of the relation between housing expenditure and income is mistaken. If anything, housing expenditure appears to increase at least proportionately with income and probably at a somewhat greater rate.[6] For this reason, the burden of higher housing prices in communities levying property taxes at above-average rates nationally does not fall disproportionately upon the poor either.

Since the view just expressed about the relation of housing expenditure to income is so different from conventional wisdom, some further explanation of it is desirable. Data on housing expenditure and income obtained from different consumers at a given time—the kind most often shown in textbooks—when plotted tend to follow the line *ES* shown in Figure 12.3. In the lowest income ranges housing expenditure is high in relation to income, and the reverse is true at higher income levels. In part, greater relative expenditures at lower income levels is due to the fact that families with lower incomes tend disproportionately to consist of those whose heads are relatively young or old and families that are smaller. For reasons apart from their income levels, such families tend to spend higher fractions of their incomes on housing than other families do. More important, though not totally unrelated, is the fact that temporary fluctuations in income about their longer-run normal values tend to convert a relation like *EL* in Figure 12.3 to one that appears to be like *ES*. This is the case whether one looks at expenditures on items of consumption such as food or housing or at all consumption expenditure in relation to income.

Suppose, for example, that one had data on expenditures made and money received by day, rather than annually. Most families would receive payments only once, twice, or four times

---

[6] For a good summary of much of the recent work on housing expenditure in relation to income see Frank De Leeuw "The Demand for Housing: A Review of Cross-Section Evidence," *Review of Economics and Statistics* 53 (February 1971), 1–10.

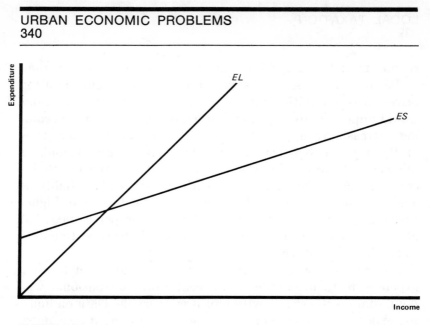

FIGURE 12.3

Short-run vs. long-run relationship between housing expenditure and income

per month. Though many bill payments are made on payday, purchases of food and many other items are made more or less regularly throughout the month. If one were to plot a family's daily expenditures against its receipts, a very weak positive association would probably result. With monthly data on expenditures and receipts, however, the effects of fluctuations in receipts tend to balance out, and the correspondence between receipts and expenditures is closer.

Is a year a long enough period to iron out all the irregularities in income receipts that families take into account in planning their expenditures? A little introspection suggests it is not. Most college students, for example, wear better clothing than they would if their past and likely future receipts were no greater than their current ones. With regard to housing, the costs of search for a new dwelling, physically moving one's possessions, and becoming acquainted with a new community are relatively high. Consequently if income is temporarily low because of, say, illness or unemployment, most families cut back on their current savings and, perhaps, expenditures for food or clothing. Few change their dwellings, however. Simi-

larly, when a family first moves to a new community, in selecting a dwelling it considers not only its current income but
also what its income is likely to be in the next three, five,
or even ten years. When data reflecting longer-run differences
rather than year-to-year ones are examined, relations more
like EL in Figure 12.3 result. Such is the case, for example,
when looking at data on average income and housing rents
or values for different cities in the United States. For whole
cities, the effects of temporary fluctuations in income tend
to average out over a large number of families.

Thus, the belief that the property tax is regressive is largely
without foundation. Of course, one must consider the alternative to the property tax in addressing the question of its
burden. The best alternative would probably be a personal
income tax. Such a tax could certainly be designed to be more
progressive than the property tax. Most people greatly over-
estimate the degree of progression in the U.S. federal income
tax, however. Several studies have suggested that, in fact,
the federal personal income tax is essentially proportional,
except in the highest income classes.[7] This fact is illustrated
by the marginal tax rates shown in the $5,000 to $10,000 income range in Table 11.3. Reducing property taxes and raising
current personal income tax rates would probably not substantially affect the progressivity of the U.S. tax system; it might
even reduce it.

Other issues related
to property taxation

It is likely that almost no one likes the property tax. Consequently a long list of indictments in addition to its alleged
regressivity has been developed against it. Some of these will
be discussed here; others will be considered later in this chapter and in the following one.

One of the most frequent complaints about the property tax
is that assessments of property values for tax purposes are
haphazard and thus inequitable. Assessed values are typically
smaller than true market values, but this would be a purely
arithmetic matter if any given class of property were assessed

---

[7] See, for example, Richard Goode, *The Individual Income Tax* (Washington,
D.C.: The Brookings Institution, 1964), chap. 9.

at a constant fraction of market value. Though this is generally thought not to be the case, the only careful study of the question suggests that the effective rate of taxation of residential property does not vary significantly with income or property value.[8] Property taxes may be consciously set at low rates on certain kinds of property to encourage what are thought to be socially desirable uses of land—low-income housing projects or open space, for example. Though perhaps not the best way to achieve the particular objective, it is hard to say that such differences are inequitable in any meaningful sense. In like manner, certain classes of property may be associated with different rates of municipal expenditure per dollar of value. Residential property has associated with it greater expenditures for public education than nonresidential property. Differences in property tax rates between the two classes of property may well be offset by differences in benefits received from the municipal services supplied the users of them.

Uneven assessment rates, moreover, are not so much an argument for eliminating the property tax as for improving assessment practices. Indeed, nobody has ever argued that the personal income tax should be eliminated because capital gains are taxed at lower rates than ordinary income. Rather, raising the rate of taxation on capital gains income is the universal prescription. There is a very simple way to improve assessments and substantially to reduce the costs of making them. This is to have each property owner declare the value of his property for tax purposes. To prevent cheating, the owner would be legally required to accept any offer to buy his property at the value declared for tax purposes. Under such a system, anyone declaring a value less than market value would be in danger of suffering a capital loss equal to the difference. However, like most simple ideas, even if good, few people are likely to take it seriously.

Another of the more serious indictments against the property tax is that municipalities with a high per capita value of nonresidential taxable property tend to have lower tax rates. The

---

[8] E. Scott Maynes and James N. Morgan, "The Effective Rate of Real Estate Taxation: An Empirical Investigation," *Review of Economics and Statistics* 39 (February 1957), 14–22.

truth of the allegation is largely arithmetic, being true only so long as municipal expenditures, intergovernmental grants, and residential property are all constant on a per capita basis. There is, of course, no reason why all should be. And, what is probably the best study of the question found, in fact, they are not. In a study of the San Francisco Bay area Julius Margolis showed that, with the exception of industrial enclaves, those municipalities with a high ratio of jobs to residents, whether central cities or not, tended to have higher tax rates.[9] This was primarily due to greater per capita municipal expenditures. Cities with low job-to-resident ratios also tended to have more residential property per capita. (That central-city expenditures are higher is related to the argument that suburbs exploit the central city, a question to be discussed in the following chapter.)

Variations in the ratios of nonresidential property per capita certainly occur, however. Some may mean lower residential property taxes or greater expenditures for schools or municipal services at given tax rates. Residents of the apparently favored communities are not necessarily better off, though, than those of other communities. For if they were, many people would seek to move into the favored community rather than nearby ones. As a result, the favored community would grow, or, if its limits were fixed and fully built up, property values in it would rise. Once an equilibrium was reached, residents of the once favored community, though perhaps paying lower taxes for a given level of municipal services, would pay higher prices for housing and other real property. The only beneficiaries of the favorable circumstances would be the owners of land and other real assets in the community at the time the circumstances resulting in lower taxes occurred.

Another frequent charge against the real property tax is that it cannot bear the load of supporting increasing local expenditures. This, too, is largely without foundation. For the economy as a whole, real capital assets have tended to grow in proportion with income. They are thus as able to bear the brunt of increasing governmental expenditures as an income tax would be. The real problem, and it is a very real one,

---

[9] "Municipal Fiscal Structure in a Metropolitan Region," *Journal of Political Economy* 65 (June 1957), 225–236.

is the mismatch between localities insofar as the location of tax sources and demands for expenditures is concerned. This last question will be explored more fully in the following chapter.

ALTERNATIVES
TO THE PROPERTY TAX

From the analysis of the preceding section one can only conclude that the property tax is not as bad as many seem to think. A property tax at uniform rates nationally probably has little effect upon resource allocation. There is little reason to believe its burden falls disproportionately upon the poor, though a personal income tax could be designed that is more progressive. It will be argued in the next chapter that the real problem, local taxation to support what are essentially income redistributive programs, is not uniquely related to the property tax. Because of its perceived shortcomings, though, many have argued for elimination of the property tax. In this section two alternatives other than the personal income tax will be examined.

The land value tax

Since the writings of Henry George about a century ago, the policy of taxing land values has had a persistent though limited appeal. In recent years, as property taxes have risen in many places, land value taxation has received increasing support even among professional economists. Though some jurisdictions attempt to tax land at higher rates than improvements, little use is made currently of the land value tax in the United States.

To examine the effects of land value taxation, first suppose it to be substituted wholly or partly for a property tax levied at uniform rates throughout the economy. As the land tax is substituted, total taxes would rise for those kinds of real estate for which land value is large relative to the structures and other improvements made to it. Total taxes would fall for those assets for which land is a relatively small part of total value. Included in the former, or land-intensive, class of assets are such minor ones as golf courses, cemeteries, and drive-in movies, and more important ones such as vacant land, farms, and housing. Removal of the tax on improvements would increase the returns to investment of nonland capital in all forms of real property, though, regardless of the relative importance of land.

It is widely believed that the higher returns to improvements would induce more to be made. For such to be the case, however, additional capital must be found somewhere in the economy. As was argued in the preceding section, though, the supply of capital to the economy as a whole is highly inelastic. Though the returns to savings invested in newly constructed improvements to land rise as the property tax is reduced, the economy's total saving would appear to be largely unresponsive to the returns to saving. Thus, if the returns to all forms of investment rise uniformly and the total amount of new investment is unchanged, the same pattern of investment that would have obtained otherwise will result when the property tax is removed. The only effect of substituting a land value tax for a property tax levied at uniform rates nationally is a change in the identity of taxpayers. The rental values of vacant land, farms, and housing net of the tax would fall, though their rentals inclusive of the tax would remain unchanged. Thus market values of the aforementioned assets would fall, whereas those of factories and stores would rise. There would thus be a transfer of wealth from one group of asset owners to another.

The situation is quite different if a single community reduces its property tax rate and institutes a land value tax to make up for the revenue lost. For if a single community does so, the returns to investment in real assets in that community rise relative to the returns to investment elsewhere in the economy. Consequently, more investment takes place in the community introducing the tax change. In the new equilibrium following the change in taxes, the returns to nonland capital net of taxes are the same throughout the economy. For this reason, the rental value of real assets to users is lower in the community substituting the land value tax for the property tax, and land in that community is more intensively developed there than it would otherwise be. If the property tax had been above the average rate nationally prior to the change, reducing it to the average level for the economy increases the efficiency of resource use in the economy. This is the case because capital is shifted from areas where its total return including the tax is below average to where it is above average. If the property tax rate in the community making the substitution had been below the national average rate, however, inefficiency in the distribution of capital would be increased.

In the community substituting a land value tax for the property tax, the returns to owners of land tend to fall because of the greater tax paid from the income to land. However, this reduction is partly offset. Because more nonland capital is invested per acre of land after the removal of the property tax, the marginal product of land rises. Consequently, the rental value of land inclusive of taxes paid rises. The rise in the price users of land pay for it, when coupled with a fall in the rental value of nonland capital, changes the pattern of relative prices of final products in the community instituting the land value tax. Housing prices would rise relative to the prices of goods and services produced and sold locally. Because of the rise in rental values of land, less of it would be devoted to farms and other forms of open space.

A frequent argument for land value taxation is that the income from land is "unearned." This particular argument is seriously deficient. It is true that the supply of land to the economy as a whole is highly inelastic. The same is the case for nonland capital and even for labor. Just as labor and nonland capital may be used to produce a variety of different commodities, so may land. In any one of these specific uses, the supply price of land reflects its value in alternative uses. In this regard, land as a productive factor is on much the same footing as labor and nonland capital.

Similarly, a growth in the population of a particular urban area increases the rental value of land in that area. In much the same way, technological changes may increase the earnings of certain classes of workers or nonland capital assets. The increased earnings in all cases may be windfalls, or unearned, if not anticipated. To the extent that population growth is anticipated, however, its effects are reflected in the market values of land at each moment. Any particular owner of land would earn the same return by purchasing land as by purchasing any other real or financial asset. The owner would then "earn" the return to land by sacrificing the opportunity to earn an equivalent return in the purchase of some other asset. Income paid out to owners of land is thus little different from income to any other form of capital. And, as was stressed in the previous discussion of education, much of labor income is simply a return to past investment in human capital. Only the income to raw or uneducated labor might be said to be qualitatively different from the returns to land. Land value taxation would seem to be much less than the panacea that is often claimed for it.

The sales tax

Unlike the tax on land values, the sales tax is widely used in the United States. Sales taxes are especially important as revenue sources for state governments. Sales and gross receipts taxes, however, provide local governments with roughly one-quarter the revenues property taxes do. Moreover, sales taxes at the state level, when coupled with state transfers of revenue to local governments, are a very real alternative to local property taxes. In discussing the sales tax, however, it is convenient to suppose it is levied in lieu of a personal income tax. Furthermore, since the issue of national average as opposed to differentially high local tax rates is of much less importance than in the case of a property tax, it will be assumed in what follows that the substitution of the sales for the personal income tax is made in a single community rather than for the nation as a whole.

If the personal income tax is reduced in a particular urban area, the spendable incomes of the residents of that area tend to rise. Thus, the demand curves for goods and services in the area rise, as from D to D' in Figure 12.4. The effect upon prices paid by consumers in the area and quantities purchased, however, depends very much upon the conditions of supply. Commodities purchased by residents of a particular city are either imported or produced domestically. Only a small part of the national or world output of imported commodities is sold in any particular city of the country. Little of Eastman Kodak's output of Kodachrome color film is sold in New York

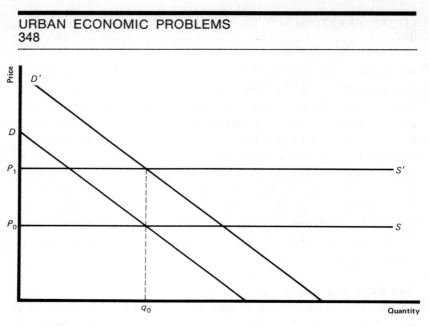

FIGURE 12.4

Substitution of a sales tax for a personal income tax at the local level

City, for example. The supply schedules of imported commodities are thus highly elastic. Imposition of a sales tax then shifts their supply schedules upward from S to S' in Figure 12.4, and prices paid by residents of the area for imported commodities rise from p_0 to p_1, the amount of the tax.

The elasticity of supply of goods and services produced locally depends, of course, on the supply elasticities of productive factors to the city in question. As was argued in Chapter 2, the rental values of capital assets used in production in the particular city are essentially fixed by national market conditions. A temporary increase in the earnings of such assets would result in a flow of capital into the city until the previous rate of earnings in relation to that elsewhere in the economy was restored. It was also noted in Chapter 2 that wage differentials as among different areas of the U.S. economy have been quite constant historically. The best explanation is that the demand for labor in the production of commodities for export is highly elastic. Hence, the wage rate producers for domestic consumption must pay is also fixed to the extent that they hire labor in the same labor market as producers for export. In consequence, the supply elasticity for commodities produced locally is also very large. Sales taxes collected on such commodities, then, like those on imported commodities, also result in vertical shifts in highly elastic supply schedules.

Sales taxes in lieu of income taxes are thus paid by consumers in the area as higher prices inclusive of the tax. It is often argued that, as such, sales taxes are regressive because lower-income families spend larger fractions of their incomes than higher-income ones. Though the conclusion is correct, the usual reason given is not. For reasons that are quite similar to those discussed in connection with the burden of higher housing prices earlier in this chapter, the apparently higher fraction of income consumed by lower-income families is largely the result of temporary fluctuations in income coupled with consumption levels geared to permanent or normal income levels. Indeed, many survey data suggest that the lowest income groups spend an amount greater than their incomes. Yet they cannot do so consistently over a long period of time. Data for the economy as a whole over the past century suggest, rather, that over a wide range of income levels, consumption expenditure increases more or less proportionally with income.

Though the term "sales tax" denotes a general tax imposed upon all commodity purchases, sales taxes as they exist in the U.S. economy are in fact selective. They are more general than excise taxes imposed upon specific commodities such as plane tickets or cosmetics, but a large part of consumption is not subject to so-called sales taxes. Housing on the average represents perhaps one-fifth of consumer expenditure, and housing is rarely subject to sales taxation. (Property taxes are sometimes said to be excise taxes on housing, but this tends to be the case only of taxes imposed at above-average rates nationally.) More generally, services, as opposed to goods, are usually not subject to sales taxes. Since medical and dental care and other personal services very likely make up larger fractions of the consumption expenditure of higher-income families, their exclusion means that lower-income families generally spend higher fractions of their incomes on sales taxes. In states such as California, however, which exempt food from sales taxes, this may well not be the case, for food is the one important class of consumption for which expenditures increase less than proportionately as income increases.

TAXES AND
LOCAL EXPENDITURE

Thus far the propositions developed regarding local taxation have all dealt with the substitution of one form of taxation for another. Yet in many instances the alternative to higher local taxes is a lower level of expenditures on goods and services produced by local governments. In local elections voters are frequently asked to approve higher property tax rates to finance airport improvements, street lights, and even greater expenditures for public education. The effects of higher property tax rates may be quite different if, instead of reducing some other tax, the community increases the expenditures it makes for public schools. Although higher property tax rates may reduce the quantity of housing purchased, better public schools make the community a more desirable place in which to live. Consequently, the demand for housing in the community increases, and one can not state unambiguously that the quantity of housing demanded declines.

The effects of taxes such as the property tax when combined with an increase in local public expenditure are not very well understood. This section concentrates on the process by which local tax levels and expenditures are simultaneously determined. The fundamental fact about public expenditure is that, unlike private expenditure, the same level of public expenditure is experienced by all families in a particular community. (Though garbage may be collected less frequently in the poorer areas of some large cities, or the streets may be more poorly lighted, the effects are felt simultaneously by large numbers of families.) First, consideration will be given to the level of local expenditure and associated tax payments any particular family would prefer if free to choose. Following this will be a discussion of how diverse preferences for local expenditure levels among different families in the community are reconciled.

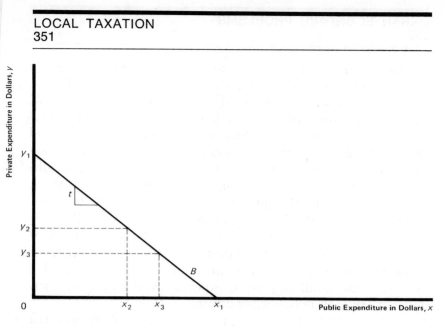

FIGURE 12.5
Relation of private to public expenditure for a family

The demand
for local expenditures

In examining an individual family's preferred level of local expenditure and taxes, it is useful to draw an analogy with the family's choice among different commodities purchased on the private market. The choice among different privately produced goods is conditioned by the family's total income, and thus the amount available for expenditure upon all commodities, and by the prices of these commodities. Typically, the greater its income, the more a family will seek to purchase privately produced commodities. Similarly, the greater the price of any particular commodity relative to those of others, the fewer the units in physical terms of the commodity that will be purchased.

In like manner, a family's choice between publicly and privately produced commodities is influenced by its total income and by the relative prices of the commodities. The price of publicly produced commodities depends, in turn, upon the family's share in the total taxes imposed by the community. This fact is illustrated in Figure 12.5, along whose axes are shown, respectively, different levels of public expenditure by the community as a whole and private expenditure by a given family. Both kinds of expenditure are measured in dollars. The choices open to the family are limited by the line B, which economists call a budget line. The family's income before any local taxes is y_1, which is the amount it could spend on private goods if the community in which it lived made no public expenditure whatsoever. The maximum level of public expenditure the family could help support is x_1, which would result if all the family's income after other tax payments were "spent" for local taxes. In general, local public expenditure can be increased by a dollar if the family gives up t dollars, where t is the family's share in the total taxes levied by the community. The latter, of course, is the amount by which the family's private expenditure declines for each dollar increase in public expenditure.

Supposing only that families prefer more to less, choices will always be made from those combinations of x and y lying along the budget line B. Points along B are preferred to points toward the origin, 0, in the set bounded by B and the coordinate axes, whereas points outside the set are unattainable. The particular point along B selected by the family depends upon what economists characterize as tastes and preferences. Families with school-age children would probably prefer greater expenditures for public schools than families without children, and hence would prefer, say, point (x_3, y_3) to (x_2, y_2). Similarly, some might prefer to take more frequent weekend trips than to have public parks, and hence would prefer greater private to public expenditure and wish to choose (x_2, y_2) in preference to (x_3, y_3). Whatever point along B the family selects as its preferred level, however, the additional satisfaction the family derives from a dollar of public expenditure when divided by its price, the family's tax share t, is equal to the additional satisfaction a dollar of private expenditure yields.

The budget constraints restricting a family's choices, however, may differ among families, as illustrated in Figure 12.6. The budget lines B_1 and B_2 compare families with the same tax share but differing incomes. (Actually, families with differing incomes are likely to pay the same share of local taxes only if taxes levied are so-called head or poll taxes). Presumably,

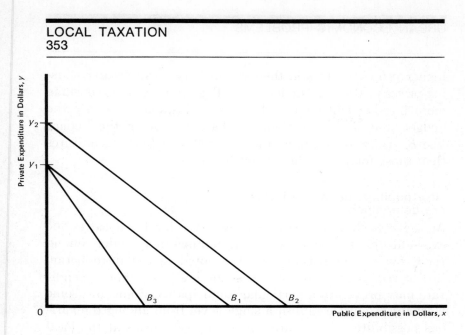

FIGURE 12.6
Budget constraints for different families

families whose incomes are y_2 rather than y_1 would prefer both greater public and greater private expenditures. The extent to which the demand for public expenditure varies with income, however, may vary considerably among different types of it. A higher-income family would probably drive a newer, more expensive car, but make roughly the same kind and number of trips with it. Higher-income families would tend to value their time more highly, however, as was discussed in Chapter 7, and hence would be willing to give up more money for local streets that permit faster trips to be made. Higher-income families may also value education more highly, and hence would desire greater expenditures on local schools. It is possible, however, that higher-income families have larger yards and would thus be less willing to make expenditures on public parks. And certainly, the higher one's income, the more likely one is to visit a private physician than a public hospital for medical treatment.

The budget lines facing any given family also depend upon their tax shares. The lines B_1 and B_3 illustrate the contrast between families of the same income but different tax shares. Suppose, for example, that local expenditures are financed by property taxes and that families correctly perceive that

higher property taxes in their community mean greater housing prices to them in the long run. Then families that consume
more housing will have higher tax shares, and thus face the
budget line B_3 rather than B_1. Families facing the budget
line B_3 will tend to prefer a lower level of public expenditures
than those for whom the budget line is B_1.

How public expenditure levels
are determined

As the preceding discussion suggests, the level of local public
expenditures desired by different families may differ among
them for several reasons. As was noted in the introduction
to this section, though, only a single level of public expenditure may prevail in a particular municipality. Somehow, some
mechanism must establish a single level from among the various possibilities. There are two such mechanisms at the local
level. In the short run, when the residences of different families are fixed, public expenditures are set by officials elected
by these families. In the long run, however, families may
select a package of local expenditures and taxes by selecting a place of residence—by voting with their feet—as
well.

Consider, first, the short run, in which the residential locations
of all families are fixed. Each family in the particular municipality will have a preferred package of public expenditure
levels and associated taxes it must pay. These will differ from
family to family. It is convenient to think of the preferred
expenditure levels as ranked in order from largest to smallest.
In such an array the median value is of particular significance.
The median is a numerical value such that no more than
half the observations of the array are larger and no more
than half are smaller. If the array consists of an odd number
of items, the median is the middle value; for an even number
it is any value between the two middle ones.

One of the few voting principles that yields usable conclusions
is "majority rule." It is fortunate that the majority-rule principle yields predictable consequences, for this mechanism ap-
proximates those by which many public choices are made.
One specific instance of majority rule is that of two candidates
for a particular election. We may suppose that each candidate

announces a platform consisting of the level of public expenditure he will undertake and the taxes he will impose to finance this expenditure. Suppose, too, that the total taxes in the candidate's platform equal the expenditures he promises to make, though this need not always be the case, and that voters pick among candidates on the basis of promised taxes and expenditures rather than on the basis of, say, foreign policy. Under these conditions, the winning platform is the median of the voters' array of preferred expenditure levels.

To see why this is the case, consider a platform characterized by some level of expenditures other than the median, say, smaller than the median. Let the other candidate adopt a platform calling for a larger local expenditure but a level that is still less than the median of the voters' array of preferred levels. Under conditions economists usually assume about people's preferences, the closer the actual outcome to a person's preferred position, the more satisfaction he derives from that outcome. Hence, the second candidate by his platform increases the satisfaction of more than half the voters, so he, rather than the first, would be elected. Thus, any platform promising a nonmedian expenditure level can be beaten by an appropriate platform chosen by the other candidate. If candidates for office wish to be elected, they will seek to adopt median platforms.

Too much should not be claimed for the principle just explained. Like all principles, it is offered only as a real-world tendency, not as a literal description of the state of affairs at any particular moment in time. Students of politics will recognize lots of complications and exceptions, which will not be listed here. However, to show that the principle does yield correct predictions of political outcomes in the United States, one need merely point to the oft-noted similarity of platforms, to say nothing of actions taken while in office, of the Democratic and Republican parties.

To the extent that similar results occur at the local level, one would expect the actual level of expenditures in any particular community and the associated level of taxes to correspond to the median of the array of those preferred by a community's voters. The median family, that whose preferred level of expenditures is the one selected by the political process, is in much the same position vis-à-vis private vs. public expenditure as it is regarding differing kinds of private expenditure. The additional satisfaction it receives, per dollar spent on local taxes, from local public expenditure is exactly the same as the additional satisfaction it receives from a dollar's private expenditure. For families preferring greater than median levels of public expenditure, though, the additional satisfaction received from public expenditure relative to taxes paid exceeds that of private expenditure. Such voters probably would complain of unmet public needs. Other families, whose preferred expenditure levels are below the median, would find taxes too high. On the average, taxpayers are just willing to pay local taxes for the services received from local government, but few will be perfectly satisfied.

In the long run, however, few individuals stay in a particular residential location. Some may move for the express purpose of placing their children in better public school systems. Few are likely to move just because the garbage isn't picked up often enough or water bills are too high. Still, families are constantly moving for a variety of other reasons, a change in the job location of the family's principal breadwinner being one of the most important. When selecting a new place of residence, people generally inquire about how high taxes are and how good the schools are in addition to other factors that affect the desirability of a particular location. In the process, municipalities offering a given bundle of public expenditure levels and taxes will come to be inhabited by persons preferring these particular levels to others. Persons preferring a given level of local expenditures thus will have similar incomes as well as similar educational and social backgrounds. When coupled with the likelihood that most people tend to feel more comfortable residing among others of similar station, a degree of residential segregation by municipality tends to result.

At the same time, to the extent that there is a best size of community, in the sense that public output is provided at the smallest average cost per family, communities will tend to that size. If some communities are so small that police and fire protection, say, require greater tax payments per family than in other communities, these communities will tend to be unstable. Their residents will either leave the community, or it will seek to attract new residents and to annex or be annexed to surrounding areas. Where other communities are too large, fewer families will seek to move in than move out. In the long run the community will decline in size. In the short run, though, property values will fall, and families who are willing to pay higher taxes in order to obtain cheaper housing will be attracted to the community that is too large.[10]

Similar kinds of considerations are relevant regarding the practice of large-lot zoning in suburban areas. Many suburban municipalities have zoning ordinances restricting large areas of them to single-family residential development on quarter-acre lots, even full-acre or larger lots in some cases. Such zoning is frequently said to exclude the poor from suburban areas by making them too expensive to live in. Though there is no technical reason why small dwellings could not be put on large lots, probably few people would choose to do so. Yet such zoning ordinances will only be established with voter approval.[11] Voters will elect officials advocating such zoning or move to such communities only if they feel that a residential area consisting of detached residences on large lots is desirable for them and they are willing to pay for it.

In Chapter 4 it was argued that segregation of land uses results when members of one particular group are willing to pay a greater premium for sites adjacent to other members of the same group than persons outside the group will pay. As applied to the present instance, it seems reasonable to suppose that persons choosing to live in detached dwellings will pay more for such residences in the vicinity of similar ones. At the same time, persons living in other types of dwellings, though perhaps having a preference for spacious surroundings, would not bid as much for dwellings in such surroundings. This would certainly seem to be the case for lower-income families. If so, large-lot residential areas would tend

---

[10] The matters discussed in this and the preceding paragraph are considered in greater detail by Charles M. Tiebout, "A Pure Theory of Local Expenditures," *Journal of Political Economy* 64 (October 1956), 416–424.

[11] In this regard see Otto A. Davis, "Economic Elements in Municipal Zoning Decisions," *Land Economics* 39 (November 1963), 375–386.

to develop in the absence of zoning. Developers of such areas could increase their attractiveness to potential buyers of such residences by including deed covenants restricting future use to large-lot residences. Municipal zoning ordinances may well be a cheaper way to achieve the same result. The extent to which large-lot residential areas develop, however, is limited by consumer demands for such residences. If too many such areas were developed, the returns to capital invested in their development would be less than that of capital invested in other residential developments. The growth of large-lot residential areas would thus be retarded.

Finally, the foregoing considerations shed some light on why lower-income families are concentrated in the central cities of urban areas. It is frequently argued that the poor and members of racial minorities are "confined" to the central cities and thus receive poorer schooling and services from local government. The principal reason why the poor are disproportionately concentrated in central cities is that housing is cheaper for them there. This is especially the case, as was argued in Chapters 3 and 4, because older housing is smaller and more easily converted from higher to lower quality. Yet most urban areas have concentrations of lower-income families outside the central city as well. If lower-income families were to offer more for housing outside the central city than they now do, these concentrations would grow more rapidly. One reason why they do not is that lower-income families will offer less of a premium for better schools and higher-quality municipal services than higher-income families will. Consequently, suburban municipalities tend to become disproportionately inhabited by middle- and upper-income families. At the same time, lower-income residents of central cities have less opportunity to choose among alternative packages of municipal expenditures and taxes, a matter that will be elaborated upon in the following chapter.

SUMMARY

The property tax is the single most important local revenue source, but it is poorly understood. In the short run, when the stock of real assets is fixed, raising the property tax merely reduces the return to real assets, leaving the before-tax return unchanged. This is also the case with the long-run effect of an increase in property taxes throughout a closed economy such as the United States. This follows because the stock of real assets of all kinds for the United States seems, empirically, to be unrelated to variations in the return to saving. The long-run effects of a differential property tax increase in a single municipality, however, are quite different. These are a higher rental value of real assets, a lower before-tax rental value of land in the taxing community, and lower after-tax returns to movable capital throughout the whole economy.

When their effects are correctly understood, there is little reason to suppose that property taxes impose a disproportionally heavy burden on the poor. To the extent that property taxes reduce the returns to owners of real wealth, their impact on the poor would be especially light, if anything. Contrary to popular belief, expenditures on housing tend to increase more than proportionally with income. Nor do many other arguments against the property tax make much sense when carefully considered. Uneven assessment rates are an argument for making them more even. A high per capita value of non-residential property reduces property tax rates only if everything else is unchanged, which appears not to be the case. In addition, low tax rates on residential property for a given level and quality of municipal services are offset by higher housing prices.

Replacing property taxes with taxes on land values has little to recommend it when the effects of property taxes are properly understood. If the substitution were made nationally, the only effect would be to change the identity of taxpayers. Asset rentals and before-tax returns both to nonland capital and to land would remain unchanged; hence, the pattern of resource use would remain unchanged. If the substitution were made in a single community, more nonland capital would be invested in that community than otherwise. This would have desirable effects only if the community's property tax rate were initially above the national average. Sales taxes in lieu of personal income taxes result in higher prices paid for goods and services in the taxing community. Hence their burden falls on members of the taxing community. The poor are not affected disproportionally because they spend a larger fraction of their incomes. Rather, items such as personal services upon which the poor spend a smaller fraction of their incomes tend not to be subject to the tax.

When a local tax increase is accompanied by an increase in local public expenditures, it is by no means clear that the community becomes a less desirable place to live. The level of public expenditures and the associated level of local taxes depends upon the desires of the community's voters. So long as majority rule prevails, the equilibrium level of public expenditures is equal to the median of the array of voters' preferred levels. For the median voter, the additional satisfaction resulting from the increase in the community's expenditures associated with an additional dollar in taxes is the same as that from an additional dollar of private expenditure. In the long run people move from one residence to another and select a community whose local tax and expenditure level corresponds most closely to their own. Large-lot zoning and segregation by income level among suburban municipalities are also outcomes of this process.

CHAPTER 13

$\mathcal{A}$bout once a month I read a quotation attributed to the mayor of some large central city to the effect that his city or cities generally are becoming ungovernable. This is probably correct to an extent. The problem, though, is not that cities are ungovernable as such but rather that they are becoming increasingly difficult to govern under current governmental arrangements. This chapter will begin by discussing certain economic factors that influence the kinds of functions local governments ought to undertake and their proper areal scope. Then specific problem areas will be examined. Throughout, however, the emphasis will be on reforms that seem desirable in enhancing the ability of governments effectively to deal with urban problems.

FUNCTIONS AND SCOPE OF LOCAL GOVERNMENT

In his classical treatise on public finance, Richard A. Musgrave classifies the functions of government into those dealing with stabilization, redistribution, and resource allocation.[1] Stabilization means those actions that influence such economic aggregates as the gross national product, the overall unemployment rate, and the general price level. Redistribution refers to actions that influence the incomes received by different persons or families. Actions that influence the way an economy's resources are used are called resource allocation.

State and local governments rarely engage in stabilization activities, nor should they. These governmental units are frequently restricted by state constitutions and in other ways as to the debt they may incur. Unlike the federal government, state and local governments have no control over the money supply. Even if they were not so limited, nonfederal governmental units would be seriously handicapped if they attempted to control short-run fluctuations in economic activity. Since states and urban areas are open regions, actions taken to stimulate economic activity in their particular jurisdictions would spill over into other jurisdictions. Coordinating fiscal

---

[1] Richard A. Musgrave, *The Theory of Public Finance* (New York: McGraw-Hill, 1959).

and monetary actions at the federal level is difficult enough. Separate stabilization efforts by a myriad of state and local governments would almost certainly be chaotic.

State and even local governments undertake a variety of actions that affect the distribution of income among different consumer units. It will be argued shortly, however, that their attempts to do so are principally responsible for the fiscal difficulties of central-city governments. Like stabilization activities, income redistribution is a matter best left to the federal government. Local governments also undertake many actions affecting the allocation of resources to different uses, and indeed they should. To the extent that problems exist in connection with local actions to influence resource allocations, these problems are frequently due to the fact that local governments either do the wrong things or are the wrong size.

Redistribution

Many expenditures made by local governments are redistributive to a greater or lesser extent. The purest examples of such expenditures are those made for public welfare. Public assistance programs, of which Aid to Families with Dependent Children or "welfare" is an important part, are state-operated, supported in part by matching federal grants. In many states these programs are operated through local governments. The latter spent over 2 billion dollars on public welfare programs in the fiscal year 1969–1970, or about one-ninth of their total expenditures that are readily allocatable to specific functions (see Table 13.1).

The other functions classified as redistributive in Table 13.1 are somewhat ambiguous. As has already been discussed in Chapter 5, urban renewal and low-income housing programs are sometimes alleged to correct resource misallocations resulting from private market activity. However, popular support for such programs results largely from the belief that they improve the well-being of the poor. At the same time, the conditions that give rise to a perceived need for such programs are very much the same as those that have led to increased expenditures for other redistributive programs. In a somewhat different vein, public health programs are largely resource-allocative, but expenditures for private health are essentially redistributive. Patients in local public hospitals are very similar to charity cases in private hospitals. To make matters even more confusing, many redistributive expenditures are made on what are sometimes called merit goods in economics, that is, commodities upon which people ought, in terms of someone else's standards, to spend more than they would of

TABLE 13.1
Expenditures of U.S. local governments, 1956 and 1969–1970, by function[a,b] (millions of dollars)

FUNCTION	1956	1969–1970	PERCENT OF INCREASE
Redistributive	$2,155	$ 8,457	292%
Education	1,039	3,999	285
Hospitals and health	569	1,836	223
Housing[c]	68	407	498
Public welfare	479	2,215	362
Allocative	3,410	9,640	183
Local	2,034	6,031	196
Fire	645	1,762	173
Police	948	2,994	216
Other[d]	441	1,275	189
Area wide	1,376	3,609	162
Highways	622	1,381	122
Sewerage and sanitation	639	1,672	162
Other[e]	115	556	383
Total[b]	5,565	18,097	225

[a] Excluding capital outlays where possible.
[b] Excluding general administration, bonded indebtedness, and others not allocatable to specific functions.
[c] Identified as "Housing and Community Development" in 1956, "Housing and Urban Renewal" in 1969–1970.
[d] Libraries plus parks and recreation.
[e] Airports plus water transportation and terminals.
Source: U.S. Bureau of the Census, *City Government Finances in 1958* (Washington, D.C.: U.S. Government Printing Office, 1959), table 1; and *City Government Finances in 1970–1971* (Washington, D.C.: U.S. Government Printing Office, 1972), table 1.

their own volition. (Since there is no merit in paternalism, the term "demerit good" seems more appropriate.)

Education, which is the largest single type of local government expenditure, is neither wholly allocative nor redistributive. As was pointed out in Chapter 9, society as a whole benefits from literacy, and perhaps good citizenship, and public support of education is one means of gaining these benefits. It seems, though, that most people think of education as producing far more than this. In most public discussion education is viewed as a means of enriching the lives and, especially, increasing the incomes of those who receive it. Much of the so-called war on poverty may be viewed as an effort to break the cycle of poverty by correcting past deficiencies in education.[2] Similarly, much of the support for governmental expenditures on special or remedial education seems to come from the desire to prevent future poverty. Recent court decisions holding that local financing of educational expenditures violates the equal protection clause of the Constitution have arisen in cases involving lower-income persons living in school districts that make relatively low expenditures on schools.

Regardless of the principal purpose one would ascribe to them, the expenditures classified as redistributive in Table 13.1 grew much more rapidly from 1956 to 1969–1970 than others. In the aggregate they increased almost 300 percent, as compared with less than 200 percent for the expenditures classified as allocative. Since prices rose almost 40 percent over this period. redistributive expenditures tripled, but allocative expenditures merely doubled in real terms. Population of U.S. cities has grown at about 2 percent per year and real family income about 3 percent, so real allocative expenditure has increased only at about the same rate as total real income in cities. Because of the differences in growth rates, redistributive expenditures accounted for 39 percent of total expenditures in 1956 but 47 percent in 1969–1970, as shown in Table 13.1.

When one examines the components of the broad expenditure classes shown in the table, only other areawide expenditures

---

[2] See Joseph A. Keishaw, *Government Against Poverty* (Chicago: Markham, 1970), pp. 24–33.

have grown more rapidly than any of those classified as redistributive. (The distinction between local and areawide allocative expenditures will be made in the second section of this chapter.) The increase in other areawide expenditures resulted mainly from expenditures for airports. The latter, in turn, have been associated with the growth in intercity air travel coupled with the fact that airports are largely publicly owned, whereas rail depots and bus terminals are privately owned. Despite all one hears of crime in the streets, police expenditures grew only slightly more rapidly in the past decade and a half than total allocative expenditures. Even more surprising is the fact that current expenditure on highways only slightly more than doubled from 1956 to 1969–1970.

Though Table 13.1 suggests that a principal source of the rise in local governmental expenditure has been increased redistributive expenditure, it fails to highlight an important aspect of the problem. To a great extent the fiscal crisis in local government has occurred in the central cities of urban areas of the United States. Historically, migrants to urban areas have tended to concentrate in the older, more centrally located parts of these areas. Migrants to cities have typically been poorer than others. Migration during and following World War II from the rural South to the urban North and West has been similar to earlier patterns in this regard. The reasons for the concentration of lower-income families in the older, more centrally located parts of urban areas have already been discussed in some detail in Chapters 3 and 4. To review, the primary reason is that lower-income families offer relatively higher rentals for smaller, older dwellings, and these are more easily converted from higher to lower quality in response to their smaller expenditures on housing.

As lower-income migrants to urban areas concentrate in central cities, the brunt of increasing redistributive expenditure is felt in the central cities. Even if benefit rates per recipient under public welfare programs are fixed, total expenditures under these programs will increase. The situation is similar with regard to public hospitals. With a greater number of poor families and a larger part of the central city's housing stock devoted to the production of what is considered slum housing, the apparent need for governmental housing programs appears more urgent. If students in public schools are more poorly prepared on the average, increased demands are made on the public schools for more costly educational programs. Thus, as lower-income families move from rural areas in the South to the urban North and West, where local redistributive expenditures are made at greater rates, total local expenditures for these purposes increase. The increased expenditures, like the lower-income population, tend disproportionately to be concentrated in the central cities.

There is good reason to believe, however, that, with a growth in the fraction of a central city's population that is lower-income, benefit rates under redistributive programs will rise. As was discussed in the last section of the preceding chapter, local public expenditure programs are conditioned by the willingness of voters to "buy" public expenditure with the taxes they pay. This willingness is in turn dependent upon the benefits conferred by such programs on a particular voter and by the voter's share in taxes collected to finance the expenditure. Regardless of what taxes are levied, except for poll taxes, the tax shares of lower-income families are smaller than those of higher-income ones. Although the "price" of a dollar's public expenditure is lower to them, the benefits to lower-income families of a dollar spent on police or fire protection, highways, and libraries may also be less valuable relative to private expenditure on food and housing. Lower-income families, however, receive more direct benefits from income-redistributive expenditure than higher-income families. (Higher-income families may also benefit indirectly, as will be discussed more fully.) For these reasons, a higher proportion of central-city voters will tend to approve redistributive-type programs with any given benefit level. In a sense, the demand for income redistribution in the central city may be said to have risen, and benefit levels will increase.

Although the demands upon central-city governments for income-redistributive expenditures have been increasing, their tax bases have been declining relative to those in the suburbs. Throughout the postwar period, population and employment have grown less rapidly in the central cities than in the suburbs. Many have argued that such urban decentralization has been a "flight from blight," that is, a response to the greater concentration of lower-income families and relatively lower-quality housing in the central cities. As stated earlier, however, especially in Chapters 3 and 10, much of the urban decentralization that has occurred in the postwar period is unrelated to so-called urban blight. Urban decentralization has been going on for at least eighty years and probably longer. It has resulted largely from improvements in urban transportation, from increases in income, and from the growth of urban areas themselves. Whatever the reason, though, urban decentralization has meant that a smaller fraction of an urban area's real property and retail sales are located, or its incomes received, in the central city. And, to the extent that central-city residents become poorer relative to those of suburban areas, the central city's share in the urban area's tax base falls as well.

To meet expenditure demands upon central-city governments that rise relative to taxes collected at given rates and other revenues received, one of three things must happen: Existing tax rates must be increased, new taxes levied, or additional revenues received from other governmental units. All three have occurred. Indeed, the most important increase in local governmental revenues from 1956 to 1969–1970 was in grants from state governments.[3] Still, property tax rates have risen in many central cities. The consequences of such increases are complicated, and the views most commonly stated are seriously in error. In the following paragraphs some of the material of the preceding chapter will be reviewed in an attempt correctly to assess these consequences.

To begin with, local public expenditures for whatever purpose are undertaken only to the extent that they meet with voter approval. As was pointed out in the last section of Chapter 12, the median voter derives the same additional satisfaction per dollar of additional taxes paid from public expenditure as from a dollar's expenditure on goods and services purchased in the market. Some voters would prefer lower taxes and expenditures, others larger ones, but on the average voters derive enough additional satisfaction from public expenditure actually undertaken to compensate them for the private expen-

---

[3] See Table 12.1.

diture they forego in the payment of local taxes. This is the case whether expenditure is made for police protection, highways, or libraries, which voters consume directly, or on expenditures for income redistribution. The beneficiaries of the latter, of course, "consume" income redistribution directly. Those voters who pay taxes to provide transfer payments to others may be thought of as consuming income redistribution indirectly in the sense that they derive satisfaction from the additional consumption it provides those who are less fortunate. In this last sense, income redistribution is quite similar to private philanthropy or charity.

In a very real sense, local redistributive expenditures are more like private philanthropy than allocative expenditure (that which produces direct benefits to all voters). Except for external effects as among local governmental units, which will be discussed later, to receive the direct benefits of police and fire protection provided by a particular municipality one must reside in that municipality. Just as it is not necessary for me to contribute to the United Fund to receive the indirect benefits it provides, however, so it is not necessary for me to reside in the central city to receive indirect satisfaction from public assistance payments made to its poorer residents. And, indeed, if I live in the central city and pay local taxes to support its public assistance programs, my tax payments have a negligible effect upon the total payments received by any welfare recipient. I and others like me thus have an incentive to move to the suburbs to avoid the payment of taxes to support redistributive expenditure. The set of conditions just described is sometimes called the "free-rider" problem and is quite similar to the prisoner's dilemma referred to in Chapter 4 in connection with the neighborhood effects of real estate investment.

Many have concluded that in such situations none of the affected activity will take place in the absence of coercion. Such a conclusion is unwarranted, however. Private philanthropy does occur, and local governments do make redistributive expenditures. It is correct, though, to conclude that less redistributive expenditure will be undertaken by local than by state or national governments. In the first place, the larger the areal region over which taxes are collected to support redistributive expenditure, the more costly it becomes for me to avoid paying taxes to support this expenditure by moving away. In addition, I would be more willing to vote for a given dollar amount of taxes for redistributive purposes where the tax is to be levied throughout the urban area rather than in the central city only. If the taxes are to be levied on an areawide basis, a given tax payment will be associated with a greater level of benefits for lower-income families. Consequently, I would vote for a higher level of taxes and benefits if the taxes were levied throughout the urban area.

It is often argued that the peculiar difficulties of central-city finances are associated with the property tax as a revenue source. This is wholly mistaken. Suppose that, instead of local income taxes, all central cities raise property tax rates to finance a given level of municipal expenditure. Following the analysis of Chapter 12, the rental values of taxable assets, especially housing prices, will be higher in central cities than outside them. Likewise, land values will be lower in central cities than in suburban and other areas. As a result, the burden of the tax will fall principally upon the residents of central cities. Much the same would be true, however, if an income or a sales tax were imposed by central cities. Though the specific distribution of the burden of these alternative taxes could well differ as among central-city residents, the burden of central-city income or sales taxes would fall on their residents. In this last sense, income, sales, and property taxes are equally regressive.

Similarly, if a property tax is imposed by central cities to finance local redistributive expenditures, some families and business firms would seek to locate outside the central city. The allocation of resources would thus tend to be distorted. Quite similar results follow if taxes other than the property tax are imposed. If sales taxes made central-city living more expensive relative to suburban areas, some residents will shift to suburban areas. The outputs of suburban retail stores will thus be larger than otherwise. Or, if income taxes are levied by central-city governments for redistributive purposes, people and business firms would also seek suburban locations in greater numbers. Though the specific resource-allocative effects would differ, depending upon the type of taxes levied, any kind of central-city tax to finance redistributive expenditure would tend to produce too much suburbanization.

Thus, the principal difficulty arises because of local taxes to finance redistributive expenditure. To avoid these difficulties, taxes for redistributive purposes should not be levied by local governments as currently constituted. Indeed, since the kinds of effects discussed would also occur, though to a lesser degree perhaps, even if urban areawide or state governments were to levy taxes for redistributive purposes, income redistribution would best be carried on by the federal government. Not only would voters approve larger taxes and benefit levels if redistributive programs were national in scope, but the resource-allocative effects of taxes imposed would be less wasteful. Regardless of what kind of income maintenance or wage subsidy programs are adopted, federal programs are more effective in achieving redistribution than local ones. Property taxes for the support of public education are not so much a problem; it is local taxes, rather, that lead to difficulties.

It is sometimes argued that the fiscal problems of local governments arise because, like the performing arts, they are labor-intensive. Since they use much labor relative to other productive factors, they have experienced little growth in productivity when compared with more capital-intensive production such as manufacturing. The argument is unsatisfactory for several reasons. In the first place, it provides no explanation at all for the special problems of central-city governments. (Indeed, central-city police forces are probably more highly automated than suburban ones.) Second, many once labor-intensive activities have subsequently exhibited rapid technological progress. Two good examples are medical care and data processing. Finally, professional football has essentially the same economic characteristics as the performing arts, yet its recent success can only be termed phenomenal.

Resource allocation

There are several reasons why local governmental actions to affect the allocation of resources might be desirable. In the absence of governmental intervention, too few resources would be devoted to the production of what have come to be called "public goods" in economics. External diseconomies of the kind discussed in Chapters 4 and 6 may require zoning and other regulatory measures to prevent certain kinds of private production from being carried too far. In addition, external economies in certain kinds of local public production may exist that require corrective action by higher governmental units. Finally, governmental activity may be required to correct the misallocation of resources that results from private monopoly in the production of certain commodities that are consumed locally.

In essence, the term "public good" refers to what might better be characterized as indivisibility in consumption. A public good is formally defined as one whose consumption by any individual does not reduce the amount available for others to consume. Among the best examples are public health measures. The fact that my children are protected from polio because enough others have been vaccinated against it does not reduce the protection of my neighbor's children. Similarly, if a nearby swamp is drained to reduce the number of mosquitoes, everyone in the area benefits equally. To take a different example, any person observing the beauty of a particular mountain need not reduce the ability of others to enjoy it, except if congestion as discussed in Chapter 6 occurs.

The notion of public goods is an abstraction, and different real-world commodities share the characteristic of indivisibility of consumption to a greater or lesser degree. This is partly because public goods may be of limited areal scope. National defense is a frequently cited example of a public good, though some readers will think it a public bad. Yet a ring of antiballistic missiles around the Washington, D.C., area would provide more protection to residents of that area than to those of Denver. Similarly, a police car, to the extent that it deters burglars or muggers, equally benefits all those along its assigned beat but may have little impact elsewhere. The situation is further complicated by the fact that some commodities have both private and public aspects. If I plant a flowering peach tree in my front yard, I preclude anyone else planting that tree, so to this extent the tree is a private good. However, the enjoyment I derive from the tree when it is flowering does not limit my neighbor's enjoyment of it; in the latter sense, then, it is a public good.

Private producers, in general, will not devote sufficient resources to the production of public goods. The reasons are quite similar to those discussed earlier in connection with the incentives taxpayers have to avoid the payment of taxes to support local redistributive expenditure. Indeed, the indirect satisfaction received from an increase in someone else's consumption is a good example of a public good. If an increase in A's consumption makes B feel better, C is in no way prevented from feeling better, too. Just as with philanthropy, however, it is a mistake to conclude that private producers will not undertake the provision of any commodities with substantial public-good characteristics. The signals from a television transmitter are a public good, yet transmitters are privately owned and operated in the United States. Private organizations maintain museums, zoos, and historical buildings, and many musical performances are supported by private subscription.

Whether private producers provide public goods at all depends to a great extent upon the costs faced by private individuals in organizing for collective consumption. The costs of private organization depend partly upon the extent to which it is technically possible to charge consumers for a public good and partly upon the number of its beneficiaries. Admissions can be charged for symphony concerts and zoos. Through relatively inexpensive scrambling devices it is technically possible to limit the enjoyment of television transmission to purchasers of the device, though such devices are not yet used very much in the United States. Similarly, in the case of many private clubs the potential membership is relatively small. Consequently, through private negotiation agreement can be reached upon the rules of the club and the sharing of its expenses.

In the case of public goods produced by local governments, such as police and fire protection and public parks, neither of these conditions holds. The number of potential beneficiaries of these goods is large, hence private negotiation is very costly. Further, it may be prohibitively expensive to limit the benefits of the public goods to those users who pay a charge. Even though all residents of a municipality benefit from, say, police protection, no single resident individually has the incentive voluntarily to subscribe to a police service.

His contribution has a negligible effect upon whether enough others subscribe to support the service. By not subscribing, though, he may still enjoy the benefits of the service. For these reasons, private producers are not likely to provide enough of the service—indeed, it might not be provided at all. The coercive powers of government, which can be used to require payment through taxes, are in effect a cheaper way to organize for collective consumption than private negotiation would be.

By their very nature, if public goods are produced at all the same level of them must be provided all the persons of some particular area. In the case of public health programs, for example, the same level of protection against infectious disease is provided residents of the area affected by them. When public goods are provided by different governmental units in different areas, though, all areas need not provide the same level of the public good. In the case of police protection, some communities may buy more patrol cars and hire more policemen. By providing more frequent patrols, a better regulation of local traffic and a higher degree of protection of persons and property would result. Residents of such municipalities would pay higher taxes and receive more or higher-quality municipal services.

External economies and diseconomies provide another class of cases in which government intervention in economic activity may improve the allocation of resources. Externalities resulting from private production imply that governmental regulation of such activities is, in principle, desirable. Several instances of such externalities have been discussed earlier in this book. Chapters 4 and 5 discussed externalities in private land use and suggested that, where boundary effects on private land use are of significant practical importance, local governmental intervention to limit the areas of cities devoted to certain uses of land could increase the rental value of urban land and thus the national income. Toll charges for the use of urban highways during periods of congestion and the establishment of property rights in air and water resources through the sale of licenses to pollute, both of which were discussed in Chapter 6, are other examples of governmental actions that could improve the allocation of resources by private markets.

Though many other examples could be cited, these three are probably the most important ones so far as urban problems are concerned.

The activities of local governments themselves may impose externalities on the residents of surrounding areas. To take a rather trivial example, garbage burned at a municipally owned garbage dump or incinerator might increase the pollution costs borne by persons outside the municipality. Cases of benefits provided to outsiders are likely to be more important. Publicly owned libraries, museums, and zoos are used by residents of other municipalities, who pay no taxes to support them. An admission charge, for outsiders at least, is a device to get around such difficulties. More important, perhaps, residents of surrounding municipalities may be benefited by the provision of public roads and the regulation of air pollution by any single local government. In many such instances it may be difficult to impose charges on external beneficiaries.

It is generally believed that if an activity of local government provides external benefits, voters will not approve a sufficiently high rate of that activity. For, although voters take into account the benefits they receive in return for the taxes they pay, they have no incentive to take into account the benefits received by outsiders. But by providing benefits to outsiders, say, cleaner air, the residents of surrounding municipalities in effect have higher incomes than they otherwise would. If air is less polluted, outsiders spend less on cleaning and medical bills to receive the same level of protection from, or amelioration of, polluted air and have more to spend on other things. The voters in surrounding areas would thus approve greater expenditures for the regulation of air pollution than they would otherwise, from which residents of the first municipality would benefit. But, though one cannot necessarily conclude that too little local governmental activity to produce external benefits will be undertaken, one can't conclude that precisely the correct amount will be undertaken either.

There are two ways of handling the problem of external benefits of local governmental activity. One is to increase the areal scope of the governmental unit undertaking the activity in question. In the case of air pollution, for example, regulation might rather be made the responsibility of county governments or special air pollution control districts that include the whole area over which the benefits of regulation are felt. The other device is matching grants to municipal governments from some higher unit of government. Suppose, for example, that the pollution regulation activities of a particular local government were to produce benefits to outsiders that were half as great as those experienced by the residents of the municipality in question. If a higher unit of government were to provide grants of $1 for every $2 spent by the local government, the price of pollution control to voters would be reduced and more of it undertaken.

The term "monopoly" typically connotes a large manufacturing corporation whose products are sold nationwide or even worldwide. Control of monopoly is thus a matter for antitrust laws and other regulatory activity by the federal government. Yet, the problem of monopoly may be more important at the local level. By monopoly economists mean the ability of a seller to affect the price at which he sells by the amount he sells. Monopoly tends to arise largely because of what are called internal economies of scale, that is, a decline in the cost per unit of output as output increases. Declining average costs of production tend to result, in turn, from the presence of some productive factor that is indivisible, one that can be used only in relatively large amounts. On the local level, the road bed and rails of a rapid transit system are such a factor of production.

Internal economies of scale are likely to be particularly important at the local level. If the output of a local rapid transit system could be sold nationally, the indivisibility of a single rail transit system would be of negligible importance relative to the size of the market. Since the output can only be sold locally, however, it may not be. Similarly, there are significant internal economies of scale in the purification of sewage and in the generation of electric power. Because of the relatively high cost of transmission of electric power and sewage, the spatial extent of the market for electric power and sewage disposal is limited. Consequently, one or at most a few producers tend to dominate the market. Local monopoly is also a more likely outcome than competition where duplication of facilities imposes additional costs. Examples are the economies to be achieved by a single set of telephone or electric power transmission lines, or perhaps, a single truck collecting garbage along a given street. Activities of the type just described are frequently referred to as public utilities.

Private producers maximize their incomes by producing a rate of output such that their marginal or additional revenues are equal to their marginal or additional cost. For if not, say marginal revenue exceeds marginal cost, the excess of revenue over cost is increased by increasing output. Where competition prevails, marginal revenue is equal to price or average revenue. Consumers, in turn, adjust their consumption to prices paid in such a way that the additional satisfaction derived per dollar spent is the same for all commodities. Where the sale of final products takes place under competitive conditions, then, the relative valuation consumers place on different items of consumption is equal to the additional costs of producing these commodities. For commodities produced under conditions of monopoly, though, price exceeds marginal revenue and hence the additional costs incurred in the production of the monopolized product. Where some products are produced competitively and others monopolistically, the values consumers place on monopolized products exceed the ratios of their marginal costs. For this reason, consumers can be made better off by increasing the outputs of and resources allocated to the production of monopolized products.

Through either governmental regulation or ownership of so-called public utilities, the misallocation of resources from private control could be corrected. In practice, however, resource allocation to public utilities may be no better under governmental than under private control. Since public utility regulation is principally aimed at eliminating monopoly profit, it results in utility rates or prices being set equal to average, not marginal, costs. The same is true of publicly operated enterprises that seek to break even. Where internal economies in production exist or average costs or production are declining, marginal costs are less than average costs. (The latter statement is simply a mathematical truism. The reader may appreciate its truth by considering what happens to a ball-

player's batting average when he goes hitless for a day.) Prices
that are set equal to average cost by public regulation or ownership thus exceed marginal cost just as under private control
of public utilities.

Setting prices equal to marginal cost when average costs are
declining, however, results in total revenues that are less than
total costs incurred. Under governmental regulation, private
utilities would have to be subsidized. Properly operated gov-
ernment-owned enterprises would likewise incur losses. In
either case the public utility for efficient operation would have
to be supported out of taxes or charges levied upon the public
at large. The funds for such subsidies might come in part
from governmentally regulated or owned enterprises where
average costs are increasing. For, if average costs are increasing, marginal cost exceeds average cost. Pricing outputs at
marginal cost, which is appropriate for efficient resource allocation, would thus yield surpluses, not deficits, where average
costs are rising.

These last considerations are equally important in considering
the proper "pricing" of the services of local governments.
Local taxes, apart from those levied for income-redistributive
purposes, may be viewed as charges or prices imposed for
municipal services produced. To the extent that local governments break even in the long run, prices are set equal to average cost. To the extent that, say, police and fire protection
are supplied under conditions of constant average cost
(whether they are is considered more fully in the second part
of the following section), no problem results. For, constant
average cost implies marginal cost equal to average cost, so
average cost-pricing is marginal cost-pricing. To the extent,
however, that relatively small urban areas face declining average cost for some municipal services, the prices charged as
taxes are too high. Living in these communities is more expensive than it ought to be, hence these communities will be
too small. Similarly, if the average cost of municipal services
is rising in relatively large communities, average cost-pricing
imposes too small a charge for living in these communities,
and they will grow too big. This second case is quite analogous
to the problem of freeway congestion discussed in Chapter
6. For efficient resource allocation as among different communities, smaller communities might thus be subsidized and

larger ones taxed by the federal government. These considerations provide a rationale for federal loans for public facilities in regional development programs, which were mentioned briefly in Chapter 2.

One other point concerning the pricing of public services is pertinent here. In the case of municipal services such as police and fire protection, which are principally public as opposed to private goods, the same level of service is provided all members of the community. However, the rate at which individuals consume other, essentially private, goods (such as public libraries, municipal swimming pools, and garbage collection) varies considerably. When supported by taxes, the average charge for the use of the library, though not necessarily the same to all users on an annual basis, varies inversely on a per-book-read basis with the number of books read. Economic efficiency would require an equal charge per book or per day, however. The latter can be achieved by imposing user charges or fees, similar to those private rental libraries would charge. The only strong objection to user charges is probably that they are injurious to the poor. The poor, however, can be helped more by real money they may spend for whatever they wish than by lower rental rates for library books.

PROBLEMS OF LOCAL GOVERNMENT

In the preceding section, the discussion of local public expenditure was organized around economic principles. Several important conclusions regarding the appropriate scope and function of local government were reached, but these grew out of a consideration of theory rather than specific problem areas. Now it would be useful to consider specific problem areas, such as education, in order to develop propositions regarding public expenditure that have a wider applicability. In addition to public education, the discussion here will be organized around problems of metropolitan government and revenue sharing.

Public education

It was pointed out in Chapter 9 that education provides external benefits to society as a whole through a higher level of literacy and, though perhaps somewhat doubtful, good citizenship. The external benefits of education are in the nature of public goods. The more efficient regulation of traffic on public roads that results from more drivers being able to read and comprehend road signs is something my benefiting from does not detract from the benefit to others. To the extent that public support of education provides income redistribution, my enjoyment of this likewise need not detract from the enjoyment others receive. Thus, there are good economic reasons for the public support of education.

Public support, however, does not require public production. To take another example, there are also good economic reasons why municipalities should require garbage to be collected. Uncollected garbage is both unsanitary and unsightly and imposes externalities that are public bads upon one's neighbors. It is also probably cheaper for a single firm to collect all the garbage along a particular street than for several to do so on the same street. Garbage collection is thus a public utility or natural monopoly as well. There is no particular advantage for municipal employees and municipally owned trucks to collect garbage, though. Indeed, in many areas private firms are awarded exclusive rights for garbage collection and bill their customers directly.

Though, like garbage collection, public education produces externalities that are public goods, education is by no means a natural monopoly. Average costs are probably more or less constant over widely different sizes of schools.[4] Indeed, larger schools differ from smaller ones primarily in that they employ more teachers and classrooms in very similar proportions. It is not at all uncommon for a public elementary school to have several separate teachers and classrooms of similar size to accommodate a given grade, and a large high school may have more than one teacher whose principal duty is to teach twelfth-grade English. Even though some high schools may be too small to keep a physics teacher fully employed at his specialty, many elementary school districts have music and art teachers

---

[4] Some evidence on the nature of average cost curves for public education is given by Werner Z. Hirsch, "The Supply of Urban Public Services," in Harvey S. Perloff and Lowdon Wingo, Jr., eds., *Issues in Urban Economics* (Baltimore: Johns Hopkins Press, 1958), especially table 2, p. 508.

who travel from school to school within the district. Nor does the existence of more than one school in any area make education more costly because duplicate facilities interfere with each other.

Public production of education is like the production of police protection in that all residents of a particular school district receive essentially the same services per child. There is certainly no technical reason why this should be the case. Apart from a few instances of specialized science or vocational high schools in some large cities, however, uniformity of output would certainly seem to be characteristic of public school systems. There is a much greater variety not only of private colleges and universities in comparison to state institutions, but of private nursery schools in comparison with publicly run elementary schools.

Public schools, as the term is used in the United States, are under much less competitive pressure to operate efficiently than are gas stations or grocery stores, which share many of the same economic characteristics of production. If the service is bad at one gas station, or the fresh produce of poor quality in a particular grocery store, one may easily make one's purchases elsewhere. However, if the taxes paid for the quality of school received are high, or, if as is frequently alleged, minority children are misclassified as retarded because of racial bias in IQ tests, the alternatives open to parents are severely limited.[5] Parents may send their children to private schools, but to do so requires payment of tuition as well as taxes to support public schools. The only other alternative is to move to another school district. The latter, however, may be expensive in terms of actual moving costs and costs of commuting to a job.

In the long run, however, many people pay special attention to the public schools in a particular area when making a move. People who place a premium on high-quality education will tend to offer more for housing in school districts offering such schooling and to pay higher taxes. Those who place less em-

---

[5] For a discussion of some of the other economic consequences of public production of education see James M. Buchanan and Nicos E. Devletoglou, *Academia in Anarchy: An Economic Diagnosis* (New York: Basic Books, 1970), chaps. 2 and 3.

phasis on high-quality public education select residences in other school districts. It seems quite likely that those who are willing and able to pay higher taxes for better education will have higher incomes and themselves be more highly educated. Tying the education one's child receives to one's residential location is thus likely to produce a greater degree of residential segregation by income level and social characteristics than would otherwise occur.

One way out of the problems posed by the public support of education by public production is the use of so-called educational vouchers. The parents of each child up to a certain age would receive a voucher or certificate that they could spend, perhaps along with some of their own funds, on "tuition" for the child's education. The parents could then select a public or even private school, without regard to their residential location, to which their child would be sent.[6] Vouchers would be rather like the state scholarships for higher education currently awarded by New York State. New York residents receiving these scholarships may use them to attend either public or private universities in the state. Vouchers would also be similar to the widely acclaimed educational benefits under the so-called G.I. Bill of Rights. An experimental educational voucher program involving six elementary schools in the Alum Rock School District of San Jose, California, was begun in the fall of 1969 with support from the Office of Economic Opportunity.

Educational vouchers would almost certainly lead to increased efficiency of resource use in public education by permitting competition among schools for students. When public support is tied to public production of education, public schools have a more or less assured market. They thus have less incentive to reduce their expenditures or improve the quality of the schooling they offer than if parents were free to switch their children to a less expensive or better-quality school. More important, perhaps, a voucher scheme would provide for a greater range of alternatives. Parents wishing to send their children to schools stressing science, music, or physical educa-

---

[6] For a fuller discussion of issues related to educational vouchers see Milton Friedman, *Capitalism and Freedom* (Chicago: University of Chicago Press, 1962), chap. 6, especially pp. 93ff.

tion could do so. Likewise, children could be sent to schools that spend more on teachers and books and less on buildings and football uniforms if their parents felt it desirable. Most important of all, perhaps, if minority parents felt that their children were not being treated fairly or properly, a change of schools would remedy the situation more easily than a sit-in at the board of education offices.

Given the widely acknowledged success of the G.I. Bill, this country's only large-scale experience with educational vouchers, the resistance sometimes encountered by the scheme is rather surprising. One of the strongest arguments voiced against the voucher system is that it would foster segregation in elementary and secondary education. It is by no means clear that such would be the case, for it is difficult to imagine a greater degree of segregation by race or by income than now exists in many large U.S. cities. Black students receiving benefits under the G.I. Bill were probably less segregated racially than black college students otherwise supported. Some white parents might well feel that their children would benefit from attending integrated schools if their children were not a minority. The opposition to low-income housing in suburban areas is partly due to the increased taxes current residents would have to pay for public education. Vouchers supported by federal taxes would eliminate this source of opposition. Even so, to increase the degree of integration in schools it would be a relatively simple matter to make the tuition for which a voucher could be exchanged greater in integrated schools. White parents would thus have a positive incentive to send their children to integrated schools.

The other major objection to voucher schemes that would allow parents to spend additional amounts for tuition out of their own funds is that inequality in education and income would be perpetuated. It is by no means clear that this would be the case either. Unlike the World War II version, the Korean War and subsequent versions of the G.I. Bill have paid students a flat sum, and these students are permitted to receive other support or to spend out of their own resources. Yet it is almost certainly the case that the post-Korean G.I. Bill has increased the education received by students from lower-income and black families more than that received by richer and white ones. Indeed, one of the greatest advantages of allowing parents to spend more than their vouchers on tuition would be for lower-income and minority families. Middle- and upper-income families currently spend more on education through music or dance lessons, private tutoring, and especially by choosing a place to live. The last alternative is probably especially costly to lower-income families. Moving from a house worth $12,500 to one valued at $25,000 would entail an additional expenditure on housing of about $125 per month before, or $1,350 per year after, the federal income tax saving on owner-occupied housing. It would be cheaper for a family to spend $500 more on tuition for each of two children than to move to the more expensive house. Under a voucher system, spending the voucher plus $500 could well make the difference between a child's attending a high-quality school instead of a low-quality one.

One means of overcoming the objections to educational vouchers would be to vary the value of the voucher inversely with the parents' income. An argument sometimes advanced for doing so is that a year's schooling at a given level is more costly for lower-income or minority children, perhaps because teachers must be paid higher salaries to teach them or because such children need enriched programs to compensate for previous deficiencies. In terms of the analysis of the determinants of amounts invested in education presented in Chapter 9, such students have lower demands for education than others. To spend more on the education of lower-income or minority children where the returns to such education are lower involves an inefficiency in the use of resources. Other programs involving an equal expenditure could benefit them more. It is by no means clear, then, that it is desirable to vary the value of vouchers with the income level of a child's family.

The use of federally financed vouchers to divorce public support from public production would probably be more important in elementary and secondary education than any other areas. The arguments for voucher or certificate-type programs are equally as strong when applied to other income-redistributive expenditures. Federal scholarships that students could use in any college or university would be a far superior means of support for higher education than low-interest loans for building dormitories or federal research funds. Medicare and other health programs that enable their beneficiaries to purchase more medical care from private physicians are likewise preferable to free health care in public hospitals. It was argued in Chapter 4 that a rent certificate program would be superior in many respects to publicly operated low-income housing projects. In all these cases, the effect would be similar to the food stamp program, which enables lower-income families to purchase more in private grocery stores than they otherwise would. Few would argue that food stamps should be redeemable only in government-operated grocery stores.

Metropolitan government

About a decade ago, much was said and written about the desirability of metropolitan areawide local government. Some of the support for areawide government came from the belief that economies of scale exist in the production of municipal services. If so, larger producing units would permit cost savings in public production. Support for areawide government also arose from the belief that public decision making is fragmented by the existence of numerous local governments. One hears much less about metropolitan-area government today, however, and there are only a few urban areas in the United States (Miami-Dade County in Florida is one) where anything approaching it exists. Here some of the economic considerations bearing on the desirable areal scope of local governments will be examined.

Based upon their economic characteristics, there is little reason to expect significant decreases in average cost for most local governmental functions as the size of population served increases. Many, if not most, local government functions are carried on by relatively small producing units and do not employ indivisible productive factors. Larger municipalities differ from smaller ones primarily in that the former operate larger numbers of essentially the same kind of producing units rather than quite different kinds of units. In addition to public education, which has just been discussed, this is also the case with police and fire protection, public parks, and libraries. Larger cities use more policemen, patrol cars, and police stations, for example, than smaller ones do. Larger and smaller cities do not differ much, however, in the number of men per police car or of cars and men assigned to a particular police station. Rather, larger cities differ from smaller ones primarily in that they have more police stations. Similarly, larger municipalities have more parks and libraries than smaller ones, but the size of either need not vary much in municipalities of different size except in some of the larger central cities. Though some economies may be realized through large-scale purchases of police cars or other equipment, these may be counterbalanced by increased difficulties in coordination and control as the size of a producing organization increases.

At the same time, most local governmental functions are characterized by relatively high transport costs. Trips to and from school are frequently made, and time is of the essence in responding to a fire alarm. Some people travel relatively great distances to scenic national or state parks, but few mothers will walk children great distances to public parks or travel very far to public libraries. The lack of significant economies in large-scale production, coupled with high transport costs, would require small, widely scattered producing units rather than a few large units. Indeed, as was pointed out in Chapter 2, such is the case with similar kinds of private production—gas stations and grocery stores, for example. Much the same kind of pattern is typically observed with public schools, police and fire stations, parks, and libraries.

At the other end of the spectrum there are a few kinds of private or public production characterized by significant indivisibility at some stage of the production process. These have already been mentioned in the first section of the chapter in connection with the notions of local and natural monopoly. Many studies have been done on the effects of population size and other factors on local government expenditure. It is frequently difficult to eliminate the effects of variations in the quality of service provided by these expenditures. In addition, there are many factors, some of which may be difficult to identify, let alone measure, that may affect local expenditure. Still, the bulk of the available evidence suggests that, apart from those areas already identified as local monopolies, the average costs of local governmental functions are more or less invariant with population served. In reviewing this evidence and the kinds of considerations discussed earlier, Werner Z. Hirsch concludes that "in terms of economies of scale, governments serving from 50,000 to 100,000 urbanites might be most efficient."[7]

Even if economies of scale in producing local governmental services were more pervasive than they appear to be, large-scale local governments would not be called for. For it is technically possible for local governments to purchase from other governmental units or even private producers, and many do. Not infrequently, local governments purchase water, electricity, or gas in bulk from other producers and distribute it to their residents. The municipality of Los Altos Hills in the San Francisco Bay area has no police force of its own, and until recently, purchased police services both from the Santa Clara County Sheriff's office and from a private firm that provides security service. Such arrangements are common in the Los Angeles area and are described in some detail by Robert L. Bish.[8] Thus small size need be no barrier at all to the efficient provision of local governmental functions.

Though there is very little evidence bearing on the matter, the external effects of local governmental activity are probably either of quite limited areal scope or are metropolitan-area- or even nationwide. To the extent that external benefits are provided by education, they are probably nationwide in scope; hence they should be the province of the federal government. Measures taken by any central-city government to regulate commuter traffic, however, affect land-use decisions and values throughout the whole metropolitan area. Similarly, the control of air pollution by one municipality may well affect much of the urban area. At the other end of the spectrum, apart from nationwide effects, the operation of one school district would seem to inflict few externalities upon surrounding districts. The number of traffic lights in a particular part of the area has little impact upon the residents of other parts. If a fire department is slow in responding to calls it may make fire insurance more expensive in the limited area it serves

[7] Perloff and Wingo, op. cit., p. 509.
[8] Robert L. Bish, *The Public Economy of Metropolitan Areas* (Chicago: Markham, 1971), pp. 81–93.

but do little to increase the risk of property damage outside that area. To take a final example, as was argued in Chapter 4, the boundary external effects of one kind of land use on another are probably felt over very small distances.

Balanced against internal economies of scale in production and external economies or diseconomies are the possibilities of varying the levels of municipal services that smaller local governments provide. As was stressed in the earlier discussion of public goods, though the output of a public good must be more or less the same throughout some particular area, levels of output may vary from area to area. By providing different levels of local expenditure and taxes, different local governments allow individuals the chance to choose those levels most nearly conforming to their incomes and preferences. In the preceding chapter it was deduced that the level of public expenditures adopted in a community will tend to the median of the array of levels desired by families in the community. By dividing any community in, say, three, in accordance with its desired expenditure levels, the new median levels will more accurately reflect the desires of the community's members. For, if desired public expenditure levels were uniformly distributed, the median level of the middle third of the array is precisely the same as that for the whole array, whereas the medians of the smallest and largest thirds of the array are closer to the desired levels for members of these groups than the median of the whole array.

Viewed from this perspective, central-city governments are like dinosaurs. Whereas technical conditions of production and external effects allow relatively small producing units and thus a wide range of public service levels, large central-city governments do not permit such variation to occur. Middle- and upper-income families already have a great deal of choice provided by the existence of a large number of suburban municipalities. Probably because housing costs relatively less in central cities than in suburban areas, though, lower-income families have little effective choice among public expenditure levels and taxes. At the same time, where significant numbers of both lower- and upper-income families live, as in the central city, imposing identical expenditure levels and tax rates inevitably results in conflict.

Based upon these considerations, breaking central-city government units up into smaller ones for the provision of many local governmental functions would have much to recommend it. Among the functions such small municipalities might assume are local traffic control, the routine protection of people and property, parks, and land-use control. Not only would some conflicts be avoided, but lower-income families would be given some of the opportunities for choice that higher-income ones now possess. The major objection to so doing, probably, would be that poorer areas would have limited tax resources to provide for the support of local expenditure. This objection loses much of its force if the financing of education and other forms of redistributive expenditure were assumed by the federal government. Regarding allocative functions, though, lower-income families may be required to spend more under existing central-city governments than they would prefer to.

Though too large for the effective provision of what are characterized as local allocative functions in Table 13.1, central-city governments in most metropolitan areas are far too small to provide true metropolitan government for those functions requiring it. Until early in this century, central cities grew by annexing populated areas that developed adjacent to them. More recently, however, such annexations have largely ceased while population growth outside the central city has continued, at faster rates if anything. Thus, though central cities may once have been metropolitan-area governments, they no longer are in many instances. Indeed, in lots of cases—the San Francisco Bay area, for example—even county governments are far too small to serve as metropolitan-areawide governments.

Where significant internal economies of scale in production or areawide externalities exist, metropolitan-area governments would have much to recommend them. The provision of rapid transit, water, sewage disposal, power, and light are previously cited examples of such functions. Because investigation of serious crimes such as murder may require highly specialized though infrequently used personnel and equipment, a metropolitan-area police force after the model of Scotland Yard in Britain might be desirable. Planning, to the extent that this means forecasting future growth or examining the effects of different transportation programs rather than detailed land-use control, has significant areawide public-good aspects. It, too, might thus be a function for a metropolitan government. Whether special districts or governmental units intermediate in size between small local governments and a metropolitan-area government would be desirable is much too complicated a question to enter into here. But it seems clear that central-city governments today perform no functions that other units could not perform better.

Revenue sharing

In the fall of 1972 Congress passed a Nixon administration proposal for the federal government to provide state and local governments with about $5 billion in grants. This particular proposal is one form of a class of intergovernmental grants that have come to be called revenue sharing. Higher levels of government have been "sharing" revenues with lower-level governments for many years, however. In 1969–1970, local governments received almost $8 billion in grants, about three-fourths from state governments. Their total grants received were only slightly smaller in the aggregate than property taxes levied. Furthermore, intergovernmental grants to local governments increased by slightly more than 400 percent from 1956 to 1969–1970, compared with an increase of only 150 percent in total taxes collected over the same period.[9] This section examines the economic effects of intergovernmental grants and their desirability as instruments for dealing with central city fiscal problems.

The effects of intergovernmental grants on local expenditures may best be illustrated in terms of the budget line relating private to public expenditure, which was described in the last section of Chapter 12. As was pointed out there, the median of voters' desired expenditure levels is the level resulting from majority rule. Hence, in Figure 13.1 the budget lines shown are those of the voter whose desired level of expenditures is the median level of the array for all voters. The budget line B_0 is that applicable before the grant is made, and x_1 is the

---

[9] See Table 12.1.

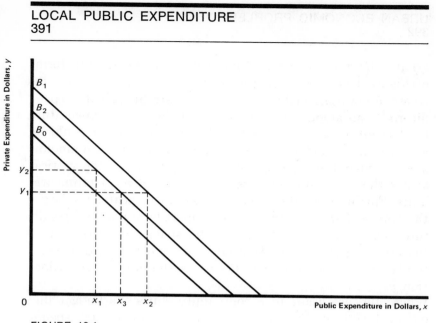

FIGURE 13.1

Inter-governmental grants and the local taxpayer's budget line

level of public expenditures of the community in dollars. A higher level of government makes a grant of $x_2 - x_1$ dollars to the local government, which enables the median voter to spend y_1 on private goods and to experience a local public expenditure level of x_2. It is all too easy to forget, though, that the higher level of government imposes taxes, some of which fall on voters in the community in question. As shown in the figure, these taxes shift the budget line down from B_1 to B_2, enabling a public expenditure level of only x_3 if y_1 dollars of private expenditure continue to be made by the median voter. The net grant is thus $x_3 - x_1$ rather than $x_2 - x_1$. For some communities, indeed, B_2 may be below B_0, so that when taken in conjunction with the taxes levied to finance the grant, the maximum possible level of public expenditure for a given private expenditure level actually declines.

One of the important features of intergovernmental grants is that they are implicit tax reductions to voters in the community receiving net grants. (Where the net grant is negative, or local taxpayers pay more in taxes to finance the set of grants to all communities than their community receives in grants, the grant is a set of implicit tax increases.) In terms of Figure 13.1, the grant, together with its associated tax increase, allows the median voter to increase his private expenditure by an amount $y_2 - y_1$ dollars if the public expenditure level is unchanged at x_1. Precisely the same result could be achieved if the median voter's taxes were cut by the amount $y_2 - y_1$, since the intercept of the budget line on the vertical axis is the voter's income less taxes paid higher governmental units. Furthermore, the size of the tax cut is greater the larger the voter's share in taxes paid to support local public expenditure. The larger this tax share, the steeper are the budget lines shown in the figure. Hence, given the net grant of $x_3 - x_1$, the larger a voter's tax share the larger the implicit tax reduction $y_2 - y_1$.

Where the net grant to a community shifts the budget line outward, as from B_0 to B_2 in Figure 13.1, in effect the spendable incomes of voters have increased. Empirically, public expenditure levels appear to be greater the higher the income level in a community. With an increase in spendable incomes, however, families also spend more on private goods. Hence one would anticipate the net grant of $x_3 - x_1$ to increase both private and desired public expenditure levels for the median voter. As a result, the new level of public expenditure chosen by the community would lie somewhere between x_1 and x_3.

The grant illustrated in Figure 13.1 is what might best be called a flat or lump-sum grant. Rather than providing a given number of dollars, irrespective of what the community does, many intergovernmental grants are matching grants. The higher level of government agrees to grant, say, $1 for every $2 the local government spends. The effects of matching grants are illustrated in Figure 13.2. Because of additional taxes levied by the higher level of government, the intercept of the postgrant budget line B_1 on the private expenditure axis lies below that of the pregrant budget line B_0. Since the higher level of government agrees to pay a fraction, which is one-third in the example cited here, the tax shares of all voters fall by this fraction. Thus the postgrant budget line, B_1, is flatter than B_0. As drawn in Figure 13.2, the median voter could increase his private expenditure if the pregrant

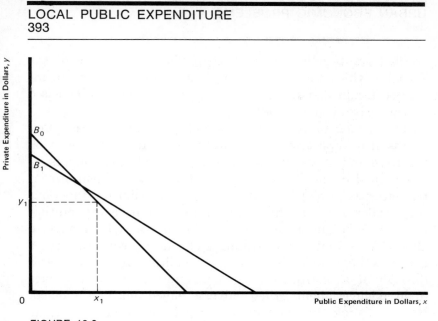

FIGURE 13.2
Matching vs. lump-sum grants

level of public expenditure, x_1, were maintained. The matching grant thus has an income effect that, if positive, tends to increase public expenditure in the same way as a flat grant does. In addition, however, the matching grant by reducing tax shares in effect reduces the "price" of public expenditure to voters. The substitution effect by itself would lead to greater public as opposed to private expenditure. For this reason, matching grants by reducing tax shares increase local public expenditure more than equivalent flat grants do.

Up to this point the discussion has focused on what might be called unrestricted grants. Many intergovernmental grants, though, impose restrictions upon the types of local public expenditure for which they may be spent. In some the acceptable types of expenditure may be very broad, say merely for schools. In others, the allowable expenditures may be very narrowly defined, perhaps for school lunches or for classrooms but not for teachers' salaries. To make matters more confusing, restricted grants may either be flat or matching grants. It becomes quite difficult to illustrate the effects of restricted grants. Many of the principles of unrestricted grants apply also to restricted grants, however. In particular, whereas restricted grants will increase local public expenditures of the kind for which the grant is made, they may also lead to increased local expenditures for other purposes and to increased private expenditure as well.

In attempting to assess the desirability of intergovernmental grants, it is important once again to distinguish between redistributive and allocative expenditure by local governments. It was argued in the first section that the fiscal problem of central cities is primarily related to the redistributive functions they undertake. The financing of redistributive expenditure by taxes levied in the central city, in turn, may have adverse allocative as well as redistributive effects. By collecting taxes for the support of redistributive expenditure at uniform rates throughout a metropolitan area and returning the revenues to local governments, these adverse effects may be avoided. However, programs for redistributing incomes ought to treat persons equally situated in equal fashion. This last goal would be far more easily achieved through federal programs for public assistance, educational vouchers, and other income-redistributive purposes than through federal grants in support of local programs. Clearly, federal support through matching grants for state and local public assistance programs to date has not produced anything resembling uniformity of benefit levels throughout the nation.

The major justification for intergovernmental grants arises in the case of allocative expenditure by local governments. If external economies of certain local governmental expenditures are experienced by residents of surrounding communities, matching grants restricted to these functions are one means of affecting the price of this kind of local expenditure to reflect the external benefits supplied by voters of the community. However, the really significant external effects of local government actions—those related to transportation and pollution control—probably are areawide and could be better handled by assigning jurisdiction over them to a metropolitan-area government.

A stronger case for intergovernmental grants can be made for those functions characterized by internal economies of scale in production. As was argued in the preceding section, optimal allocation of resources requires pricing—either user charges or taxes—that is equal to marginal costs. Marginal cost-pricing, however, results in deficits where average costs exceed marginal cost. Intergovernmental grants are one way of covering such deficits. Since the smaller urban areas for which internal scale economies in water and sewage systems, electric and gas companies, and rail transit systems are likely to exist may be disproportionately concentrated in certain regions of the country, federal grants may be better suited for this purpose. At the same time, negative grants would be called for to tax away the surpluses in those larger cities where internal scale economies in the aforementioned activities have been exhausted.

Intergovernmental grants are sometimes justified as providing poorer communities the resources to finance needed local governmental services. A little consideration, however, suggests that there is little justification for grants for such purposes. To the extent that the local functions in question are redistributive, it has been argued that federal programs are superior to federally supported local ones. To the extent that they are allocative, such grants are similar in their attempt to provide income in kind, but in their effect they may be viewed as an implicit set of tax cuts to the voters of the poorer areas. If redistributive programs are doing their job, there is no additional justification for a program of disguised tax cuts to poorer areas.

In sum, intergovernmental grants generally are inferior solutions to public finance problems. To the extent that grants are made to support redistributive expenditures or those allocative expenditures of local governments where genuine externalities exist, assigning these expenditures to the appropriate higher level of government is a better solution. Since grants may be viewed as an implicit set of tax cuts to the voters of the community receiving the grant, they need also be judged by their equity and allocative effects as tax cuts. Grants may be favorable to the extent that they replace regressive local taxes with progressive state or federal taxes, but the reverse effect could well be true in some cases. Though the allocative effects of differentially high local property taxes may indeed be bad, replacement by differentially low ones may worsen their allocative effects.

SUMMARY

As lower-income families have come to be concentrated in
the central cities of the United States, local public expenditures for redistributive purposes have increased. In part this
has been the case because benefit levels are higher in the areas
receiving lower-income migrants; in part it has occurred because the demand for redistributive expenditures and hence
benefit levels have risen. At the same time, the central city's
share in the urban area's tax base has fallen as decentralization of population and production has occurred, largely for
other reasons. Higher central-city taxes to support growing
redistributive expenditure, however, have produced incentives
for too much decentralization. The fiscal problems of central
cities are frequently ascribed to local reliance on the property
tax, but any other local tax would fall on central-city residents
and provide similar incentives for decentralization. The best
remedy for the fiscal problems of central cities would be for
the federal government to assume redistributive expenditures
now made locally and to levy the taxes that finance these
expenditures.
A public good is one whose consumption by any one individual
does not reduce the amount available for others. Where the
number of potential beneficiaries is large and excluding non-
subscribers from benefits is difficult, public goods are more
cheaply produced using the coercive powers of government.
Though constant within a given community, the level of pub-
lic-goods production may vary from community to community. Not only do local governments regulate private production in the presence of external economies, but the activities
of one local government may impose externalities on the residents of other communities. Local monopoly provides a justification for local regulation or operation of activities characterized by economies of scale. Either regulation of public operation, however, tends to result in prices equal to average costs,
but marginal cost-pricing would better promote efficient use
of resources. User charges are preferable to tax support of
activities such as garbage collection and libraries, which,
though publicly produced, are essentially private goods.
Education is a far more important case of a commodity that,

though deserving of public support, does not require public production. Providing public support through vouchers, which could be used to pay tuition in publicly or privately operated schools, would lead to increased efficiency in education. Integration could be promoted by providing larger vouchers to children attending integrated schools, and vouchers would give lower-income families a much wider choice of schools than they now have. Most local governmental activities are characterized by constant returns to scale and high transport costs. Small-scale governmental units thus enhance consumer choice among different levels of public service at no sacrifice in productive efficiency. A few are characterized by economies of scale in production that are large relative to the size of most urban areas and/or areawide external effects. The latter class would most efficiently be produced by urban areawide governments. Net intergovernmental grants are an implicit set of tax reductions, shared in proportion to local taxes paid. Though net grants stimulate local public expenditure, they stimulate private expenditure as well. Generally they are inferior solutions to public finance problems.

INDEX